SUICIDE RESEARCH: SELECTED READINGS

Volume 15

November 2015 — April 2016

Y. W. Koo, M. McDonough, V. Ross, D. De Leo

Australian Institute for Suicide Research and Prevention

Griffith
UNIVERSITY

WHO Collaborating Centre for
Research and Training in Suicide Prevention

National Centre of Excellence in Suicide Prevention

First published in 2016
Australian Academic Press
18 Victor Russell Drive,
Samford QLD 4520, Australia
Australia
www.australianacademicpress.com.au

ISBN: 978 1 9221 1772 4

Book and cover design by Maria Biaggini — The Letter Tree.

Contents

Recommended readings

Citation list

Foreword

This volume contains quotations from internationally peer-reviewed suicide research published during the semester November 2015 – April 2016; it is the fifteenth of a series produced biannually by our Institute with the aim of assisting the Commonwealth Department of Health to be constantly updated on new evidences from the scientific community.

As usual, the initial section of the volume collects a number of publications that could have particular relevance for the Australian people in terms of potential applicability. These publications are accompanied by a short comment from us, and an explanation of the motives that justify why we have considered of interest the implementation of studies' findings in the Australian context. An introductory part provides the rationale and the methodology followed in the identification of papers.

The central part of the volume represents a selection of research articles of particular significance; their abstracts are reported *in extenso*, underlining our invitation to read those papers in full text: they represent a remarkable advancement of suicide research knowledge.

The last section reports all items retrievable from major electronic databases. We have catalogued them on the basis of their prevailing reference to fatal and non-fatal suicidal behaviours, with various sub-headings (e.g. epidemiology, risk factors, etc.). The deriving list guarantees a level of completeness superior to any individual system; it can constitute a useful tool for all those interested in a quick update of what was most recently published on the topic.

Our intent was to make suicide research more approachable to non-specialists, and in the meantime provide an opportunity for a *vademecum* of quotations credible also at the professional level. A compilation such as the one that we provide here is not easily obtainable from usual sources and can save a considerable amount of time to readers. We believe that our effort in this direction may be an appropriate interpretation of one of the technical support roles to the Government that the status of National Centre of Excellence in Suicide Prevention – which has deeply honoured our commitment – entails for us.

The significant growth of our centre, the Australian Institute for Suicide Research and Prevention, and its influential function, both nationally and internationally, in the fight against suicide, could not happen without the constant support of Queensland Health and Griffith University. We hope that our passionate dedication to the cause of suicide prevention may compensate their continuing trust in our work.

Diego De Leo, DSc

Emeritus Professor, Australian Institute for Suicide Research and Prevention

Acknowledgments

This report has been produced by the Australian Institute for Suicide Research and Prevention, WHO Collaborating Centre for Research and Training in Suicide Prevention and National Centre of Excellence in Suicide Prevention. The assistance of the Commonwealth Department of Health in the funding of this report is gratefully acknowledged.

Introduction

Context

Suicide places a substantial burden on individuals, communities and society in terms of emotional, economic and health care costs. In Australia, about 2000 people die from suicide every year, a death rate well in excess of transport-related mortality. At the time of preparing this volume, the latest available statistics released by the Australian Bureau of Statistics[1] indicated that, in 2013, 2,522 deaths by suicide were registered in Australia, representing an age-standardised rate of 10.7 per 100,000.

Despite the estimated mortality, the prevalence of suicide and self-harming behaviour in particular remains difficult to gauge due to the often secretive nature of these acts. Without a clear understanding of the scope of suicidal behaviours and the range of interventions available, the opportunity to implement effective initiatives is reduced. Further, it is important that suicide prevention policies are developed on the foundation of evidence-based empirical research, especially as the quality and validly of the available information may be misleading or inaccurate. Additionally, the social and economic impact of suicide underlines the importance of appropriate research-based prevention strategies, addressing not only significant direct costs on health system and lost productivity, but also the emotional suffering for families and communities.

The Australian Institute for Suicide Research and Prevention (AISRAP) has, through the years, gained an international reputation as one of the leading research institutions in the field of suicide prevention. The most important recognition came via the designation as a World Health Organization (WHO) Collaborating Centre in 2005. In 2008, the Commonwealth Department of Health (DoH) appointed AISRAP as the National Centre of Excellence in Suicide Prevention. This latter recognition awards not only many years of high quality research, but also of fruitful cooperation between the Institute and several different governmental agencies.

As part of this mandate, AISRAP is committed to the creation of a databank of the recent scientific literature documenting the nature and extent of suicidal and self-harming behaviour and recommended practices in preventing and responding to these behaviours. The key output for the project is a critical bi-annual review of the national and international literature outlining recent advances and promising developments in research in suicide prevention, particularly where this can help to inform national activities. This task is not aimed at providing a critique of new researches, but rather at drawing attention to investigations that may have particular relevance to the Australian context. In doing so, we are committed to a user-friendly language, in order to render research outcomes and their interpretation accessible also to a non-expert audience.

In summary, these reviews serve three primary purposes:

1. To inform future State and Commonwealth suicide prevention policies;
2. To assist in the improvement of existing initiatives, and the development of new and innovative Australian projects for the prevention of suicidal and self-harming behaviours within the context of the Living is for Everyone (LIFE) Framework (2008);
3. To provide directions for Australian research priorities in suicidology.

The review is presented in three sections. The first contains a selection of the best articles published in the last six months internationally. For each article identified by us (see the method of choosing articles described below), the original abstract is accompanied by a brief comment explaining why we thought the study was providing an important contribution to research and why we considered its possible applicability to Australia. The second section presents the abstracts of the most relevant literature — following our criteria — collected between November 2015 to April 2016; while the final section presents a list of citations of all literature published over this time-period.

Methodology

The literature search was conducted in four phases.

Phase 1

Phase one consisted of weekly searches of the academic literature performed from November 2015 to April 2016. To ensure thorough coverage of the available published research, the literature was sourced using several scientific electronic databases including: PubMed, ProQuest, Scopus, SafetyLit and Web of Science, using the following key words: *suicide OR suicidal OR self-harm OR self-injury OR parasuicide.*

Results from the weekly searches were downloaded and combined into one database (deleting duplicates).

Specific inclusion criteria for Phase 1 included:

- Timeliness: the article was published (either electronically or in hard-copy) between November 2015 to April 2016;
- Relevance: the article explicitly referred to fatal and/or non-fatal suicidal behaviour and related issues and/or interventions directly targeted at preventing/treating these behaviours;
- The article was written in English.

Articles about euthanasia, assisted suicide, suicide terrorist attacks, and/or book reviews, abstracts and conference presentations were excluded.

Also, articles that have been published in electronic versions (ahead of print) and therefore included in the previous volume (Volumes 1 to 14 of *Suicide Research: Selected Readings*) were excluded to avoid duplication.

Phase 2

Following an initial reading of the abstracts (retrieved in Phase 1), the list of articles was refined down to the most relevant literature. In Phase 2 articles were only included if they were published in an international, peer-reviewed journal.

Allocation to these categories was not always straightforward, and where papers spanned more than one area, consensus of the research team determined which domain the article would be placed in. Within each section of the report (i.e., Key articles, Recommended readings, Citation list) articles are presented in alphabetical order by author.

Endnotes

1   Australian Bureau of Statistics (2015). *Causes of death, Australia, 2013. Suicides.* Cat. no. 3303.0. Canberra: ABS.

Key Articles

Suicide and the Internet: Changes in the accessibility of suicide-related information between 2007 and 2014

Biddle, L, Derges J, Mars B, Heron J, Donovan JL, Potokar J, Piper M, Wyllie C, Gunnell D (United Kingdom).

Journal of Affective Disorders 190, 370-375, 2016

Background: Following the ongoing concerns about cyber-suicide, we investigate changes between 2007 and 2014 in material likely to be accessed by suicidal individuals searching for methods of suicide.

Methods: 12 search terms relating to suicide methods were applied to four search engines and the top ten hits from each were categorised and analysed for content. The frequency of each category of site across all searches, using particular search terms and engines, was counted.

Results: Key changes: growth of blogs and discussion forums (from 3% of hits, 2007 to 18.5% of hits, 2014); increase in hits linking to general information sites – especially factual sites that detail and evaluate suicide methods (from 9%, 2007 to 21.7%, 2014). Hits for dedicated suicide sites increased (from 19% to 23%), while formal help sites were less visible (from 13% to 6.5%). Overall, 54% of hits contained information about new high-lethality methods.

Limitations: We did not search for help sites so cannot assess the balance of suicide promoting versus preventing sites available online. Social media was beyond the scope of this study.

Conclusions: Working with ISPs and search engines would help optimise support sites. Better site moderation and implementation of suicide reporting guidelines should be encouraged

Comment

Main findings: Information about suicide is easily accessible through news sites, factual information-based sites and within dedicated or pro-suicide sites. However there has also been a surge of user-generated suicide content (e.g., personal websites, interactive discussion forums, chat rooms), allowing opportunities for users to exchange information on a global scale. Replicating the researchers' previous work in 2007 that examined what a suicidal person might find on searching the internet for information on suicide methods[1], the present study examined changes between 2007 and 2014 in online material. This study also examined in more detail the content of these sites by focusing on themes such as peer support, images, site moderation, help within discussion forum and blogs. Searches were conducted using the same 12 search terms as their previous study, (i.e., suicide; suicide methods; suicide sure methods; most effective methods of suicide; methods of suicide; ways to commit suicide; how to commit suicide; how to kill yourself; easy suicide methods; best suicide methods; pain-free suicide, and quick suicide). These searches were applied to the four most popular search engines: Google, Bing, Yahoo and Ask. The top 10 hits from each were categorised and analysed for content. The content analysis provided additional information on the nature of the sites; such as references to celebrity suicides, links to help sites or services, images relating to suicide (i.e., video clips, pictures and photographs), and information about novel high lethality methods. This yielded a total of 135 unique websites (after accounting for duplicates). Results showed a slight increase from 90 hits (19%) for suicide sites in 2007, to 111 (23.1%) in 2014. The biggest increase was in the number of hits leading to websites providing factual information about suicide methods; a three-fold increase from 24 (5%) to 73 (15.2%). These websites provided suicide method lists, detailed information and sometimes evaluation of suicide methods and information on implementation. There was also a six-fold increase in the number of chat rooms and blogs discussing suicide methods during this period from 12 (3%) to 89 (18.5%). Conversely, there was a 50% decrease in suicide prevention and support sites hits from 62 (13%) to 31 (6.5%). Furthermore, a new category of websites containing explicit images of self-harm, suicide and suicide methods also emerged in 2014, accounting for 1.7% of all hits. Content analysis revealed that over half of the hits (54%) contained information about new high-lethality suicide methods. The overall intent behind some sites was often blurred. For example, some sites promote themselves as offering suicide method information whilst also encouraging users to seek help. In contrast, other sites claim to provide support to individuals yet also list explicit and detailed information on suicide methods.

Implications: This the first study to employ a comparative and longitudinal approach to analyse trends in online content relating to suicide methods across two time-points, mimicking types of internet usage by a suicidal individual. As suicide method information is disseminated widely on the internet, this creates challenges for suicide prevention initiatives given the difficulties in moderating content on the World Wide Web. These findings are not without limitations, given that search engines may personalise results according to previous search history, potentially increasing the volume of suicide-related information in subsequent searches. Thus this study may have underestimated the accessibility of material to returning search engine users. Additionally, as the keywords were used to mimic internet users researching suicide methods rather than those seeking help, the results did not reflect the balance of suicide promoting versus suicide preventing sites. From a policy perspective, a potential strategy would be to work with internet service providers and search engines to optimise supportive sites and minimise pro-suicide sites. However, it could be argued that this approach could violate rights to freedom of expression and also potentially remove suicide prevention peer support blogs and discussion-based forums. It is clear that this is a complex issue, requiring multiple approaches to address. Information sites (e.g., Wikipedia, News sites) are usually sourced by people researching and seeking to perfect suicide methods[2], thus it is important that website moderators follow media reporting guidelines, and are made accountable for the type of information approved and published online. Given that online support is an important part of Australia's current suicide prevention initiatives[3], it is important that this research area is not neglected, in order to improve future suicide prevention initiatives regarding online content.

Endnotes

1. Biddle L, Donovan J, Hawton K, Kapur N, Gunnell D (2008). Suicide and the internet. *BMJ* 336, 800.

2. Biddle L, Gunnell D, Owen-Smith A, Potokar J, Longson D, Hawton K, Kapur N, Donovan J (2012). Information sources used by the suicidal to inform choice of method. *Journal of Affective Disorders* 136, 702-709.

3. Department of Health (2015). *Australian government response to contributing lives, thriving communities – review of mental health programmes and services.* Retrieved 27 April 2016 from http://www.health.gov.au/internet/main/publishing.nsf/Content/0DBEF2D78F7CB9E7CA25 7F07001ACC6D/$File/response.pdf

Do suicide attempts occur more frequently in the spring too? A systematic review and rhythmic analysis

Coimbra DG, Pereira E Silva AC, de Sousa-Rodrigues CF, Barbosa FT, de Siqueira Figueredo D, Araújo Santos JL, Barbosa MR, de Medeiros Alves V, Nardi AE, de Andrade TG (Brazil)

Journal of Affective Disorders 196, 125-137, 2016

Background: Seasonal variations in suicides have been reported worldwide, however, there may be a different seasonal pattern in suicide attempts. The aim of this study was to perform a systematic review on seasonality of suicide attempts considering potential interfering variables, and a statistical analysis for seasonality with the collected data.

Method: Observational epidemiological studies about seasonality in suicide attempts were searched in PubMed, Web of Science, LILACS and Cochrane Library databases with terms attempted suicide, attempt and season. Monthly or seasonal data available were evaluated by rhythmic analysis softwares.

Results: Twenty-nine articles from 16 different countries were included in the final review. It was observed different patterns of seasonality, however, suicide attempts in spring and summer were the most frequent seasons reported. Eight studies indicated differences in sex and three in the method used for suicide attempts. Three articles did not find a seasonal pattern in suicide attempts. Cosinor analysis identified an overall pattern of seasonal variation with a suggested peak in spring, considering articles individually or grouped and independent of sex and method used. A restricted analysis with self-poisoning in hospital samples demonstrated the same profile.

Limitations: Grouping diverse populations and potential analytical bias due to lack of information are the main limitations.

Conclusions: The identification of a seasonal profile suggests the influence of an important environmental modulator that can reverberate to suicide prevention strategies. Further studies controlling interfering variables and investigating the biological substrate for this phenomenon would be helpful to confirm our conclusion.

Comment

Main findings: There is mixed evidence regarding seasonality of suicide attempts, and to date, no systematic review has been published on this topic. This systematic review aimed to explore which season reports the highest incident rates while considering potential confounding variables such as sex, suicide methods and source of data. A statistical analysis for seasonality was also conducted with the collected data to examine the rhythmic phenomena. Searches were limited to articles published in English, Portuguese and Spanish. A total of 208 potentially relevant articles were found, with only 29 studies which satisfied all criteria. The majority of studies were cross-sectional in design, with one prospective study of case series and one case-control study. An overall pattern was found for a peak in spring, independent of sex, region and type of method used. The majority of studies (n=23) identified seasonality in suicide attempts, while three did not find this association. Moreover, when applying methods for the analysis of rhythmic patterns to each article, the peak of suicide attempts was most frequent in spring. However, there were three articles that presented a significant peak in winter and one that presented a peak in summer. Statistical analyses revealed no differences between sexes in seasonality of suicide attempts. The results suggest that suicidal behaviour may be strongly modulated by endogenous or environmental factors associated with seasonal variation rather than sex. Only two studies analysed suicide methods by sex, and they found that among males, seasonality occurred regardless of method used. Meanwhile in females only one study identified seasonality in non-violent methods.

Implications: This systematic review found that a pattern of peak suicide attempts occurred in mid-late spring, irrespective of country. The authors suggest that this association may be a consequence of the increasing photoperiod and light intensity in spring. Although these findings can serve as a starting point for further investigation, the strength and generalisability of these results are limited as this systematic review grouped globally diverse populations (e.g., different ages, suicide methods, ethnic groups, social/economic statuses, cultural differences) and different data sources for their analyses. Thus, to further investigate this association, future studies should aim to employ a significant sample size from various countries, and include measures of different latitudes, photoperiod variation, sex and suicide methods, while controlling for psychiatric disorders and analysing for rhythmic variation. The results would help inform future suicide prevention initiatives[1,2], by providing relevant bodies such as public health agencies and health professionals with a better understanding of seasonal variations in suicide attempts in order to provide assistance to vulnerable individuals when they are most at risk.

Endnotes

1. Queensland Mental Health Commission (2015). *Queensland Suicide Prevention Action Plan 2015-2017.* Retrieved 27 April 2016 from https://www.qmhc.qld.gov.au/wp-content/uploads/2015/09/Queensland-Suicide-Prevention-Action-Plan-2015-17_WEB.pdf
2. Department of Health (2015). *Australian government response to contributing lives, thriving communities – review of mental health programmes and services.* Retrieved 27 April 2016 from http://www.health.gov.au/internet/main/publishing.nsf/Content/0DBEF2D78F7CB9E7CA25 7F07001ACC6D/$File/response.pdf

Evaluation of benefit to patients of training mental health professionals in suicide guidelines: Cluster randomised trial

de Beurs DP, de Groot MH, de Keijser J, van Duijn E, de Winter RF, Kerkhof AJ (Netherlands)

British Journal of Psychiatry 208, 477-483, 2016

Background: Randomised studies examining the effect on patients of training professionals in adherence to suicide guidelines are scarce.

Aims: To assess whether patients benefited from the training of professionals in adherence to suicide guidelines.

Method: In total 45 psychiatric departments were randomised (Dutch trial register: NTR3092). In the intervention condition, all staff in the departments were trained with an e-learning supported train-the-trainer programme. After the intervention, patients were assessed at admission and at 3-month follow-up. Primary outcome was change in suicide ideation, assessed with the Beck Scale for Suicide Ideation.

Results: For the total group of 566 patients with a positive score on the Beck Scale for Suicide Ideation at baseline, intention-to-treat analysis showed no effects of the intervention on patient outcomes at 3-month follow-up. Patients who were suicidal with a DSM-IV diagnosis of depression (n = 154) showed a significant decrease in suicide ideation when treated in the intervention group. Patients in the intervention group more often reported that suicidality was discussed during treatment.

Conclusions: Overall, no effect of our intervention on patients was found. However, we did find a beneficial effect of the training of professionals on patients with depression.

Comment

Main findings: In order to strengthen suicide prevention in Dutch mental healthcare, an evidence-based multidisciplinary practice guideline for the assessment and treatment of suicidal behaviour (PGSB) was implemented in 2012. It has been argued that training of professionals in guideline recommendations improves adherence to guidelines and thus improves patient care. However, to date, randomised control trials (RCT) examining the effectiveness of suicide guideline training is limited. Therefore, an RCT was conducted examining the effectiveness of an e-learning supported train-the-trainer program (TtT-e), delivered to multidisciplinary teams of mental healthcare departments. TtT-e is based on the premise that adults learn more effectively where the education is relevant to their work, where it draws on their previous experience[1] and where it is delivered through a trusted social network[2]. The TtT-e combines 1-day face-to-face training with an additional e-learning module. It was hypothesised that suicidal individuals who received treatment from TtT-e trained professionals would recover more quickly from suicidal ideation than patients treated by professionals who did not receive the TtT-e training (control), but received information on the release of the guideline via the usual methods (e.g., internet, conferences, workshops). Secondary measures were self-reported suicide attempts, treatment satisfaction and discussion of suicidal thoughts. Mental healthcare departments were included in the study where they treated patients 18 years and older and where professionals felt the need for suicide prevention skill training. Forty-five departments were deemed eligible, 22 being randomly allocated to the TtT-e group and 23 to the control group. Departments were matched on patients' DSM-IV main diagnosis and on comparable average length of treatment. Data were collected from patients at admission (baseline) and then three months after admission (follow-up). Of the 881 patients included, 556 (64%) had a baseline suicide ideation score greater than one, and 250 (28%) reported at least one suicide attempt. Results showed there was no significant effect of TtT-e on either suicide ideation or suicide attempts between baseline and follow-up. However, TtT-e did have an effect on depressed patients, recording an 8.4 point decrease in suicidal ideation between baseline and follow-up, compared to a 4.8 point decrease in the control group. There was also no effect of TtT-e on suicide attempts or treatment satisfaction for depressed patients. Suicidal thoughts were more likely to be discussed in the TtT-e group than in the control group.

Implications: These findings align with previous research demonstrating the effectiveness of guideline training for general practitioners treating older adults with depression[3]. It is possible that the TtT-e training was only effective with depressed patients because its focus on making contact with patients and discussing suicidality might be more appropriate for suicidal patients with a depressive disorder than for those with other disorders such as borderline or psychotic disorder. The finding that suicidality was discussed more during treatment indicates that professionals changed their behaviour during individual treatment sessions, and is consistent with previous research that found that general practitioners assessed more patients for suicide risk following the implementation of a tailored depression guideline[4]. A limitation of this study was that 37% of patient diagnoses were missing, preventing the authors from testing the effectiveness of TtT-e on subgroups other than patients with depression. The results of this study provide evidence for the effectiveness of TtT-e training for depressed patients, and support the use of training to reinforce suicide prevention guidelines amongst mental health professionals. This is particularly relevant in the Australian context given that both Federal[5] and State[6] governments plan to implement effective mental health guidelines for community and clinical services.

Endnotes

1. Knowles MS (1970). *The modern practice of adult education* (Vol. 41). New York: New York Association Press.
2. Rogers EM (2010). *Diffusion of innovations.* Simon and Schuster.
3. Alexopoulos GS, Reynolds CF III, Bruce ML, Katz IR, Raue PJ, Mulsant BH, Oslin DW, Ten Have T (2009). Reducing suicidal ideation and depression in older primary care patients: 24-

month outcomes of the PROSPECT study. *American Journal of Psychiatry* 166, 882–890.

4. Baker R, Reddish S, Robertson N, Hearnshaw H, Jones B (2001). Randomised controlled trial of tailored strategies to implement guidelines for the management of patients with depression in general practice. *British Journal of General Practice* 51, 737-741.

5. Department of Health (2015). *Australian government response to contributing lives, thriving communities – review of mental health programmes and services.* Retrieved 29 April 2016 from http://www.health.gov.au/internet/main/publishing.nsf/Content/0DBEF2D78F7CB9E7CA25 7F07001ACC6D/$File/response.pdf

6. Queensland Mental Health Commission (2015). *Queensland Suicide Prevention Action Plan 2015-2017.* Retrieved 27 April 2016 from https://www.qmhc.qld.gov.au/wp-content/uploads /2015/09/Queensland-Suicide-Prevention-Action-Plan-2015-17_WEB.pdf

The Impact of a Suicide Prevention Strategy on Reducing the Economic Cost of Suicide in the New South Wales Construction Industry

Doran CM, Ling R, Gullestrup J, Swannell S, Milner A (Australia)
Crisis 37, 121–129, 2016

Background: Little research has been conducted into the cost and prevention of self-harm in the workplace.

Aims: To quantify the economic cost of self-harm and suicide among New South Wales (NSW) construction industry (CI) workers and to examine the potential economic impact of implementing Mates in Construction (MIC).

Method: Direct and indirect costs were estimated. Effectiveness was measured using the relative risk ratio (RRR). In Queensland (QLD), relative suicide risks were estimated for 5-year periods before and after the commencement of MIC. For NSW, the difference between the expected (i.e., using NSW pre-MIC [2008–2012] suicide risk) and counterfactual suicide cases (i.e., applying QLD RRR) provided an estimate of potential suicide cases averted in the post-MIC period (2013–2017). Results were adjusted using the average uptake (i.e., 9.4%) of MIC activities in QLD. Economic savings from averted cases were compared with the cost of implementing MIC.

Results: The cost of self-harm and suicide in the NSW CI was AU $527 million in 2010. MIC could potentially avert 0.4 suicides, 1.01 full incapacity cases, and 4.92 short absences, generating annual savings of AU $3.66 million. For every AU $1 invested, the economic return is approximately AU $4.6.

Conclusion: MIC represents a positive economic investment in workplace safety.

Comment

Main findings: Current literature suggests that suicide rates are differentially distributed across industry and occupational groups. Low-skilled occupation groups and construction industry (CI) workers are said to experience higher rates of suicide[1,2]. Unfortunately, suicide prevention in the workplace has not yet been adequately addressed. This study therefore aimed to quantify the economic impact of suicide and self-harm in the New South Wales (NSW) CI, and to examine the potential economic impact of implementing the suicide prevention strategy Mates in Construction (MIC). The study calculated the total economic cost of CI self-harm and suicide by multiplying the average indirect and direct costs by cases of self-harm and suicide. The classification structure for economic costs was comprised of production disturbance costs (workplace costs), human capital costs (lost future earnings), medical costs, administrative costs, transfer costs and other costs. Also relevant to cost was the outcome severity of suicidal behaviours. Three levels of outcome severity were used: short absence involving less than five days off work, full incapacity resulting in the individual being permanently unable to return to work, and a fatality.

The study utilised the MIC prevention strategy to assess the economic impact of reducing CI suicides and suicide attempts. MIC is an early intervention program consisting of three components: general awareness training, connector training and applied suicide intervention skills training. It has been primarily implemented in Queensland and has been shown to be effective at reducing suicide rates[3]. Intervention effectiveness for the NSW CI was estimated using the change in suicide cases experienced following the implementation of MIC in Queensland; which was a reduction of 9.64%. In Queensland, 9.4% of CI workers were exposed to MIC. Therefore, to calculate the effect of MIC on suicide and suicide attempts in NSW, the authors attributed 9.4% of the 9.64% estimated decrease in suicide cases to MIC.

In 2010, the cost of self-harm and suicide in the NSW CI was calculated at $527 million; this included 145 self-harm incidents resulting in full incapacity, 710 self-harm incidents resulting in short work absences, and 57 deaths by suicide. The per person costs for suicide cases were estimated to be $925 for short term absences, $2.78 million for full incapacity and $2.14 million due to death. Moreover, for every 15 suicide attempts there was one fatality, 2.55 incapacity cases and 12.45 short absence cases. Hence, it was estimated that if implemented, MIC would avert 0.4 suicide fatalities, 1.01 full incapacitations and 4.92 short absences from work, potentially saving $3.66 million each year. Given the cost of implementing MIC is $800,000, the return on investment would be $4.60 for every $1.00.

Implications: These findings are consistent with research from Beyond Blue which found that workplace mental health investment resulted in a benefit-cost ratio of $2.30 for every $1 spent[4]. The current study provides a strong economic case to increase expenditure in suicide prevention and mental health programs aimed at not only the CI but other at-risk occupations. It highlights the significant impact that suicide prevention investments can have, and further validates the need to provide support to people working in low skilled and CI occupations[1,2]. The study captured the wide ranging costs of suicide, such as the costs associated with suicide bereavement and counselling. However, a limitation of this study is that its benefit-cost estimations are based on Queensland data and not NSW data. Therefore, it is unclear whether the same outcomes seen in Queensland would apply to NSW. The study also adopted very conservative estimates in assessing MIC uptake in the CI. It is possible that MIC would have greater uptake in the NSW CI, especially over time, given Queensland's positive experience.

Endnotes

1. Milner A, Spittal MJ, Pirkis J, La Montagne AD (2013). Suicide by occupation: Systematic review and meta-analysis. *The British Journal of Psychiatry* 203, 409–416.
2. Milner A, Niven H, LaMontagne A (2014). Suicide by occupational skill level in the Australian construction industry: Data from 2001 to 2010 *Australian and New Zealand Journal of Public Health* 38, 281-285.
3. Gullestrup J, Lequertier B, Martin G (2011). MATES in construction: Impact of a multimodal, community-based program for suicide prevention in the construction industry. *International Journal of Environmental Research and Public Health* 8, 4180-4196.
4. Beyond Blue (2014). *Creating a mentally healthy workplace: Return on investment analysis.* Canberra, Australia: Australian Government National Health Commission.

The impact of self-harm by young people on parents and families: A qualitative study

Ferrey AE, Hughes ND, Simkin S, Locock L, Stewart A, Kapur N, Gunnell D, Hawton K (United Kingdom)

BMJ Open 6, e009631, 2016

Objectives: Little research has explored the full extent of the impact of self-harm on the family. This study aimed to explore the emotional, physical and practical effects of a young person's self-harm on parents and family.

Design and Participants: We used qualitative methods to explore the emotional, physical and practical effects of a young person's self-harm on their parents and family. We conducted a thematic analysis of thirty-seven semistructured narrative interviews with parents of young people who had self-harmed.

Results: After the discovery of self-harm, parents described initial feelings of shock, anger and disbelief. Later reactions included stress, anxiety, feelings of guilt and in some cases the onset or worsening of clinical depression. Social isolation was reported, as parents withdrew from social contact due to the perceived stigma associated with self-harm. Parents also described significant impacts on siblings, ranging from upset and stress to feelings of responsibility and worries about stigma at school. Siblings had mixed responses, but were often supportive. Practically speaking, parents found the necessity of being available to their child often conflicted with the demands of full-time work. This, along with costs of, for example, travel and private care, affected family finances. However, parents generally viewed the future as positive and hoped that with help, their child would develop better coping mechanisms.

Conclusions: Self-harm by young people has major impacts on parents and other family members. Clinicians and staff who work with young people who self-harm should be sensitive to these issues and offer appropriate support and guidance for families.

Comment

Main findings: Most research on self-harm has examined the characteristics, intentions and outcomes of the individuals involved[1]. A person's self-harm may have significant impacts on their parents and family; yet there has been a lack of research in this area. This study addressed this gap by examining the emotional and practical impacts on family and parents of young people who self-harmed. This qualitative study employed semistructured narrative interviews with 37 parents of 35 young people who had self-harmed. These interviews began with an uninterrupted open-ended section where participants described their experiences of caring for a young person who self-harmed. Interviewers asked follow-up questions if more information was required. Participants were purposively sampled through mental health charities, support groups, clinicians, adverts, social media, personal contacts and snowballing through existing contacts in England, Scotland

and Wales. The average age of the young people who self-harmed was 15.1 years, and all young persons had engaged in multiple acts of self-harm. Although ranging in severity, self-harm included self-cutting, overdoses, burning and strangulation. Twenty-nine of the young people were female and six were male.

Parents reported that they often discovered their child's self-harm from teachers, their children, friends of their children, or through searching for information (such as reading their child's diary). Their initial reaction to discovering their child self-harmed included shock, horror, frustration, annoyance, anger. Parents also described feelings of shame, guilt or embarrassment. Depression was common among parents, which some related directly to their child's self-harm. One parent reported that the impact of her child self-harming lead to a relapse of her own self-harm. Some parents experienced physical symptoms as a result (e.g., feeling sick, panic attacks, physical exhaustion, chest pains, and losing a lot of weight). The stresses associated with self-harm also put strain on relationships between family members and sometimes led to marriage problems. The reactions of other siblings to the child's self-harm behaviour varied as several experienced distress, anger, resentment and frustration, while others were extremely supportive, and became overprotective of their sibling. Some siblings felt responsible and avoided irritating their sibling in case they self-harmed, while school-aged siblings worried about stigma at school. Relationships with parents (child's grandparents) were also affected as some family members were reportedly unsupportive. However some grandparents were determined to help, and as a result developed stronger relationships with their children and grandchildren.

A common theme observed was a profound sense of isolation and a desire to keep a child's problems private. Some parents withdrew socially due to their perceived stigma of self-harm, which could potentially lead to temporary or permanent loss of social support. Several parents reported that friendships function as an important source of support, especially when hearing about the experiences of others in similar situations. Many parents found themselves in financial strain as it was difficult to manage work commitments while wanting to be available for their children. In addition, parents often spent large amounts of money on private psychiatric care or counselling for their child. Nevertheless, parents mostly thought about the future in a guardedly positive light. Another common theme was "taking life one day at a time". Parents were aware of their child's problems, concerned about their vulnerabilities and ability to cope as an adult and worried about the effect stigma might have on others' opinions of their child.

Implications: This is one of the first qualitative studies to explore the emotional, physical and practical effects of young peoples' self-harm on their parents and family. Results showed that self-harm can have extensive effects on parents' emotional states, as well as mental health, relationships with partners and others, employment and finances. A common worry was that their child self-harming was a result of what they did or did not do as a parent, which resulted in feelings of shame, embarrassment or guilt. It should be noted that this study relied on self-reported data from one parent, which may be subject to a number of biases. There was also limited diversity as only one participant was from a minority ethnic background. In order to capture the full impact of a child's self-harming behaviour on their families, future research should aim for wider ethnic diversity and include other family members such as fathers, siblings and grandparents. The findings from this study should help inform organisations such as Parentline[2] in providing support and guidance to parents whose children are self-harming.

Endnotes

1. Hawton K, Rodham K, Evans E, Weatherall R (2002). Deliberate self-harm in adolescents: self report survey in schools in England. *BMJ* 325, 1207–11.
2. Parentline (2016). *Tip sheets – Self-injury/self-harm*. Retrieved on 29 April 2016 from http://www.parentline.com.au/parenting-information/tip-sheets/self-harm.php

Effect of the Garrett Lee Smith memorial suicide prevention program on suicide attempts among youths

Garraza LG, Walrath C, Goldston DB, Reid H, McKeon R (United States)

JAMA Psychiatry 72, 1143-1149, 2015

Importance: Youth suicide prevention is a major public health priority. Studies documenting the effectiveness of community-based suicide prevention programs in reducing the number of nonlethal suicide attempts have been sparse.

Objective: To determine whether a reduction in suicide attempts among youths occurs following the implementation of the Garrett Lee Smith Memorial Suicide Prevention Program (hereafter referred to as the GLS program), consistent with the reduction in mortality documented previously.

Design, Setting, and Participants: We conducted an observational study of community-based suicide prevention programs for youths across 46 states and 12 tribal communities. The study compared 466 counties implementing the GLS program between 2006 and 2009 with 1161 counties that shared key preintervention characteristics but were not exposed to the GLS program. The unweighted rounded numbers of respondents used in this analysis were 84000 in the control group and 57000 in the intervention group. We used propensity score-based techniques to increase comparability (on background characteristics) between counties that implemented the GLS program and counties that did not. We combined information on program activities collected by the GLS national evaluation with information on county characteristics from several secondary sources. The data analysis was performed between April and August 2014. P < .05 was considered statistically significant.

Exposures: Comprehensive, multifaceted suicide prevention programs, including gatekeeper training, education and mental health awareness programs, screening activities, improved community partnerships and linkages to service, programs for suicide survivors, and crisis hotlines.

Main Outcomes and Measures: Suicide attempt rates for each county following implementation of the GLS program for youths 16 to 23 years of age at the time the program activities were implemented. We obtained this information from the National Survey on Drug Use and Health administered to a large national probabilistic sample between 2008 and 2011.

Results: Counties implementing GLS program activities had significantly lower suicide attempt rates among youths 16 to 23 years of age in the year following implementation of the GLS program than did similar counties that did not implement GLS program activities (4.9 fewer attempts per 1000 youths [95% CI, 1.8-8.0 fewer attempts per 1000 youths]; P = .003). More than 79000 suicide attempts may have been averted during the period studied following implementation of the GLS program. There was no significant difference in suicide attempt rates among individuals older than 23 years during that same period. There was no evidence of longer-term differences in suicide attempt rates.

Conclusions and Relevance: Comprehensive GLS program activities were associated with a reduction in suicide attempt rates. Sustained suicide prevention programming efforts may be needed to maintain the reduction in suicide attempt rates.

Comment

Main findings: The Garrett Lee Smith Memorial Suicide Prevention Program (GLS program) funds competitive grants for suicide prevention activities throughout the United States. These activities include mental health awareness programs, screening activities, gate-keeper training, crisis hotlines, programs for suicide survivors and improved community partnerships and linking services. Limited research has been published on the effectiveness of community-based suicide prevention programs, such as those funded by the GLS program. This study sought to address this deficiency by examining the differences in suicide attempts between communities that implemented a GLS funded program and those with similar characteristics that did not. The study aimed to complement an earlier report investigating the effectiveness of the GLS program on suicide mortality among young people. Community gatekeeper training was used as an indicator of GLS program implementation due to its ubiquity in GLS funded programs. The study investigated the effectiveness of GLS programs targeting youth and therefore examined suicide attempts in youth within the age range targeted by the program (i.e., those who were between 16 and 23 years old during the implementation of the programs). Given that previous findings have shown GLS programs to be ineffective beyond one year, suicide attempts over time were also examined. Data were collected from 466 counties in America that were exposed to GLS programs between 2006 and 2009, as well as 1161 counties that shared similar characteristics but did not have GLS programs. Analysis was based on data from the National Survey on Drug Use and Health (NSDUH) conducted between 2008 and 2011. The primary variable of interest was the suicide attempt rate post GLS program implementation. Suicide attempt rates for adults aged 24 years and older were used as a control outcome, as this demographic group was not the target of the GLS programs. Several county level and individual level covariates, such as demographics and economic indicators, were also included for the purpose of sample selection and weighting prior to the main analysis. Results showed a significant reduction in suicide attempts in youths aged 16 to 23 years in counties that implemented a GLS funded program compared to those that did not. It is estimated that these suicide prevention programs resulted 39% fewer suicide attempts or 4.9 fewer attempts per 1000 youths. The absence of change in youths aged 24 years and older provides support for the premise that the changes were due to GLS program activities. However, consistent with previous research these results were temporary, with no effect on suicide attempts two or more years after the implementation of GLS programs.

Implementation: These findings contribute to the evidence base regarding the effectiveness of a comprehensive approach to suicide prevention. They also highlight the temporary impact of these initiatives on suicidality and the importance of continued implementation of suicide prevention program activities to ensure results over time. However, it is important that these findings are interpreted within the limitations of the study. Causality cannot be definitively inferred from this study given the lack of experimental randomisation, and whilst the authors did account for potential confounding variables prior to their main analysis, it is still possible that other variables may have influenced the results. Furthermore, information concerning lifetime suicide attempts was not available to the authors, meaning they could not determine whether the effectiveness of the GLS programs differed based upon one's history of suicidal behaviour. The apparent success of these programs in reducing suicide attempts lends further support to the implementation of community-based suicide prevention programs in Australia. The Queensland Suicide Prevention Action Plan 2015-17 recommends the use of gatekeeper training as a way to improve the screening and detection of suicidal ideation and behaviour[1]. Whilst gatekeeper training has been implemented in Australia, this study suggests that more extensive and ongoing training is needed through community-based suicide prevention programs.

Endnotes

1. Queensland Mental Health Commission (2015). *Queensland Suicide Prevention Action Plan 2015-17.* Retrieved 28 April 2016 from https://www.qmhc.qld.gov.au/wp-content/uploads/2015/09/Queensland-Suicide-Prevention-Action-Plan-2015-17_WEB.pdf

Incidence of suicide among persons who had a parent who died during their childhood: A population-based cohort study.

Guldin MB, Li J, Pedersen HS, Obel C, Agerbo E, Gissler M, Cnattingius S, Olsen J, Vestergaard M (Denmark)

JAMA Psychiatry 72, 1227-1234, 2015

Importance: Parental death from suicide is associated with increased risk of suicide in the bereaved child, but little is known about the long-term risks of suicide after parental death from other causes. A better understanding of this association may improve suicide prevention efforts.

Objective: To examine the long-term risks of suicide after parental death and how the risk trajectories differed by cause of parental death while accounting for major potential confounding variables.

Design, Setting, and Participants: A population-based matched cohort study was performed using information from nationwide registers (data from 1968 to 2008) in 3 Scandinavian countries (for a total of 7 302 033 persons). We identified 189 094 children (2.6%) who had a parent who died before the child reached 18 years of age (ie, the bereaved cohort). Each bereaved child was matched by sex and age to 10 children who did not have a parent who died before they reached 18 years of age (for a total of 1 890 940 children) (ie, the reference cohort). Both cohorts were followed for up to 40 years. Poisson regression was used to calculate the incidence rate ratio (IRR), while accounting for age at parental death, sex, time since bereavement, maternal/paternal death, birth order, family history of psychiatric illness, and socioeconomic status. Data analyses were finalized June 24, 2015.

Exposure: The main exposure was death of a parent within the first 18 years of life.

Main Outcomes And Measures: Incidence of suicide among persons who had a parent who died during their childhood.

Results: During follow-up, 265 bereaved persons (0.14%) and 1342 non-bereaved persons (0.07%) died of suicide (IRR = 2.02 [95%CI, 1.75-2.34]); IRR = 3.44 (95%CI, 2.61-4.52) for children who had a parent who died of suicide, and IRR = 1.76 (95%CI, 1.49-2.09) for children who had a parent who died of other causes. The IRR tended to be higher for children who had a parent who died before they reached 6 years of age, and the IRR remained high for at least 25 years. During 25 years of follow-up, the absolute risk of suicide was 4 in 1000 persons for boys who experienced parental death and 2 in 1000 persons for girls who experienced parental death.

Conclusions and Relevance: Parental death in childhood is, irrespective of cause, associated with an increased long-term risk of suicide. The consequences of parental death in childhood are far-reaching, and suicide risk trajectories may be influenced by early-life conditions. Future public health efforts should consider helping highly distressed children to cope with bereavement.

Comment

Main findings: Experiencing the death of a parent can be extremely damaging to children, resulting in mental health problems and suicidality[1,2]. Research on the long-term effects of parental death is limited, with few studies of sufficient size and follow-up time. This large population-based matched cohort study was therefore conducted with the aim of investigating the long-term suicide risk of parental death and how the risk trajectories differ due to different factors.

Population cohort data was collected from Denmark, Finland and Sweden by linking data from the national registers of these countries. Unique personal identification numbers used in the Nordic countries allows linkage of individual-level data between different registers. Cohort data consisted of persons born in Denmark from 1968 to 2008, Sweden between 1973 and 2006 and a random sample of 89.3% of persons born in Finland from 1987 to 2007. Each of the 189 094 children who were found to have experienced parental death before 18 years of age (i.e., the bereaved cohort) were then matched to 10 children who did not have a parent who died before they reached 18 years of age (1 890 940 in total for the reference cohort). Matching was based upon age at the time of parental death, gender and country of residence. Citizen data was collected from the time of their parent's death (or equivalent in the reference cohort) until either their own death, emigration from their country or the end of the study (December 31, 2009, in Denmark; December 31, 2008, in Sweden; and December 31, 2010, in Finland). The authors were interested in whether incidence rate ratios (IRRs) varied according to specific suicide risk factors: sex, age at time of parental death, time since parental death, maternal or paternal death, parity, family history of psychiatric illness, socioeconomic status, and parental education level. Based upon the *International Classification of Diseases (ICD)*, cause of death was categorised as either suicides, accidents or other causes.

Overall, 265 (0.14%) bereaved children died by suicide compared to 1342 (0.07%) non-bereaved children in the reference cohort. This equates to an IRR of 2.02 bereaved suicides for every one non-bereaved suicide. Suicide risk remained high for at least 25 years after parental death, with the absolute suicide risk for boys being four in 1000 and for girls, two in 1000. Suicide risk was over three times higher for children who experience parental suicide compared to non-bereaved children. Comparatively, suicide risk for children whose parents died by other causes was 1.76 times greater and for those whose parents died by accident it was 1.89 times higher. The incident rate of suicide was higher for: boys whose mother had died (IRR = 2.52 [95% CI, 1.93-3.27]), children who experienced parental death before reaching six years of age (IRR = 2.83 [95% CI, 2.12-3.78]), and for first-born children (IRR = 2.22 [95% CI, 1.75-2.82]).

Implications: These findings have important public health implications as they highlight the increased suicide risks facing survivors of parental death. This study reinforces the need for mental health services to provide support for children bereaved by parental death, particularly for those whose parents died by suicide.

These findings are consistent with other studies that have investigated the impact of parental death on children[3,4]. Furthermore, the study's large sample size and access to precise longitudinal data is unparalleled. However, it is important to note that investigation of the interaction between psychiatric disorders and suicides was challenged due to the rarity of psychiatric disorders in offspring who died by suicide. Furthermore, specific data was limited to particular countries, with data on parent education levels only available for Denmark, and data on socioeconomic status and psychiatric disorders only available for Denmark and Sweden. The underlying causal mechanism for the association between parental death and subsequent suicide risk in offspring remains unclear. However, the findings do suggest that the pathway leading to suicide can have its beginnings in early life experiences, such as the death of a parent.

Endnotes

1. Wilcox HC, Kuramoto SJ, Lichtenstein P, Långström N, Brent DA, Runeson B (2010). Psychiatric morbidity, violent crime, and suicide among children and adolescents exposed to parental death. *Journal of the American Academy of Child & Adolescent Psychiatry*, 49, 514-523.
2. Geulayov G, Gunnell D, Holmen TL, Metcalfe C (2012). The association of parental fatal and non-fatal suicidal behaviour with offspring suicidal behaviour and depression: a systematic review and meta-analysis. *Psychological medicine* 42, 1567-1580.
3. Jakobsen IS, Christiansen E (2011). Young people's risk of suicide attempts in relation to parental death: A population-based register study. *Journal of Child Psychology and Psychiatry* 52, 176-183.
4. Kuramoto SJ, Brent DA, Wilcox HC (2009). The impact of parental suicide on child and adolescent offspring. *Suicide and Life-Threatening Behavior* 39, 137–151.

A novel brief therapy for patients who attempt suicide: A 24-months follow-up randomized controlled study of the Attempted Suicide Short Intervention Program (ASSIP)

Gysin-Maillart A, Schwab S, Soravia L, Megert M, Michel K (Switzerland)

PLoS Medicine 13, e1001968, 2016

Background: Attempted suicide is the main risk factor for suicide and repeated suicide attempts. However, the evidence for follow-up treatments reducing suicidal behavior in these patients is limited. The objective of the present study was to evaluate the efficacy of the Attempted Suicide Short Intervention Program (ASSIP) in reducing suicidal behavior. ASSIP is a novel brief therapy based on a patient-centered model of suicidal behavior, with an emphasis on early therapeutic alliance.

Methods and Findings: Patients who had recently attempted suicide were randomly allocated to treatment as usual (n = 60) or treatment as usual plus ASSIP (n = 60). ASSIP participants received three therapy sessions followed by regular contact through personalized letters over 24 months. Participants considered to be at high risk of suicide were included, 63% were diagnosed with an affective disorder, and 50% had a history of prior suicide attempts. Clinical exclusion criteria were habitual self-harm, serious cognitive impairment, and psychotic disorder. Study participants completed a set of psychosocial and clinical questionnaires every 6 months over a 24-month follow-up period. The study represents a real-world clinical setting at an outpatient clinic of a university hospital of psychiatry. The primary outcome measure was repeat suicide attempts during the 24-month follow-up period. Secondary outcome measures were suicidal ideation, depression, and health-care utilization. Furthermore, effects of prior suicide attempts, depression at baseline, diagnosis, and therapeutic alliance on outcome were investigated. During the 24-month follow-up period, five repeat suicide attempts were recorded in the ASSIP group and 41 attempts in the control group. The rates of participants reattempting suicide at least once were 8.3% (n = 5) and 26.7% (n = 16). ASSIP was associated with an approximately 80% reduced risk of participants making at least one repeat suicide attempt (Wald χ^2_1 = 13.1, 95% CI 12.4-13.7, p < 0.001). ASSIP participants spent 72% fewer days in the hospital during follow-up (ASSIP: 29 d; control group: 105 d; W = 94.5, p = 0.038). Higher scores of patient-rated therapeutic alliance in the ASSIP group were associated with a lower rate of repeat suicide attempts. Prior suicide attempts, depression, and a diagnosis of personality disorder at baseline did not significantly affect outcome. Participants with a diagnosis of borderline personality disorder (n = 20) had more previous suicide attempts and a higher number of reattempts. Key study limitations were missing data and dropout rates. Although both were generally low, they increased during follow-up. At 24 months, the group difference in dropout rate was significant: ASSIP, 7% (n = 4); control, 22% (n = 13). A further limitation is that we do not have detailed information of the co-active follow-up treatment apart from participant self-reports every 6 months on the setting and the duration of the co-active treatment.

Conclusions: ASSIP, a manual-based brief therapy for patients who have recently attempted suicide, administered in addition to the usual clinical treatment, was efficacious in reducing suicidal behavior in a real-world clinical setting. ASSIP fulfils the need for an easy-to-administer low-cost intervention. Large pragmatic trials will be needed to conclusively establish the efficacy of ASSIP and replicate our findings in other clinical settings.

Comment

Main findings: Attempted Suicide Short Intervention Program (ASSIP) is a novel brief treatment composed of three 60-90 minute therapy sessions, and follow-up over two years via personalised mailed letters for those who had recently attempted suicide. It is based on a patient-centred model of suicidal behaviour, focusing on early therapeutic alliance. This program includes psychoeducation, cognitive case conceptualisation, safety planning and continued long-term out-reach contact. The aim of this randomised control trial was to evaluate the efficacy of the ASSIP in reducing the rate of repeated suicide attempts. The researchers also made comparisons between the groups on suicidal ideation, levels of depression, and how often people were hospitalised. A total of 120 patients were randomly assigned to ASSIP (n=60) or control group (n=60). Treatment as usual (inpatient, day patient and individual outpatient care) continued in both groups. Patients who had habitual self-harm, serious cognitive impairment, psychotic disorder, insufficient fluency of German, and resided outside the hospital catchment area were excluded. There was a 5% dropout rate for ASSIP and a 22% dropout rate for the control group at 12 months. At 24 months, there was a significant difference in dropout rates between groups: 7% and 22%, for ASSIP and the control group respectively. During the 24-month follow-up period, there were five repeat suicide attempts in ASSIP and 41 in the control group. The rates of patients reattempting suicide at least once were 8.3% (n=5) and 26.7% (n=16), respectively. Moreover, ASSIP was associated with an approximately 80% reduced risk of patients making at least one repeat suicide attempt (95% CI 12.4-13.7, p < 0.001). The ASSIP group spent 72% fewer days in the hospital than controls during follow-up (ASSIP: 29 days; control group: 105 days). However, there were no differences between groups in self-reported suicidal ideation or levels of depression.

Implications: The results of this study showed that ASSIP significantly reduced suicidal behaviour up to the 24-month follow up in patients who had recently attempted suicide. This treatment was based on a published manual, which, according to the authors is highly structured and easy to adhere to for both therapists and patients. The findings from this study are promising given the real-world clinical setting (a university hospital) and the potential to reduce suicide attempts, deaths from suicide and health-care costs. A limitation of the study was the use of small trials which may have impacted the effect sizes. In addition, measurements of suicidal ideation and depression were primarily based on self-reports (although the authors attempted to minimise this problem by supplementing the self-reported data with medical records etc). Further testing using large clinical trials is recommended in order to establish the efficacy of ASSIP in reducing suicidal behaviours. These findings may help inform Australia's suicide prevention programs, and potentially lower the healthcare costs of suicide, which was estimated to be $1.7 billion in 2012[1]. Moreover, further investigation into the efficacy and efficiency of programs like ASSIP in treatment settings would be in line with Australia's mental health reform, by identifying opportunities for better use of services, reducing duplication and removing inefficiencies in the mental health system, and improving post-discharge care for people at high risk of suicide[2].

Endnotes

1. KPMG Health Economics (2013). *The economic cost of suicide in Australia.* Retrieved 28 April 2016 from http://menslink.org.au/wp-content/uploads/2013/10/KPMG-Economic-cost-of-suicide -in-Australia-Menslink.pdf
2. Department of Health (2015). *Australian government response to contributing lives, thriving communities – review of mental health programmes and services.* Retrieved 27 April 2016 from http://www.health.gov.au/internet/main/publishing.nsf/Content/0DBEF2D78F7CB9E7CA25 7F07001ACC6D/$File/response.pdf

Exploring synergistic interactions and catalysts in complex interventions: Longitudinal, mixed methods case studies of an Optimised Multi-Level Suicide Prevention Intervention in four European countries (OSPI-Europe)

Harris FM, Maxwell M, O'Connor R, Coyne JC, Arensman E, Coffey C, Koburger N, Gusmão R, Costa S, Szekely A, Cserháti Z, McDaid D, Van Audenhove C, Hegerl U (United Kingdom, Netherlands, Ireland, Germany, Portugal, Hungary, Belgium)

BMC Public Health 16, 1-9, 2016

Background: The Medical Research Council (MRC) Framework for complex interventions highlights the need to explore interactions between components of complex interventions, but this has not yet been fully explored within complex, non-pharmacological interventions. This paper draws on the process evaluation data of a suicide prevention programme implemented in four European countries to illustrate the synergistic interactions between intervention levels in a complex programme, and to present our method for exploring these.

Methods: A realist evaluation approach informed the process evaluation, which drew on mixed methods, longitudinal case studies. Data collection consisted of 47 semi-structured interviews, 12 focus groups, one workshop, fieldnoted observations of six programme meetings and 20 questionnaires (delivered at six month intervals to each of the four intervention sites). Analysis drew on the framework approach, facilitated by the use of QSR NVivo (v10). Our qualitative approach to exploring synergistic interactions (QuaSIC) also developed a matrix of hypothesised synergies that were explored within one workshop and two waves of data collection.

Results: All four implementation countries provided examples of synergistic interactions that added value beyond the sum of individual intervention levels or components in isolation. For instance, the launch ceremony of the public health campaign (a level 3 intervention) in Ireland had an impact on the community-based professional training, increasing uptake and visibility of training for journalists in particular. In turn, this led to increased media reporting of OSPI activities (monitored as part of the public health campaign) and also led to wider dissemination of editorial guidelines for responsible reporting of suicidal acts. Analysis of the total process evaluation dataset also revealed the new phenomenon of the OSPI programme acting as a catalyst for externally generated (and funded) activity that shared the goals of suicide prevention.

Conclusions: The QuaSIC approach enabled us to develop and refine our definition of synergistic interactions and add the innovative concept of catalytic effects. This represents a novel approach to the evaluation of complex interventions. By exploring synergies and catalytic interactions related to a complex intervention or programme, we reveal the added value to planned activities and how they might be maximised.

Comment

Main findings: Complex suicide prevention strategies consist of multiple components which are thought to interact to produce synergistic outcomes. However, little is known about which of these components are the most effective, or of the synergistic interactions that arise from these interactions. This paper therefore examined the interactions between the components of a multi-level suicide intervention program implemented in Germany, Hungary, Ireland and Portugal (OPSI-Europe). The program consisted of five levels: primary care (e.g., training general practitioners), community-based professionals (e.g., training social workers, teachers); a public health campaign; support for patients and families (e.g., self-help groups and signposting sources of help to those at risk); and reducing access to lethal means (in this case, mostly restricted to the identification of suicide hotspots). Process evaluation data gathered from participating countries was used to explore synergistic interactions between these five levels and to identify any added value that emerged from their interactions. A longitudinal, mixed method case study design was applied to the process evaluation. Four waves of qualitative and quantitative data were collected at six monthly intervals (January 2010 – December 2011). This was comprised of semi-structured interviews (n = 47) and focus groups (n = 12); field notes recorded at six intervention team meetings; and five waves of questionnaires (to track progress of implementation in each country). Quantitative analysis involved charting and summarising data, distilling it into major themes and then developing an analytical matrix where each intervention level was broken down into components. Based on existing evidence of synergistic interactions, hypotheses about further potential synergies were generated and workshopped by experts in each participant country.

Synergistic interactions were evident in all four countries providing added value beyond the sum of OPSI-Europe program's individual levels. For example, in Germany self-help group participants became volunteers for the program, increasing the visibility of its public awareness campaign through distributing flyers and helping with public events etc. In both Ireland and Germany there was evidence that inviting members of the press to attend public launches of OSPI-Europe activities developed media interest prior to the launch which in turn enhanced subsequent press coverage. Analysis also revealed that the program acted as a catalyst for externally generated activities that shared the goals of suicide prevention (referred to as catalytic interactions). For example, in Portugal, initiating suicide prevention training and rolling out a public awareness campaign resulted in complimentary activities being developed by professionals with a shared interest in suicide prevention.

Implications: These findings have important implications for maximising the effectiveness of suicide prevention initiatives. It is important that multi-level suicide initiatives are structured in a way that maximises both synergistic and catalytic interactions. For example, these initiatives should approach and engage with service user groups and local volunteers where possible, and co-ordinate activities to maximise impact. Public launches of initiatives should also be close to the actual delivery of suicide prevention training in order to maximise the potential synergies between media reporting, take-up of public awareness messages and recruitment for training. Adopting a complex suicide intervention program similar to the OPSI-Europe program could aid the Australian government in its goal to better integrate mental health services, particularly at the regional level[1]. This study had several limitations. It did not measure the intervention's actual impact on suicidal behaviours, limiting the conclusions one can draw regarding its effectiveness. The study did not take into account pre-existing health programs that might have already generated the conditions for synergy. Finally, the study did not consider the possibility of aversive consequences arising from multiple inter-actions which could reduce their overall effectiveness due to being 'crowded out' by other factors.

Endnotes

1. Department of Health (2015). *Australian government response to contributing lives, thriving communities – review of mental health programmes and services.* Retrieved 27 May 2016 from http://www.health.gov.au/internet/main/publishing.nsf/Content/0DBEF2D78F7CB9E7CA25 7F07001ACC6D/$File/response.pdf

Interventions for self-harm in children and adolescents

Hawton K, Witt KG, Taylor Salisbury TL, Arensman E, Gunnell D, Townsend E, van Heeringen K, Hazell P (United Kingdom)

Cochrane Database of Systematic Reviews 12, CD012013, 2015

Background: Self-harm (SH; intentional self-poisoning or self-injury) is common in children and adolescents, often repeated, and strongly associated with suicide. This is an update of a broader Cochrane review on psychosocial and pharmacological treatments for deliberate SH first published in 1998 and previously updated in 1999. We have now divided the review into three separate reviews; this review is focused on psychosocial and pharmacological interventions for SH in children and adolescents.

Objectives: To identify all randomised controlled trials of psychosocial interventions, pharmacological agents, or natural products for SH in children and adolescents, and to conduct meta-analyses (where possible) to compare the effects of specific treatments with comparison types of treatment (e.g. treatment as usual (TAU), placebo, or alternative pharmacological treatment) for children and adolescents who SH.

Search Methods: For this update the Cochrane Depression, Anxiety and Neurosis Group (CCDAN) Trials Search Co-ordinator searched the CCDAN Specialised Register (30 January 2015).

Selection Criteria: We included randomised controlled trials comparing psychosocial or pharmacological treatments with treatment as usual, alternative treatments, or placebo or alternative pharmacological treatment in children and adolescents (up to 18 years of age) with a recent (within six months) episode of SH resulting in presentation to clinical services.

Data Collection and Analysis: Two reviewers independently selected trials, extracted data, and appraised study quality, with consensus. For binary outcomes, we calculated odds ratios (OR) and their 95% confidence intervals (CI). For continuous outcomes measured using the same scale we calculated the mean difference (MD) and 95% CI; for those measured using different scales we calculated the standard mean difference (SMD) and 95% CI. Meta-analysis was only possible for two interventions: dialectical behaviour therapy for adolescents and group-based psychotherapy. For these analyses, we pooled data using a random-effects model.

Main Results: We included 11 trials, with a total of 1,126 participants. The majority of participants were female (mean = 80.6% in 10 trials reporting gender). All trials were of psychosocial interventions; there were none of pharmacological treatments. With the exception of dialectical behaviour therapy for adolescents (DBT-A) and group-based therapy, assessments of specific interventions were based on single trials. We downgraded the quality of evidence owing to risk of bias or imprecision for many outcomes. Therapeutic assessment appeared to increase adherence with subsequent treatment compared with TAU (i.e. standard assessment; n = 70; k = 1; OR = 5.12, 95% CI 1.70 to 15.39), but this had no apparent impact on repetition of SH at either 12 (n = 69; k = 1; OR 0.75, 95% CI 0.18 to 3.06; GRADE: low quality) or 24 months (n = 69; k = 1; OR = 0.69, 05% CI 0.23 to 2.14; GRADE: low quality evidence). These results are based on a single cluster randomised trial, which may overestimate the effectiveness of the intervention. For patients with multiple episodes of SH or emerging personality problems, mentalisation therapy was associated with fewer adolescents scoring above the cut-off for repetition of SH based on the Risk-Taking and Self-Harm Inventory 12 months post-intervention (n = 71; k = 1; OR = 0.26, 95% CI 0.09 to 0.78; GRADE: moderate quality). DBT-A was not associated with a reduction in the proportion of adolescents repeating SH when compared to either TAU or enhanced usual care (n = 104; k = 2; OR 0.72, 95% CI 0.12 to 4.40; GRADE: low quality). In the latter trial, however, the authors reported a significantly greater reduction over time in frequency of repeated SH in adolescents in the DBT condition, in whom there were also significantly greater reductions in depression, hopelessness, and suicidal ideation. We found no significant treatment effects for group-based therapy on repetition of SH for individuals with multiple episodes of SH at either the six (n -= 430; k = 2; OR 1.72, 95% CI 0.56 to 5.24; GRADE: low quality) or 12 month (n = 490; k = 3; OR 0.80, 95% CI 0.22 to 2.97; GRADE: low quality) assessments, although considerable heterogeneity was associated with both (I(2) = 65% and 77% respectively). We also found no significant differences between the following treatments and TAU in terms of reduced repetition of SH: compliance enhancement (three month follow-up assessment: n = 63; k = 1; OR = 0.67, 95% CI 0.15 to 3.08; GRADE: very low quality), CBT-based psychotherapy (six month follow-up assessment: n = 39; k = 1; OR = 1.88, 95% CI 0.30 to 11.73; GRADE: very low quality), home-based family intervention (six month follow-up assessment: n = 149; k = 1; OR = 1.02, 95% CI 0.41 to 2.51; GRADE: low quality), and provision of an emergency card (12 month follow-up assessment: n = 105, k = 1; OR = 0.50, 95% CI 0.12 to 2.04; GRADE: very low quality). No data on adverse effects, other than the planned outcomes relating to suicidal behaviour, were reported.

Authors' Conclusions: There are relatively few trials of interventions for children and adolescents who have engaged in SH, and only single trials contributed to all but two comparisons in this review. The quality of evidence according to GRADE criteria was mostly very low. There is little support for the effectiveness of group-based psychotherapy for adolescents with multiple episodes of SH based on the results of three trials, the evidence from which was of very low quality according to GRADE criteria. Results for therapeutic assessment, mentalisation, and dialectical behaviour therapy indicated that these approaches warrant further evaluation. Despite the scale of the problem of SH in children and adolescents there is a paucity of evidence of effective interventions. Further large-scale trials, with a range of outcome measures including adverse events, and investigation of therapeutic mechanisms underpinning these interventions, are required. It is increasingly apparent that development of new interventions should be done in collaboration with patients to ensure that these are likely to meet their needs. Use of an agreed set of outcome measures would assist evaluation and both comparison and meta-analysis of trials.

Comment

Main findings: It is concerning that children and adolescents suffer from high rates of self-harm, which is strongly linked to risk of future suicide[1]. This paper was one of three systematic reviews evaluating the effectiveness of self-harm interventions for children and adolescents. Randomised control trials (RCTs) testing the efficacy of psychosocial and pharmacological treatments were reviewed and where possible, meta-analyses were conducted to compare the effects of specific treatments for children and adolescents who self-harm. A total of 11 RCTs comprised of 1,126 participants were included in the systematic review. Participants were children and adolescents up to 18 years of age whom had recently (within six months) self-harmed resulting in presentation to clinical services. Of the 10 trials that recorded gender, the majority of participants (80.6%) were female, which reflects the typical gender proportions of self-harm in children and adolescents. Measures of treatment effectiveness included self-harm repetition, suicide, depression, hopelessness, treatment adherence, suicidal ideation and problem solving. All trials in the review were of psychosocial interventions; none of the trials evaluated pharmacological treatments. RCTs were included where they compared psychosocial treatments to treatment as usual, alternative treatments or placebo. Results showed that only one therapeutic approach had a significant impact on episodes of self-harm. Mentalisation therapy for patients with multiple self-harm episodes or emerging personality problems, led to fewer self-harm repetitions in the three months leading up to 12 months post-intervention. Mentalisation is a therapy that aims to improve patients' ability to empathise with others through developing an understanding of their own behaviour, as well as better regulating their emotions[2]. Although there was some suggestion of beneficial effects of dialectical behaviour therapy (DBT) for adolescents, the evidence was regarded as ambiguous. Similarly, therapeutic assessment appeared to increase adherence with subsequent treatment, but had no apparent effect on repetition of self-harm.

Implications: Mentalisation was the only therapeutic intervention found to be associated with a reduction in the frequency of repetition of self-harm in children and adolescents. It should be noted however, that the effect was modest and the trial was small, thus limiting the ability to make any firm conclusions about the effectiveness of this approach. Nevertheless, given that mentalisation, DBT and therapeutic assessment showed some promise, the authors recommend that these interventions warrant further evaluation. Limitations of the study include relatively small sized trials and potential bias (as it is generally not possible to blind patients or clinicians for psychological interventions). In addition, independent reviewers rated the RCTs to be low in quality overall. The lack of eligible pharmacological RCTs meant the effectiveness of these treatments could not be gauged. The authors note that there are surprisingly few trials examining this population given the significant problem of self-harm in children and adolescents worldwide. These results highlight the need for further investigation into psychosocial and pharmacological interventions for self-harm in children and adolescents. Given the extent of self-harming behaviour in children and adolescents, greater attention should be paid to the development and evaluation of specific therapies for this population. This is particularly important given the elevated suicide risk young people already face[3].

Endnotes

1. Hawton K, Saunders KEA, O'Connor R (2012). Self-harm and suicide in adolescents. *Lancet* 379, 2373–2382.
2. Rossouw TI (2013). Mentalization-based treatment: Can it be translated into practice in clinical settings and teams? *Journal of the American Academy of Child and Adolescent Psychiatry* 52, 220–222.
3. World Health Organisation (2014). *Preventing suicide: A global imperative.* Geneva, Switzerland.

Childhood predictors of lifetime suicide attempts and non-suicidal self-injury in depressed adults

Johnstone JM, Carter JD, Luty SE, Mulder RT, Frampton CM, Joyce PR (United States, New Zealand)

Australian and New Zealand Journal of Psychiatry 50, 135-144, 2016

Objective: Adverse childhood experiences are well-recognized risk factors for a variety of mental health issues, including depression, suicide attempts and non-suicidal self-injury. However, less is known about whether childhood adversity, in the form of low parental care, overprotection and abuse, is associated with suicide attempt and non-suicidal self-injury within a sample of depressed adults.

Method: The sample of outpatients (n = 372) was drawn from two randomized depression trials. Childhood adversity variables, depression severity, age of first depressive episode (major depression episode onset), lifetime suicide attempt and non-suicidal self-injury were recorded at baseline. The association between variables and outcome measures was examined using partial correlations, univariate and multivariate logistic regressions.

Results: Low maternal care was significantly associated with suicide attempt; low paternal care was associated with non-suicidal self-injury; overprotection was not associated with either outcome. Other risk factors for suicide attempt were major depression episode onset and baseline depression severity. Major depression episode onset was also a risk factor for non-suicidal self-injury. Abuse, regardless of how it was measured, was not significantly associated with either behaviour after adjusting for its correlations with low maternal or paternal care.

Conclusion: In this sample of depressed adults, the quality of ongoing, intra-familial relationships, as measured by levels of parental care, had a greater impact on suicide attempt and non-suicidal self-injury than abuse. As the findings were not a priori hypotheses, they require replication. Although the cross-sectional study design limits causal determination, the findings suggest different childhood risk factors for suicide attempt and non-suicidal self-injury and underscore the impact of low parental care on these two behaviours. These findings signal to clinicians the importance of asking specifically about suicide attempts, and non-suicidal self-injury, as well as levels of parental care in childhood. When endorsed, low parental care may be considered an important factor in contextualizing a patient's depression and potential risk for suicide and non-suicidal self-injury.

Comment

Main findings: Childhood adversity is a risk factor for developing depression and other mental health problems in adulthood. In this study the authors investigated the link between childhood adversity and suicide attempts (SA) and non-suicidal self-injury (NSSI) in people with depression. Childhood adversity was examined in three categories: low parental care, overprotection and abuse (psychological, sexual and physical). The authors were interested in the significance of these risk factors in predicting SA and NSSI. Participants were recruited by inviting clinically depressed outpatients to participate in two consecutive clinical studies investigating the effectiveness of medication and psychotherapy for depression. Between the two trials there were 372 participants (133 males and 239 females). In this study the authors were not interested in the clinical trials outcomes regarding the effectiveness of medication and psychotherapy (the results of which were published separately); rather, the clinical trials were used by the authors to collect pre-trial measures of depression (age of onset, score on depression scale), maternal and paternal care, overprotection, childhood abuse (psychological, physical and sexual), lifetime SA and NSSI and demographics.

Univariate analyses found participant age, age of depression onset, score on depression scale, level of maternal care, level of paternal care, maternal protection, abuse, and child sexual abuse (CSA) to be significantly associated with SA. When controlling for related variables, only maternal care, age of depression onset and score on depression scale were associated with SA. In total, these three variables helped explain 11-16% of the variance in SA. Maternal care was the only childhood adversity variable to independently predict SA. Participants who reported low maternal care were 2.3 times more likely to have attempted suicide than those who reported high maternal care. Results also showed that participant age, age of depression onset, paternal care, and abuse were associated with NSSI. However, when controlling for related variables, only age of depression onset and level of paternal care were associated with NSSI. Participants reporting low scores in paternal care (i.e., parental neglect) were 2.7 times more likely to engage in NSSI than those reporting high parental care.

Implications: These findings align with previous research establishing a link between poor parental care and SA and NSSI[1]. They reinforce the negative impact that insecure parental attachment and disruptive family environments can have on one's emotional well-being over the lifetime[2-4]. Interestingly, contrary to previous research, abuse was not found to be independently associated with SA or NSSI. A possible explanation is that because childhood abuse usually occurs in neglectful parental care environments[5], the impact of the abuse on SA and NSSI may be simply overshadowed by the poor parental care received by the child. This paper was not without its limitations. The cross-sectional design limits the ability to infer causality, and the use of retrospective measures is problematic as they may be subject to memory bias and potential reporting bias. These findings highlight the relationship between low parental care (characterised by emotional neglect) and increased risk of SA and NSSI in adults with depression. It is important that children's services are aware of children who are at risk of parental neglect and ensure that they provide early support to families and conduct interventions where necessary. The Queensland Suicide Prevention Action Plan recommends the use of mobile outreach, extended hours of service delivery and school-based emotional and social learning programs that focus on building supportive environments and providing interventions to those who need them[6]. These strategies could greatly assist in preventing or limiting the negative effect of poor parental care.

Endnotes

1. Wichstrom L (2009). Predictors of non-suicidal self-injury versus attempted suicide: Similar or different? *Archives of Suicide Research* 13, 105–122.

2. Van Orden KA, Witte TK, Cukrowicz KC, Braithwaite SR, Selby EA, Joiner Jr TE (2010). The interpersonal theory of suicide. *Psychological Review* 117, 575–600.

3. Bowlby J (1977). The making and breaking of affectional bonds. I. Aetiology and psychopathology in the light of attachment theory. An expanded version of the Fiftieth Maudsley Lecture, delivered before the Royal College of Psychiatrists, 19 November 1976. *British Journal of Psychiatry* 130, 201–210.

4. Gratz KL, Conrad SD, Roemer L (2002). Risk factors for deliberate self-harm among college students. *American Journal of Orthopsychiatry* 72, 128–140.

5. Spinhoven P, Slee N, Garnefski N, Arensman E (2009). Childhood sexual abuse differentially predicts outcome of cognitive-behavioral therapy for deliberate self-harm. *Journal of Nervous and Mental Disease* 197, 455–457.

6. Queensland Mental Health Commission (2015). *Queensland Suicide Prevention Action Plan 2015-17*. Retrieved 28 April 2016 from https://www.qmhc.qld.gov.au/wp-content/uploads/2015/09/Queensland-Suicide-Prevention-Action-Plan-2015-17_WEB.pdf

Adolescent suicide rates between 1990 and 2009: Analysis of age group 15-19 years worldwide

Kõlves, K, De Leo, D (Australia)

Journal of Adolescent Health, 58, 69-77

Purpose: The aim of the current analysis is to analyze suicide rates in adolescents aged 15-19 years in decades between 1990 and 2009 worldwide.

Methods: Suicide data were obtained from the World Health Organization Mortality Database and population data from the World Bank Data set. In total, 81 countries or territories, having data at least for 5 years in 1990-1999 and in 2000-2009, were included in the analysis. Additional analysis for regional trends with 57 countries was performed.

Results: Over the decades considered, analysis showed a declining trend in the overall suicide rate for males from 10.30 to 9.51 per 100,000 (p = .076), and for females from 4.39 to 4.18 (p = .472). The average suicide rate showed a significant decline for both genders in Europe, dropping from 13.13 to 10.93 (p = .001) in males and from 3.88 to 3.34 in females (p = .038). There was a significant increase in South American countries for males, from 7.36 to 11.47 (p = .016), and a close to significant rise for females, from 5.59 to 7.98 (p = .053). Although other world regions did not show significant trends, there were several significant changes at country level.

Conclusions: Reasons behind the decrease in Western countries could potentially be related to the overall improvements in global health; the possible contribution of suicide prevention activities remains unclear. Increases in several South American countries might be related to economic recession and its impact on adolescents from diverse cultural backgrounds, and partly also to improvements in mortality registration

Comment

Main findings: Given that suicide rates have been shown to be high in the 15-19 year age group in some countries, the aim of this study was to analyse suicide rates in adolescents aged 15-19 years worldwide in the last two decades, 1990-1999 and 2000-2009. Suicide data were obtained from the World Health Organization Mortality Database and population data obtained from the World Bank dataset. A total of 81 countries or territories with available data at least for 5 years from 1990-1999 and from 2000-2009 were included in the analyses. Additional analyses were also conducted for regional trends for 57 countries. Results showed that average suicide rates of youth aged 15-19 years in 81 countries declined for both genders in these two decades. Globally, the average suicide rate for males dropped from 10.32 to 9.50 (per 100,000) (close to significance level: p = .066) and remained steady for females from 4.41 to 4.19 (per 100,000). Significant changes were detected in a number of countries. In Europe, the average suicide rate showed a significant decline for both genders, dropping from 13.13 to 10.93 (per

100,000) (p<.001) in males and from 3.88 to 3.34 (per 100,000) in females (p=.038). There was a significant increase in South American countries for males, from 7.36 to 11.47 (per 100,000) (p=.016), and a close to significant rise for females, (5.59 to 7.98 per 100,000) (p=.053). In Northern America, there was a significant decrease in suicide rates for males (16.13 to 11.81 per 100,000) (p<.001) and females (3.31 to 2.82 per 100,000) (p<.001) in the United States. Moreover, in Canada a significant drop was observed for males from 19.56 to 13.32 (per 100,000) (p<.001) but not for females. In Australia there was a significant decline in suicides for males 15-19 years (16.79 to 11.10 per 100,000) (p<.001), while rates were stable for females (4.12 to 4.17 per 100,000). There was also a decline for males in New Zealand (28.23 to 22.38 per 100,000)(p<.001), and a nonsignificant decline for females (9.71 to 9.55 per 100,000).

Implications: It is important to acknowledge that a key limitation of this study is the availability of data. Although western countries (e.g., Europe and America) are well covered, there is limited data available from African and Asian countries, especially heavily populated countries such as India and China. The WHO estimates high suicide rates in India and some African countries; however, most African countries have no official registration of suicide mortality, and estimates for India and China are based on population samples[1]. The prevalence of suicide is also likely to be underestimated due to misclassification and under-reporting[2]. Nevertheless, monitoring youth suicide is important as it can help inform future suicide prevention strategies. This worldwide analysis provides a snapshot of adolescent suicide trends and serves as a guideline for future investigations. Of interest, are Australia and New Zealand's suicide rates, which showed a significant decline throughout the study for males. For females, a significant upward trend was observed until 1998, followed by nonsignificant decline up to 2009. Australia's suicide prevention youth position statement was last updated in 2010[3]. The observed declining trends for both genders in the latter years may reflect the effectiveness of suicide prevention initiatives, thus it is important to further develop, evaluate and improve these initiatives for adolescents in Australia.

Endnotes

1. World Health Organization (2014). *Preventing suicide: A global imperative.* World Health Organization, Geneva, Switzerland.

2. De Leo D (2015). Can we rely on suicide mortality data? *Crisis 36*, 1-3.

3. Suicide Prevention Australia (2010). Position Statement: Youth Suicide Prevention. Retrieved 28 April 2016 from: https://www.suicidepreventionaust.org/sites/default/ files/resources/2016/ SPA-Youth-Suicide-Prevention-Position-Statement%5B1%5D.pdf

Ten years of suicide mortality in Australia: Socio-economic and psychiatric factors in Queensland

Kõlves K, Potts B, De Leo D (Australia)

Journal of Forensic and Legal Medicine 36, 136-143, 2015

Background: With the exception of the United States, in recent years suicide rates have been declining in most western countries. Notoriously, suicide rates fluctuate – especially in males – in response to a range of socio-political and environmental factors, some of them difficult to identify. Our aim was to obtain an updated profile of main commonalities in suicide cases of Queensland residents between 2002 and 2011 to inform prevention strategies.

Methods: Data were obtained from the Queensland Suicide Register (QSR), including police and toxicology reports, post-mortem autopsy and Coroner's findings. Data are crosschecked with records from the National Coronial Information System. Age-standardised rates (ASR) of suicide, Poisson regression and Chi^2 tests are presented.

Results: A total of 5,752 suicides by Queensland residents was registered between 2002 and 2011; 76.9% by males and 23.1% by females. The average ASR was 14.3 per 100,000, with a significant decrease between 2002 and 2011. Rates declined significantly in males, not in females. On average, rates were 3.41-times higher in males. ASR for Aboriginal and Torres Strait Islander peoples was significantly higher than for other Australians. Overall, male suicide rates were particularly high in remote areas, as well as in the most disadvantaged ones. One third of suicide cases presented history of previous suicidal behaviour, and half a detected and treated mental disorder. Hanging was the most common method.

Conclusions: Suicide rates have declined in Queensland, Australia. It is problematic to say if this was due to suicide prevention programs or other factors.

Comment

Main findings: A recent World Health Organization (WHO) report found that suicide rates have declined in most western countries except for the Unites States. The report recommended that in order to continuously improve suicide prevention programs for communities and countries, it is imperative to improve data quality to ensure effectiveness evaluation of interventions[1]. The aim of this study was to analyse recent suicide trends to inform suicide prevention planning in Queensland. Suicide trends were analysed by age and gender, and in vulnerable populations. Socio-demographic characteristics, psychiatric characteristics, life events and physical health of people who died by suicide in Queensland were explored. Data over a 10-year period (2002-2011) was collated from the Queensland Suicide Register (QSR).

Between 2002 and 2011, a total of 5,752 people died by suicide. The average ASR for this period was 14.3 suicides per 100,000. A significant decrease in the ASRs was observed from 2002 to 2011. Male suicides decreased significantly from 2002 to 2011 (25.5 to 19.5), while females suicides remained relatively stable during the same period (6.8 to 7.2). Suicide rates for males were significantly higher than female suicide rates, being 3.41 times more likely to die by suicide (95%CI 3.21-3.62). Both genders had the highest suicide rates in the 35-44 years age group and the lowest suicide rates in the below 15 years age group. The ASR rate for Aboriginal and Torres Strait Islander peoples was significantly higher than for other Australians (20.5 and 13.3 per 100,000 respectively). Suicide rates increased with remoteness (i.e., metropolitan, regional and remote areas). For males rates increased from 18.6, 23.9 and 33.6 (per 100,000), respectively. Similarly for females suicide rates increased with remoteness from 6.8, 7.4 and 12.0 (per 100,000). The highest suicide rates were in the most disadvantaged areas (in terms of relative socioeconomic disadvantage, economic resources, education and occupation) and the lowest in the most advantaged areas; this was significant for both genders, with differences most noticeable in males.

Overall, hanging was the most frequent method (45.1%), followed by drug poisoning (16.3%), carbon monoxide poisoning (11.4%), firearms and explosives (8.9%) and jumping from height (3.4%). Furthermore, 49.2% of all people who died by suicide suffered from at least one psychiatric disorder. Unipolar depression was the most frequent psychiatric diagnosis (34.7%), followed by psychotic disorders (6.8%), substance use disorders (5.4%), anxiety disorders (4.9%) and bipolar disorders (4.5%). Almost half of the people (49%) who died by suicide during this period were observed to have received psychiatric treatment, while almost one-third (27.4%) had consulted a health professional with regards to their mental health in the three months previous to suicide. Physical illness was reported in 34.9% of people who died by suicide. Regarding life events, relationship separation was reported in 22.6% of those who died by suicide. This was followed by financial problems (12.7%), bereavement (10.4%), pending legal matters (8.9%), recent/pending unemployment (7.4%), and work/school related problems (6.9%).

Implications: Despite the QSR being a comprehensive suicide mortality database, several limitations may affect the accuracy of these results. The information in the QSR is gathered from various sources (e.g., police, Coroners, next-of-kins, autopsy reports and toxicology reports) and the accuracy of information provided depends on the quality of investigation into the possible suicide cases. Thus, some information that may have been relevant to the person's death may be unrecorded. The findings from this study indicate an overall decline in suicide rates in Queensland, particularly for males over the time period 2002-2011, in line with the WHO (2014) report[1]. It remains unclear if higher suicide rates in Aboriginal and Torres Strait Islander people are related to cultural, social, political or environmental factors. There is no clear understanding how Aboriginal and Torres Strait Islander people define, describe or understand mental health problems or how they would correlate with Western concepts and diagnoses[2]. It is therefore important for suicide prevention researchers to gain a better understanding of Aboriginal and

Torres Strait Islander concepts of mental health and suicide to inform culturally appropriate suicide prevention measures. Despite the decline in rates, it is important to continue to improve suicide prevention initiatives and stay updated with key risk factors for suicide. In Queensland, those at risk have socio-economic disadvantage, poor resources, poor education and poor occupations. Moreover, men with relationship separations are at high risk, and should also be targeted for prevention programs. Thus, a range of approaches, rather than a single approach is necessary for prevention[1]. In a recent mental health review, the Australian Government highlighted existing inefficiencies in the current system, stating that we often wait too long to intervene and offer services, and employ a one size fits all approach which does not cater to individuals' needs[3]. Similarly, the Queensland Suicide Prevention Action Plan 2015-17 also prioritises support for vulnerable groups (i.e., those who are experiencing higher rates and at greater risk of suicide)[4]. The authors of this paper concluded that reduction of suicide rates could be achievable with the coordination of the health sector with other key-sectors such as education, employment, social welfare and the judiciary.

Endnote

1. World Health Organization (2014). *Preventing suicide: A global imperative.* WHO, Geneva.
2. Ypinazar V, Margolis S, Haswell-Elkins M, Tsey K (2007). Indigenous Australian's understanding regarding mental health and disorders. *Australian and New Zealand Journal of Psychiatry* 41, 467-478.
3. Department of Health (2015). *Australian government response to contributing lives, thriving communities – review of mental health programmes and services.* Retrieved 27 April 2016. http://www.health.gov.au/internet/main/publishing.nsf/Content/0DBEF2D78F7CB9E7CA25 7F07001ACC6D/$File/response.pdf
4. Queensland Mental Health Commission (2015). *Queensland Suicide Prevention Action Plan 2015-2017.* Retrieved 27 April 2016 from http://www.health.gov.au/internet/main/publishing.nsf/Content/0DBEF2D78F7CB9E7CA25 7F07001ACC6D/$File/response.pdf

Allergies and suicidal behaviors: A systematic literature review

Kõlves K, Barker E, De Leo D (Australia)

Allergy and Asthma Proceedings 36, 433-438, 2015

Background: Allergies are among the most common chronic conditions. In addition to physical and social impacts, a number of studies have consistently linked allergies to poor psychological outcomes, including depression and anxiety.

Objectives: The aim of the present systematic literature review was to analyze the existing literature about the relationship between allergies and fatal and nonfatal suicidal behaviors.

Methods: Data sources include articles retrieved from Scopus, PubMed, ProQuest, and Web of Knowledge. Search terms: "suicid* and (allerg* or hay fever or atop* or eczema or aeroallergen*)" in English-language peer-reviewed journals between 1990 and 2014.

Eligibility Criteria: Original research articles that provide empiric evidence about the potential link between allergies and suicidal behaviors.

Results: The initial search identified a total of 769 articles with 17 original research articles that present empiric evidence. Nine articles analyzed the relationship between allergies and fatal suicidal behavior, and nine analyzed nonfatal suicidal behaviors (one article included both). There currently is little research into the relationship between allergies and suicidal behavior.

Limitations: The review was restricted to English-language articles published within the chosen time period; other limitations included the small number of articles that involve suicide mortality, and the fact that the majority of articles originated from the United States and Scandinavia.

Conclusions: Analysis of the results indicates a link between allergies and suicidality, particularly suicide mortality; however, results for nonfatal suicidal behaviors are mixed. It is important that further research by using more rigorous study designs be carried out to lend strength to these findings.

Comment

Main findings: Allergies are associated with various physical effects, as well as other consequences such as reduced cognitive ability, work/school performance, increased daytime sleepiness, impoverished quality of life, and poor psychological outcomes, including major depression and anxiety. The most common conditions in Western countries are allergic rhinitis (AR), asthma, and atopic dermatitis (AD). This systematic literature review aimed to investigate whether there is an association between allergies and fatal and nonfatal suicidal behaviours. A total of 17 original research articles on suicidal behaviours were identified. One article included self-harm as well as fatal suicidal behaviour, nine articles focused on the relationship between allergies and fatal suicidal behaviour, and the remaining nine articles focused on nonfatal suicidal behaviour (five measured suicide ideation, two measured suicide attempts, and two, both suicide ideation and attempts).

There is mixed evidence for an association between fatal suicidal behaviours and allergies. Some studies found an association between suicide rates and peak pollen periods, however this became non-significant when controlling for psychosocial factors and other potential confounding factors (urban or rural location, income, psychiatrists in area)[1]. Another study found an increase relative risk of suicide during pollen increases, even when controlling for other factors[2]. A significant gender difference was also found, where males responded immediately to small increases in pollen counts, while females responded gradually, in line with increasing pollen counts. Another study found that as prescriptions for intranasal corticosteroids increased, suicide rates declined. This association also remained significant when antidepressant use was controlled for. However, the authors suggest that prescription rates of nonsedating antihistamines may indicate higher prevalence of allergies in the community, but have little association with suicide. Two articles found associations between hospital related atopic disorders (AD, AR, and asthma) and suicide. Those who were treated for atopic disorder died significantly more often during the first half of the year than the second half; and AR was found to predict suicide in patients who had received inpatient treatment for their allergy and those who had AR in combination with bronchial asthma. Other studies investigating AR found an association between AR and increased risk of suicide at a 12 year follow up in young people aged 11-15 years; however this relationship was attenuated after controlling for current and previous asthma, and smoking. Another study found no evidence for an association between atopy without asthma, eczema-uritcaria only, or hay fever only, and suicide. However, individuals with combination of eczema-urticaria and hay fever showed a higher risk of suicide, and this remained significant after adjusting for demographic variables and current smoking. A further study found that persons with eczema were more likely to die by suicide than those without, and this was significant while controlling for demographic variables.

The evidence for the association between nonfatal suicidal behaviour and allergies is mixed, such that significant increases in suicidal ideation were found in adults and adolescents with AD. In contrast, three studies did not support the association between AR and nonfatal suicidal behaviours, and only one study each among children and adults supported an association with ideation but not suicide attempts. Several studies also found gender differences in the association such that allergies were associated with increased depression in women but not men, or that there was a higher prevalence of suicidal ideation in women compared to men. Although one study found an association with suicidal ideation in patients with AD and various other skin conditions, they did not have a comparison or control group[3].

Implications: This systematic review highlighted the lack of research into the association between allergies and suicidal behaviour. Most studies did not control for psychosocial factors which may have affected the results, and those that did control for these factors found mixed results. Reasons for the potential link between allergies and suicidal behaviours are still poorly understood. The findings presented should be interpreted with caution due to the small number of studies and the restriction to only English-language articles. A number of articles employed ecological designs or cross-sectional designs which do not allow inferences of causality, and relied on self-reported data which may hinder the accuracy and reliability of these results. Moreover, the majority of studies were conducted in North America and Scandinavia, and therefore differences in climates, seasonal conditions and the prevalence of allergies may not be transferable to Australia. Future research should aim to explore the association between allergies and suicide more thoroughly by controlling for psychosocial and demographic variables, and severity of allergies. The results would help inform future suicide prevention strategies to support those at risk.

Endnotes

1. Woo JM, Gibbons RD, Rogers CA, Qin P, Kim JB, Roberts DW, Noh ES, Mann JJ, Postolache TT (2012). Pollen counts and suicide rates. Association not replicated. *Acta Psychiatrica Scandinavica* 125, 168-175.
2. Qin P, Waltoft BL, Mortensen PB, Postolache TT (2013). Suicide risk in relation to air pollen counts: A study based on data from Danish registers. *BMJ Open* 3, e002462.
3. Gupta MA, Gupta AK (1998). Depression and suicidal ideation in dermatology patients with acne, alopecia areata, atopic dermatitis and psoriasis. *British Journal of Dermatology*. 139, 846-850.

Serotonergic medication enhances the association between suicide and sunshine

Makris GD, Reutfors J, Larsson R, Isacsson G, Osby U, Ekbom A, Ekselius L, Papadopoulos FC (Sweden)

Journal of Affective Disorders 189, 276-281, 2015

Background: An association between suicide and sunshine has been reported. The effect of sunshine on hormones and neurotransmitters such as serotonin has been hypothesized to exert a possible triggering effect on susceptible individuals. The aim of this study is to examine if there is an association between sunshine and suicide, adjusting for season, and if such an association differs between individuals on different antidepressants.

Methods: By using Swedish Registers and the Swedish Meteorological and Hydrological Institute we obtained information, including forensic data on antidepressive medication for 12,448 suicides and data on monthly sunshine duration. The association between monthly suicide and sunshine hours was examined with Poisson regression analyses while stratifying for sex and age and controlling for time trend and season. These analyses were repeated in different groups of antidepressant treatment.

Results: We found a significantly increased suicide risk with increasing sunshine in both men and women. This finding disappeared when we adjusted for season. Among both men and women treated with selective serotonin reuptake inhibitors (SSRIs) there was a positive association between sunshine and suicide even after adjustment for season and time trend for suicide. Pair comparisons showed that the sunshine-suicide association was stronger among men treated with SSRIs compared to other antidepressant medications or no medication at all.

Limitations: Other meteorological factors were not controlled (i.e. temperature) for in the analyses.

Conclusions: There is an enhanced association between sunshine and suicide among those with SSRI medication, even after adjusting for season. This may have interesting theoretical and clinical implications.

Comment

Main findings: The aim of this study was to investigate the relationship between sunshine and suicide, controlling for season, and whether this relationship differs for those on different antidepressants (selective serotonin reuptake inhibitors (SSRIs) or other antidepressants). It was hypothesized that sunlight and serotonergic medication act upon the same neurobiological system, and may have an amplifying effect, thus leading to an increased risk for suicide in vulnerable individuals. Monthly data was obtained from the Swedish Cause of Death Register and The Swedish Meteorological and Hydrological Institute between 1992-2003. For counties which no sunshine data was obtained, the average number of sunshine hours form neighbouring counties were used instead. Suicides with toxic levels of antidepressants were excluded from the analyses since it would be difficult to ascertain whether these patients were adhering to prescribed treatment.

A total of 12,448 suicides (72.4% male, 27.6% female) with information about blood levels of antidepressants, month of death and gender were identified. For males, 8.7% screened positive for any SSRI, compared to 13.3% of females. Moreover, 7.2% of males and 14.6% of females were positive for another antidepressant. In addition, 81.7% of males and 69.1% of females were not positive for any antidepressant drug. An increase by one hour of sunshine a day was significantly associated with an increase of average monthly number of suicides by in men (1.6%) and women (1.2%). However, this association disappeared after adjusting for season. Meanwhile for those treated with SSRIs, a significant association was found between sunshine and suicide even after adjusting for season and time trend for suicide. That is, an increase by one hour of sunshine a day was significantly associated with an increase of average monthly number of suicides by men (5.4%) and women (3.1%). This association was largely driven by the age group of 65 years and older, which presented monthly increases of 10.4% in men and 4.75% in women. No association was observed between sunshine and suicide for those treated with other antidepressants.

Implications: This study showed that there is an association between sunshine duration and suicide, although this association is attenuated when controlling for season. However, for those treated with SSRI antidepressants, the association between sunshine duration and suicide remains significant, even when adjusting for age, and especially among older adults aged 65 and over. The authors postulated that in the short-term, increased sunshine and treatment with SSRIs may further reduce serotonin transporter binding capacity, which could foster impulsivity or anxiety in some individuals who might be prone to suicidal behaviour. However the generalisability of these findings are limited to only those who adhered to prescribed antidepressant treatment, since those with toxic levels of antidepressants were excluded. A limitation of this study is that other meteorological variables (e.g., temperature) or other factors such as ethnicity were not available for analyses, which may have contributed to the associations observed. Moreover, this study was of an observational design, therefore causality cannot be inferred. Although a previous meta-analysis found no significant association between sunshine and monthly suicide when controlling for seasonality in Australia, Greece and Norway[1], future research should aim to investigate this association using a case-control design including variables such as antidepressant treatment, psychiatric disorders, demographic variables, and temperature, as this would help inform our future mental health programmes and services. The results of such research in Australia may have clinical implications in terms of identifying and monitoring individuals who could potentially be at risk (e.g., those being treated with SSRIs who are older and living in areas experiencing prolonged sunshine). This would be in line with the Australian Government's response to the current mental health programmes and services, to provide effective early intervention and shifting the balance to provide the right care when it is needed[2].

Endnotes

1. White RA, Azrael D, Papadopoulos FC, Lambert GW, Miller M (2015). Does suicide have a stronger association with seasonality than sunlight? *BMJ Open* 5, e007403.

2. Department of Health (2015). *Australian government response to contributing lives, thriving communities – review of mental health programmes and services.* Retrieved 27 April 2016 from http://www.health.gov.au/internet/main/publishing.nsf/Content/0DBEF2D78F7CB9E7CA25 7F07001ACC6D/

Direct versus indirect psychosocial and behavioural interventions to prevent suicide and suicide attempts: A systematic review and meta-analysis

Meerwijk EL, Parekh A, Oquendo MA, Allen IE, Franck LS, Lee KA

Lancet Psychiatry 3, 544-554, 2016

Background: Psychosocial and behavioural interventions that address suicidal thoughts and behaviour during treatment (direct interventions) might be more effective in preventing suicide and suicide attempts than indirect interventions that address symptoms associated with suicidal behaviour only (eg, hopelessness, depression, anxiety, quality of life). To test this hypothesis, we did a systematic review and meta-analysis of psychosocial and behavioural interventions aimed at preventing suicide and suicide attempts.

Methods: For this systematic review and meta-analysis, we searched MEDLINE and PsycINFO from inception to Dec 25, 2015, for randomised controlled trials that reported suicides or suicide attempts as an outcome, irrespective of participants' diagnoses or the publication language. We excluded studies with pharmacological or device-based interventions, those that targeted communities or clinicians, primary prevention trials, and trials that reported events of non-suicidal self-injury as suicide attempts. Trials that had no suicides or suicide attempts in both groups were also excluded. Data were extracted by one investigator and independently verified by a second investigator. We used random-effects models of the odds ratio (OR) based on a pooled measure of suicides and the number of individuals who attempted suicide, immediately post-treatment and at longer-term follow-up.

Findings: Of 2024 unique abstracts screened, 53 articles met eligibility criteria and reported on 44 studies; 31 studies provided post-treatment data with 6658 intervention group participants and 6711 control group participants at baseline, and 29 studies provided follow-up data. The post-treatment difference between direct interventions and indirect interventions did not reach statistical significance at the 0.05 level (OR 0.62 [95% CI 0.45-0.87] vs 0.93 [0.77-1.12], p=0.06) and represented a large effect size (Cohen's d=0.77). At longer-term follow-up, the difference was not significant (OR 0.65 [0.46-0.91] vs 0.82 [0.70-0.96], p=0.25) but still represented a medium effect size (Cohen's d=0.47). These effect sizes emphasise the clinical importance of direct interventions. Post-hoc subgroup and sensitivity analyses showed that our results are robust and unlikely to be notably affected by between-study heterogeneity or publication bias.

Interpretation: Psychosocial and behavioural interventions that directly address suicidal thoughts and behaviour are effective immediately post-treatment and long term, whereas treatments indirectly addressing these components are only effective long term. Moreover, although the differences shown between direct and indirect strategies were non-significant, the difference in favour of direct interventions represented a large post-treatment improvement and medium improvement at longer-term follow-up. On the basis of these findings, clinicians working with patients at risk of suicide should address suicidal thoughts and behaviours with the patient directly. Although direct interventions are effective, they are not sufficient, and additional efforts are needed to further reduce death by suicide and suicide attempts. Continued patient contact might be necessary to retain long-term effectiveness.

Comment

Main findings: Suicide interventions are classified as either direct or indirect interventions, with direct interventions directly targeting a person's suicidal ideation and behaviours, and indirect interventions targeting the symptoms associated with suicide (e.g., hopelessness, depression, anxiety) but not the suicidality itself. Whilst direct interventions have been posited as more effective than indirect interventions[1], to date no meta-analyses or studies have tested this assertion. In order to examine this issue, the authors conducted a systematic review and meta-analysis of psychosocial and behavioural interventions to prevent suicide and suicide attempts. The MEDLINE and PsycINFO databases were used to conduct literature searches for randomised controlled trials (RCTs), with RCTs being included if they reported suicides or suicide attempts as outcome variables for direct or indirect interventions. RCTs of pharmacological interventions, interventions that used devices, interventions that targeted communities or clinicians, and primary prevention were excluded. RCTs with a control group with no form of treatment were also excluded.

Forty-four eligible RCTs were identified, with 31 including post-treatment data (mean treatment duration being 11.3 months) and 29 including follow-up data (the mean follow-up duration being 13.6 months post-treatment). A significant proportion of RCTs investigated the effectiveness of direct interventions based on dialectical or cognitive behaviour therapy. Direct interventions were shown to significantly reduce the likelihood of suicidality at post-treatment compared to control groups (OR = 0.62, 95% CI: 0.45–0.87). However, for indirect interventions there was no significant post-treatment reduction in suicidality (OR = 0.93, 95% CI: 0.77–1.12). Whilst there was no effect of indirect interventions overall, in isolation active outreach treatments (e.g., telephone calls, home visits) had a significant preventative effect at post-treatment compared to control groups (OR = 0.75, 95% CI: 0.57–0.99). At post-treatment there was no significant difference between direct and indirect interventions (OR = 0.62 *vs* 0.93; *p*=0.06). For studies including follow-up data both direct interventions (OR = 0.65, 95% CI: 0.46–0.91) and indirect interventions (OR = 0.82, 95% CI: 0.70–0.96) were shown to significantly lower the likelihood of suicidality in participants compared to controls. However, in isolation, for indirect interventions only active outreach treatments were effective in reducing suicidality (OR = 0.80, 95% CI: 0.66–0.97). There was no difference in suicidality between direct and indirect interventions at follow-up (OR = 0.65 *vs* 0.82, *p*=0.25).

Implications: The findings demonstrate that directly addressing a person's suicidal ideation and behaviour was effective both immediately post-treatment and long-term; whereas indirect treatments were effective long-term only. It is therefore recommended that clinicians utilise direct interventions that include discussing a client's suicidal thoughts and behaviours, as well as strategies to reduce suicidality. Given the high proportion of direct interventions based on cognitive and dialectical therapy, the findings from this paper align with a prior meta-analysis demonstrating the effectiveness of cognitive-based interventions in reducing suicidal behaviour[2]. This review is not without its limitations. Half of the studies reported more than 10% missing data due to attrition, potentially biasing the results. Furthermore, the paper did not differentiate between psychological disorders when examining the effectiveness of the interventions. It is possible that direct and indirect interventions might vary in their effectiveness across different disorders. In addition, the analysis was unable to rule out whether medication use may have affected suicidal behaviour in some studies. Further research is needed to investigate these issues.

Endnotes

1. Rudd MD, Williams B, Trotter D (2009). The psychological and behavioural treatment of suicidal behaviour. In Wasserman D, Wasserman C (Eds). *Oxford Textbook of Suicidology and Suicide Prevention*. New York, NY: Oxford University Press, 427–438.
2. Tarrier N, Taylor K, Gooding P (2008). Cognitive-behavioral interventions to reduce suicide behavior: A systematic review and meta-analysis. *Behavior Modificiation* 32, 77–108.

Occupational class differences in suicide: Evidence of changes over time and during the global financial crisis in Australia

Milner AJ, Niven H, LaMontagne AD (Australia)

BMC Psychiatry 15, 223, 2015

Background: Previous research showed an increase in Australian suicide rates during the Global Financial Crisis (GFC). There has been no research investigating whether suicide rates by occupational class changed during the GFC. The aim of this study was to investigate whether the GFC-associated increase in suicide rates in employed Australians may have masked changes by occupational class.

Methods: Negative binomial regression models were used to investigate Rate Ratios (RRs) in suicide by occupational class. Years of the GFC (2007, 2008, 2009) were compared to the baseline years 2001-2006.

Results: There were widening disparities between a number of the lower class occupations and the highest class occupations during the years 2007, 2008, and 2009 for males, but less evidence of differences for females.

Conclusions: Occupational disparities in suicide rates widened over the GFC period. There is a need for programs to be responsive to economic downturns, and to prioritise the occupational groups most affected.

Comment

Main findings: Previous research has established that economic downturns, such as the Global Financial Crisis (GFC), are associated with an increase in population-level suicide rates[1]. More recently, studies have revealed that economic downturns also have an impact on suicide rates in the working population. For example, in Australia suicide rates during the GFC slightly increased for the working population[2]. The current study extended this research by investigating whether the increase in suicide rates may have masked changes by occupational class. The researchers also assessed whether gender modified the association between the GFC and suicide. Given that previous research showed that compared to females, male suicides increased in response to labour market changes (e.g., unemployment), it was hypothesised that males would be more affected by the GFC than females.

Data were retrieved from the National Coroners Information System (NCIS) and Australian Bureau of Statistics. The GFC years (2007, 2008, 2009) were compared to the baseline years (2001-2006). 2010 was also included to assess possible post-GFC related changes in suicide. A retrospective time trend analysis of suicide rates was conducted with gender, age and eight major occupational groupings from the Australian and New Zealand Standard Classification of Occupations (ANZSCO) as the variables of interest. The highest occupation class (managers) was used as the reference group.

Results showed that between 2001-2010, male suicide rates were highest amongst labourers, farmers, machinery operators and technical and trade workers, while for females, suicides were highest amongst labourers, farmers, machinery operators, and professionals. Overall males had a four-fold higher rate ratio (RR) than females over the 10-year period. Compared to the reference group (managers) the ratio of suicide in professionals, technical and trade workers, community service workers, sales workers, machinery operators, labourers and farmers increased for males during the GFC and remained high in 2010. There was also a three-fold increase in the disparity of suicide rates for male technical and trade workers and community workers during the GFC. For females there was a four-fold increase in suicide rates for technical and trade workers compared to managers during 2007 and 2008, and a nonsignificant decline in 2009 and 2010.

Implications: This study suggests that a disparity in suicide rates exists between occupational class, particularly among men. This disparity widens during economically challenging times. In general males had higher suicide rates in occupations which involved physical work (i.e., labouring, agriculture, machine operators, and technical and trades employment). The findings from this study have important implications for improving suicide prevention. Initiatives should target those working in these high-risk occupational groups both before and during economic downturns. This is particularly relevant to Australia given the current slowdown in the mining sector[3] and the pending closure of Australian car manufacturing[4]. Based on these findings and the fact that men are three times more likely to die by suicide than women in first world countries like Australia[5], a focus on male suicide prevention in these areas will be important. A limitation of this study was that in some occupations small numbers of suicides meant that the authors were unable to assess statistical significance. Other potential limitations include the underreporting of suicides and the possible misclassification of occupation codes.

Endnotes

1. Chang S-S, Stuckler D, Yip P, Gunnell D (2013). Impact of 2008 global economic crisis on suicide: Time trend study in 54 countries. *BMJ* 347, 1-15.
2. Milner A, Morrell S, LaMontagne AD (2014). Economically inactive, unemployed and employed suicides in Australia by age and sex over a 10-year period: what was the impact of the 2007 economic recession? *International Journal of Epidemiology* 43, 1500-1507.
3. Neubauer I (2015). The Aussie towns destroyed by China's economic slowdown. *news.com.au.* Retrieved from http://www.news.com.au/finance/business/mining/the-aussie-towns-destroyed-by-chinas-economic-slowdown/news-story/58e32a724a97f2ddda8ff9e54d34ef57
4. Lynch J, Hawthorne M (2015). Australia's car industry one year from closing its doors. *The Sydney Morning Herald.* Retrieved from http://www.smh.com.au/business/the-economy/australias-car-industry-one-year-from-closing-its-doors-20151012-gk7ip0.html
5. World Health Organisation (2014). *Preventing suicide: A global imperative.* Geneva, Switzerland.

Suicide among male road and rail drivers in Australia: A retrospective mortality study

Milner A, Page K, LaMontagne AD (Australia)
Road and Transport Research 24, 26-31, 2015

Objectives: This paper aims to describe the epidemiology of suicide among males employed in driving occupations (road and rail) compared to other male occupations in Australia.

Methods: Suicide cases among road and rail drivers were extracted from a national dataset of occupationally coded suicide cases for the period 2001 to 2010. Suicide rates per 100 000 were calculated and standardised using the Australian standard population (2001). Incidence rate ratios (IRR) with 95% confidence intervals were calculated using Mantell Haenszel rates and compared to all employed suicide cases.

Results: The majority of suicides in this occupational category occurred in truck drivers, followed by road and rail drivers. 98% of these suicides were among males; hence only males were included in further analyses. The age-standardised rate of male suicide among Road and Rail drivers over the period 2001 to 2010 was 22.6 per 100 000 (95% CI 19.2 to 25.9). The IRR of suicide in this occupational group compared to other male occupations was 1.42 (95% CI 1.26 to 1.60).

Conclusions: Suicide among Road and Rail drivers is higher than in the other male occupations. Suicide prevention initiatives addressing these risk factors, while also providing access to treatment for those at risk, are clearly needed.

Comment

Main findings: Studies have found that road and rail drivers, like other people in lower skilled and lower status occupations have elevated suicide rates compared to higher skilled occupations[1]. To date, however, studies have not examined road and rail driver suicide rates independently from other low skilled occupations. Therefore, this study sought to describe the epidemiology of suicide among road and rail drivers compared to other male occupations in Australia. It was hypothesised that rates of suicide among road and rail drivers will be higher than other occupational groups.

Data were obtained from the National Coroners Information System for the years 2001-2010. Road and rail drivers were defined as drivers of cars, buses, coaches, trains, trams, vans and trucks to transport passengers and freight. All other occupations represented the study's comparison group. To categorise the data, occupations were coded by two researchers according to the Australian and New Zealand Standard Classification of Occupations, with consensus between coders being reached via discussion. Age standardised suicide rates per 100 000 persons were calculated based on the 2001 census data for average number of people per occupation. Between 2001-2010 there were 513 suicides among all road and rail drivers. Truck drivers accounted for the majority of suicides (63%), followed by drivers of automobiles (10%), rail drivers (9.9%), bus and coach drivers (7.6%), delivery drivers (6.24%) and train and tram drivers (2.73%). Given that 98% of road and rail suicides were men, only male suicide was analysed in this study. Whilst there were differences in age for road and rail driver suicides compared to other occupations, with road and rail drivers being slightly older, this difference was not statistically significant. Overall, the age standardised suicide rate for road and rail drivers was 22.6 per 100 000, compared to 15.9 per 100 000 for all other occupations. Results from the statistical analysis supported the hypothesis that road and rail drivers had a significantly higher suicide rate than all other male occupational groups over the 2001-2010 period. The suicide rate for road and rail drivers was also considerably higher than the general male suicide rate (between 15 and 17.5 per 100 000).

Implications: These findings align with prior studies investigating suicide rates for low skilled and low status occupations. As suggested, road and rail suicide rates are likely the result of drivers facing a greater number of suicide risk factors compared to other occupations. Road and rail drivers are more likely to engage in poor health behaviours, such as alcohol consumption and smoking, and suffer from poor working conditions such as irregular hours, fatigue, limited psychosocial support and job dissatisfaction[2,3]. Furthermore, given the low status and low skilled nature of their work, drivers tend to have lower socio-economic status which has been shown to be associated with poor mental health[4]. It is therefore important that rail and road workplaces (with the help of industry and government) identify and manage occupational stressors, promote mental health and foster organisational support for its employees. The findings from this research could also help inform suicide prevention strategies in the workplace for specific occupations. It is also important that organisations such as Suicide Prevention Australia develop suicide guidelines for specific occupations[5]. This paper is not without limitations. Firstly, this study only calculated the suicide rates for broad categories of road and rail occupations and not specific road and rail occupations. This is problematic because specific occupations within each category (e.g., short distance versus long-distance truck drivers) often face different occupational risk factors, which may in turn lead to different suicide rates. This lack of specificity could limit the ability of these findings to inform suicide initiatives for specific occupations (e.g., taxi drivers). Therefore, future research should investigate the suicide rates of specific road and rail occupations. It is also likely that given the problems with the underreporting and miscoding of suicide that incident rates were higher than reported in this study[6].

Endnote

1. Milner A, Spittal MJ, Pirkis J, Lamontagne AD (2013). Suicide by occupation: A systematic review and meta-analysis. *British Journal of Psychiatry* 203, 409-416.
2. Blonk RWB, Broersen JPJ, De Croon EM, Frings-Dresen MHW, De Zwart BCH (2002). Job stress, fatigue, and job dissatisfaction in Dutch lorry drivers: Towards an occupation specific model of job demands and control. *Occupational and Environmental Medicine* 59, 356-61.

3. De Croon EM, Sluiter JK, Blonk RWB, Broersen JPJ, Frings-Dresen MHW (2004). Stressful work, psychological job strain, and turnover: A 2-year prospective cohort study of truck drivers. *Journal of Applied Psychology* 89, 442-454.

4. Lorant V, Deliege D, Eaton W, Robert A, Philippot P, Ansseau M (2003). Socioeconomic inequalities in depression: A meta-analysis. *American Journal of Epidemiology* 157, 98-112.

5. Suicide Prevention Australia (2014). *Work and suicide prevention: Position Statement.* Sydney: Suicide Prevention Australia.

6. De Leo D, Dudley MJ, Aebersold CJ, Mendoza JA, Barnes MA, Harrison JE, Ranson DL (2010). Achieving standardised reporting of suicide in Australia: Rationale and program for change. *Medical Journal of Australia* 192, 452-456.

Comparison of the effects of telephone suicide prevention help by volunteers and professional paid staff: Results from studies in the USA and Quebec, Canada

Mishara, BL, Daigle M, Bardon C, Chagnon F, Balan B, Raymond S, Campbell J (Canada)
Suicide & Life-Threatening Behavior. Published online: 6 March 2016. doi: 10.1111/sltb.12238

Research since the 1960s has consistently found that lay volunteers are better at helping suicidal callers than professionals. Yet, professional degrees are increasingly becoming requirements for helpline workers. In our first study, we conducted post hoc comparisons of U.S. helplines with all professional paid staff, all lay volunteers, and a mix of both, using silent monitoring and standardized assessments of 1,431 calls. The volunteer centers more often conducted risk assessments, had more empathy, were more respectful of callers, and had significantly better call outcome ratings. A second study of five Quebec suicide prevention centers used silent monitoring to compare telephone help in 1,206 calls answered by 90 volunteers and 39 paid staff. Results indicate no significant differences between the volunteers and paid employees on outcome variables. However, volunteers and paid staff with over 140 hours of call experience had significantly better outcomes. Unlike the United States, Quebec paid employees were not required to have advanced professional degrees. We conclude from these results and previous research that there is no justification for requiring that suicide prevention helpline workers be mental health professionals. In fact, the evidence to date indicates that professionals may be less effective in providing telephone help to suicidal individuals when compared to trained lay volunteers.

Comment

Main findings: Despite professional degrees increasingly becoming requirements for telephone helplines, previous research has found that volunteers/lay persons are more effective in providing help to suicidal people than professionals. This study aimed to assess the relative effectiveness of using volunteers and professional paid staff to work on telephone helplines. Results from two separate previous studies were re-examined and compared centres with volunteers or "professional" staff. These two studies examined whether there was a difference between effectiveness of telephone help provided to suicidal callers by volunteers and paid professional staff. The first study involved conducting post hoc analyses on effectiveness of staff of telephone helplines regarding intervention styles in the United States (US). A total of 14 centres were contacted and asked whether they used all volunteers to answer their calls, all professionals or a mix of volunteers and professionals. Four of the centres employed all professionals, with a total of 168 professional helpline workers participating in the study. Three centres used 131 helpline workers, which was a mix of professionals and volunteers. In the remaining 7 centres only volunteers answered calls which was a total of 493 helpers. A total of 2,611 calls to 14 U.S helplines were silently monitored. Two trained research assistants listened to all calls and rated the characteristics of the helper's behaviours, and the observed impact on the callers using standardised rating scales. Post hoc analyses revealed that centres with all professional staff showed the highest number of calls with low empathy and low respect for callers. Meanwhile, all volunteer centres had higher levels of respect and empathy, and had higher ratings of help effectiveness than centres with all professional centres or a mix of professional and volunteers.

The second study involved a survey conducted in Quebec, Canada and aimed to compare practices and outcomes by volunteers and paid staff in telephone helplines. A total of 129 helpers participated in the study, with 90 (69.7%) volunteers and 39 (30.3%) paid staff. At the end of calls, helpers were instructed to ask callers for consent to call back as part of an evaluation study. Two clusters of intervention style were identified: the first was a nondirective approach characterised by more acceptance and approval; the second was a directive approach characterised by more orientation/investigation, more silence, reassurance, judgments, reflection, clarification, interpretation and telling a personal experience and telling about the experience of others. There were no significant differences between intervention styles between paid staff and volunteers. The directive approach was used by half the volunteers (52.7%) and paid staff (46%), the remaining used the nondirective approach (47.3% and 54%, respectively). No differences in changes in suicide urgency from beginning to the end of call when answered by volunteer or paid staff, and no changes in measures of psychological symptoms or of depression. Although services were rated higher when paid staff answered the call compared to volunteers (78.6% vs. 58.3%, p<.026), no differences in satisfaction ratings at follow-up was observed for those with more or less experience. In other words, both volunteers and paid staff were equally effective in answering calls from suicidal individuals. However, volunteers and paid staff with over 140 hours of call experience were found to have significantly better outcomes than those with less experience.

Implications: The authors conclude from the results of these two studies (and previous research) that there is no justification for requiring that suicide prevention helpline workers need to be mental health professionals. Future research is needed to investigate why professional qualifications are not showing advantages over volunteers, given the years of specialised training involved in becoming a professional. The authors suggested that this observed non-advantage of professional training may be due to the fact that lay persons are able to relate with experiences of callers, and that interacting as a peer rather than an expert helps connect to the caller better. As both volunteers and paid staff with more experience had better outcomes, Mishara et al. also highlight the importance of retaining volunteers and staff long-term rather than focussing on recruiting and training new personnel. Currently, Lifeline Australia accepts volunteers without requiring a tertiary degree, and trains volunteers according to guidelines and standards[1]. In line with these findings, Lifeline's only requirement is that volunteers should have the ability to express empathy, respect for others and have a strong sense of self-awareness. A key limitation of this study was that ad hoc analyses were applied to a study that was not designed to compare volunteers and professionals. It would be useful to extend this research in Australia using a more systematic approach and controlling for confounding variables, in order to investigate whether volunteers or professionals for telephone support lines are more effective in helping suicidal callers.

Endnotes

1. Lifeline (2016). Crisis Supporter Training. Retrieved 21 April 2016 from https://www.lifeline.org.au/About-Lifeline/Training-Opportunities/Telephone-Volunteer-Training/Telephone-Volunteer-Training

The association of physical illness and self-harm resulting in hospitalisation among older people in a population-based study

Mitchell R, Draper B, Harvey L, Brodaty H, Close J (Australia)

Aging and Mental Health. Published online: 15 October 2015. doi: 10.1080/13607863.2015.1099610

Objectives: With population ageing, self-harm injuries among older people are increasing. Further examination of the association of physical illness and self-harm among older people is warranted. This research aims to identify the association of physical illness with hospitalisations following self-harm compared to non-self-harm injury among older people.

Method: A population-based cohort study of individuals aged 50+ years admitted to hospital either for a self-harm or a non-self-harm injury using linked hospital admission and mortality records during 2003-2012 in New South Wales, Australia was conducted. Logistic regression and survival plots were used to examine the association of 21 physical illnesses and mortality at 12 months by injury intent, respectively. Age-adjusted health outcomes, including length of stay, readmission and mortality were examined by injury intent.

Results: There were 12,111 hospitalisations as a result of self-harm and 474,158 hospitalisations as a result of non-self-harm injury. Self-harm compared to non-self-harm hospitalised injury was associated with higher odds of mental health conditions (i.e. depression, schizophrenia, bipolar and anxiety disorders), neurological disorders (excluding dementia), other disorders of the nervous system, diabetes, chronic lower respiratory disease, liver disease, tinnitus and pain. Tinnitus, pain, malignancies and diabetes all had a higher likelihood of occurrence for self-harm compared to non-self-harm hospitalisations even after adjusting for mental health conditions, number of comorbidities and alcohol and drug dependency.

Conclusion: Older people who are experiencing chronic health conditions, particularly tinnitus, malignancies, diabetes and chronic pain may be at risk of self-harm. Targeted screening may assist in identifying older people at risk of self-harm.

Comment

Main findings: In most countries suicide rates peak in older adults. Surprisingly, recent evidence suggests that self-harm, something traditionally associated with younger people, is increasing in older adults as well. Risk factors for older adult self-harm include psychiatric illnesses, social isolation, previous suicidal behaviour, alcohol misuse, personality factors, bereavement and relationship problems. However, the extent that physical health acts as a risk factor for self-harm is unclear. Previous research examining this link has been limited by small sample sizes, no comparison cohort and a focus on suicide and suicidal ideation as opposed to self-harm. This paper aimed to identify the link between physical illness and subsequent hospitalisations due to self-harm compared to non-self-harm injury among older adults. A retrospective analysis was conducted on self-harm and non-self-harm injuries in New South Wales (NSW) residents aged 50 years and above. Data was gathered from linked hospital admission and mortality records from January 2003 to December 2012. Diagnoses, external cause codes and substance type were classified using the International Classification of Diseases, 10th Revision, Australian Modification (ICD-10-AM).

There were 12,111 instances of self-harm and 474,158 instances of non-self-harm hospitalisations during the 10-year study period. In people aged 50-59 years there was over twice the proportion of self-harm hospitalisations compared to non-self-harm hospitalisations, whereas for people aged 70+ years there was a much smaller proportion. Twelve physical illnesses were identified as being associated with self-harm in older people, and after adjusting for mental health conditions, alcohol and drug dependence and number of comorbidities, four of these remained associated with self-harm. Tinnitus (2.9 times more likely), pain (1.3 times more likely), malignancies (1.3 times more likely) and diabetes (1.2 times more likely) had a higher likelihood of occurrence in older adults hospitalised for self-harm as opposed to those hospitalised for non-self-harm injuries.

Implications: These findings are not only consistent with previous research[1,2] but they also have serious implications for Australia's public health system. The findings reinforce the need for an easily accessible health system that provides targeted screening and subsequent treatment so to ensure that deteriorating physical health does not lead self-harm. This is particularly important for physical illnesses which are associated with significant pain. Debilitating physical illnesses can be a tipping point which leads to imminent suicide risk[3]. Therefore, implementing effective suicide and self-harm screening for older adults with physical conditions could help identify the risk factors for self-harm before it occurs. This paper is not without its limitations. As data validity was not able to be assessed it is possible that hospital records could have either been misclassified or inconsistently classified. It is also possible that some individuals may have chosen not to disclose that their injuries were the result of self-harm. Furthermore, the paper did not examine individuals who self-harmed, died and were not hospitalised, which may have led to an under-estimation of the number of self-harm and suicides amongst older adults.

Endnotes

1. Draper B (1996). Attempted suicide in old age. *International Journal of Geriatric Psychiatry* 11, 577-587.
2. Fassberg M, Cheung G, Canetto S, Erlangsen A, Lapierre S, Lindner R, Draper B, Gallo JJ, Wong C, Wu J, Duberstein P, Waern M. (2015). A systematic review of physical illness, functional disability and suicidal behaviour among older adults. *Aging and Mental Health* 20, 166-194.
3. Queensland Mental Health Commission (2015). *Queensland Suicide Prevention Action Plan 2015-17.* Retrieved 28 April 2016 from https://www.qmhc.qld.gov.au/wp-content/uploads/2015/09/Queensland-Suicide-Prevention-Action-Plan-2015-17_WEB.pdf.

Interventions to reduce suicides at suicide hotspots: A systematic review and meta-analysis

Pirkis J, Too LS, Spittal MJ, Krysinska K, Robinson J, Cheung YTD (Australia)

Lancet Psychiatry 2, 994-1001, 2015

Background: Various interventions have been introduced to try to prevent suicides at suicide hotspots, but evidence of their effectiveness needs to be strengthened.

Methods: We did a systematic search of Medline, PsycINFO, and Scopus for studies of interventions, delivered in combination with others or in isolation, to prevent suicide at suicide hotspots. We did a meta-analysis to assess the effect of interventions that restrict access to means, encourage help-seeking, or increase the likelihood of intervention by a third party.

Findings: We identified 23 articles representing 18 unique studies. After we removed one outlier, interventions that restricted access to means were associated with a reduction in the number of suicides per year (incidence rate ratio 0.09, 95% CI 0.03-0.27; $p < 0.0001$), as were interventions that encourage help-seeking (0.49, 95% CI 0.29-0.83; $p = 0.0086$), and interventions that increase the likelihood of intervention by a third party (0.53, 95% CI 0.31-0.89; $p = 0.0155$). When we included only those studies that assessed a particular intervention in isolation, restricting access to means was associated with a reduction in the risk of suicide (0.07, 95% CI 0.02-0.19; $p < 0.0001$), as was encouraging help-seeking (0.39, 95% CI 0.19-0.80; $p = 0.0101$); no studies assessed increasing the likelihood of intervention by a third party as a lone intervention.

Interpretation: The key approaches that are currently used as interventions at suicide hotspots seem to be effective. Priority should be given to ongoing implementation and assessment of initiatives at suicide hotspots, not only to prevent so-called copycat events, but also because of the effect that suicides at these sites have on people who work at them, live near them, or frequent them for other reasons.

Comment

Main findings: There are four general approaches to suicide prevention at suicide hot spots: (1) restricting access to means, (2) encouraging help-seeking, (3) increasing the likelihood of intervention by a third party, and (4) encouraging responsible media reporting of suicide[1]. A previous meta-analysis by the authors revealed unequivocal evidence for the effectiveness of restricting access to means (i.e., barriers on bridges and cliffs)[2], while the evidence for the other approaches was weaker. In order to strengthen the evidence for the effectiveness of suicide hot-spot interventions, this systematic review and meta-analysis examined the relative effectiveness of each of the four main approaches to intervention (delivered in isolation or combined with other interventions). Search results for the systematic literature review yielded 23 articles representing 18 unique studies. Thirteen studies assessed restricting access to means (11 in isolation, and two in combination with other interventions), six assessed encouraging help-seeking (three in isolation, three in combination with other interventions), and four assessed increasing the likelihood of intervention by a third party (all in combination with other interventions). There were no studies that assessed increasing the likelihood of intervention by a third party delivered as an isolated intervention. In six of the 18 studies, the number of suicides dropped to zero in the post-intervention period. For each group of studies, a pooled incidence rate ratio (IRR) was estimated with a random-effects conditional model. This estimated the average population change in the incidence from pre to post-intervention period while accounting for between-study differences. Results revealed that there was an association between interventions that restricted access to the means and a reduction in number of suicides per year (IRR= 0.09, 95% CI 0.03-0.27; p<0.0001). Similarly, interventions that encouraged help-seeking (IRR=0.49, 95% CI 0.29-0.83; p=0.0086), and interventions that increase the likelihood of intervention by a third party (IRR=0.53, 95% CI 0.31-0.89; p=0.0155) was also associated with a reduction in number of suicides per year. Analysing studies with one type of intervention only showed that restricting access to means (IRR=0.07, 95% CI 0.02-0.19; p<0.0001) and interventions that encouraged help-seeking (IRR=0.39, 95% CI 0.19-0.80; p=0.0101) was associated with a reduction of suicide risk.

Implications: These findings reveal that restricting access to means, encouraging help-seeking, and increasing the likelihood of intervention by a third party are effective in reducing deaths by suicide at hotspots. The evidence for the effectiveness of both encouraging help-seeking and increasing the likelihood of intervention by a third party is very promising, given that restricting access to means is not always feasible (e.g., due to natural cliffs, tourist locations). Nevertheless, the authors note a potential limitation of this study is the source data for the meta-analysis (where not all relevant studies may have been identified). In addition, the study was unable to assess whether particular combinations of interventions produced the best outcomes, because the outcomes that were studied were not exhaustive. Future research should aim to disaggregate the effects of these different interventions to pinpoint the key approaches to suicide prevention at suicide hotspots. The authors argue that although intervention at suicide hotspots may only have a small effect on the total suicide rate, suicide prevention at hotspots is important in preventing copycat events, and in reducing the adverse impact that suicides at these sites have on people who work at them, live near them, or frequent them for other reasons. In 2015, suicide prevention barriers were installed for Queensland's Story Bridge, as well as safety telephone systems and a 24-hour CCTV system. An evaluation of the effectiveness of these barriers would be useful to inform future suicide hotspot interventions in Australia.

Endnotes

1. Cox GR, Owens C, Robinson J, Nicholas A, Lockley A, Williamson M, Cheung YT, Pirkis J (2013). Interventions to reduce suicides at suicide hotspots: a systematic review. *BMC Public Health* 13, 214.
2. Pirkis J, Spittal M, Cox G, Robinson J, Cheung Y-T, Studdert D (2013). The effectiveness of structural interventions at suicide hotspots: a meta-analysis. *International Journal of Epidemiology* 42, 541–548.

Bereavement by suicide as a risk factor for suicide attempt: A cross-sectional national UK-wide study of 3432 young bereaved adults

Pitman AL, Osborn DP, Rantell K, King MB (United Kingdom)
BMJ Open, 6, 1-11, 2016

Objectives: US and UK suicide prevention strategies suggest that bereavement by the suicide of a relative or friend is a risk factor for suicide. However, evidence is lacking that the risk exceeds that of any sudden bereavement, is specific to suicide, or applies to peer suicide. We conducted the first controlled UK-wide study to test the hypothesis that young adults bereaved by suicide have an increased risk of suicidal ideation and suicide attempt compared with young adults bereaved by other sudden deaths.

Design: National cross-sectional study.

Setting: Staff and students at 37 UK higher educational institutions in 2010.

Participants: 3432 eligible respondents aged 18-40 exposed to sudden bereavement of a friend or relative after the age of 10.

Exposures: Bereavement by suicide (n=614), by sudden unnatural causes (n=712) and by sudden natural causes (n=2106).

Primary Outcome Measures: Incident suicidal ideation and suicide attempt.

Findings: Adults bereaved by suicide had a higher probability of attempting suicide (adjusted OR (AOR)=1.65; 95% CI 1.12 to 2.42; p=0.012) than those bereaved by sudden natural causes. There was no such increased risk in adults bereaved by sudden unnatural causes. There were no group differences in probability of suicidal ideation. The effect of suicide bereavement was similar whether bereaved participants were blood-related to the deceased or not. The significant association between bereavement by suicide and suicide attempt became non-significant when adding perceived stigma (AOR=1.11; 95% CI 0.74 to 1.67; p=0.610). When compared with adults bereaved by sudden unnatural causes, those bereaved by suicide did not show significant differences in suicide attempt (AOR=1.48; 95% CI 0.94 to 2.33; p=0.089).

Conclusions: Bereavement by suicide is a specific risk factor for suicide attempt among young bereaved adults, whether related to the deceased or not. Suicide risk assessment of young adults should involve screening for a history of suicide in blood relatives, non-blood relatives and friends.

Comment

Main findings: Close friends and relatives of people who die by suicide are a high risk group for suicide. This population-based study employed an online cross-sectional survey to compare the impact of specific modes of self-reported sudden death bereavement on non-fatal suicide-related outcomes. It was hypothesised that: 1) young adults who had been bereaved by suicide would have a higher risk of suicidal thoughts and attempts, compared to those bereaved by sudden death; 2) suicide bereavement would be a risk factor for secondary clinical and occupational measures (postbereavement, nonsuicidal self-harm, depression, occupational drop-out, and social dysfunction) which would reflect policy concerns about the contribution of bereavement to workplace mental ill health and sickness absence; 3) the impact of suicide bereavement would extend beyond genetic relatedness to peer suicides; and 4) associations with clinical or occupational outcomes would be attenuated by perceived stigma, as a marker for reduced help seeking.

A total of 5085 people of the 659 572 sampled responded to the questionnaire, and only 68% (n=3432) were eligible to participate. Participants were grouped into those bereaved by sudden natural death (n=2106), bereaved by sudden unnatural death (n=712) and bereaved by suicide (n=314). Participants were primarily female and blood-related to the deceased. Those bereaved by suicide were significantly more likely to report prebereavement psychopathology, and family history of psychiatric problems compared to those bereaved by sudden death. There were no significant differences in mean time elapsed since bereavement between the two groups (M=4.9 years). Results showed that those bereaved by suicide had a greater risk of postbereavement suicide attempt (adjusted OR (AOR)=1.65; 95% CI 1.12 to 2.42; p=0.012), but not of suicidal ideation. Moreover, those bereaved by suicide had a greater risk of occupational drop-out (AOR=1.80; 95% CI 1.20 to 2.71; p=0.005), but there was no evidence for group differences in postbereavement non-suicidal self-harm, depression or social functioning.

Implications: This is the first study to show that irrespective of blood-relatedness, bereavement by suicide is a specific risk factor for suicide attempts compared to those bereaved due to sudden natural causes. These findings have important clinical implications for assessing suicide risk, and highlight the need for clinicians to enquire about suicide history not only in blood relatives, but in friends and non-blood relatives. It is important to note that the relationship between suicide bereavement and suicide attempt became non-significant when controlling for perceived stigma, which suggests that perceived stigma may reduce help seeking. However, further investigation is warranted to determine causality. A strength of the study was the national, population-based sample size; however, sampling from UK higher education institutes resulted in a highly educated sample which limits the generalisability of the findings. The results of this study may be more generalisable to young bereaved women than men, and to the more highly educated. Currently there are no evidence-based interventions for this risk group. Future research should aim to develop prevention interventions and guidelines for this population, especially investigating the role of stigma in reducing help-seeking. This would help inform organisations like StandBy in their bereavement support care[1].

Endnotes

1. United Synergies (2016). Standby response service. Retrieved 26 April 2016 from http://www.unitedsynergies.com.au/program/standby-response-service/

Suicidal ideation, suicide attempts and non-suicidal self-injury among lesbian, gay, bisexual and heterosexual adults: Findings from an Australian national study

Swannell S, Martin G, Page, A (Australia)

Australian & New Zealand Journal of Psychiatry 50, 145-153, 2016

Objectives: This study investigated associations between sexual orientation and measures of suicidality and non-suicidal self-injury in Australian adults. Previous studies of sexual orientation and suicidality have been limited by unclear conceptualisations of suicidal intent, failure to differentiate between homosexuality and bisexuality, inattention to gender differences and use of convenience-based samples.

Methods: A large ($N = 10,531$) representative national sample of Australian adults was used to investigate associations between sexual orientation (heterosexual, homosexual, bisexual) and (1) suicidal ideation, (2) attempted suicide and (3) non-suicidal self-injury, for males and females separately, in a series of sequentially adjusted logistic regression models.

Results: Sexual minority participants were at greater risk of suicidality and self-injury than heterosexuals, after adjusting for age and other covariates, with patterns of risk differing by sexual orientation and gender. Compared with their heterosexual counterparts, gay men, but not bisexual men, were more likely to report suicidal ideation (odds ratio = 3.05, 95% confidence interval = [1.65, 5.60]) and suicide attempts (odds ratio = 4.16, confidence interval = [2.18, 7.93]). Bisexual women, but not lesbian women, were more likely to report suicidal ideation (odds ratio = 4.40, confidence interval = [3.00, 6.37]) and suicide attempts (odds ratio = 4.46, confidence interval = [2.41, 8.24]). Neither bisexual nor gay men were more likely than heterosexual men to report self-injury. However, bisexual women, but not lesbian women, were more likely than heterosexual women to report self-injury (odds ratio = 19.59, confidence interval = [9.05, 42.40]). Overall, bisexual females were at greatest risk of suicidality and self-injury.

Conclusion: Clinicians working with sexual minority populations are encouraged to openly discuss suicidal and self-injurious thoughts and behaviours with their clients and may consider using therapeutic strategies to reduce internalised stigma and enhance personal and social resources.

Comment

Main findings: Non-heterosexual orientation has been shown to be associated with increased risk of non-suicidal self-injury (NSSI)[1] which is in turn linked to suicidal behaviour[2]. Previous studies investigating the link between sexual orientation and NSSI, have been limited by the use of convenience samples, combining homosexual and bisexual orientation into the one category, inattention to gender differences, and unclear conceptualisations of suicidal intent. This study aimed to investigate the link between sexual orientation and suicidal ideation, suicide attempts and NSSI in a large nationally representative sample. A total of 12,006 Australians were sampled in a national telephone survey of self-injury conducted in 2008. Data pertaining to NSSI, suicidal ideation, suicide attempts, psychological distress, demographics, sexual orientation, alcohol use and illicit drug use in adults aged 18-100 years were analysed. Logistic regression models were used to investigate associations between sexual orientation and NSSI, suicidal ideation, and suicide attempts. Overall, homosexuality and bisexuality was associated with a higher risk of suicidal ideation, suicide attempts and NSSI. Important differences emerged when gender (males, females) and sexuality (homosexual and bisexual) were considered separately and where age, psychological distress, alcohol and illicit drug use were controlled for. Homosexual males, but not bisexual males, were more likely to attempt suicide (OR = 4.16, 95% CI = [2.18, 7.93], $p<0.001$) and experience suicidal ideation (OR = 3.05, 95% CI = [1.65, 5.60], $p<0.001$). Whereas, bisexual women, but not lesbian women, were more likely to attempt suicide (OR = 4.46, 95% CI = [2.41, 8.24], $p<0.001$), experience suicidal ideation (OR = 4.40, 95% CI = [3.00, 6.37], $p<0.001$) and engage in NSSI (OR = 19.59, 95% CI = [9.05, 42.40], $p<0.001$).

Implications: These findings expand upon previous research by refining our understanding of the relationship between non-heterosexual orientation and suicidal ideation, suicide attempts and NSSI. The results highlight the importance of considering gay and bisexual males and females as distinct groups and the need to implement mental health initiatives that are tailored to their needs. Suicide Prevention Australia recommends a comprehensive approach to non-heterosexual suicidality and NSSI, implementing a range of initiatives such as community education campaigns and anti-discrimination legislation[3]. A strength of the study was the use of a nationally representative sample of the Australian population; however, the study was limited to a relatively small sample of homosexual and bisexual participants. Furthermore, as the research relied on self-report measures, it is possible that the results may have been influenced by recall and social desirability biases (the latter which could lead to an underreporting of non-heterosexual orientation).

Endnotes

1. Deliberto TL, Nock MK (2008). An exploratory study of correlates, onset, and offset of non-suicidal self-injury. *Archives of Suicide Research* 12, 219–231.
2. Andover M. S, Pepper CM, Ryabchenko KA, Orrico EG, Gibb BE (2005). Self-mutilation and symptoms of depression, anxiety, and borderline personality disorder. *Suicide and Life-Threatening Behavior* 35, 581–591.
3. Suicide Prevention Australia (2009). *Suicide and self-harm among gay, lesbian and transgender communities: Position Statement.* Retrieved 31 May 2016 from https://www.suicidepreventionaust.org/sites/default/files/resources/2016/SPA-GayLesbian-PositionStatement%5B1%5D.pdf

Is case management effective for long-lasting suicide prevention? A community cohort study in Northern Taiwan

Wang L-J, Wu Y-W, Chen C-K (Taiwan)

Crisis 36, 194-201, 2015

Background: Case management services have been implemented in suicide prevention programs.

Aims: To investigate whether case management is an effective strategy for reducing the risks of repeated suicide attempts and completed suicides in a city with high suicide rates in northern Taiwan.

Method: The Suicide Prevention Center of Keelung City (KSPC) was established in April 2005. Subjects included a consecutive sample of individuals (N = 2,496) registered in KSPC databases between January 1, 2006, and December 31, 2011, with at least one episode of nonfatal self-harm. Subjects were tracked for the duration of the study.

Results: Of all the subjects, 1,013 (40.6%) received case management services; 416 (16.7%) had at least one other deliberate self-harm episode and 52 (2.1%) eventually died by suicide. No significant differences were found in the risks of repeated self-harm and completed suicides between suicide survivors who received case management and those who refused the services. However, a significant reduction in suicide rates was found after KSPC was established.

Conclusion: Findings suggest that case management services might not reduce the risks of suicide repetition among suicide survivors during long-term follow-up. Future investigation is warranted to determine factors impacting the downward trend of suicide rates.

Comment

Main findings: Although recent community studies have demonstrated that case management is an effective strategy to prevent repeated suicide attempts in those who have had one prior nonfatal attempt, there has been mixed evidence from studies using various types of case management services (e.g., telephone contact, home visits, brief educational interventions, and post card interventions). This study aimed to investigate whether a case management program is effective in reducing repeated suicide attempts and completed suicides. The study was conducted with The Suicide Prevention Center of Keelung City (KSPC), with a total of 2,496 participants (who survived an episode of self-harm between the study period of January 1 2006 to December 31 2011). If an individual had made several attempts of self-harm during the study period, the first attempt recorded in the database was defined as the index attempt. Methods of suicide were categorised as low-lethality (drug overdose, self-cutting); charcoal-burning (poisoning using other gases and vapors); and a third group involving poisoning by gases used domestically, hanging, drowning, firearms, air guns, explosives, jumping from high places, and other and unspecified means. Case managers contacted individuals via telephone or home visit within one week of the attempt and then followed them up for six months. Case management was discontinued if issues leading up to the deliberate self-harm were resolved, if psychiatric treatment had been taken up or individuals clearly refused services more than three times. Of the participants enrolled in this study, 1,483 (59.4%) refused services.

The sample was comprised of 1,686 (67.5%) females, and 810 (32.5%) males. The most common methods chosen for the first suicide attempt were low-lethality methods (82.7%), charcoal-burning (7.5%) and other highly lethal methods (9.9%). Compared to those who refused case management services, participants receiving services had a higher rate of choosing charcoal-burning or other highly lethal methods as their first self-harm episode, and were more likely to have a pre-existing mental illness. In total, 416 (16.7%) participants carried out further deliberate self-harm and 52 (2.1%) individuals completed suicide during the study period. Repeated self-harm episodes were more likely to occur in individuals aged between 35 and 49 years and those with a history of mental illness, and less likely to occur among men, those older than 65 years old, individuals who used charcoal-burning, and those who used other high-lethality methods.

Implications: The study showed that the risk of repeated self-harm and subsequent suicide mortality did not differ between those who refused or accepted case management services. The authors suggest that a possible explanation was the lack of relevant prior training and experience in the newly recruited case managers. In addition, although the case management program offered psychological support to patients, it did not include support on adverse life events that may have triggered the suicide. Lastly, the observation period for this study cohort was up to six years, which is much longer than six-month follow-ups in previous studies showing positive results. Given that those receiving case management services had a more serious index episode of self-harm and more serious mental illness than those who received services, it is possible that this difference might have counteracted the benefits of the case management services. The authors highlight the importance of modifying and improving case management models to achieve long-term effects on suicide prevention (e.g., not only linking people to resources, but also providing novel approaches to care in transition). Currently, in Australia, only some Department of Health guidelines[1,2,3] include case management as part of their practices. Replication of this research in Australia would assist in evaluating and improving current case management practices, and provide evidence for inclusion of case management in all Department of Health guidelines.

Endnotes

1. New South Wales Department of Health (2004). *Framework for Suicide Risk Assessment and Management for New South Wales Health Staff.* North Sydney: Better Health Centre.
2. Victoria Department of Health (2010). *Working with the suicidal person: A summary guide for emergency departments and mental health services.* Melbourne: Mental Health, Drugs and Regions branch, Victorian Government.
3. South Australia Department of Health (2012). *Guidelines for working with the suicidal person.* South Australia: Department for Health and Ageing.

Ultra-low-dose buprenorphine as a time-limited treatment for severe suicidal ideation: A randomized controlled trial

Yovell Y, Bar G, Mashiah M, Baruch Y, Briskman I, Asherov J, Lotan A, Rigbi A, Panksepp J
(Israel)

American Journal of Psychiatry 173, 497-198, 2016

Objective: Suicidal ideation and behavior currently have no quick-acting pharmacological treatments that are suitable for independent outpatient use. Suicidality is linked to mental pain, which is modulated by the separation distress system through endogenous opioids. The authors tested the efficacy and safety of very low dosages of sublingual buprenorphine as a time-limited treatment for severe suicidal ideation.

Method: This was a multisite randomized double-blind placebo-controlled trial of ultra-low-dose sublingual buprenorphine as an adjunctive treatment. Severely suicidal patients without substance abuse were randomly assigned to receive either buprenorphine or placebo (in a 2:1 ratio), in addition to their ongoing individual treatments. The primary outcome measure was change in suicidal ideation, as assessed by the Beck Suicide Ideation Scale at the end of each of 4 weeks of treatment.

Results: Patients who received ultra-low-dose buprenorphine (initial dosage, 0.1 mg once or twice daily; mean final dosage=0.44 mg/day; N=40) had a greater reduction in Beck Suicide Ideation Scale scores than patients who received placebo (N=22), both after 2 weeks (mean difference -4.3, 95% CI=-8.5, -0.2) and after 4 weeks (mean difference=-7.1, 95% CI=-12.0, -2.3). Concurrent use of antidepressants and a diagnosis of borderline personality disorder did not affect the response to buprenorphine. No withdrawal symptoms were reported after treatment discontinuation at the end of the trial.

Conclusions: The time-limited, short-term use of very low dosages of sublingual buprenorphine was associated with decreased suicidal ideation in severely suicidal patients without substance abuse. Further research is needed to establish the efficacy, safety, dosing, and appropriate patient populations for this experimental treatment.

Comment

Main findings: Currently there are no quick-acting drugs for suicide ideation and behaviour that are suitable for independent outpatient use. Although most standard antidepressants relieve suicidal ideation, this effect may take several weeks, and patient response varies. As suicidality has been associated with mental pain, modulated by the separation distress system through endogenous opioids, it was hypothesized that opioids in very low dosages may help reduce suicidal ideation. A randomised, double-blind placebo-control study was applied to test whether very low doses of buprenorphine were associated with decreased suicidal ideation in severely suicidal patients. In four medical and psychiatric centres in Israel, a total of 265 patients were screened, with 88 randomly allocated to treatment groups (57 to the buprenorphine and 31 to the placebo). Patients were eligible to participate if they were between ages of 18 to 65 and suffered from clinically significant suicidal ideation. However, they were excluded if they were pregnant or lactating, suffered from a severe medical condition, had a lifetime history of opioid abuse, a lifetime diagnosis of schizophrenia, current psychosis, ECT within past month, substance or alcohol abuse within the past two years, and benzodiazepine dependence within the past two years. More than half of the participants (56.8%) met the criteria for borderline personality disorder. In the four weeks of treatment, questionnaires were administered once a week, along with assessment of severity of suicidality, screening for adverse events and adjustment of medication dosages (i.e., daily dose could be raised in 0.1-0.2 mg increments, at maximum of 0.8 mg) by a psychiatrist. Medication dose was not raised if participants reached full remission or if they experienced significant adverse events. There was a high dropout rate of 29.5% during the first week of treatment due to the fact that almost all participants were clinically unstable, which compromised their ability to participate.

Results revealed that the effect of low-dose buprenorphine on suicidal ideation did not differ between patients who were also taking antidepressants. Overall, the buprenorphine group had a greater reduction in suicidal ideation compared to placebo, at the end of week two (mean difference=24.3, 95% CI=28.5, 20.2; p=0.04) and at the end of week four (mean difference=27.1, 95% CI=212.0, 22.3; p=0.004). One or more adverse events (i.e., dry mouth, fatigue, nausea, constipation) were reported in the buprenorphine group compared to placebo (77.2% vs. 54.8%, p=0.03).

Implications: This study found that very low doses of buprenorphine were associated with decreased suicidal ideation in severely suicidal patients. Suicidal ideation did not differ between patients who were also being treated with antidepressants and those who were not. Unlike previous research which showed that those with borderline personality disorder were associated with poorer clinical outcomes, patients with borderline personality disorder responded to the treatment similarly to those who had no diagnosis. The authors speculate that buprenorphine may address a sub-set of symptoms associated with painful feelings of rejection and abandonment and therefore might be more effective against 'atypical/borderline' suicidality than against 'melancholic' suicidality. However, these results should be interpreted with caution due to a number of limitations. The outcome measures were based on self-reports, and there was a high dropout rate in the first week of treatment due to participants being clinically unstable. Moreover, non-suicidal self-injury was not measured in this study. Thus, these findings may not be generalisable as it is unclear whether this treatment is effective for more stable, less severely suicidal patients, or those who self-harm. There was also no follow-up period to investigate long term effects (i.e., drug cravings or rebound suicidality). Future research is necessary to address these methodological issues and identify appropriate patient populations. Despite these promising results, there is a need for caution given that buprenorphine is potentially addictive and possibly lethal[1]. Further investigation into the use of this drug will clarify whether ultra-low dose buprenorphine treatments may be a safe and feasible treatment for suicidal ideation.

Endnotes

1. Butler S (2013). Buprenorphine: clinically useful but often misunderstood. *Scandinavian Journal of Pain* 4, 148–152.

Self-harm: Prevalence estimates from the second Australian Child and Adolescent Survey of Mental Health and Wellbeing

Zubrick SR, Hafekost J, Johnson SE, Lawrence D, Saw S, Sawyer M, Ainley J, Buckingham WJ (Australia)

Australian and New Zealand Journal of Psychiatry. Published online: 30 November 2015. doi: 10.1177/0004867415617837

Objective: To (1) estimate the lifetime and 12-month prevalence of self-harm without suicide intent in young people aged 12-17 years, (2) describe the co-morbidity of these behaviours with mental illness and (3) describe their co-variation with key social and demographic variables.

Method: A nationally representative random sample of households with children aged 4-17 years recruited in 2013-2014. The survey response rate was 55% with 6310 parents and carers of eligible households participating. In addition, 2967 (89%) of young people aged 11-17 completed a self-report questionnaire with 2653 of the 12- to 17-year-olds completing questions about self-harm behaviour.

Results: In any 12-month period, about 8% of all 12- to 17-year-olds (an estimated 137,000 12- to 17-year-olds) report engaging in self-harming behaviour without suicide intent. This prevalence increases with age to 11.6% in 16- to 17-year-olds. Eighteen percent (18.8%; 95% confidence interval [CI] = [14.5, 23.0]) of all 12- to 17-year-old young people with any mental health disorder measured by parent or carer report said that they had engaged in self-harm in the past 12 months. Among young people who were measured by self-report and met criteria for the Diagnostic and Statistical Manual of Mental Disorders' major depressive disorder almost half (46.6%; 95% CI = [40.0, 53.1]) also reported that they had engaged in self-harm in the past 12 months. Suicide risk among those who self-harm is significantly elevated relative to the general population.

Conclusion: The demonstrated higher risks in these young people for continued harm or possible death support the need for ongoing initiatives to reduce self-harm through mental health promotion, improved mental health literacy and continuing mental health reform to ensure services are accessible to, and meet the needs of families and young persons.

Comment

Main findings: There is a lack of population data on non-suicidal self-harm in Australian youth. This paper provides the first contemporary, community-based Australian population estimates of lifetime and 12-month prevalence for self-reported self-harm in young people. The paper aimed to: 1) estimate the lifetime and 12-month prevalence of self-harm without suicide intent in young people aged 12-17 years; 2) describe the co-morbidity of these behaviours with mental illness and; 3) describe their co-variation with key social and demographic variables. Participants were from a nationally representative random sample of households with children aged 4–17 years recruited in 2013–2014. The response rate was 55% with 6310 parents and carers of eligible households participating. In addition, 2967 (89%) young people aged 11–17 years completed a self-report questionnaire with 2653 of 12-17 year olds completing questions about self-harm behaviour.

A total of 201 (7.5%) participants aged 12 years and over reported 'prefer not to say' to a question on self-harm and were therefore excluded from results. Results revealed that 10.9% of people aged 12-17 years reported lifetime self-harm (95% confidence interval [CI] = [9.7, 12.2]), and of these, 8% also reported self-harm in the past 12 months (95% CI = [6.9, 9.1]). Compared to 12-15 year olds, significantly higher proportions of 16-17 year olds reported having ever self-harmed (8.2%; 95% CI = [6.7, 9.8] vs 16.1%; 95% CI = [14.1, 18.2]), having ever done so four times or more (3.8%; 95% CI = [2.7, 5.0] vs 9.8%; 95% CI = [8.1, 11.5]) and having self-harmed within the previous 12 months (6.2%; 95% CI = [4.8, 7.5] vs 11.6%; 95% CI = [9.9, 13.4]). Only 1% (95% CI = [0.4, 1.2]) of all young people received medical treatment for self-harm in the previous 12 months. Among all young people (aged 12-17), 69.2% reported cutting in their last episode of self-harm.

In both groups (12-15 and 16-17 year olds) there were higher proportions of females than males who reported ever having self-harmed, having self-harmed four or more times and having self-harmed within the last 12 months. In addition, when a mental disorder was present, the young people with the highest proportions of self-harming behaviours were female and older (16–17 years). Many young persons reported that their self-harm behaviour was not intended to end their life; however they also went on to report having engaged in suicidal behaviour(s), including suicide attempt(s).

Implications: This is one of the first Australian studies which estimated the prevalence of youth self-harm behaviours. These findings support the improvement of mental health literacy and current mental health services, which may in turn reduce self-harm among young people. A limitation of this study is that it relied on self-reported data from a survey, and thus findings may be subjected to biases and reliability issues. It is also difficult to ascertain how respondents interpreted the question, 'self-harm without intending to end your own life', since many who did report self-harm without intention of death also reported engaging in high levels of suicidal behaviour including suicide attempt(s). Limitations notwithstanding, these findings can help update The Royal Australian and New Zealand College of Psychiatrist's self-harm treatment guide as it is currently outdated (published in 2009), and does not provide guidelines for children and youth[1]. These guidelines may especially cater for teenage females (especially 16-17 years old), since those who also have a mental disorder present had the highest suicide risk relative to the general population.

Endnotes

1. The Royal Australian & New Zealand College of Psychiatrist (2009). *Self-harm: Australian treatment guide for consumers and carers.* Melbourne: Australia.

Recommended Readings

Prior suicide attempts are less common in suicide decedents who died by firearms relative to those who died by other means

Anestis MD (United States)

Journal of Affective Disorders 189, 106-109, 2016

Background: Suicide prevention efforts often center on the identification of risk factors (e.g. prior suicide attempts); however, lists of risk factors without consideration of context may prove incapable of impacting suicide rates. One contextual variable worth considering is attempt method.

Methods: Utilizing data from the National Violent Death Reporting System (2005-2012), I examined suicide deaths (n=71,775) by firearms and other means to determine whether prior suicide attempts were more common in one group versus the other.

Results: Significantly fewer suicide decedents who died by firearms reported a prior history of suicide attempts (12.10%) than did decedents who died by other means (28.66%). This result was further replicated within each state that contributed data to the NVDRS.

Limitations: Only 17 states have contributed to the NVDRS thus far and, within those states, not all suicide deaths were reported. Due to the nature of the data, I was unable to test proposed mediators within our model.

Conclusions: Suicide decedents who die by firearms may die on their first attempt more often than other decedents due to a capability and willingness to utilize a highly lethal means. Current risk assessment protocols may be ill equipped to identify such individuals prospectively on their own. Broader methods of implementing means restriction (e.g. legislation) may thus be pivotal in suicide prevention efforts.

Factors associated with suicide outcomes 12 months after screening positive for suicide risk in the emergency department

Arias SA, Miller I, Camargo CA, Jr. Sullivan AF, Goldstein AB, Allen MH, Manton AP, Boudreaux ED (United States)

Psychiatric Services 67, 206-213, 2016

Objective: The main objective was to identify which patient characteristics have the strongest association with suicide outcomes in the 12 months after an index emergency department (ED) visit.

Methods: Data were analyzed from the first two phases of the Emergency Department Safety Assessment and Follow-up Evaluation (ED-SAFE). The ED-SAFE study, a quasi-experimental, interrupted time-series design, involved participation from eight general medical EDs across the United States. Participants included adults presenting to the ED with active suicidal ideation or an attempt in the past week. Data collection included baseline interview; six- and 12-month chart reviews; and six-, 12-, 24-, 36-, and 52-week telephone follow-up assessments. Regression analyses were conducted.

Results: Among 874 participants, the median age was 37 years (interquartile range 27-47), with 56% of the sample being female (N=488), 74% white (N=649), and 13% Hispanic (N=113). At baseline, 577 (66%) participants had suicidal ideation only, whereas 297 (34%) had a suicide attempt in the past week. Data sufficient to determine outcomes were available for 782 (90%). In the 12 months after the index ED visit, 195 (25%) had documentation of at least one suicide attempt or suicide. High school education or less, an ED visit in the preceding six months, prior nonsuicidal self-injury, current alcohol misuse, and suicidal intent or plan were predictive of future suicidal behavior.

Conclusions: Continuing to build an understanding of the factors associated with future suicidal behaviors for this population will help guide design and implementation of improved suicide screening and interventions in the ED and better allocation of scarce resources.

An exploratory randomised trial of a simple, brief psychological intervention to reduce subsequent suicidal ideation and behaviour in patients admitted to hospital for self-harm

Armitage CJ, Abdul Rahim W, Rowe R, O'Connor RC (United Kingdom)
British Journal of Psychiatry 208, 470-476, 2016

Background: Implementation intentions link triggers for self-harm with coping skills and appear to create an automatic tendency to invoke coping responses when faced with a triggering situation.AimsTo test the effectiveness of implementation intentions in reducing suicidal ideation and behaviour in a high-risk group.

Method: Two hundred and twenty-six patients who had self-harmed were randomised to: (a) forming implementation intentions with a 'volitional help sheet'; (b) self-generating implementation intentions without help; or (c) thinking about triggers and coping, but not forming implementation intentions. We measured self-reported suicidal ideation and behaviour, threats of suicide and likelihood of future suicide attempt at baseline and then again at the 3-month follow-up.

Results: All suicide-related outcome measures were significantly lower at follow-up among patients forming implementation intentions compared with those in the control condition (ds>0.35). The volitional help sheet resulted in fewer suicide threats (d = 0.59) and lowered the likelihood of future suicide attempts (d = 0.29) compared with patients who self-generated implementation intentions.

Conclusions: Implementation intention-based interventions, particularly when supported by a volitional help sheet, show promise in reducing future suicidal ideation and behaviour.

Geographic variation in suicide rates in Australian farmers: Why is the problem more frequent in Queensland than in New South Wales?

Arnautovska U, McPhedran S, Kelly B, Reddy P, De Leo D (Australia)

Death Studies 40, 367-372, 2016

Research on farmer suicide is limited in explaining the variations in farmers' demographic characteristics. This study examines farmer suicides in two Australian states: Queensland (QLD) and New South Wales (NSW). Standardised suicide rates over 2000-2009 showed a two times higher prevalence of suicide in QLD than NSW (147 vs. 92 cases, respectively). Differences in age and suicide method were observed between states, although they do not appear to account for the sizeable intra- and inter-state variations. Suicide prevention initiatives for farmers should account for different age groups, and also specific place-based risk factors that may vary between and within jurisdictions.

Population trends in substances used in deliberate self-poisoning leading to intensive care unit admissions from 2000 to 2010

Bhaskaran J, Johnson E, Bolton JM, Randall JR, Mota N, Katz C, Rigatto C, Skakum K, Roberts D, Sareen J (Canada)

Journal of Clinical Psychiatry 76, e1583-e1589, 2015

Objective: To examine population trends in serious intentional overdoses leading to admission to intensive care units (ICUs) in Winnipeg, Manitoba, Canada.

Method: Participants consisted of 1,011 individuals presenting to any of the 11 ICUs in Winnipeg, Canada, with deliberate self-poisonings from January 2000 to December 2010. Eight categories of substances were created: poisons, over-the-counter medications, prescription medications, tricyclic antidepressants (TCAs), sedatives and antidepressants, anticonvulsants, lithium, and cocaine. Using the population of Winnipeg as the denominator, we conducted generalized linear model regression analyses using the Poisson distribution with log link to determine significance of linear trends in overdoses by substance over time.

Results: Women accounted for more presentations than men (57.8%), and the largest percentage of overdoses occurred among individuals in the 35- to 54-year age range. A large proportion of admissions were due to multiple overdoses, which accounted for 65.7% of ICU admissions. At the population level, multiple overdoses increased slightly over time (incidence rate ratio [IRR] = 1.02, P <.05), whereas use of poisons (IRR = 0.897, P <.01), over-the-counter medications (IRR = 0.910, P <.01), nonpsychotropic prescription medications (IRR = 0.913, P <.01), anticonvulsants (IRR = 0.880, P <.01), and TCAs (IRR = 0.920, P <.01) decreased over time. Overdoses did not change over time as a function of age or sex. However, severity of overdoses classified by length of stay increased over time (IRR = 1.08, P <.01).

Conclusions: It is important for physicians to exercise vigilance while prescribing medication, including being aware of other medications their patients have access to.

Self-harm emergencies after bariatric surgery: A population-based cohort study.

Bhatti JA, Nathens AB, Thiruchelvam D, Grantcharov T, Goldstein BI, Redelmeier DA (Canada)
JAMA Surgery 151, 226-232, 2016

Importance: Self-harm behaviors, including suicidal ideation and past suicide attempts, are frequent in bariatric surgery candidates. It is unclear, however, whether these behaviors are mitigated or aggravated by surgery.

Objective: To compare the risk of self-harm behaviors before and after bariatric surgery.

Design, Setting, and Participants: In this population-based, self-matched, longitudinal cohort analysis, we studied 8815 adults from Ontario, Canada, who underwent bariatric surgery between April 1, 2006, and March 31, 2011. Follow-up for each patient was 3 years prior to surgery and 3 years after surgery.

Main Outcomes and Measures: Self-harm emergencies 3 years before and after surgery.

Results: The cohort included 8815 patients of whom 7176 (81.4%) were women, 7063 (80.1%) were 35 years or older, and 8681 (98.5%) were treated with gastric bypass. A total of 111 patients had 158 self-harm emergencies during follow-up. Overall, self-harm emergencies significantly increased after surgery (3.63 per 1000 patient-years) compared with before surgery (2.33 per 1000 patient-years), equaling a rate ratio (RR) of 1.54 (95% CI, 1.03-2.30; P = .007). Self-harm emergencies after surgery were higher than before surgery among patients older than 35 years (RR, 1.76; 95% CI, 1.05-2.94; P = .03), those with a low-income status (RR, 2.09; 95% CI, 1.20-3.65; P = .01), and those living in rural areas (RR, 6.49; 95% CI, 1.42-29.63; P = .02). The most common self-harm mechanism was an intentional overdose (115 [72.8%]). A total of 147 events (93.0%) occurred in patients diagnosed as having a mental health disorder during the 5 years before the surgery.

Conclusions and Relevance: In this study, the risk of self-harm emergencies increased after bariatric surgery, underscoring the need for screening for suicide risk during follow-up.

Trends from the surveillance of suicidal behaviour by the Belgian Network of Sentinel General Practices over two decades: A retrospective observational study

Boffin N, Moreels S, Van Casteren V (Belgium)

BMJ Open 5, e008584, 2015

Objectives: First, we describe trends in characteristics of suicidal events using new (2011-2012) and previous (1993-1995, 2000-2001 and 2007-2008) data reported by the Belgian Network of Sentinel General Practices (SGP); second, we examine patient age-related trends in on-site attendance of sentinel general practitioners (GPs) as first professional caregivers following suicidal behaviour; third, we investigate the accuracy of suicide incidence estimates derived from the SGP data.

Design: Retrospective observational study.

Setting: General practices from the nationwide representative Belgian Network of SGP.

Outcome Measures: Patient gender and age, suicide methods, whether the patient was new, whether the GP was the first caregiver on-site, and the outcome of the suicidal behaviour (fatal or not) were recorded on standard registration forms. The accuracy of suicide incidence estimates was tested against suicide mortality data.

Results: Over the four time periods, 1671 suicidal events were reported: 275 suicides, 1287 suicide attempts and 109 events of suicidal behaviour of unknown outcome. In 2011-2012, sentinel GPs' on-site attendance following the suicidal behaviour of patients <65 years had continued to decrease (from 71% in 1993-1995 to 58% in 2000-2001, 39% in 2007-2008 and 25% in 2011-2012). In 2011-2012, it had also decreased steeply in the population ≥65 years (from 70% in 1993-1995, 76% in 2000-2001 and 79% in 2007-2008 to 35% in 2011-2012). No significant differences were found between the SGP-based suicide incidence estimates for 2011-2012 and the available suicide mortality rates for people <65 and ≥65 years.

Conclusions: GPs' on-site attendance as first professional caregivers following suicidal behaviour continues to decline since 2011-2012 also in the population ≥65 years. Unawareness of patients' suicidal behaviour endangers both care for surviving patients and the completeness of SGP surveillance data. Yet, the incidence of suicide for 2011-2012 was estimated accurately by the SGP.

Self-harm following release from prison: A prospective data linkage study.

Borschmann R, Thomas E, Moran P, Carroll M, Heffernan E, Spittal MJ, Sutherland G, Alati R, Kinner SA (Australia, United States, United Kingdom)

Australian and New Zealand Journal of Psychiatry. Published online: 24 March 2016. doi: 10.1177/0004867416640090

Objective: Prisoners are at increased risk of both self-harm and suicide compared with the general population, and the risk of suicide after release from prison is three times greater than for those still incarcerated. However, surprisingly little is known about the incidence of self-harm following release from prison. We aimed to determine the incidence of, identify risk factors for and characterise emergency department presentations resulting from self-harm in adults after release from prison.

Method: Cohort study of 1325 adults interviewed prior to release from prison, linked prospectively with State correctional and emergency department records. Data from all emergency department presentations resulting from self-harm were secondarily coded to characterise these presentations. We used negative binomial regression to identify independent predictors of such presentations.

Results: During 3192 person-years of follow-up (median 2.6 years per participant), there were 3755 emergency department presentations. In all, 83 (6.4%) participants presented due to self-harm, accounting for 165 (4.4%) presentations. The crude incidence rates of self-harm for males and females were 49.2 (95% confidence interval: [41.2, 58.7]) and 60.5 (95% confidence interval: [44.9, 81.6]) per 1000 person-years, respectively. Presenting due to self-harm was associated with being Indigenous (incidence rate ratio: 2.01; 95% confidence interval: [1.11, 3.62]), having a lifetime history of a mental disorder (incidence rate ratio: 2.13; 95% confidence interval: [1.19, 3.82]), having previously been hospitalised for psychiatric treatment (incidence rate ratio: 2.68; 95% confidence interval: [1.40, 5.14]) and having previously presented due to self-harm (incidence rate ratio: 3.91; 95% confidence interval: [1.85, 8.30]).

Conclusion: Following release from prison, one in 15 ex-prisoners presented to an emergency department due to self-harm, within an average of 2.6 years of release. Demographic and mental health variables help to identify at-risk groups, and such presentations could provide opportunities for suicide prevention in this population. Transition from prison to the community is challenging, particularly for those with a history of mental disorder; mental health support during and after release may reduce the risk of adverse outcomes, including self-harm.

Improving suicide risk screening and detection in the emergency department

Boudreaux ED, Camargo CA, Arias SA, Sullivan AF, Allen MH, Goldstein AB, Manton AP, Espinola JA, Miller IW (United States)

American Journal of Preventive Medicine 50, 445-453, 2016

Introduction: The Emergency Department Safety Assessment and Follow-up Evaluation Screening Outcome Evaluation examined whether universal suicide risk screening is feasible and effective at improving suicide risk detection in the emergency department (ED).

Methods: A three-phase interrupted time series design was used: Treatment as Usual (Phase 1), Universal Screening (Phase 2), and Universal Screening + Intervention (Phase 3). Eight EDs from seven states participated from 2009 through 2014. Data collection spanned peak hours and 7 days of the week. Chart reviews established if screening for intentional self-harm ideation/behavior (screening) was documented in the medical record and whether the individual endorsed intentional self-harm ideation/behavior (detection). Patient interviews determined if the documented intentional self-harm was suicidal. In Phase 2, universal suicide risk screening was implemented during routine care. In Phase 3, improvements were made to increase screening rates and fidelity. Chi-square tests and generalized estimating equations were calculated. Data were analyzed in 2014.

Results: Across the three phases (N=236,791 ED visit records), documented screenings rose from 26% (Phase 1) to 84% (Phase 3) (χ^2 [2, n=236,789]=71,000, p<0.001). Detection rose from 2.9% to 5.7% (χ^2 [2, n=236,789]=902, p<0.001). The majority of detected intentional self-harm was confirmed as recent suicidal ideation or behavior by patient interview.

Conclusions: Universal suicide risk screening in the ED was feasible and led to a nearly twofold increase in risk detection. If these findings remain true when scaled, the public health impact could be tremendous, because identification of risk is the first and necessary step for preventing suicide.

Association between victimization by bullying and direct self injurious behavior among adolescence in Europe: A ten-country study

Brunstein Klomek A, Snir A, Apter A, Carli V, Wasserman C, Hadlaczky G, Hoven CW, Sarchiapone M, Balazs J, Bobes J, Brunner R, Corcoran P, Cosman D, Haring C, Kahn JP, Kaess M, Postuvan V, Sisask M, Tubiana A, Varnik A, Ziberna J, Wasserman D (Israel, Sweden, United Sates, Italy, Hungary, Spain, Germany, Ireland, Romania, Austria, France, Slovenia, Estonia)
European Child and Adolescent Psychiatry. Published online: 24 March 2016. doi: 10.1007/s00787-016-0840-7

Previous studies have examined the association between victimization by bullying and both suicide ideation and suicide attempts. The current study examined the association between victimization by bullying and direct-self-injurious behavior (D-SIB) among a large representative sample of male and female adolescents in Europe. This study is part of the Saving and Empowering Young Lives in Europe (SEYLE) study and includes 168 schools, with 11,110 students (mean age = 14.9, SD = 0.89). Students were administered a self-report survey within the classroom, in which they were asked about three types of victimization by bullying (physical, verbal and relational) as well as direct self-injurious behavior (D-SIB). Additional risk factors (symptoms of depression and anxiety, suicide ideation, suicide attempts, loneliness, alcohol consumption, drug consumption), and protective factors (parent support, peer support, pro-social behavior) were included. The three types of victimization examined were associated with D-SIB. Examination of gender as moderator of the association between victimization (relational, verbal, and physical) and D-SIB yielded no significant results. As for the risk factors, depression, but not anxiety, partially mediated the effect of relational victimization and verbal victimization on D-SIB. As for the protective factors, students with parent and peer support and those with pro-social behaviors were at significantly lower risk of engaging in D-SIB after being victimized compared to students without support/pro-social behaviors. This large-scale study has clearly demonstrated the cross-sectional association between specific types of victimization with self-injurious behavior among adolescents and what may be part of the risk and protective factors in this complex association.

The epidemiology of self-harm in a UK-wide primary care patient cohort, 2001-2013

Carr MJ, Ashcroft DM, Kontopantelis E, Awenat Y, Cooper J, Chew-Graham C, Kapur N, Webb RT (United Kingdom)
BMC Psychiatry 16, 53, 2016

Background: Most of the research conducted on people who harm themselves has been undertaken in secondary healthcare settings. Little is known about the frequency of self-harm in primary care patient populations. This is the first study to describe the epidemiology of self-harm presentations to primary care using broadly representative national data from across the United Kingdom (UK).

Methods: Using the Clinical Practice Research Datalink (CPRD), we calculated directly standardised rates of incidence and annual presentation during 2001-2013. Rates were compared by gender and age and across the nations of the UK, and also by degree of socioeconomic deprivation measured ecologically at general practice level.

Results: We found significantly elevated rates in females vs. males for incidence (rate ratio - RR, 1.45, 95 % confidence interval - CI, 1.42-1.47) and for annual presentation (RR 1.56, CI 1.54-1.58). An increasing trend over time in incidence was apparent for males ($P < 0.001$) but not females ($P = 0.08$), and both genders exhibited rising temporal trends in presentation rates ($P < 0.001$). We observed a decreasing gradient of risk with increasing age and markedly elevated risk for females in the youngest age group (aged 15-24 years vs. all other females: RR 3.75, CI 3.67-3.83). Increasing presentation rates over time were observed for males across all age bands ($P < 0.001$). We found higher rates when comparing Northern Ireland, Scotland, and Wales with England, and increasing rates of presentation over time for all four nations. We also observed higher rates with increasing levels of deprivation - most vs. least deprived male patients: RR 2.17, CI 2.10-2.25.

Conclusions: Incorporating data from primary care yields a more comprehensive quantification of the health burden of self-harm. These novel findings may be useful in informing public health programmes and the targeting of high-risk groups toward the ultimate goal of lowering risk of self-harm repetition and premature death in this population.

Clinical management following self-harm in a UK-wide primary care cohort

Carr MJ, Ashcroft DM, Kontopantelis E, While D, Awenat Y, Cooper J, Chew-Graham C, Kapur N, Webb RT (United Kingdom)

Journal of Affective Disorders 197, 182-188, 2016

Background: Little is known about the clinical management of patients in primary care following self-harm.

Methods: A descriptive cohort study using data from 684 UK general practices that contributed to the Clinical Practice Research Datalink (CPRD) during 2001-2013. We identified 49,970 patients with a self-harm episode, 41,500 of whom had one complete year of follow-up.

Results: Among those with complete follow-up, 26,065 (62.8%, 62.3-63.3) were prescribed psychotropic medication and 6318 (15.2%, 14.9-15.6) were referred to mental health services; 4105 (9.9%, CI 9.6-10.2) were medicated without an antecedent psychiatric diagnosis or referral, and 4,506 (10.9%, CI 10.6-11.2) had a diagnosis but were not subsequently medicated or referred. Patients registered at practices in the most deprived localities were 27.1% (CI 21.5-32.2) less likely to be referred than those in the least deprived. Despite a specifically flagged NICE 'Do not do' recommendation in 2011 against prescribing tricyclic antidepressants following self-harm because of their potentially lethal toxicity in overdose, 8.8% (CI 7.8-9.8) of individuals were issued a prescription in the subsequent year. The percentage prescribed Citalopram, an SSRI antidepressant with higher toxicity in overdose, fell sharply during 2012/2013 in the aftermath of a Medicines and Healthcare products Regulatory Agency (MHRA) safety alert issued in 2011.

Conclusions: A relatively small percentage of these vulnerable patients are referred to mental health services, and reduced likelihood of referral in more deprived localities reflects a marked health inequality. National clinical guidelines have not yet been effective in reducing rates of tricyclic antidepressant prescribing for this high-risk group.

Newspaper reporting and the emergence of charcoal burning suicide in Taiwan: A mixed methods approach

Chen Y-Y, Tsai C-W, Biddle L, Niederkrotenthaler T, Wu KC-C, Gunnell D (Taiwan, United Kingdom, Austria)

Journal of Affective Disorders 193, 355-361, 2016

Background: It has been suggested that extensive media reporting of charcoal burning suicide was a key factor in the rapid spread of this novel method in many East Asian countries. But very few empirical studies have explored the relationship between media reporting and the emergence of this new method of suicide.

Aims: We investigated the changing pattern of media reporting of charcoal burning suicides in Taiwan during 1998-2002 when this method of suicide increased most rapidly, assessing whether the characteristics of media reporting were associated with the changing incidence of suicide using this method.

Methods: A mixed method approach, combining quantitative and qualitative analysis of newspaper content during 1998-2002 was used. We compared differences in reporting characteristics before and after the rapid increase in charcoal burning suicide. Point-biserial and Pearson correlation coefficients were calculated to quantify the associations between the media item content and changes in suicide rates.

Results: During the period when charcoal burning suicide increased rapidly, the number of reports per suicide was considerably higher than during the early stage (0.31 vs. 0.10). Detailed reporting of this new method was associated with a post-reporting increase in suicides using the method. Qualitative analysis of news items revealed that the content of reports of suicide by charcoal burning changed gradually; in the early stages of the epidemic (1999-2000) there was convergence in the terminology used to report charcoal burning deaths, later reports gave detailed descriptions of the setting in which the death occurred (2001) and finally the method was glamourized and widely publicized (2001-2002).

Limitations: Our analysis was restricted to newspaper reports and did not include TV or the Internet.

Conclusions: Newspaper reporting was associated with the evolution and establishment of charcoal burning suicide. Working with media and close monitoring of changes in the incidence of suicide using a new method might help prevent a suicide epidemic such as charcoal burning suicide seen in Taiwan.

Geographical and temporal variations in the prevalence of mental disorders in suicide: Systematic review and meta-analysis

Cho SE, Na KS, Cho SJ, Im JS, Kang SG (Korea)

Journal of Affective Disorders 190, 704-713, 2016

Background: In contrast to the previous studies reporting that most suicides occur among people with mental disorders, recent studies have reported various rates of mental disorders in suicide in different geographical regions. We aimed to comprehensively investigate the factors influencing the variation in the prevalence of mental disorders reported among suicide victims.

Method: The authors searched Embase, Medline, Web of Science, and the Cochrane Library to identify psychological autopsy studies reporting the prevalence of any mental disorders among suicide victims. A meta-regression analysis was conducted to identify the potential effects of geographical regions, the year of publication, measurements of personality disorder, measurements of comorbidity, and the ratio of females on the prevalence of mental disorders in addition to examining the heterogeneity across studies.

Results: From 4475 potentially relevant studies, 48 studies met eligibility criteria, with 6626 suicide victims. The studies from East Asia had a significantly lower mean prevalence (69.6% [95% CI=56.8 to 80.0]) than those in North America (88.2% [95% CI=79.7-93.5]) and South Asia (90.4% [95% CI=71.8-97.2]). The prevalence of any mental disorder decreased according to the year of publication (coefficients=-0.0715, p<0.001).

Limitations: Substantial heterogeneities were identified within all subgroup analyses.

Conclusions: The prevalence of mental disorders among suicide cases seemed relatively low in the East Asia region, and recently published studies tended to report a lower prevalence of mental disorders. The link between the risk factors and suicide in the absence of a mental disorder should be examined in different geographical and sociocultural contexts.

Patterns of health care usage in the year before suicide: A population-based case-control study.

Chock MM, Bommersbach TJ, Geske JL, Bostwick JM (United States)

Mayo Clinic Proceedings 90, 1475-1481, 2015

Objective: To compare the type and frequency of health care visits in the year before suicide between decedents and controls.

Patients and Methods: Cases (n=86) were Olmsted County, Minnesota, residents whose death certificates listed "suicide" as the cause of death from January 1, 2000, through December 31, 2009. Each case had 3 age- and sex-matched controls (n=258). Demographic, diagnostic, and health care usage data were abstracted from medical records. Conditional logistic regression was used to analyze differences in the likelihood of having had psychiatric and nonpsychiatric visits in the year before death, as well as in visit types and frequencies 12 months, 6 months, and 4 weeks before death.

Results: Cases and controls did not significantly differ in having had any health care exposure (P=.18). Suicide decedents, however, had a significantly higher number of total visits in the 12 months, 6 months, and 4 weeks before death (all P<.001), were more likely to have carried psychiatric diagnoses in the previous year (odds ratio [OR], 8.08; 95% CI, 4.31-15.17; P<.001), and were more likely to have had outpatient and inpatient mental health visits (OR, 1.24; 95% CI, 1.05-1.47; P=.01 and OR 6.76; 95% CI, 1.39-32.96; P=.02, respectively). Only cases had had emergency department mental health visits; no control did.

Conclusion: Given that suicide decedents did not differ from controls in having had any health care exposure in the year before death, the fact alone that decdents saw a doctor provides no useful information about risk. Compared with controls, however, decedents had more visits of all types including psychiatric ones. Higher frequencies of health care contacts were associated with elevated suicide risk.

Nonsuicidal self-injury and suicide attempts among ED patients older than 50 years: Comparison of risk factors and ED visit outcomes

Choi NG, DiNitto DM, Marti CN, Choi BY (United States)
American Journal of Emergency Medicine. Published online: 26 February 2016. doi: 10.1016/j.ajem.2016.02.058

Background: Although the number of older adults who engage in nonsuicidal self-injury (NSSI) is not insignificant, research on older adults' NSSI is scant. The current study examined the prevalence and characteristics of NSSI compared to suicide attempt (SA) in adults older than 50 years who were seen at Emergency Departments (EDs) and their ED visit outcomes.

Methods: Data came from the 2012 Nationwide Emergency Department Sample. We used binary logistic regression analysis to examine demographic and clinical characteristics of NSSI versus SA among 67,069 visits with a diagnosis of either SA or NSSI, and multinomial logistic regression analysis to examine associations between NSSI versus SA and ED outcomes.

Results: Of self-inflicted intentional injuries, 76.89% were SA and 23.11% were NSSI. Visits for NSSI were associated with lower levels of psychiatric disorders and alcohol use disorders than SA and were more likely than SA visits to occur among older age groups (65-74 and 75. +), females, and those with multiple injuries and drug use disorders. NSSI visits were also associated with greater risks of hospital admission (relative risk ratio [RRR] = 1.45, 95% CI = 1.36-1.54) and death (RRR = 18.64, 95% CI = 14.19-24.49), as opposed to treat-and-release, but lower risks of facility transfer/discharge with home health care (RRR = 0.77, 95% CI = 0.72-0.83).

Conclusions: The findings of higher hospitalization and death rates among those with NSSI than SA show how lethal intentional self-destructive behaviors in late life can be even if they are not classified as suicide attempts. The need for mental health and substance abuse treatment is discussed.

Rates of self-harm presenting to general hospitals: A comparison of data from the multicentre study of self-harm in England and hospital episode statistics

Clements C, Turnbull P, Hawton K, Geulayov G, Waters K, Ness J, Townsend E, Khundakar K, Kapur N (United Kingdom)

BMJ Open 6, e009749, 2016

Objective: Rates of hospital presentation for self-harm in England were compared using different national and local data sources.

Design: The study was descriptive and compared bespoke data collection methods for recording self-harm presentations to hospital with routinely collected hospital data.

Setting: Local area data on self-harm from the 3 centres of the Multicentre Study of Self-harm in England (Oxford, Manchester and Derby) were used along with national and local routinely collected data on self-harm admissions and emergency department attendances from Hospital Episode Statistics (HES).

Primary Outcome: Rate ratios were calculated to compare rates of self-harm generated using different data sources nationally and locally (between 2010 and 2012) and rates of hospital presentations for self-harm were plotted over time (between 2003 and 2012), based on different data sources.

Results: The total number of self-harm episodes between 2010 and 2012 was 13 547 based on Multicentre Study data, 9600 based on HES emergency department data and 8096 based on HES admission data. Nationally, routine HES data underestimated overall rates of self-harm by approximately 60% compared with rates based on Multicentre Study data (rate ratio for HES emergency department data, 0.41 (95% CI 0.35 to 0.49); rate ratio for HES admission data, 0.42 (95% CI 0.36 to 0.49)). Direct local area comparisons confirmed an overall underascertainment in the HES data, although the difference varied between centres. There was a general increase in self-harm over time according to HES data which contrasted with a fall and then a rise in the Multicentre Study data.

Conclusions: There was a consistent underestimation of presentations for self-harm recorded by HES emergency department data, and fluctuations in year-on-year figures. HES admission data appeared more reliable but missed non-admitted episodes. Routinely collected data may miss important trends in self-harm and cannot be used in isolation as the basis for a robust national indicator of self-harm.

Risk factors for suicide in bipolar I disorder in two prospectively studied cohorts

Coryell W, Kriener A, Butcher B, Nurnberger J, McMahon F, Berrettini W, Fiedorowicz J (United States)

Journal of Affective Disorders 190, 1-5, 2016

Background: These analyses were undertaken to determine whether similar risk factors for suicide emerged across two prospectively studied cohorts of individuals with bipolar I disorder.

Methods: The NIMH Collaborative Study of Depression (CDS) recruited 288 patients with bipolar I disorder from 1978-1981 as they sought treatment. Subjects were followed semiannually and then annually for up to 30 years. The Bipolar Genomics studies identified individuals through clinical referrals and advertisement. Clinical follow-up did not occur but personal identifiers of 1748 were matched with National Death Index (NDI) records. Kaplan-Meier survival analyses tested ten potential risk factors.

Results: The CDS and Genomic follow-ups encompassed 12,667 and 4529 person-years, respectively. Suicides/100 person-years were 0.26 and 0.055. The demographic or clinical variables that predicted suicide differed considerably in the two cohorts. The odds ratio for suicide for those with any history of suicide attempt was 2.3 and 2.8, respectively, and was the third highest odds ratio of the tested risk factors in both studies.

Limitations: Conclusions: Differences in the sources of participants in studies of suicide risk may result in marked differences across studies in both rates of suicide and in risk factors. A history of suicide attempt is a relatively robust risk factor across samples.

Development of suicide postvention guidelines for secondary schools: A Delphi study

Cox GR, Bailey E, Jorm AF, Reavley NJ, Templer K, Parker A, Rickwood D, Bhar S, Robinson J (Australia)

BMC Public Health 16, 180, 2016

Background: Suicide of school-aged adolescents is a significant problem, with serious implications for students and staff alike. To date, there is a lack of evidence regarding the most effective way for a secondary school to respond to the suicide of a student, termed postvention [(Crisis 33:208-214, 2012), (Crisis 34:164-182, 2013)]. The aim of this study was to employ the expert consensus (Delphi) methodology to the development of a set of guidelines, to assist English-speaking secondary schools to develop a plan to respond to a student suicide, or to respond to a suicide in the absence of a predetermined plan.

Methods: The Delphi methodology was employed, which involved a two-stage process. Firstly, medical and research databases, existing postvention guidelines developed for schools, and lay literature were searched in order to identify potential actions that school staff could carry out following the suicide of a student. Based on this search, an online questionnaire was produced. Secondly, 40 experts in the area of suicide postvention from English-speaking countries were recruited and asked to rate each action contained within this questionnaire, in terms of how important they felt it was to be included in the postvention guidelines. A set of guidelines was developed based on these responses. In total, panel members considered 965 actions across three consensus rounds.

Results: Five hundred fourty-eight actions were endorsed for inclusion into the postvention guidelines based on an 80 % consensus agreement threshold. These actions were groups according to common themes, which are presented in the following sections: 1. Developing an Emergency Response Plan; 2. Forming an Emergency Response Team; 3. Activating the Emergency Response Team; 4. Managing a suspected suicide that occurs on school grounds; 5. Liaising with the deceased student's family; 6. Informing staff of the suicide; 7. Informing students of the suicide; 8. Informing parents of the suicide; 9. Informing the wider community of the suicide; 10. Identifying and supporting high-risk students; 11. Ongoing support of students; 12. Ongoing support of staff; 13. Dealing with the media; 14. Internet and social media; 15. The deceased student's belongings; 16. Funeral and memorial; 17. Continued monitoring of students and staff; 18. Documentation; 19. Critical Incident Review and annual review of the ER Plan; 20. Future prevention. Panel members frequently commented on every suicide being 'unique', and the need for flexibility in the guidelines, in order to accommodate the resources available, and the culture of the school community.

Conclusion: In order to respond effectively and safely to the suicide of a student, schools need to undertake a variety of postvention actions. These are the first set of postvention guidelines produced worldwide for secondary schools that are based on expert opinion using the Delphi method.

Socio-demographic, health, and psychological correlates of suicidality severity in Australian adolescents

Delfabbro PH, Malvaso C, Winefield AH, Winefield HR (Australia)

Australian Journal of Psychology. Published online: 5 November 2015. doi: 10.1111/ajpy.12104

Objective: Few studies have examined whether factors related to suicide ideation alone are also related to suicide plans and attempts. The aim of this study was to examine the psychological and social factors associated with different levels of suicide risk in Australian adolescents.

Method: A sample of 2,552 young people aged 14-16 years completed a detailed survey that included demographic, social, and psychological indicators as well as a four-tier measure of suicidality: occasional ideation, regular ideation, suicide plans, and suicide attempts. Separate statistical models were developed for each level of suicide risk as well as an overall multinomial logistic regression to compare more severe levels of suicidality against occasional ideation.

Results: The results showed that while most well-established predictors were indicative of elevations of each level of suicide risk, only some factors predicted suicide attempts. The highest suicide attempt risk was observed in girls, those who smoked, had romantic relationships, and who had poorer health. Students with concerns about their weight, who used marijuana, who had more negative mood states, and who were in romantic relationships were more likely to have suicide plans.

Conclusions: The results suggest that the identification of young people at highest risk of suicide attempts can be enhanced by focusing on specific indicators, including gender (females higher), smoking and marijuana use, and declines in physical health.

Re-examination of classic risk factors for suicidal behavior in the psychiatric population

Dennis BB, Roshanov PS, Bawor M, ElSheikh W, Garton S, DeJesus J, Rangarajan S, Vair J, Sholer H, Hutchinson N, Lordan E, Thabane L, Samaan Z (Canada)
Crisis 36, 231-240, 2015

Background: For decades we have understood the risk factors for suicide in the general population but have fallen short in understanding what distinguishes the risk for suicide among patients with serious psychiatric conditions.

Aims: This prompted us to investigate risk factors for suicidal behavior among psychiatric inpatients.

Method: We reviewed all psychiatric hospital admissions (2008-2011) to a centralized psychiatric hospital in Ontario, Canada. Using multivariable logistic regression we evaluated the association between potential risk factors and lifetime history of suicidal behavior, and constructed a model and clinical risk score to predict a history of this behavior.

Results: The final risk prediction model for suicidal behavior among psychiatric patients (n = 2,597) included age (in three categories: 60-69 [OR = 0.74, 95% CI = 0.73-0.76], 70-79 [OR = 0.45, 95% CI = 0.44-0.46], 80+ [OR = 0.31, 95% CI = 0.30-.31]), substance use disorder (OR = 1.30, 95% CI = 1.27-1.32), mood disorder (OR = 1.49, 95% CI = 1.47-1.52), personality disorder (OR = 2.30, 95% CI = 2.25-2.36), psychiatric disorders due to general medical condition (OR = 0.52, 95% CI = 0.50-0.55), and schizophrenia (OR = 0.42, 95% CI = 0.41-0.43). The risk score constructed from the risk prediction model ranges from -9 (lowest risk, 0% predicted probability of suicidal behavior) to +5 (highest risk, 97% predicted probability).

Conclusion: Risk estimation may help guide intensive screening and treatment efforts of psychiatric patients with high risk of suicidal behavior.

Suicides during pregnancy and 1 year postpartum in Sweden, 1980-2007

Esscher A, Essen B, Innala E, Papadopoulos FC, Skalkidou A, Sundstrom-Poromaa I, Hogberg U (Sweden)

British Journal of Psychiatry 208, 462-469, 2016

Background: Although the incidence of suicide among women who have given birth during the past 12 months is lower than that of women who have not given birth, suicide remains one of the most common causes of death during the year following delivery in high-income countries, such as Sweden.

Aims: To characterise women who died by suicide during pregnancy and postpartum from a maternal care perspective.

Method: We traced deaths (n = 103) through linkage of the Swedish Cause of Death Register with the Medical Birth and National Patient Registers. We analysed register data and obstetric medical records.

Results: The maternal suicide ratio was 3.7 per 100 000 live births for the period 1980-2007, with small magnitude variation over time. The suicide ratio was higher in women born in low-income countries (odds ratio 3.1 (95% CI 1.3-7.7)). Violent suicide methods were common, especially during the first 6 months postpartum. In all, 77 women had received psychiatric care at some point, but 26 women had no documented psychiatric care. Antenatal documentation of psychiatric history was inconsistent. At postpartum discharge, only 20 women had a plan for psychiatric follow-up.

Conclusions: Suicide prevention calls for increased clinical awareness and cross-disciplinary maternal care approaches to identify and support women at risk.

Meta-analysis of risk factors for nonsuicidal self-injury

Fox KR, Franklin JC, Ribeiro JD, Kleiman EM, Bentley KH, Nock MK (United States)

Clinical Psychology Review 42, 156-167, 2015

Nonsuicidal self-injury (NSSI) is a prevalent and dangerous phenomenon associated with many negative outcomes, including future suicidal behaviors. Research on these behaviors has primarily focused on correlates; however, an emerging body of research has focused on NSSI risk factors. To provide a summary of current knowledge about NSSI risk factors, we conducted a meta-analysis of published, prospective studies longitudinally predicting NSSI. This included 20 published reports across 5078 unique participants. RESULTS from a random-effects model demonstrated significant, albeit weak, overall prediction of NSSI (OR=1.59; 95% CI: 1.50 to 1.69). Among specific NSSI risk factors, prior history of NSSI, cluster b, and hopelessness yielded the strongest effects (ORs>3.0); all remaining risk factor categories produced ORs near or below 2.0. NSSI measurement, sample type, sample age, and prediction case measurement type (i.e. binary versus continuous) moderated these effects. Additionally, results highlighted several limitations of the existing literature, including idiosyncratic NSSI measurement and few studies among samples with NSSI histories. These findings indicate that few strong NSSI risk factors have been identified, and suggest a need for examination of novel risk factors, standardized NSSI measurement, and study samples with a history of NSSI.

Perceptions of suicide stigma

Frey LM, Hans JD, Cerel J (United States)
Crisis 37, 95-103, 2016

Background: Previous research has failed to examine perceptions of stigma experienced by individuals with a history of suicidal behavior, and few studies have examined how stigma is experienced based on whether it was perceived from treatment providers or social network members.

Aims: This study examined stigma experienced by individuals with previous suicidal behavior from both treatment providers and individuals in one's social and family networks.

Method: Individuals (n = 156) with a lifetime history of suicidal behavior were recruited through the American Association of Suicidology listserv.

Results: Respondents reported the highest rates of perceived stigma with a close family member (57.1%) and emergency department personnel (56.6%). Results indicated that individuals with previous suicidal behavior were more likely to experience stigma from non-mental health providers and social network members than from mental health providers. A hierarchical regression model including both source and type of stigma accounted for more variance (R2 = .14) in depression symptomology than a model (R2 = .06) with only type of stigma. Prevalence of stigma perceived from social network members was the best predictor of depression symptom severity.

Conclusion: These findings highlight the need for future research on how social network members react to suicide disclosure and potential interventions for improving interactions following disclosure.

Associations between peer victimization and suicidal ideation and suicide attempt during adolescence: Results from a prospective population-based birth cohort

Geoffroy MC, Boivin M, Arseneault L, Turecki G, Vitaro F, Brendgen M, Renaud J, Seguin JR, Tremblay RE, Cote SM (Canada, Russia, United Kingdom)

Journal of the American Academy of Child and Adolescent Psychiatry 55, 99-105, 2016

Objective: To test whether adolescents who are victimized by peers are at heightened risk for suicidal ideation and suicide attempt, using both cross-sectional and prospective investigations.

Method: Participants are from the Quebec Longitudinal Study of Child Development, a general population sample of children born in Quebec in 1997 through 1998 and followed up until 15 years of age. Information about victimization and serious suicidal ideation and suicide attempt in the past year was obtained at ages 13 and 15 years from self-reports (N = 1,168).

Results: Victims reported concurrently higher rates of suicidal ideation at age 13 years (11.6-14.7%) and suicide attempt at age 15 years (5.4-6.8%) compared to those who had not been victimized (2.7-4.1% for suicidal ideation and 1.6-1.9% for suicide attempt). Being victimized by peers at 13 years predicted suicidal ideation (odds ratio [OR] = 2.27; 95% CI = 1.25-4.12) and suicide attempt (OR = 3.05, 95% CI = 1.36-6.82) 2 years later, even after adjusting for baseline suicidality and mental health problems and a series of confounders (socioeconomic status, intelligence, family's functioning and structure, hostile-reactive parenting, maternal lifetime suicidal ideation/suicide attempt). Those who were victimized at both 13 and 15 years had the highest risk of suicidal ideation (OR = 5.41, 95% CI = 2.53-11.53) and suicide attempt (OR = 5.85, 95% CI = 2.12-16.18) at 15 years.

Conclusion: Victimization is associated with an increased risk of suicidal ideation and suicide attempt over and above concurrent suicidality and prior mental health problems. The longer the history of victimization, the greater the risk.

How parental reactions change in response to adolescent suicide attempt

Greene-Palmer FN, Wagner BM, Neely LL, Cox DW, Kochanski KM, Perera KU, Ghahramanlou-Holloway M (United States)

Archives of Suicide Research 19, 414-421, 2015

This study examined parental reactions to adolescents' suicide attempts and the association of reactions with future suicidal self-directed violence. Participants were 81 mothers and 49 fathers of 85 psychiatric inpatient adolescents. Maternal hostility and paternal anger and arguing predicted future suicide attempts. From pre- to post-attempt, mothers reported feeling increased sadness, caring, anxiety, guilt, fear, and being overwhelmed; fathers reported increased sadness, anxiety, and fear. Findings have clinical implications; improving parent-child relationships post suicide attempt may serve as a protective factor for suicide.

Structured follow-up by general practitioners after deliberate self-poisoning: A randomised controlled trial

Grimholt TK, Jacobsen D, Haavet OR, Sandvik L, Jorgensen T, Norheim AB, Ekeberg O
(Norway)

BMC Psychiatry 15, 245, 2015

Background: General Practitioners (GPs) play an important role in the follow-up of patients after deliberate self-poisoning (DSP). The aim was to examine whether structured follow-up by GPs increased the content of, adherence to, and satisfaction with treatment after discharge from emergency departments.

Methods: This was a multicentre, randomised trial with blinded assignment. Five emergency departments and general practices in the catchment area participated. 202 patients discharged from emergency departments after DSP were assigned. The intervention was structured follow-up by the GP over a 6-month period with a minimum of five consultations, accompanied by written guidelines for the GPs with suggestions for motivating patients to follow treatment, assessing personal problems and suicidal ideation, and availability in the case of suicidal crisis. Outcome measures were data retrieved from the Register for the control and payment of reimbursements to health service providers (KUHR) and by questionnaires mailed to patients and GPs. After 3 and 6 months, the frequency and content of GP contact, and adherence to GP consultations and treatment in general were registered. Satisfaction with general treatment received and with the GP was measured by the EUROPEP scale.

Results: Patients in the intervention group received significantly more consultations than the control group (mean 6.7 vs. 4.5 (p = 0.004)). The intervention group was significantly more satisfied with the time their GP took to listen to their personal problems (93.1 % vs. 59.4 % (p = 0.002)) and with the fact that the GP included them in medical decisions (87.5 % vs. 54. 8 % (p = 0.009)). The intervention group was significantly more satisfied with the treatment in general than the control group (79 % vs. 51 % (p = 0.026)).

Conclusions: Guidelines and structured, enhanced follow-up by the GP after the discharge of the DSP patient increased the number of consultations and satisfaction with aftercare in general practice. Consistently with previous research, there is still a need for interventional studies.

Problem-solving therapy reduces suicidal ideation in depressed older adults with executive dysfunction

Gustavson KA, Alexopoulos GS, Niu GC, McCulloch C, Meade T, Arean PA (United States)

American Journal of Geriatric Psychiatry 24, 11-17, 2016

Objective: To test the hypothesis that Problem Solving Therapy (PST) is more effective than Supportive Therapy (ST) in reducing suicidal ideation in older adults with major depression and executive dysfunction. We further explored whether patient characteristics, such as age, sex, and additional cognitive impairment load (e.g. memory impairments) were related to changes in suicidal ideation over time.

Design: Secondary data analysis using data from a randomized clinical trial allocating participants to PST or ST at 1:1 ratio. Raters were blind to patients' assignments.

Setting: University medical centers.

Participants: 221 people aged 65 years old and older with major depression determined by Structured Clinical Interview for DSM-III-R diagnosis and executive dysfunction as defined by a score of 33 or less on the Initiation-Perseveration Score of the Mattis Dementia Rating Scale or a Stroop Interference Task score of 25 or less.

Interventions: 12 weekly sessions of PST or ST.

Main Outcome Measures: The suicide item of the Hamilton Depression Rating Scale.

Results: Of the 221 participants, 61% reported suicidal ideation (SI). The ST group had a lower rate of improvement in SI after 12 weeks (44.6%) than did the PST group (60.4%, Fisher's exact test p = 0.031). Logistic regression showed significantly greater reductions in SI in elders who received PST at both 12 weeks (OR: .50, Z = -2.16, p = 0.031) and 36 weeks (OR: 0.5, Z = -1.96, p = 0.05) after treatment.

Conclusions: PST is a promising intervention for older adults who are at risk for suicide.

What happens when you tell someone you self-injure? The effects of disclosing NSSI to adults and peers

Hasking P, Rees CS, Martin G, Quigley J (Australia)

BMC Public Health 15, 1039, 2015

Background: Non-suicidal self-injury (NSSI) is associated with significant adverse consequences, including increased risk of suicide, and is a growing public health concern. Consequently, facilitating help-seeking in youth who self-injure is an important goal. Although young people who disclose their NSSI typically confide in peers and family, it is unclear how this disclosure and related variables (e.g. support from family and friends, coping behaviours, reasons for living) affect help-seeking over time. The aim of this study was to advance understanding of the impact of disclosure of NSSI by young people and to investigate these effects over time.

Methods: A sample of 2637 adolescents completed self-report questionnaires at three time points, one year apart.

Results: Of the sample, 526 reported a history of NSSI and 308 of those who self-injured had disclosed their behaviour to someone else, most commonly friends and parents.

Conclusions: Overall, we observed that disclosure of NSSI to parents facilitates informal help-seeking, improves coping and reduces suicidality, but that disclosure to peers might reduce perceived social support and encourage NSSI in others. We discuss these findings in light of their clinical and research implications.

Impact of the recent recession on self-harm: Longitudinal ecological and patient-level investigation from the multicentre study of self-harm in England

Hawton K, Bergen H, Geulayov G, Waters K, Ness J, Cooper J, Kapur N (United Kingdom)
Journal of Affective Disorders 191, 132-138, 2016

Background: Economic recessions are associated with increases in suicide rates but there is little information for non-fatal self-harm.

Aims: To investigate the impact of the recent recession on rates of self-harm in England and problems faced by patients who self-harm.

Method: Analysis of data from the Multicentre Study of Self-harm in England for 2001-2010 and local employment statistics for Oxford, Manchester and Derby, including interrupted time series analyses to estimate the effect of the recession on rates of self-harm.

Results: Rates of self-harm increased in both genders in Derby and in males in Manchester in 2008-2010, but not in either gender in Oxford, results which largely followed changes in general population unemployment. More patients who self-harm were unemployed in 2008-10 compared to before the recession. The proportion in receipt of sickness or disability allowances decreased. More patients of both genders had employment and financial problems in 2008-2010 and more females also had housing problems, changes which were also largely found in employed patients.

Limitations: We have assumed that the recession began in 2008 and information on problems was only available for patients having a psychosocial assessment.

Conclusions: Increased rates of self-harm were found in areas where there were greater rises in rates of unemployment. Work, financial and housing problems increased in people who self-harmed. Changes in welfare benefits may have contributed.

Psychotic experiences and risk of self-injurious behaviour in the general population: A systematic review and meta-analysis

Honings S, Drukker M, Groen R, van Os J (The Netherlands)

Psychological Medicine 46, 237-251, 2016

Background: Recent studies suggest that psychotic experiences (PE) in the general population are associated with an increased risk of self-injurious behaviour. Both the magnitude of this association and the level of adjustment for confounders vary among studies. A meta-analysis was performed to integrate the available evidence. The influence of possible confounders, including variably defined depression, was assessed.

Method: A systematic review and meta-analysis was conducted including general population studies reporting on the risk of self-injurious behaviour in individuals with PE. Studies were identified by a systematic search strategy in Pubmed, PsycINFO and Embase. Reported effect sizes were extracted and meta-analytically pooled.

Results: The risk of self-injurious behaviour was 3.20 times higher in individuals with PE compared with those without. Subanalyses showed that PE were associated with self-harm, suicidal ideation as well as suicidal attempts. All studies had scope for considerable residual confounding; effect sizes adjusted for depression were significantly smaller than effect sizes unadjusted for depression. In the longitudinal studies, adjustment for psychopathology resulted in a 74% reduction in excess risk.

Conclusions: PE are associated with self-injurious behaviour, suggesting they have potential as passive markers of suicidality. However, the association is confounded and several methodological issues remain, particularly how to separate PE from the full range of connected psychopathology in determining any specific association with self-injurious behaviour. Given evidence that PE represent an indicator of severity of non-psychotic psychopathology, the association between PE and self-injurious behaviour probably reflects a greater likelihood of self-injurious behaviour in more severe states of mental distress.

Risk factors for repetition of a deliberate self-harm episode within seven days in adolescents and young adults: A population-level record linkage study in Western Australia

Hu N, Glauert RA, Li J, Taylor CL (Australia)

Australian and New Zealand Journal of Psychiatry 50, 154-166, 2016

Objective: The risk of repetition of deliberate self-harm peaks in the first 7 days after a deliberate self-harm episode. However, thus far no studies have examined the risk factors for repeating deliberate self-harm during this short-term period. We aimed to investigate the effects of socio-demographic factors, self-harm method and mental health factors in adolescents (10-19 years old) and young adults (20-29 years old).

Methods: We used data linkage of population-wide administrative records from hospital inpatients and emergency departments to identify all the deliberate self-harm-related episodes that occurred in adolescents and young adults in Western Australia from 2000 to 2011. Logistic regression with generalised estimating equations was used for the analyses.

Results: The incidence of repeating deliberate self-harm within the first 7 days after an index episode was 6% (403/6,768) in adolescents and 8% (842/10,198) in young adults. Socio-demographic risk factors included female gender and socioeconomic disadvantage. Compared with non-poisoning, self-poisoning predicted increased risk of having a repeated deliberate self-harm episode in males, but not in females. Borderline personality, impulse-control and substance use disorders diagnosed within one week before and one week after an index deliberate self-harm episode conferred the highest risk, followed by depressive and anxiety disorders. Having a preceding deliberate self-harm episode up to 7 days before an index episode was a strong predictor for the future repetition of a deliberate self-harm episode.

Conclusion: Having a repeated deliberate self-harm episode within the first 7 days was related to a wide range of factors present at an index deliberate self-harm episode including socio-demographic characteristics, deliberate self-harm method and co-existing psychiatric conditions. These factors can inform risk assessments tailored to adolescents and young adults respectively to reduce the repetition of deliberate self-harm within a short but critical period, potentially contributing to reduce the repetition of deliberate self-harm in the long term.

Clinical features, impulsivity, temperament and functioning and their role in suicidality in patients with bipolar disorder

Jimenez E, Arias B, Mitjans M, Goikolea JM, Ruiz V, Brat M, Saiz PA, Garcia-Portilla MP, Buron P, Bobes J, Oquendo MA, Vieta E, Benabarre A (Spain, Germany, United States)

Acta Psychiatrica Scandinavica 133, 266-276, 2016

Objective: Our aim was to analyse sociodemographic and clinical differences between non-suicidal (NS) bipolar patients (BP), BP reporting only suicidal ideation (SI) and BP suicide attempters according to Columbia-Suicide Severity Rating Scale (C-SRSS) criteria. Secondarily, we also investigated whether the C-SRSS Intensity Scale was associated with emergence of suicidal behaviour (SB).

Method: A total of 215 euthymic bipolar out-patients were recruited. Semistructured interviews including the C-SRSS were used to assess sociodemographic and clinical data. Patients were grouped according to C-SRSS criteria: patients who scored ≤1 on the Severity Scale were classified as NS. The remaining patients were grouped into two groups: 'patients with history of SI' and 'patients with history of SI and SB' according to whether they did or did not have a past actual suicide attempt respectively.

Results: Patients from the three groups differed in illness onset, diagnosis, number of episodes and admissions, family history, comorbidities, rapid cycling and medication, as well as level of education, functioning, impulsivity and temperamental profile.

Conclusion: Our results suggest that increased impulsivity, higher rates of psychiatric admissions and a reported poor controllability of SI significantly increased the risk for suicidal acts among patients presenting SI.

Trajectories of suicidal ideation in depressed older adults undergoing antidepressant treatment

Kasckow J, Youk A, Anderson SJ, Dew MA, Butters MA, Marron MM, Begley AE, Szanto K, Dombrovski AY, Mulsant BH, Lenze EJ, Reynolds CF (United States)

Journal of Psychiatric Research 73, 96-101, 2015

Suicide is a public health concern in older adults. Recent cross sectional studies suggest that impairments in executive functioning, memory and attention are associated with suicidal ideation in older adults. It is unknown whether these neuropsychological features predict persistent suicidal ideation. We analyzed data from 468 individuals ≥ age 60 with major depression who received venlafaxine XR monotherapy for up to 16 weeks. We used latent class growth modeling to classify groups of individuals based on trajectories of suicidal ideation. We also examined whether cognitive dysfunction predicted suicidal ideation while controlling for time-dependent variables including depression severity, and age and education. The optimal model using a zero inflated Poisson link classified individuals into four groups, each with a distinct temporal trajectory of suicidal ideation: those with 'minimal suicidal ideation' across time points; those with 'low suicidal ideation'; those with 'rapidly decreasing suicidal ideation'; and those with 'high and persistent suicidal ideation'. Participants in the 'high and persistent suicidal ideation' group had worse scores relative to those in the "rapidly decreasing suicidal ideation" group on the Color-Word 'inhibition/switching' subtest from the Delis-Kaplan Executive Function Scale, worse attention index scores on the Repeatable Battery for the Assessment of Neuropsychological Status (RBANS) and worse total RBANS index scores. These findings suggest that individuals with poorer ability to switch between inhibitory and non-inhibitory responses as well as worse attention and worse overall cognitive status are more likely to have persistently higher levels of suicidal ideation.

The impact of intimate partner relationships on suicidal thoughts and behaviours: A systematic review

Kazan D, Calear AL, Batterham PJ (Australia)
Journal of Affective Disorders 190, 585-598, 2016

Background: A systematic review was conducted to identify the impact of intimate partner relationships on suicidality. The aim of the review was to identify factors within intimate partner relationships that influence suicidal ideation, attempts and completion.

Method: Fifty-one articles were identified through Scopus, PubMed and PsycINFO databases. Due to the high heterogeneity of the included studies, a narrative data synthesis was conducted.

Results: The research drew attention to specific contingents of the population, for example examining suicide risk in individuals under the age of 35 or lesbian, gay, bisexual and transgender (LGBT) individuals who are experiencing relationship discord, and in males who have recently separated.

Limitations: Interpretation of these findings is constrained by methodological limitations prevalent in much of the literature. Limitations of the existing literature and corresponding directions for future research are discussed.

Conclusions: Relationship separation and poor quality relationships are likely to be important risk factors for suicidal thoughts and behaviours and are frequent triggers for a suicide attempt. This review highlights intimate partner relationships as a significant component in a suicide risk assessment, regardless of the clinical setting. Consequently, clinicians should be aware that individuals reporting relationship problems are likely to be at increased risk of suicidal thoughts and behaviours.

Suicidality in schizophrenia spectrum disorders: The relationship to hallucinations and persecutory delusions

Kjelby E, Sinkeviciute I, Gjestad R, Kroken RA, Løberg EM, Jørgensen HA, Hugdahl K, Johnsen E (Norway)

European Psychiatry 30, 830-836, 2015

Background: Assessment of suicide risk is crucial in schizophrenia and results concerning risk contributed by hallucinations and persecutory delusions are inconsistent. We aimed to determine factors associated with suicidal ideation and plans at the time of acute admission in patients suffering from schizophrenia spectrum disorders.

Methods: One hundred and twenty-four patients older than 18 years admitted to an acute psychiatric ward due to psychosis were consecutively included. Predictors of suicidal ideation and suicide plans at the time of admission were examined with multinominal logistic regression and structural equation modelling (SEM). The study design was pragmatic, thus entailing a clinically relevant representation.

Results: Depression Odds Ratio (OR) 12.9, Drug use OR 4.07, Hallucinations OR 2.55 and Negative symptoms OR 0.88 significantly predicted Suicidal ideation. Suspiciousness/ Persecution did not. Only Depression and Hallucinations significantly predicted Suicide plans. In the SEM-model Anxiety, Depression and Hopelessness connected Suspiciousness/Persecution, Hallucinations and Lack of insight with Suicidal ideation and Suicide plans.

Conclusions: The study contributes to an increasing evidence base supporting an association between hallucinations and suicide risk. We want to emphasise the importance of treating depression and hallucinations in psychotic disorders, reducing hopelessness while working with insight and reducing drug abuse in order to lower suicide risk.

Differences in the effectiveness of psychosocial interventions for suicidal ideation and behaviour in women and men: A systematic review of randomised controlled trials

Krysinska K, Batterham P, Christensen H (Australia)

Archives of Suicide Research. Published online: 16 March 2016. doi: 10.1080/13811118.2016.1162246

Objectives: To explore outcomes of preventive programs and psychosocial treatments for suicidal ideation and behaviour in gender sub-groups in mixed gender studies and in studies limited to one gender.

Methods: A systematic review of randomised controlled trials (RCTs) which included women or men only, or reported and/or examined outcomes of psychosocial interventions in mixed gender samples.

Results: Twenty-seven (18%) of RCTs reported or examined differences in intervention outcomes. Five (33%) of the mixed gender RCTs reported greater effectiveness for females than males. The review identified promising interventions in female-only samples. None of the trials reported greater effectiveness of the intervention in men.

Conclusion: The majority of reviewed studies looking at treatment outcomes in gender sub-groups showed no differences between women and men or indicated that some psychosocial interventions are effective for women. There is a need for studies which look at gender effects and development of interventions more effective and appealing for men at risk of suicide.

Dialectical behavior therapy for high suicide risk in individuals with borderline personality disorder: A randomized clinical trial and component analysis

Linehan MM, Korslund KE, Harned MS (United States)
JAMA Psychiatry 72, 475-482, 2015

Importance: Dialectical behavior therapy (DBT) is an empirically supported treatment for suicidal individuals. However, DBT consists of multiple components, including individual therapy, skills training, telephone coaching, and a therapist consultation team, and little is known about which components are needed to achieve positive outcomes.

Objective: To evaluate the importance of the skills training component of DBT by comparing skills training plus case management (DBT-S), DBT individual therapy plus activities group (DBT-I), and standard DBT which includes skills training and individual therapy.

Design, Setting, and Participants: We performed a single-blind randomized clinical trial from April 24, 2004, through January 26, 2010, involving 1 year of treatment and 1 year of follow-up. Participants included 99 women (mean age, 30.3 years; 69 [71%] white) with borderline personality disorder who had at least 2 suicide attempts and/or nonsuicidal self-injury (NSSI) acts in the last 5 years, an NSSI act or suicide attempt in the 8 weeks before screening, and a suicide attempt in the past year. We used an adaptive randomization procedure to assign participants to each condition. Treatment was delivered from June 3, 2004, through September 29, 2008, in a university-affiliated clinic and community settings by therapists or case managers. Outcomes were evaluated quarterly by blinded assessors. We hypothesized that standard DBT would outperform DBT-S and DBT-I.

Interventions: The study compared standard DBT, DBT-S, and DBT-I. Treatment dose was controlled across conditions, and all treatment providers used the DBT suicide risk assessment and management protocol.

Main Outcomes and Measures: Frequency and severity of suicide attempts and NSSI episodes.

Results: All treatment conditions resulted in similar improvements in the frequency and severity of suicide attempts, suicide ideation, use of crisis services due to suicidality, and reasons for living. Compared with the DBT-I group, interventions that included skills training resulted in greater improvements in the frequency of NSSI acts ($F_{1,85} = 59.1$ [$P < .001$] for standard DBT and $F_{1,85} = 56.3$ [$P < .001$] for DBT-S) and depression ($t_{399} = 1.8$ [$P = .03$] for standard

DBT and t399 = 2.9 [P = .004] for DBT-S) during the treatment year. In addition, anxiety significantly improved during the treatment year in standard DBT (t94 = −3.5 [P < .001]) and DBT-S (t94 = −2.6 [P = .01]), but not in DBT-I. Compared with the DBT-I group, the standard DBT group had lower dropout rates from treatment (8 patients [24%] vs 16 patients [48%] [P = .04]), and patients were less likely to use crisis services in follow-up (ED visits, 1 [3%] vs 3 [13%] [P = .02]; psychiatric hospitalizations, 1 [3%] vs 3 [13%] [P = .03]).

Conclusions and Relevance: A variety of DBT interventions with therapists trained in the DBT suicide risk assessment and management protocol are effective for reducing suicide attempts and NSSI episodes. Interventions that include DBT skills training are more effective than DBT without skills training, and standard DBT may be superior in some areas.

No correlation between rates of suicidal ideation and completed suicides in Europe: Analysis of 49,008 participants (55+ years) based on the Survey of Health, Ageing and Retirement in Europe (SHARE)

Lukaschek K, Engelhardt H, Baumert J, Ladwig KH (Germany)
European Psychiatry 30, 874-879, 2015

Background: Little is known about country-specific variations in suicidal ideation (SID) by sex and how they correspond with completed suicide rate. Therefore, the aim of the present study was to assess variations in SID prevalence rates by sex and its correlation to completed suicide rates across European countries.

Method: SHARE is a cross-national European survey of individuals over the age of 50 and their spouse of any age. The present study relied on wave 4 conducted in 2010-2012 including 49,008 participants aged 55 to 104 years from 16 countries. SID was evaluated using a single item from the Euro-D. Data on completed suicide rates were taken from the WHO mortality database.

Results: Of the study population (n=49,008, 44.3% men, mean age 68.2±9.1years), a total of 4139 (8.5%, 95% CI 8.2-8.7) reported suicidal ideation within the last month. The women:men ratio in SID prevalence ranged from 1.30 in Estonia to 2.25 in Spain and Portugal. Regarding country-specific variation, the SID prevalence patterns of both men and women did not correspond to the completed suicide rates for males and females aged 55+ reported by the WHO (2013). Correlations were rather moderate in men (r=0.45) and especially weak in women (r=0.16).

Conclusion: The study showed remarkable differences in SID prevalence by sex. The most exciting finding was that SID rates did not correspond with completed suicide rates in each country under investigation. However, the strength of these patterns substantially differs across countries. This unexpected finding need to be further evaluated.

Is suicide an option?: The impact of disability on suicide acceptability in the context of depression, suicidality, and demographic factors

Lund EM, Nadorff MR, Samuel Winer E, Seader K (United States)
Journal of Affective Disorders 189, 25-35, 2015

Background: Suicide is a major clinical and public health issue, especially in people with disabilities. However, research on the acceptability of suicide in people with disabilities has not directly compared the relative acceptability of suicidality in people with and without disabilities.

Method: An online sample of five hundred American adults read five pairs of vignettes about individuals who were experiencing suicidal ideation following a life stressor. Each pair contained a disability and no-disability condition; a sixth pair of vignettes discussed suicidal ideation in an elderly individual and contained physical and cognitive disability conditions. Participants completed questions regarding the relative acceptability of suicidality for each vignette as well as demographic items and measures of suicidality, depressive symptoms, and attitude towards disability.

Results: In all vignette five pairs, suicidality was seen as significantly more acceptable in the disability condition; this was true even when the participants themselves had disabilities or friends or family members with disabilities. Suicidality, depressive symptomology, and more negative attitudes towards disability predicted greater acceptability in both conditions; no factors predicted greater differences between the two conditions.

Limitations: The vignettes in this study focused primarily on individuals in their 20s and most did not compare two disabling conditions.

Conclusions: The greater social acceptability of suicidality in people with disabilities may be taken by individuals with disabilities who are suicidal as implicit permission to end their lives. The potential impact of such social influences should be assessed and addressed by clinicians and suicide prevention advocates.

'Our care through our eyes': A mixed-methods, evaluative study of a service-user, co-produced education programme to improve inpatient care of children and young people admitted following self-harm

Manning JC, Latif A, Carter T, Cooper J, Horsley A, Armstrong M, Wharrad H (United Kingdom)
BMJ Open 5, e009680, 2015

Introduction: Within Europe, the UK has one of the highest rates of self-harm, with a particularly high prevalence in children and young people (CYP). CYP who are admitted to paediatric hospital wards with self-harm are cared for by registered children's nurses who have been identified to lack specific training in caring for this patient group. This may impede the delivery of high quality care. Therefore, this study aims to co-produce, implement and evaluate an education programme for registered children's nurses to improve their knowledge, attitudes and confidence when caring for CYP admitted with self-harm.

Methods and Analysis: This mixed-methods evaluative study will involve a three-stage design. Stage 1: A priority-setting workshop will be conducted with 19 registered children's nurses. A Delphi technique will be used to establish consensus of information needs. Stage 2: An online educational intervention will be co-produced with 25 CYP and 19 registered children's nurses based on the priorities identified in Stage 1. Stage 3: The intervention will be implemented and evaluated with 250 registered children's nurses at a single hospital. Online Likert scale questionnaires will be administered at baseline and postintervention to assess levels of knowledge, attitudes and confidence in caring for CYP who self-harm. Descriptive and inferential statistics will be used to analyse the data. Statistical significance will be assessed at the 5% (two-sided) level. One-to-one qualitative interviews will also be undertaken with approximately 25 participants to explore any perceived impact on clinical practice. An interpretive descriptive approach will guide qualitative data collection and analysis.

Blunted HPA axis activity in suicide attempters compared to those at high-risk for suicidal behavior

Melhem NM, Keilp JG, Porta G, Oquendo MA, Burke A, Stanley B, Cooper TB, Mann JJ, Brent DA (United States)
Neuropsychopharmacology, 41, 1447-1456, 2015

Studies looking at the relationship of the hypothalamic-pituitary-adrenal axis (HPA) to suicidal behavior and its risk factors, such as depression, childhood abuse, and impulsive aggression, report inconsistent results. These studies also do not always differentiate between subjects who go on to attempt suicide, suicidal subjects who never attempted suicide, and non-suicidal subjects with psychiatric disorders. In this study, we examined cortisol responses to an experimental stressor, the Trier Social Stress Test (TSST), in 208 offspring of parents with mood disorder. Offspring suicide attempters showed lower total cortisol output [beta=-0.47, 95% CI (-0.83, -0.11), p=0.01] compared to offspring with suicide-related behavior but never attempted, non-suicidal offspring, and a healthy control group. The result remained significant even after controlling for sex, age, race, ethnicity, site, socioeconomic status, and hour of the day when the TSST was conducted. Suicide attempters also showed lower baseline cortisol prior to the TSST [beta=-0.45, 95% CI (-0.74, -0.17), p=0.002]. However, there were no significant differences between the groups on cortisol reactivity to stress [beta=4.5, 95% CI (-12.9, 22), p=0.61]. Although subjects with suicide attempt and suicide-related behavior have similar clinical and psychosocial characteristics, this is the first study to differentiate them biologically on HPA axis indices. Blunted HPA axis activity may increase risk for suicide attempt among individuals with psychopathology by reducing their ability to respond adaptively to ongoing stressors. These results may help better identify subjects at high-risk for suicidal behavior for targeted prevention and intervention efforts.

Suicides in visually impaired persons: A nation-wide register-linked study from Finland based on thirty years of data

Meyer-Rochow VB, Hakko H, Ojamo M, Uusitalo H, Timonen M (Finland)
PLoS One 10, e0141583, 2015

Focusing on seasonality, gender, age, and suicide methods a Finnish nation-wide cohort-based study was carried out to compare suicide data between sighted, visually-impaired (WHO impairment level I-II, i.e. visual acuity >0.05, but <0.3) and blind (WHO impairment level III-V, i.e. visual acuity <0.05) victims. Standardized mortality ratios (SMR) of age- and gender-matched populations from official 1982-2011 national registers were used. Group differences in categorical variables were assessed with Pearson's Chi-square or Fisher's Exact test and in continuous variables with Mann-Whitney U-test. Seasonality was assessed by Chi-square for multinomials; ratio of observed to expected number of suicides was calculated with 95% confidence level. Hanging, poisoning, drowning, but rarely shooting or jumping from high places, were preferred suicide methods of the blind. Mortality was significantly increased in the visually impaired (SMR = 1.3; 95% CI 1.07-1.61), but in gender-stratified analyses the increase only affected males (1.34; 95% CI = 1.06-1.70) and not females (1.24; 95% CI 0.82-1.88). Age-stratified analyses identified blind males of working age rather than older men (as in the general population) as a high risk group that requires particular attention. The statistically significant spring suicide peak in blind subjects mirrors that of sighted victims and its possible cause in the blind is discussed.

Single-item measurement of suicidal behaviors: Validity and consequences of misclassification

Millner AJ, Lee MD, Nock MK (United States)

PLoS One 10, e0141606, 2015

Suicide is a leading cause of death worldwide. Although research has made strides in better defining suicidal behaviors, there has been less focus on accurate measurement. Currently, the widespread use of self-report, single-item questions to assess suicide ideation, plans and attempts may contribute to measurement problems and misclassification. We examined the validity of single-item measurement and the potential for statistical errors. Over 1,500 participants completed an online survey containing single-item questions regarding a history of suicidal behaviors, followed by questions with more precise language, multiple response options and narrative responses to examine the validity of single-item questions. We also conducted simulations to test whether common statistical tests are robust against the degree of misclassification produced by the use of single-items. We found that 11.3% of participants that endorsed a single-item suicide attempt measure engaged in behavior that would not meet the standard definition of a suicide attempt. Similarly, 8.8% of those who endorsed a single-item measure of suicide ideation endorsed thoughts that would not meet standard definitions of suicide ideation. Statistical simulations revealed that this level of misclassification substantially decreases statistical power and increases the likelihood of false conclusions from statistical tests. Providing a wider range of response options for each item reduced the misclassification rate by approximately half. Overall, the use of single-item, self-report questions to assess the presence of suicidal behaviors leads to misclassification, increasing the likelihood of statistical decision errors. Improving the measurement of suicidal behaviors is critical to increase understanding and prevention of suicide.

Perception of mattering and suicide ideation in the Australian working population: Evidence from a cross-sectional survey

Milner A, Page KM, LaMontagne AD (Australia)

Community Mental Health Journal. Published online: 3 March 2016. doi: 10.1007/s10597-016-0002-x

Thoughts about suicide are a risk factor for suicide deaths and attempts and are associated with a range of mental health outcomes. While there is considerable knowledge about risk factors for suicide ideation, there is little known about protective factors. The current study sought to understand the role of perceived mattering to others as a protective factor for suicide in a working sample of Australians using a cross-sectional research design. Logistic regression analysis indicated that people with a higher perception that they mattered had lower odds of suicide ideation than those with lower reported mattering, after controlling for psychological distress, demographic and relationship variables. These results indicate the importance of further research and intervention studies on mattering as a lever for reducing suicidality. Understanding more about protective factors for suicide ideation is important as this may prevent future adverse mental health and behavioural outcomes.

Systematic review of research on railway and urban transit system suicides

Mishara BL, Bardon C (Canada)

Journal of Affective Disorders 193, 215-226, 2015

Introduction: We critically review research on railway suicides to inform suicide prevention initiatives and future studies, including who is at risk and why, and behaviours at track locations.

Method: Literature was identified from Scopus, Web of Science, Google Scholar and our documentation centre, and contacting 71 railway companies, resulting in 716 articles and eight unpublished reports, with 94 having empirical data on 55 unique studies. Research quality was critically assessed.

Results: The quality of studies varies greatly with frequent shortcomings: no justification of sample size, lacking information on the reliability and validity of measures, no explanation nor theoretical understanding of findings. Railway suicides resemble closely people who use other methods, although they tend to be younger. As with other suicide methods, mental health problems are likely to be present. Railway suicide attempters usually die, but most urban transportation systems attempters survive. Railway suicides are rarely impulsive; people usually go to the railway for the purpose of killing themselves. Hotspots have been the focus of some prevention measures. We know little about why people choose railway suicide, but studies of survivors suggest they often thought they would have an immediate, certain and painless death. Media reports on railway suicides can increase their incidence.

Conclusions: Most research focuses on the incidence and characteristics of events and attempters. Research has not shown that railway suicides are different from suicides by other means. Better quality research is needed, particularly studies that investigate why people use railways to kill themselves and how railway suicides can be effectively prevented, as well as more evaluations of prevention programmes. Because of significant variations by country and region in characteristics of railway suicides, prevention programmes should conduct a local assessment of the characteristics of attempters and incidents.

Practical Implications: We need more research on indicators of suicide risk in attempters on railway property, and studies of how suicidal people on railway property are prevented from suicide. Changing beliefs and attitudes about railway suicides, reducing media reports, offering help onsite, controlling access at hotspots and better staff training in mental health facilities near tracks are promising prevention strategies. However, local specificities must be considered in planning prevention strategies.

Secret society 123: Understanding the language of self-harm on Instagram

Moreno MA, Ton A, Selkie E, Evans Y (United States)

Journal of Adolescence Health 58, 78-84, 2016

Purpose: Nonsuicidal self-injury (NSSI) content is present on social media and may influence adolescents. Instagram is a popular site among adolescents in which NSSI-related terms are user-generated as hashtags (words preceded by a #). These hashtags may be ambiguous and thus challenging for those outside the NSSI community to understand. The purpose of this study was to evaluate the meaning, popularity, and content advisory warnings related to ambiguous NSSI hashtags on Instagram.

Methods: This study used the search term "#selfharmmm" to identify public Instagram posts. Hashtag terms co-listed with #selfharmmm on each post were evaluated for inclusion criteria; selected hashtags were then assessed using a structured evaluation for meaning and consistency. We also investigated the total number of Instagram search hits for each hashtag at two time points and determined whether the hashtag prompted a Content Advisory warning.

Results: Our sample of 201 Instagram posts led to identification of 10 ambiguous NSSI hashtags. NSSI terms included #blithe, #cat, and #selfinjuryy. We discovered a popular image that described the broader community of NSSI and mental illness, called "#MySecretFamily." The term #MySecretFamily had approximately 900,000 search results at Time 1 and >1.5 million at Time 2. Only one-third of the relevant hashtags generated Content Advisory warnings.

Conclusions: NSSI content is popular on Instagram and often veiled by ambiguous hashtags. Content Advisory warnings were not reliable; thus, parents and providers remain the cornerstone of prompting discussions about NSSI content on social media and providing resources for teens.

A longitudinal study of suicidal ideation among homeless, mentally ill individuals

Noel F, Moniruzzaman A, Somers J, Frankish J, Strehlau V, Schutz C, Krausz M (Canada)

Social Psychiatry and Psychiatric Epidemiology 51, 107-114, 2016

Purpose: Previous cross-sectional studies have indicated that homeless individuals may present with high rates of suicidal ideation, which are strongly associated with completed suicide. We conducted the first known longitudinal study of suicidal ideation in the homeless.

Methods: We used data collected over 24 months in the Vancouver At Home project (N = 497), comprised two randomized-controlled trials of housing interventions for homeless individuals with mental disorders. Presence of suicidal ideation was determined using the Colorado symptom index.

Results: Suicidal ideation significantly decreased over time [odds ratio (OR) = 0.31 at 24 months, 95 % confidence interval (CI) 0.21-0.46]. Baseline diagnoses of mood (OR = 2.18, 95 % CI 1.48-3.21) and anxiety disorders (OR = 2.05, 95 % CI 1.42-2.97), as well as depressive mood (OR = 2.52, 95 % CI 1.90-3.33), use of any substance (OR = 1.59, 95 % CI 1.09-2.32), and polysubstance use (OR = 1.90, 95 % CI 1.40-2.60) were significantly associated with suicidal ideation in the multi-variate model. Baseline diagnosis of a psychotic disorder (protective effect), daily substance use, intravenous drug use, recent arrest, multiple physical illnesses and history of traumatic brain injury were significantly associated with suicidal ideation in the unadjusted model only.

Conclusions: Interventions targeting depressive symptoms and substance use could help decrease suicide risk in homeless individuals. Mental health services need to be tailored to address the complex needs of socially marginalized individuals.

Cortisol levels and suicidal behavior: A meta-analysis

O'Connor D, Ferguson E, Green J, O'Carroll R, O'Connor R (United Kingdom)
Psychoneuroendocrinology 63, 370-379, 2016

Suicide is a major cause of death worldwide, responsible for 1.5% of all mortality. The causes of suicidal behavior are not fully understood. Dysregulated hypothal-amic–pituitary–adrenal (HPA) axis activity, as measured by cortisol levels, is one potential risk factor. This meta-analytic review aimed (i) to estimate the strength and variability of the association between naturally fluctuating cortisol levels and suicidal behavior and (ii) to identify moderators of this relationship. A systematic literature search identified 27 studies (N = 2226; 779 suicide attempters and 1447 non-attempters) that met the study eligibility criteria from a total of 417 unique records initially examined. Estimates of effect sizes (r) obtained from these studies were analysed using Comprehensive Meta-Analysis. In these analyses, we com-pared participants identified as having a past history of suicide attempt(s) to those with no such history. Study quality, mean age of sample and percentage of male participants were examined as potential moderators. Overall, there was no signif-icant effect of suicide group on cortisol. However, significant associations between cortisol and suicide attempts were observed as a function of age. In studies where the mean age of the sample was below 40 years the association was positive (i.e., higher cortisol was associated with suicide attempts; r = .234, p < .001), and where the mean age was 40 or above the association was negative (i.e., lower cortisol was associated with suicide attempts; r = −.129, p < .001). These findings confirm that HPA axis activity, as indicated by age-dependent variations in cortisol levels, is associated with suicidal behavior. The challenge for theory and clinical practice is to explain the complete reversal of the association with age and to identify its clin-ical implications.

Suicidal ideation in family carers of people with dementia

O'Dwyer ST, Moyle W, Zimmer-Gembeck M, De Leo D (Australia)

Aging and Mental Health 20, 222-230, 2016

Objective: Two small studies have suggested that family carers of people with dementia may be a high-risk group for suicide. The objective of this study was to further explore the rate of suicidal ideation in a large sample of carers and identify psychosocial risk and protective factors.

Method: A cross-sectional survey was conducted with 566 family carers. The survey included measures of suicidality, self-efficacy, physical health, depression, anxiety, hopelessness, optimism, burden, coping strategies, and social support.

Results: Sixteen percent of carers had contemplated suicide more than once in the previous year. There were univariate differences between suicidal and non-suicidal carers on self-efficacy, social support, coping, burden, depression, anxiety, hopelessness, optimism, reasons for living, and symptoms of dementia, as well as age and income management. In a multivariate model, age, depression, and reasons for living predicted suicidal ideation. In tests for mediation, satisfaction with social support and dysfunctional coping had indirect effects on suicidal ideation via depression.

Conclusion: Family carers of people with dementia have high rates of suicidal ideation, with depression a risk factor and increasing age and reasons for living as protective factors. Depression and reasons for living should be targeted in interventions to reduce suicide risk in dementia carers.

Mental illness stigma, secrecy and suicidal ideation

Oexle N, Ajdacic-Gross V, Kilian R, Muller M, Rodgers S, Xu Z, Rossler W, Rusch N (Germany, Switzerland, Brazil)

Epidemiology and Psychiatric Sciences. Published online: 26 November 2015. doi: 10.1017/S2045796015001018

Aims: Whether the public stigma associated with mental illness negatively affects an individual, largely depends on whether the person has been labelled 'mentally ill'. For labelled individuals concealing mental illness is a common strategy to cope with mental illness stigma, despite secrecy's potential negative consequences. In addition, initial evidence points to a link between stigma and suicidality, but quantitative data from community samples are lacking.

Methods: Based on previous literature about mental illness stigma and suicidality, as well as about the potential influence of labelling processes and secrecy, a theory-driven model linking perceived mental illness stigma and suicidal ideation by a mediation of secrecy and hopelessness was established. This model was tested separately among labelled and unlabelled persons using data derived from a Swiss cross-sectional population-based study. A large community sample of people with elevated psychiatric symptoms was examined by interviews and self-report, collecting information on perceived stigma, secrecy, hopelessness and suicidal ideation. Participants who had ever used mental health services were considered as labelled 'mentally ill'. A descriptive analysis, stratified logistic regression models and a path analysis testing a three-path mediation effect were conducted.

Results: While no significant differences between labelled and unlabelled participants were observed regarding perceived stigma and secrecy, labelled individuals reported significantly higher frequencies of suicidal ideation and feelings of hopelessness. More perceived stigma was associated with suicidal ideation among labelled, but not among unlabelled individuals. In the path analysis, this link was mediated by increased secrecy and hopelessness.

Conclusions: Results from this study indicate that among persons labelled 'mentally ill', mental illness stigma is a contributor to suicidal ideation. One explanation for this association is the relation perceived stigma has with secrecy, which introduces negative emotional consequences. If our findings are replicated, they would suggest that programmes empowering people in treatment for mental illness to cope with anticipated and experienced discrimination as well as interventions to reduce public stigma within society could improve suicide prevention.

Needs and fears of young people presenting at accident and emergency department following an act of self-harm: Secondary analysis of qualitative data

Owens C, Hansford L, Sharkey S, Ford T (United Kingdom)
British Journal of Psychiatry 207, 1-6, 2015

Background: Presentation at an accident and emergency (A&E) department is a key opportunity to engage with a young person who self-harms. The needs of this vulnerable group and their fears about presenting to healthcare services, including A&E, are poorly understood.

Aims: To examine young people's perceptions of A&E treatment following self-harm and their views on what constitutes a positive clinical encounter.

Method: Secondary analysis of qualitative data from an experimental online discussion forum. Threads selected for secondary analysis represent the views of 31 young people aged 16-25 with experience of self-harm.

Results: Participants reported avoiding A&E whenever possible, based on their own and others' previous poor experiences. When forced to seek emergency care, they did so with feelings of shame and unworthiness. These feelings were reinforced when they received what they perceived as punitive treatment from A&E staff, perpetuating a cycle of shame, avoidance and further self-harm. Positive encounters were those in which they received 'treatment as usual', i.e. non-discriminatory care, delivered with kindness, which had the potential to challenge negative self-evaluation and break the cycle.

Conclusions: The clinical needs of young people who self-harm continue to demand urgent attention. Further hypothesis testing and trials of different models of care delivery for this vulnerable group are warranted.

International comparison of death place for suicide; a population-level eight country death certificate study

Rhee Y, Houttekier D, MacLeod R, Wilson DM, Cardenas-Turanzas M, Loucka M, Aubry R, Teno J, Roh S, Reinecke MA, Deliens L, Cohen J (United States, Belgium, Australia, Canada, Czech Republic, France, South Korea)

Social Psychiatry and Psychiatric Epidemiology, 51, 101-106, 2016

Purpose: The places of death for people who died of suicide were compared across eight countries and socio-demographic factors associated with home suicide deaths identified.

Methods: Death certificate data were analyzed; using multivariable binary logistic regression to determine associations.

Results: National suicide death rates ranged from 1.4 % (Mexico) to 6.4 % (South Korea). The proportion of suicide deaths occurring at home was high, ranging from 29.9 % (South Korea) to 65.8 % (Belgium). Being older, female, widowed/separated, highly educated and living in an urban area were risk factors for home suicide.

Conclusions: Home suicide deaths need specific attention in prevention programs.

Variable classification of drug-intoxication suicides across US states: A partial artifact of forensics?

Rockett IRH, Hobbs GR, Wu D, Jia H, Nolte KB, Smith GS, Putnam SL, Caine ED (United States, China)

PLoS One 10, e0135296, 2015

Background: The 21st-century epidemic of pharmaceutical and other drug-intoxication deaths in the United States (US) has likely precipitated an increase in misclassified, undercounted suicides. Drug-intoxication suicides are highly prone to be misclassified as accident or undetermined. Misclassification adversely impacts suicide and other injury mortality surveillance, etiologic understanding, prevention, and hence clinical and public health policy formation and practice.

Objective: To evaluate whether observed variation in the relative magnitude of drug-intoxication suicides across US states is a partial artifact of the scope and quality of toxicological testing and type of medicolegal death investigation system.

Methods: This was a national, state-based, ecological study of 111,583 drug-intoxication fatalities, whose manner of death was suicide, accident, or undetermined. The proportion of (nonhomicide) drug-intoxication deaths classified by medical examiners and coroners as suicide was analyzed relative to the proportion of death certificates citing one or more specific drugs and two types of state death investigation systems. Our model incorporated five sociodemographic covariates. Data covered the period 2008–2010, and derived from NCHS's Multiple Cause-of-Death public use files.

Results: Across states, the proportion of drug-intoxication suicides ranged from 0.058 in Louisiana to 0.286 in South Dakota and the rate from 1 per 100,000 population in North Dakota to 4 in New Mexico. There was a low correlation between combined accident and undetermined drug-intoxication death rates and corresponding suicide rates (Spearman's rho = 0.38; p<0.01). Citation of 1 or more specific drugs on the death certificate was positively associated with the relative odds of a state classifying a nonhomicide drug-intoxication death as suicide rather than accident or undetermined, adjusting for region and type of state death investigation system (odds ratio, 1.062; 95% CI,1.016–1.110). Region, too, was a significant predictor. Relative to the South, a 10% increase in drug citation was associated with 43% (95% CI,11%-83%), 41% (95% CI,7%-85%), and 33% (95% CI,1%-76%) higher odds of a suicide classification in the West, Midwest, and Northeast, respectively.

Conclusion: Large interstate variation in the relative magnitude of nonhomicide drug-intoxication deaths classified as suicide by medical examiners and coroners in the US appears partially an artifact of geographic region and degree of toxicological assessment in the case ascertainment process. Etiologic understanding and prevention of drug-induced suicides and other drug-intoxication deaths first require rigorous standardization involving accurate concepts, definitions, and case ascertainment.

Evictions and suicide: A follow-up study of almost 22 000 Swedish households in the wake of the global financial crisis

Rojas Y, Stenberg S-A (Sweden)
Journal of Epidemiology and Community Health 70, 409-413, 2016

Background: Millions of families across the world are evicted every year. However, very little is known about the impact that eviction has on their lives. This lack of knowledge is also starting to be noticed within the suicidological literature, and prominent scholars are arguing that there is an urgent need to explore the extent to which suicides may be considered a plausible consequence of being faced with eviction.

Method: The present study's sample consists of all persons served with an application for execution of an eviction order during 2009-2012. This group is compared to a random 10% sample of the general Swedish population, ages 16 years and over. The analysis is based on penalised maximum likelihood logistic regressions.

Results: Those who had lost their legal right to their dwellings and for whom the landlord had applied for the eviction to be executed were approximately four times more likely to commit suicide than those who had not been exposed to this experience (OR=4.42), controlling for several demographic, socioeconomic and mental health conditions prior to the date of the judicial decision.

Conclusions: Home evictions have a significant and detrimental impact on individuals' risk of committing suicide, even when several other well-known suicidogenic risk factors are controlled for. Our results reinforce the importance of ongoing attempts to remove the issue of evictions from its status as a hidden and neglected social problem.

Suicide risk after nonfatal self-harm: A national cohort study, 2000-2008

Runeson B, Haglund A, Lichtenstein P, Tidemalm D (Sweden)

Journal of Clinical Psychiatry 77, 240-246, 2016

Objective: To study the short-term risk of suicide after nonfatal deliberate self-harm and its association with coexisting mental disorders and with the method of self-harm used.

Method: We used linked Swedish national registers to design a cohort study with 34,219 individuals (59% females) who were admitted to hospital in 2000-2005 after deliberate selfharm (ICD-10defined). They were followed for 39 years. The studied outcome was completed suicide; Cox regression models yielded hazard ratios (HRs) for suicide risk. Temporal patterns were plotted with Kaplan-Meier survival curves, calculated separately for each mental disorder and for the method used at the previous selfharm event.

Results: 1,182 subjects committed suicide during follow-up (670 males and 512 females). Coexisting bipolar disorder (in males, adjusted HR = 6.3; 95% confidence interval [CI], 3.810.3; in females, adjusted HR = 5.8; 95% CI, 3.49.7) and nonorganic psychotic disorder (in males, adjusted HR = 5.1; 95% CI, 3.57.4; in females, adjusted HR = 4.6; 95% CI, 2.87.7) implied the highest risk of suicide after previous self-harm. Hanging as index self-harm method was a strong predictor of later suicide in both males (adjusted HR = 5.3; 95% CI, 4.07.0) and females (adjusted HR = 4.5; 95% CI, 2.58.1). Of those with bipolar disorder who used a method other than poisoning at the index event, 20.4% had already committed suicide after 39 years.

Conclusion: Individuals with severe mental disorders (affective and psychotic disorders) have a poor prognosis in the first years after hospital admission due to self-harm. The risk of subsequent suicide is higher after attempts by hanging and other self-injury methods (vs selfpoisoning). Aftercare for those with a self-harm episode should focus on treatment of the mental disorder present at the time of the episode.

What might interrupt men's suicide? Results from an online survey of men

Shand FL, Proudfoot J, Player MJ, Fogarty A, Whittle E, Wilhelm K, Hadzi-Pavlovic D, McTigue I, Spurrier M, Christensen H (Australia)

BMJ Open 5, *e008172, 2015*

Objectives: Men are almost two times more likely to die by suicide than women, yet little research has focused on what is required to prevent suicide among men. This paper aims to investigate what factors interrupt suicidal behaviour in men, and to examine differences according to known suicide risk factors.

Setting: Australia.

Participants: 251 Australian men aged 18 years and over who had made a suicide attempt 6-18 months prior to completing the survey.

Outcomes: The survey canvassed the language men use to describe their depression and suicidality, warning signs, barriers to accessing help and what is needed to interrupt a suicide attempt. ORs and chi2 were used to test for differences by age, geographic location and current depression severity.

Results: Of 299 men screened and eligible to participate, 251 completed all or part of the survey. Participants identified different words and warning signs for depression compared with suicidality. The most commonly endorsed barriers to accessing help were not wanting to burden others (66%) and having isolated themselves (63%). Men overwhelmingly endorsed 'I thought about the consequences for my family' as the factor which stopped a suicide attempt (67%). 'I need support from someone I really trust and respect' was also strongly endorsed. There were few differences by age, region or depression severity.

Conclusions: Participants were able to identify signs, albeit often subtle ones, that they were becoming depressed or suicidal. Similarly, most were able to identify active strategies to interrupt this downward spiral. Men wanted others to notice changes in their behaviour, and to approach them without judgement.

Trace lithium is inversely associated with male suicide after adjustment of climatic factors

Shiotsuki I, Terao T, Ishii N, Takeuchi S, Kuroda Y, Kohno K, Mizokami Y, Hatano K, Tanabe S, Kanehisa M, Iwata N, Matusda S (Japan)

Journal of Affective Disorders 189, 282-286, 2016

Background: Previously, we showed the inverse association between lithium in drinking water and male suicide in Kyushu Island. The narrow variation in meteorological factors of Kyushu Island and a considerable amount of evidence regarding the role of the factors on suicide provoked the necessities of adjusting the association by the wide variation in sunshine, temperature, rain fall, and snow fall.

Methods: To keep the wide variation in meteorological factors, we combined the data of Kyushu (the southernmost city is Itoman, 26°) and Hokkaido (the northernmost city is Wakkanai, 45°). Multiple regression analyses were used to predict suicide SMRs (total, male and female) by lithium levels in drinking water and meteorological factors.

Results: After adjustment of meteorological factors, lithium levels were significantly and inversely associated with male suicide SMRs, but not with total or female suicide SMRs, across the 153 cities of Hokkaido and Kyushu Islands. Moreover, annual total sunshine and annual mean temperature were significantly and inversely associated with male suicide SMRs whereas annual total rainfall was significantly and directly associated with male suicide SMRs.

Limitations: The limitations of the present study include the lack of data relevant to lithium levels in food and the proportion of the population who drank tap water and their consumption habits. Conclusions The present findings suggest that trace lithium is inversely associated with male but not female suicide after adjustment of meteorological factors.

Information-seeking on the internet: An investigation of websites potentially accessed by distressed or suicidal adolescents

Singaravelui V, Stewart A, Adams J, Simkin S, Hawton K (United Kingdom)

Crisis 36, 211-219, 2015

Background: The Internet is used by young people at risk of self-harm to communicate, find information, and obtain support.

Aims: We aimed to identify and analyze websites potentially accessed by these young people.

Method: Six search terms, relating to self-harm/suicide and depression, were input into four search engines. Websites were analyzed for access, content/purpose, and tone.

Results: In all, 314 websites were included in the analysis. Most could be accessed without restriction. Sites accessed by self-harm/suicide search terms were mostly positive or preventive in tone, whereas sites accessed by the term ways to kill yourself tended to have a negative tone. Information about self-harm methods was common with specific advice on how to self-harm in 15.8% of sites, encouragement of self-harm in 7.0%, and evocative images of self-harm/suicide in 20.7%. Advice on how to get help was given in 56.1% of sites.

Conclusion: Websites relating to suicide or self-harm are easily accessed. Many sites are potentially helpful. However, a significant proportion of sites are potentially harmful through normalizing or encouraging self-harm. Enquiry regarding Internet use should be routinely included while assessing young people at risk.

Understanding women who self-harm: Predictors and long-term outcomes in a longitudinal community sample

Stanford S, Jones MP, Loxton DJ (Australia)

Australian and New Zealand Journal of Psychiatry. Published online: 26 February 2016. doi: 10.1177/0004867416633298

Objective: There is growing awareness of the range of psychosocial, lifestyle, and sociodemographic factors related to self-harm, however this research is often limited by using cross-sectional or convenience samples. And while we generally assume that young adults who self-harm experience poorer long-term outcomes, longitudinal research is needed. This paper builds on prior research using a large, representative, longitudinal sample.

Methods: 5765 Australian women completed 5 surveys (age 18-23 to 31-36). Six-month self-harm was measured by self-report. We had two aims: firstly to predict future self-harm, separately for women with and without prior self-harm. Secondly, to identify outcomes 3 and 6 years following self-harm.

Results: Six-month self-harm prevalence was 2.5%. Predictors among women without recent self-harm included depression, dieting behaviours, number of male sexual partners, and abuse. Among women with recent or current self-harm, predictors were number of dieting behaviours, tiredness of life, and stress. Women who self-harmed reported poorer outcomes, namely greater difficulties in relationships at 3- and 6-year follow-up.

Conclusions: Longitudinal risk factors for self-harm differed depending on prior self-harm status, and included depression, dieting behaviours, tiredness of life and stress. These factors may serve as warning signs for new or continued self-harm. This study offers new insight into long-term outcomes up to six years after self-harm, particularly with relationships.

Assisted and unassisted suicide in men and women: Longitudinal study of the Swiss population

Steck N, Egger M, Zwahlen M (Switzerland)

British Journal of Psychiatry 208, 484-490, 2016

Background: In Switzerland assisted suicide is legal if no self-interest is involved. *Aims:* To compare the strength and direction of associations with sociodemographic factors between assisted and unassisted suicides. *Method:* We calculated rates and used Cox and logistic regression models in a longitudinal study of the Swiss population. *Results:* Analyses were based on 5 004 403 people, 1301 assisted and 5708 unassisted suicides from 2003 to 2008. The rate of unassisted suicides was higher in men than in women, rates of assisted suicides were similar in men and women. Higher education was positively associated with assisted suicide, but negatively with unassisted. Living alone, having no children and no religious affiliation were associated with higher rates of both. *Conclusions:* Some situations that indicate greater vulnerability such as living alone were associated with both assisted and unassisted suicide. Among the terminally ill, women were more likely to choose assisted suicide, whereas men died more often by unassisted suicide.

Suicide prevention through online gatekeeping using search advertising techniques

Sueki H, Ito J (Japan)

Crisis 36, 267-273, 2015

Background: Nurturing gatekeepers is an effective suicide prevention strategy. Internet-based methods to screen those at high risk of suicide have been developed in recent years but have not been used for online gatekeeping. *Aims:* A preliminary study was conducted to examine the feasibility and effects of online gatekeeping. *Method:* Advertisements to promote e-mail psychological consultation service use among Internet users were placed on web pages identified by searches using suicide-related keywords. We replied to all emails received between July and December 2013 and analyzed their contents. *Results:* A total of 139 consultation service users were analyzed. The mean age was 23.8 years (SD = 9.7), and female users accounted for 80% of the sample. Suicidal ideation was present in 74.1%, and 12.2% had a history of suicide attempts. After consultation, positive changes in mood were observed in 10.8%, 16.5% showed intentions to seek help from new supporters, and 10.1% of all 139 users actually took help-seeking actions. *Conclusion:* Online gatekeeping to prevent suicide by placing advertisements on web search pages to promote consultation service use among Internet users with suicidal ideation may be feasible.

Problems with the coronial determination of 'suicide'

Tait G, Carpenter B, De Leo D, Tatz C (Australia)
Mortality 20, 233-247, 2015

After over 100 years of constant dissatisfaction with the accuracy of suicide data, this paper suggests that the problem may actually lie with the category of suicide itself. In almost all previous research, 'suicide' is taken to be a self-evidently valid category of death, not an object of study in its own right. Instead, the focus in this paper is upon the presupposition that how a social fact like suicide is counted depends upon norms for its governmental regulation, leading to a reciprocal relationship between social norms and statistical norms. Since this relationship is centred almost entirely in the coroner's office, this paper examines governmental, definitional and categorisational issues relating to how coroners reach findings of suicide. The intention of this paper is to contribute to international debates over how suicide can best be conceptualised and adjudged.

Self-harm and life problems: Findings from the multicentre study of self-harm in England

Townsend E, Ness J, Waters K, Kapur N, Turnbull P, Cooper J, Bergen H, Hawton K (United Kingdom)
Social Psychiatry and Psychiatric Epidemiology 51, 183-192, 2016

Purpose: Self-harm is a major clinical problem and is strongly linked to suicide. It is important to understand the problems faced by those who self-harm to design effective clinical services and suicide prevention strategies. We investigated the life problems experienced by patients presenting to general hospitals for self-harm.

Methods: Data for 2000–2010 from the Multicentre Study of Self-harm in England were used to investigate life problems associated with self-harm and their relationship to patient and clinical characteristics, including age, gender, repeat self-harm and employment status.

Results: Of 24,598 patients (36,431 assessed episodes), 57 % were female and with a mean age of 33.1 years (SD 14.0 years), 92.6 % were identified as having at least one contributing life problem. The most frequently reported problems at first episode of self-harm within the study period were relationship difficulties (especially with partners). Mental health issues and problems with alcohol were also very common (especially in those aged 35–54 years, and those who repeated self-harm). Those who repeated self-harm were more likely to report problems with housing, mental health and dealing with the consequences of abuse.

Conclusions: Self-harm usually occurs in the context of multiple life problems. Clinical services for self-harm patients should have access to appropriate care for provision of help for relationship difficulties and problems concerning alcohol and mental health issues. Individualised clinical support (e.g. psychological therapy, interventions for alcohol problems and relationship counselling) for self-harm patients facing these life problems may play a crucial role in suicide prevention.

Cognitive vulnerabilities and development of suicidal thinking in children of depressed mothers: A longitudinal investigation.

Tsypes A, Gibb BE (United States)

Psychiatry Research 239, 99-104, 2016

Although children of depressed parents are at heightened risk for suicidal ideation, little is known about specific risk factors. This study focused on the relation between a broad range of cognitive vulnerabilities proposed by the leading cognitive theories and the development of suicidal ideation in children. Participants were 209 mothers (aged 24-55) and their 8-14 year old children. Children of depressed mothers who had previously experienced suicidal ideation themselves reported higher levels of brooding rumination than children of depressed mothers who had not experienced suicidal ideation as well as children of never depressed mothers who had not experienced suicidal ideation. Further, among children of depressed mothers with no prior history of suicidal ideation, higher levels of hopelessness and lower global self-worth predicted first onset of suicidal ideation over a 2-year follow-up. Importantly, these results were maintained even after taking the occurrence of major depressive disorder in children during the follow-up into account. The findings highlight specific cognitive vulnerabilities that could be targeted in early suicide prevention and intervention efforts.

Comparison of antidepressant classes and the risk and time course of suicide attempts in adults: Propensity matched, retrospective cohort study.

Valuck RJ, Libby AM, Anderson HD, Allen RR, Strombom I, Marangell LB, Perahia D (United States, United Kingdom)

British Journal of Psychiatry 208, 271-290, 2016

Background: Placebo-controlled clinical trials have led to concern over possible increased risk of suicide-related events in some populations exposed to antidepressants.

Aims: To evaluate the risk of suicide attempts by antidepressant drug class and the presence or absence of depression.

Method: A retrospective propensity-matched new-user cohort study was used to compare participants with incident depression classified by antidepressant treatment with each other and with the general population.

Results: Among the treated group, the suicide attempt rate peaked in the month prior to diagnosis then decreased steadily over the next 6 months. Among the pharmacologically untreated group, the highest rate was seen in the second month after diagnosis. Cohorts with depression had significantly higher suicide attempt risk than the general population, but the treated group did not differ significantly from the untreated group.

Conclusions: Patients on antidepressants did not have significantly higher risk compared with untreated patients. No significant differences were observed for patients treated with individual serotonin-noradrenaline reuptake inhibitors (SNRIs) or selective serotonin reuptake inhibitors (SSRIs) or by class (SSRI v. SNRI cohorts).

Exploring the validity of the fantastic lifestyle checklist in an inner city population of people presenting with suicidal behaviours

Wilhelm K, Handley T, Reddy P (Australia)
Australian and New Zealand Journal of Psychiatry 50, 128-134, 2015

Purpose: Although patients demonstrate a range of problematic health-related lifestyle behaviours preceding suicidal behaviour, there is little research that routinely measure these behaviours. This paper seeks to establish the utility of health-related lifestyle measure (Fantastic Lifestyle Checklist) in people presenting to a major inner city Emergency Department with a range of suicidal behaviours.

Methods: From 2007-2014, data from the 366 patients who had completed the Fantastic Lifestyle Checklist, after referral by the Emergency Department to a service for people with deliberate self-harm or suicidal ideation, were included in the analysis study. A Maximum Likelihood factor analysis was performed to assess the factor structure of the Fantastic Lifestyle Checklist and the resultant factors were explored in relation to measures of health; namely the Depression, Anxiety and Stress Scale and the 12-item Short-Form Health Survey.

Results: A three-component factor structure emerged comprising Component 1 'positive life investments', Component 2 'poor emotional regulation' and Component 3 'poor health behaviours'. There was a significant negative correlation between 'positive life investments' and each of the Depression, Anxiety and Stress scales subscales and significant positive associations with 'poor emotional regulation' and Short Form Health Survey-12 mental health scores. Only the Short Form Health Survey-12 physical health subscale was weakly correlated with 'poor health behaviours', in females.

Conclusion: Our findings support the construct and concurrent validity of the Fantastic Lifestyle Checklist measure. The three factors obtained for the Fantastic Lifestyle Checklist were coherent and seem useful for research and clinical practice.

Permissive beliefs and attitudes about older adult suicide: A suicide enabling script?

Winterrowd E, Canetto SS, Benoit K (United States)
Aging and Mental Health. Published online: 23 October 2015. doi: 10.1080/13607863.2015.1099609

Objectives: In the United States, suicide rates are highest among European American older adults. This phenomenon calls attention to cultural factors, specifically, the suicide beliefs and attitudes of European Americans. Beliefs and attitudes matter in the vulnerability to suicide. As predicted by cultural scripts of suicide theory, suicide is most likely among individuals and in communities where it is expected and is most acceptable. This study examined beliefs about the precipitants of, and protectors against older adult suicide, as well as suicide attitudes, in a predominantly European American community.

Design and Methods: Two hundred and fifty-five older adults (86% European

American) and 281 younger adults (81% European American) indicated what they thought were the most likely older adult suicide precipitants and protectors, and their opinion about older adult suicide, depending on precipitant.

Results: Health problems were the most endorsed older adult suicide precipitants. Suicide precipitated by health problems was also rated most positively (e.g. rational, courageous). Older adults, persons with more education, and persons who did not identify with a religion expressed the most favorable attitudes about older adult suicide, across suicide precipitants. Men viewed older adult suicide as more admissible, and women, with more sympathy. Perceived suicide protectors included religiosity among older adults, and supportive relationships among younger adults.

Conclusions: The belief, in this study's predominantly European American community, that older adult suicide is triggered by health problems, together with favorable attitudes about older adult suicide, suggest an enabling older adult suicide script, with implications for suicide risk and prevention.

Does psychosis increase the risk of suicide in patients with major depression? A systematic review

Zalpuri I, Rothschild AJ (United States)

Journal of Affective Disorders 198, 23-31, 2016

Objective: Over the years studies have shown conflicting results about the risk of suicide in psychotic depression (MD-psych). To understand this association, we undertook a comprehensive review of the literature to ascertain whether individuals with MD-psych have higher rates of completed suicides, suicide attempts or suicidal ideation compared to those with non-psychotic depression (MD-nonpsych).

Methods: We searched Pubmed, PsycINFO and Ovid in English language, from 1946-October 2015. Studies were included if suicidal ideation, attempts or completed suicides were assessed.

Results: During the acute episode of depression, patients with MD-psych have higher rates of suicide, suicide attempts, and suicidal ideation than patients with MD-nonpsych, especially when the patient is hospitalized on an inpatient psychiatric unit. Studies done after the acute episode has resolved are less likely to show this difference, likely due to patients having received treatment.

Limitations: Diagnostic interviews were not conducted in all studies. Many studies did not report whether psychotic symptoms in MD-psych patients were mood-congruent or mood-incongruent; hence it is unclear whether the type of delusion increases suicide risk. Studies did not describe whether MD-psych patients experienced command hallucinations encouraging them to engage in suicidal behavior. Only 24 studies met inclusion criteria; several of them had small sample size and a quality score of zero, hence impacting validity.

Conclusions: This review indicates that the seemingly conflicting data in suicide risk between MD-psych and MD-nonpsych in previous studies appears to be related to whether one looks at differences during the acute episode or over the long-term.

Suicidal behavior-related hospitalizations among pregnant women in the USA, 2006-2012

Zhong QY, Gelaye B, Miller M, Fricchione GL, Cai T, Johnson PA, Henderson DC, Williams MA (United States)

Archives of Women's Mental Health 19, 463-472, 2016

Suicide is one of the leading causes of maternal mortality in many countries, but little is known about the epidemiology of suicide and suicidal behavior among pregnant women in the USA. We sought to examine trends and provide nationally representative estimates for suicidal behavior (including suicidal ideation and suicide and self-inflicted injury) among pregnant women from 2006 to 2012 in the USA. Pregnant women aged 12-55 years were identified through pregnancy- and delivery-related hospitalization records from the National (Nationwide) Inpatient Sample. Suicidal behavior was identified by the International Classification of Diseases, Ninth Revision, Clinical Modification codes. Annual, nationwide estimates and trends were determined using discharge and hospital weights. The prevalence of suicidal ideation more than doubled from 2006 to 2012 (47.5 to 115.0 per 100,000 pregnancy- and delivery-related hospitalizations), whereas the prevalence of suicide and self-inflicted injury remained stable. Nearly 10 % of suicidal behavior occurred in the 12-18-year group, showing the highest prevalence per 100,000 pregnancy- and delivery-related hospitalizations (158.8 in 2006 and 308.7 in 2012) over the study period. For suicidal ideation, blacks had higher prevalence than whites; women in the lowest income quartile had the highest prevalence. Although the prevalence of suicidal behavior was higher among hospitalizations with depression diagnoses, more than 30 % of hospitalizations were for suicidal behavior without depression diagnoses. Our findings highlight the increasing burden and racial differences in suicidal ideation among US pregnant women. Targeted suicide prevention efforts are needed for high-risk pregnant women including teens, blacks, and low-income women.

Citation List

FATAL SUICIDAL BEHAVIOR

Epidemiology

Akhgari M, Baghdadi F, Kadkhodaei A (2016). Cyanide poisoning related deaths, a four-year experience and review of the literature. *Australian Journal of Forensic Sciences* 48, 186-194.

Aldana MC, Navarrete N (2015). Epidemiology of a decade of pediatric fatal burns in Colombia, South America. *Burns* 41, 1587-1592.

Alexopoulos EC, Kavalidou K, Messolora F (2015). Suicide mortality across broad occupational groups in Greece: A descriptive study. *Safety and Health at Work* 7, 1-5.

Anestis M, Capron DW (2015). The associations between state veteran population rates, handgun legislation, and statewide suicide rates. *Journal of Psychiatric Research* 74, 30-34.

Arnautovska U, McPhedran S, Kelly B, Reddy P, De Leo D (2016). Geographic variation in suicide rates in Australian farmers: Why is the problem more frequent in Queensland than in New South Wales? *Death Studies* 40, 367-372.

Ashwini Narayan K, Vaidyam B (2016). An autopsy study conducted at district hospital mortuary, Mims Mandya on violent asphyxial deaths. *Journal of South India Medicolegal Association* 8, 26-31.

Aziz UBA, Aslami AN, Ali SM (2016). Profile of acute paediatric poisoning cases admitted in a tertiary care centre in North India. *Indian Journal of Forensic Medicine and Toxicology* 10, 217-222.

Bacopoulou F, Petridou E, Korpa TN, Deligeoroglou E, Chrousos GP (2015). External-cause mortality among adolescents and young adults in Greece over the millennium's first decade 2000-09. *Journal of Public Health* 37, 70-77.

Bishop-Freeman SC, Miller A, Hensel EM, Winecker RE (2015). Postmortem metaxalone (skelaxin) data from North Carolina. *Journal of Analytical Toxicology* 39, 629-636.

Blessing MM, Lin PT (2015). Suicide by shotgun in Southeastern Minnesota. *Journal of Forensic Sciences* 61, S159-S162.

Blosnich JR, Brown GR, Wojcio S, Jones KT, Bossarte RM (2014). Mortality among veterans with transgender-related diagnoses in the veterans health administration, FY2000-2009. *LGBT Health* 1, 269-276.

Bridge JA, Asti L, Horowitz LM (2015). Suicide trends among elementary school-aged children in the United States from 1993 to 2012. *JAMA Pediatrics* 169, 673-677.

Bustamante F, Ramirez V, Urquidi C, Bustos V, Yaseen Z, Galynker I (2015). Trends and most frequent methods of suicide in Chile between 2001 and 2010. *Crisis* 37, 21-30.

Case A, Deaton A (2015). Rising morbidity and mortality in midlife among white non-Hispanic Americans in the 21st century. *Proceedings of the National Academy of Sciences* 112, 15078-15083.

Cavanagh B, Ibrahim S, Roscoe A, Bickley H, While D, Windfuhr K, Appleby L, Kapur N (2016). The timing of general population and patient suicide in England, 1997-2012. *Journal of Affective Disorders* 197, 175-181.

Cha ES, Chang SS, Gunnell D, Eddleston M, Khang YH, Lee WJ (2015). Impact of paraquat regulation on suicide in South Korea. *International Journal of Epidemiology.* Published online: 18 November 2015. doi: 10.1093/ije/dyv304.

Cha ES, Chang SS, Lee WJ (2015). Potential underestimation of pesticide suicide and its impact on secular trends in South Korea, 1991-2012. *Injury Prevention.* 22, 189-194.

Chan CH, Caine ED, You S, Yip PS (2015). Changes in South Korean urbanicity and suicide rates, 1992 to 2012. *British Medical Journal Open* 5, e009451.

Chang SS, Cheng Q, Lee ES, Yip PS (2015). Suicide by gassing in Hong Kong 2005-2013: Emerging trends and characteristics of suicide by helium inhalation. *Journal of Affective Disorders* 192, 162-166.

Chapman S, Alpers P, Agho K, Jones M (2015). Australia's 1996 gun law reforms: Faster falls in firearm deaths, firearm suicides, and a decade without mass shootings. *Injury Prevention* 21, 355-362.

Chasimpha S, McLean E, Chihana M, Kachiwanda L, Koole O, Tafatatha T, Mvula H, Nyirenda M, Crampin AC, Glynn JR (2015). Patterns and risk factors for deaths from external causes in rural Malawi over 10 years: A prospective population-based study. *BMC Public Health* 15, 1036.

Crudele GDL, Di Candia D, Gentile G, Marchesi M, Rancati A, Zoja R (2016). One hundred and one cases of plastic bag suffocation in the Milan area between 1993 and 2013-correlations, circumstances, pathological and forensic evidences and literature review. *Journal of Forensic Sciences* 61, 361-366.

Datir S, Petkar M, Farooqui J, Makhani C, Hussaini SN, Chavan K, Bangal R (2015). Profile of acute poisoning cases at Pravara Rural Hospital, Loni. *Journal of Indian Academy of Forensic Medicine* 37, 400-404.

Eskin M, Sun JM, Abuidhail J, Yoshimasu K, Kujan O, Janghorbani M, Flood C, Carta MG, Tran US, Mechri A, Hamdan M, Poyrazli S, Aidoudi K, Bakhshi S, Harlak H, Moro MF, Nawafleh H, Phillips L, Shaheen A, Taifour S, Tsuno K, Voracek M (2016). Suicidal behavior and psychological distress in university students: A 12-nation study. *Archives of Suicide Research*. Published online: 8 March 2016. doi: 10.1080/13811118.2015.1054055.

Esscher A, Essen B, Innala E, Papadopoulos FC, Skalkidou A, Sundstrom-Poromaa I, Hogberg U (2015). Suicides during pregnancy and 1 year postpartum in Sweden, 1980-2007. *British Journal of Psychiatry* 208, 462-469.

Etemadi-Aleagha A, Akhgari M, Iravani FS (2015). Aluminum phosphide poisoning-related deaths in Tehran, Iran, 2006 to 2013. *Medicine* 94, e1637.

Fernandez-Nino JA, Astudillo-Garcia CI, Bojorquez-Chapela I, Morales-Carmona E, Montoya-Rodriguez AA, Palacio-Mejia LS (2016). The Mexican cycle of suicide: A national analysis of seasonality, 2000-2013. *PLoS One* 11, e0146495.

Fond G, Llorca PM, Boucekine M, Zendjidjian X, Brunel L, Lancon C, Auquier P, Boyer L (2016). Disparities in suicide mortality trends between United States of America and 25 European countries: Retrospective analysis of who mortality database. *Scientific Report* 6, 20256.

Fragkouli K, Boumba V, Vougiouklakis T (2016). Survey of medico-legal investigation of homicide in the region of Epirus (Northwest Greece). *Journal of Forensic and Legal Medicine* 37, 39-44.

Franchi A, Bagur J, Lemoine P, Maucort-Boulch D, Malicier D, Maujean G (2016). Forensic autopsy of people having committed suicide in 2002 and in 2012: Comparison of epidemiological and sociological data. *Journal of Forensic Sciences* 61, 109-115.

Granski M, Keller A, Venters H (2015). Death rates among detained immigrants in the United States. *International Journal of Environmental Research and Public Health* 12, 14414-14419.

Grinshteyn E, Hemenway D (2015). Violent death rates: The US compared with other high-income OECD countries, 2010. *American Journal of Medicine* 129, 266-273.

Gurm J, Samji H, Nophal A, Ding E, Strehlau V, Zhu J, Montaner JSG, Hogg RS, Guillemi S (2015). Suicide mortality among people accessing highly active antiretroviral therapy for HIV/AIDS in British Columbia: A retrospective analysis. *Canadian Medical Association Journal Open* 3, E140-E148.

Harris KM, Thandrayen J, Samphoas C, Se P, Lewchalermwongse B, Ratanashevorn R, Perry ML, Britts C (2016). Estimating suicide rates in developing nations: A low-cost newspaper capture-recapture approach in Cambodia. *Asia-Pacific Journal of Public Health* 28, 262-270.

Herbert A, Gilbert R, Gonzalez-Izquierdo A, Pitman A, Li L (2015). 10-y risks of death and emergency re-admission in adolescents hospitalised with violent, drug- or alcohol-related, or self-inflicted injury: A population-based cohort study. *Public Library of Science Medicine* 12, e1001931.

Heron M (2015). Deaths: Leading causes for 2012. *National Vital Statistics Reports* 64, 1-93.

Howard SJ, Surtees W (2016). A case series review of suicides associated with social media use in South Tyneside, England. *JRSM Open* 7, e2054270415619322.

Ilic M, Ilic I (2016). Suicide in Serbia. *Journal of Affective Disorders* 193, 187-193.

Isabel RP, Miguel RB, Antonio RG, Oscar MG (2016). Economic crisis and suicides in Spain. Socio-demographic and regional variability. *European Journal of Health Economics*. Published online: 2 March 2016. doi: 10.1007/s10198-016-0774-5.

Jadhao VT, Tatiya HS, Taware AA, Punpale SB, Bandgar AL (2015). An overview of custodial deaths in Pune six years retrospective study. *Journal of Indian Academy of Forensic Medicine* 37, 268-271.

Kalesan B, Mobily ME, Keiser O, Fagan JA, Galea S (2016). Firearm legislation and firearm mortality in the USA: A cross-sectional, state-level study. *Lancet* 387, 1847-1855.

Kanamuller J, Riipinen PMDPD, Riala KMDPD, Paloneva E, Hakko H (2015). Hanging suicides in Northern Finland: A descriptive epidemiological study. *Death Studies* 40, 205-210.

Kanchan T, Bakkannavar SM, Acharya PR (2015). Paraquat poisoning: Analysis of an uncommon cause of fatal poisoning from Manipal, South India. *Toxicology International* 22, 30-34.

Kenny DT, Asher A (2016). Life expectancy and cause of death in popular musicians: Is the popular musician lifestyle the road to ruin? *Medical Problems of Performing Artists* 31, 37-44.

Kõlves K, De Leo D (2015). Adolescent suicide rates between 1990 and 2009: Analysis of age group 15-19 years worldwide. *Journal of Adolescent Health* 58, 69-77.

Kõlves K, Potts B, De Leo D (2015). Ten years of suicide mortality in Australia: Socio-economic and psychiatric factors in Queensland. *Journal of Forensic and Legal Medicine* 36, 136-143.

Krzyżak M, Maślach D, Szpak A, Piotrowska K, Florczyk K, Skrodzka M, Owoc A, Bojar I (2015). Trends of potential years of life lost due to main causes of deaths in urban and rural population in Poland, 2002–2011. *Annals of Agricultural and Environmental Medicine* 22, 564-571.

Lawson CJ (2015). Mortality in American hip-hop and rap recording artists, 1987-2014. *Medical Problems of Performing Artists* 30, 211-216.

Lovrecic M, Lovrecic B, Semerl JS, Maremmani I (2015). Suicide by narcotic poisoning in Slovenia, according to gender, during the period 2004-2007. *Heroin Addiction and Related Clinical Problems* 17, 77-83.

Lozano JG, Molina DK (2015). Deaths in custody a 25-year review of jail deaths in Bexar County, Texas. *American Journal of Forensic Medicine and Pathology* 36, 285-289.

Lukaschek K, Engelhardt H, Baumert J, Ladwig KH (2015). No correlation between rates of suicidal ideation and completed suicides in Europe: Analysis of 49,008 participants (55+ years) based on the Survey of Health, Ageing and Retirement in Europe (SHARE). *European Psychiatry* 30, 874-879.

Manninen M, Pankakoski M, Gissler M, Suvisaari J (2015). Adolescents in a residential school for behavior disorders have an elevated mortality risk in young adulthood. *Child and Adolescent Psychiatry and Mental Health* 9, 46.

Meera T, Nandeibam P, Slong D, Nabachandra H (2015). Burn deaths: A study on female victims in Manipur. *Journal of Indian Academy of Forensic Medicine* 37, 358-360.

Meyer-Rochow VB, Hakko H, Ojamo M, Uusitalo H, Timonen M (2015). Suicides in visually impaired persons: A nation-wide register-linked study from Finland based on thirty years of data. *PLoS One* 10, e0141583.

Mihailović Z, Savić S, Damjanjuk I, Jovanović A, Vuković S (2015). Suicides among Serbian war veterans - an autopsy study. *Srpski Arhiv Za Celokupno Lekarstvo* 143, 590-594.

Mills PD, Gallimore BI, Watts BV, Hemphill RR (2015). Suicide attempts and completions in veterans affairs nursing home care units and long-term care facilities: A review of root-cause analysis reports. *International Journal of Geriatric Psychiatry* 31, 518-525.

Milner A, Page K, LaMontagne AD (2015). Suicide among male road and rail drivers in Australia: A retrospective mortality study. *Road and Transport Research* 24, 26-31.

Milner AJ, Niven H, LaMontagne AD (2015). Occupational class differences in suicide: Evidence of changes over time and during the global financial crisis in Australia. *BMC Psychiatry* 15, 223.

Mohamadian F, Delpisheh A, Shiry F, Faramarzi S, Direkvand-Moghadam A (2015). Epidemiological aspects of suicide lead to death in Iranian population during 2004-2008; a retrospective study. *Der Pharmacia Lettre* 7, 154-158.

Mok PLH, Antonsen S, Pedersen CB, Appleby L, Shaw J, Webb RT (2015). National cohort study of absolute risk and age-specific incidence of multiple adverse outcomes between adolescence and early middle age. *BMC Public Health* 15, e920.

Nahar Q, Arifeen SE, Jamil K, Streatfield PK (2015). Causes of adult female deaths in Bangladesh: Findings from two national surveys. *BMC Public Health* 15, 911.

Olfson M, Gerhard T, Huang C, Crystal S, Stroup TS (2015). Premature mortality among adults with schizophrenia in the United States. *Journal of the American Medical Association Psychiatry* 72, 1172-1181.

Park C, Jee YH, Jung KJ (2016). Age-period-cohort analysis of the suicide rate in Korea. *Journal of Affective Disorders* 194, 16-20.

Parkkari J, Sievanen H, Niemi S, Mattila VM, Kannus P (2015). Injury deaths in the adolescent population of Finland: A 43-year secular trend analysis between 1971 and 2013. *Injury Prevention*. Published online: 23 December 2015. doi: 10.1136/injuryprev-2015-041798.

Pathak AG, Gadhari RK, Chaudhari KM, Chavan SS, Shejwal DK, Devraj NA (2016). Unnatural deaths in police lockup/prisons of North Maharashtra region: A 15 year retrospective study. *Indian Journal of Forensic Medicine and Toxicology* 10, 74-79.

Patil B, Patil D (2016). Profile of deaths due to poisoning in a medical college teaching hospital. *Indian Journal of Forensic Medicine and Toxicology* 10, 181-183.

Puzo Q, Qin P, Mehlum L (2016). Long-term trends of suicide by choice of method in Norway: A joinpoint regression analysis of data from 1969 to 2012. *BMC Public Health* 16, 255.

Rahimi R, Ali N, Md Noor S, Mahmood MS, Zainun KA (2015). Suicide in the elderly in Malaysia. *Malaysian Journal of Pathology* 37, 259-263.

Rhee Y, Houttekier D, MacLeod R, Wilson DM, Cardenas-Turanzas M, Loucka M, Aubry R, Teno J, Roh S, Reinecke MA, Deliens L, Cohen J (2015). International comparison of death place for suicide; a population-level eight country death certificate study. *Social Psychiatry and Psychiatric Epidemiology* 51, 101-106.

Roberts SE, Carter T (2015). Mortality from accidents, disease, suicide and homicide in the British fishing industry from 1900 to 2010. *International Maritime Health* 66, 211-219.

Rostami M, Jalilian A, Rezaei-Zangeneh R, Salari A (2016). Factors associated with the choice of suicide method in Kermanshah Province, Iran. *Annals of Saudi Medicine* 36, 7-16.

Sahoo AK, Sastry AS, Rauta S, Patanaik AMM, Mahapatra SC (2014). Study of organophospho-rous poisoning cases at Maharajah Institute of Medical Sciences, AP. *Journal of Evolution of Medical and Dental Sciences* 3, 9201-9206.

Salari S, Sillito CL (2016). Intimate partner homicide-suicide: Perpetrator primary intent across young, middle, and elder adult age categories. *Aggression and Violent Behavior* 26, 26-34.

Savage I (2016). Analysis of fatal train-pedestrian collisions in metropolitan Chicago 2004-2012. *Accident Analysis and Prevention* 86, 217-228.

Segu S, Tataria R (2016). Paediatric suicidal burns: A growing concern. *Burns* 35, 9201-9206.

Seo E-W, Kwak J-M, Kim D-Y, Lee K-S (2015). Regional disparities of suicide mortality by gender. *Health Policy and Management* 25, 285-294.

Shojaei A, Moradi S, Alaeddini F, Khodadoost M, Abdizadeh A, Khademi A (2016). Evaluating the temporal trend of completed suicides referred to the Iranian forensic medicine organiza-tion during 2006-2010. *Journal of Forensic and Legal Medicine* 39, 104-108.

Sonmez I, Bozkurt A, Akbirgun A (2015). Suicide rate in a Mediterranean Island: North Cyprus. *Journal of Psychiatry* 18, 273.

Spiller HA, Strauch J, Essing-Spiller SJ, Burns G (2015). Thirteen years of oxcarbazepine expo-sures reported to US poison centers: 2000 to 2012. *Human and Experimental Toxicology*. Pub-lished online: 26 November 2015. doi: 10.1177/0960327115618246.

Steck N, Egger M, Zwahlen M (2016). Assisted and unassisted suicide in men and women: Lon-gitudinal study of the Swiss population. *British Journal of Psychiatry* 208, 484-90.

Sumarokov YA, Brenn T, Kudryavtsev AV, Nilssen O (2015). Variations in suicide method and in suicide occurrence by season and day of the week in Russia and the Nenets Autonomous Okrug, Northwestern Russia: A retrospective population-based mortality study. *BMC Psychiatry* 15, 224.

Szymanski LJ, Aurelius MB, Szymanski SA, Lathrop SL (2016). Suicidal drug overdoses in New Mexico: A 5-year retrospective review. *Journal of Forensic Sciences* 61, 661-665.

Tanner AK, Hasking P, Martin G (2014). Effects of rumination and optimism on the relationship between psychological distress and non-suicidal self-injury. *Prevention Science* 15, 860-868.

Taylor AK, Knipe DW, Thomas KH (2016). Railway suicide in England and Wales 2000-2013: A time-trends analysis. *BMC Public Health* 16, e270.

Thibodeau L (2015). Suicide mortality in Canada and Quebec, 1926-2008: An age-period-cohort analysis. *Canadian Studies in Population* 42, 1-23

Tollefsen IM, Helweg-Larsen K, Thiblin I, Hem E, Kastrup MC, Nyberg U, Rogde S, Zahl PH, Ostevold G, Ekeberg O (2015). Are suicide deaths under-reported? Nationwide re-evalua-tions of 1800 deaths in Scandinavia. *British Medical Journal Open* 5, e009120.

Tyagi S, Sukhadeve RB, Parchake MB, Pathak HM (2015). Mumbai local: Life line or life steal-ing. *Journal of Indian Academy of Forensic Medicine* 37, 246-249.

Verma RK, Srivastava PC, Sinha US, Kaul A (2015). Study of unnatural deaths in married females within seven years of marriage in Allahabad. *Journal of Indian Academy of Forensic Medicine* 37, 405-409.

Wada K, Gilmour S (2016). Inequality in mortality by occupation related to economic crisis from 1980 to 2010 among working-age Japanese males. *Scientific Reports* 6, 22255.

Yoshioka E, Hanley SJ, Kawanishi Y, Saijo Y (2016). Time trends in method-specific suicide rates in Japan, 1990-2011. *Epidemiology and Psychiatric Sciences* 25, 58-68.

Yoshioka E, Saijo Y, Kawachi I (2016). Spatial and temporal evolution of the epidemic of char-coal-burning suicide in Japan. *Social Psychiatry and Psychiatric Epidemiology* 51, 857-868.

Yur'yev A, Yur'ye L (2015). Suicide mortality at time of armed conflict in Ukraine. *European Journal of Public Health*. Published online: 29 September 2016. doi: 10.1093/eurpub/ckv188.

Risk and protective factors

Anderberg J, Bogren M, Mattisson C, Bradvik L (2016). Long-term suicide risk in anxiety-The Lundby Study 1947-2011. *Archives of Suicide Research*. Published online: 8 March 2016. doi: 10.1080/13811118.2015.1057663.

Andrade-Machado R, Benjumea-Cuartas V, Santos-Santos A, Sosa-Dubon MA, Garcia-Espinosa A, Andrade-Gutierrez G (2015). Mortality in patients with refractory temporal lobe epilepsy at a tertiary center in Cuba. *Epilepsy and Behavior* 53, 154-160.

Andronicos M, Beauchamp G, Robert M, Besson J, Séguin M (2016). Male gamblers – suicide victims and living controls: Comparison of adversity over the life course. *International Gambling Studies* 16, 140-155.

Anestis MD (2015). Prior suicide attempts are less common in suicide decedents who died by firearms relative to those who died by other means. *Journal of Affective Disorders* 189, 106-109.

Antonakakis N, Collins A (2015). The impact of fiscal austerity on suicide mortality: Evidence across the 'Eurozone periphery'. *Social Science and Medicine* 145, 63-78.

Arias SA, Miller I, Camargo CA, Jr., Sullivan AF, Goldstein AB, Allen MH, Manton AP, Boudreaux ED (2015). Factors associated with suicide outcomes 12 months after screening positive for suicide risk in the emergency department. *Psychiatric Services* 62, 206-213.

Arnautovska U, McPhedran S, De Leo D (2015). Differences in characteristics between suicide cases of farm managers compared to those of farm labourers in Queensland, Australia. *Rural Remote Health* 15, 3250.

Arora VS, Stuckler D, McKee M (2016). Tracking search engine queries for suicide in the United Kingdom, 2004-2013. *Public Health*. Published online: 11 March 2016. doi: 10.1016/j.puhe.2015.10.015.

Bach H, Arango V, Kassir SA, Dwork AJ, Mann JJ, Underwood MD (2016). Cigarette smoking and tryptophan hydroxylase 2 mRNA in the dorsal raphe nucleus in suicides. *Archives of Suicide Research*. Published online: 8 March 2016. doi: 10.1080/13811118.2015.1048398.

Bálint L, Osváth P, Rihmer Z, Döme P (2016). Associations between marital and educational status and risk of completed suicide in Hungary. *Journal of Affective Disorders* 190, 777-783.

Barr B, Taylor-Robinson D, Stuckler D, Loopstra R, Reeves A, Whitehead M (2016). 'First, do no harm': Are disability assessments associated with adverse trends in mental health? A longitudinal ecological study. *Journal of Epidemiology and Community Health* 70, 339-345.

Bjorksten KS, Bjerregaard P (2015). Season of birth in Inuit suicide victims born in traditional or modern lifestyle are different. *International Psychogeriatrics* 27, S126-S127.

Blázquez-Fernández C, Cantarero-Prieto D, Pascual-Sáez M (2016). What does it drive the relationship between suicides and economic conditions? New evidence from Spain. *Social Indicators Research*. Published online: 9 January 2016. doi: 10.1007/s11205-016-1236-2.

Boffin N, Moreels S, Van Casteren V (2015). Trends from the surveillance of suicidal behaviour by the Belgian Network of Sentinel General Practices over two decades: A retrospective observational study. *British Medical Journal Open* 5, e008584.

Bozsonyi K, Osvath P, Fekete S, Balint L (2015). The effects of significant international sports events on Hungarian suicide rates. *Crisis*. Published online: 17 November 2015. doi: 10.1027/0227-5910/a000352.

Branas CC, Han S, Wiebe DJ (2016). Alcohol use and firearm violence. *Epidemiologic Reviews* 38, 32-45.

Bryleva EY, Brundin L (2016). Kynurenine pathway metabolites and suicidality. *Neuropharmacology*. Published online: 26 January 2016. doi: 10.1016/j.neuropharm.2016.01.034.

Bullman T, Hoffmire C, Schneiderman A, Bossarte R (2015). Time dependent gender differences in suicide risk among Operation Enduring Freedom and Operation Iraqi Freedom veterans. *Annals of Epidemiology* 25, 964-965.

Carretta CM, Burgess AW, Welner M (2015). Gaps in crisis mental health: Suicide and homicide-suicide. *Archives of Psychiatric Nursing* 29, 339-345.

Castelein S, Liemburg EJ, de Lange JS, van Es FD, Visser E, Aleman A, Bruggemans R, Knegtering H (2015). Drop in suicide rate after first psychosis: A comparison with the situation two decades ago. *Nederlands Tijdschrift Voor Geneeskunde* 159, A9565.

Castelpietra G, Gobbato M, Valent F, Bovenzi M, Barbone F, Clagnan E, Pascolo-Fabrici E, Balestrieri M, Isacsson G (2015). Somatic disorders and antidepressant use in suicides: A population-based study from the Friuli Venezia Giulia region, Italy, 2003-2013. *Journal of Psychosomatic Research* 79, 372-377.

Cerel J, Singleton MD, Brown MM, Brown SV, Bush HM, Brancado CJ (2015). Emergency department visits prior to suicide and homicide. *Crisis* 37, 5-12.

Chang SS, Bjorngaard JH, Tsai MK, Bjerkeset O, Wen CP, Yip PS, Tsao CK, Gunnell D (2015). Heart rate and suicide: Findings from two cohorts of 533 000 Taiwanese and 75 000 Norwegian adults. *Acta Psychiatrica Scandinavicaa* 133, 277-288.

Chen Y-Y, Tsai C-W, Biddle L, Niederkrotenthaler T, Wu KC-C, Gunnell D (2016). Newspaper reporting and the emergence of charcoal burning suicide in Taiwan: A mixed methods approach. *Journal of Affective Disorders* 193, 355-361.

Cheng Q, Chang SS, Guo Y, Yip PS (2015). Information accessibility of the charcoal burning suicide method in mainland China. *PLoS One* 10, e0140686.

Cho SE, Na KS, Cho SJ, Im JS, Kang SG (2016). Geographical and temporal variations in the prevalence of mental disorders in suicide: Systematic review and meta-analysis. *Journal of Affective Disorders* 190, 704-713.

Chock MM, Bommersbach TJ, Geske JL, Bostwick JM (2015). Patterns of health care usage in the year before suicide: A population-based case-control study. *Mayo Clinic Proceedings* 90, 1475-1481.

Chung RY, Yip BH, Chan SS, Wong SY (2015). Cohort effects of suicide mortality are sex specific in the rapidly developed Hong Kong Chinese population, 1976-2010. *Depression and Anxiety.* Published online: 28 September 2015. doi: 10.1002/da.22431.

Cleary A (2016). Help-seeking patterns and attitudes to treatment amongst men who attempted suicide. *Journal of Mental Health.* Published online: 4 March 2016. doi: 10.3109/09638237.2016.1149800.

Clerici CA, Gentile G, Marchesi M, Muccino E, Veneroni L, Zoja R (2016). Two decades of adolescent suicides assessed at Milan University's Medicolegal Unit: Epidemiology, forensic pathology and psychopathology. *Journal of Forensic and Legal Medicine* 37, 15-21.

Coimbra DG, Pereira E Silva AC, de Sousa-Rodrigues CF, Barbosa FT, de Siqueira Figueredo D, Araújo Santos JL, Barbosa MR, de Medeiros Alves V, Nardi AE, de Andrade TG (2016). Do suicide attempts occur more frequently in the spring too? A systematic review and rhythmic analysis. *Journal of Affective Disorders* 196, 125-137.

Conner KR, Lathrop S, Caetano R, Silenzio V, Nolte KB (2016). Blood alcohol concentrations in suicide and motor vehicle crash decedents ages 18 to 54. *Alcoholism: Clinical and Experimental Research* 40, 772-775.

Coryell W, Kriener A, Butcher B, Nurnberger J, McMahon F, Berrettini W, Fiedorowicz J (2015). Risk factors for suicide in bipolar I disorder in two prospectively studied cohorts. *Journal of Affective Disorders* 190, 1-5.

Cuadrado C, Zitko P, Covarrubias T, Hernandez D, Sade C, Klein C, Gomez A (2015). Association between adolescent suicide and sociodemographic factors in Chile: Cross-sectional ecological study. *Crisis* 36, 281-290.

Dalela D, Krishna N, Okwara J, Preston MA, Abdollah F, Choueiri TK, Reznor G, Sammon JD, Schmid M, Kibel AS, Nguyen PL, Menon M, Trinh QD (2015). Suicide and accidental deaths among patients with non-metastatic prostate cancer. *BJU International.* Published online: 19 September 2015. doi: 10.1111/bju.13257.

Denneson LM, Williams HB, Kaplan MS, McFarland BH, Dobscha SK (2016). Treatment of veterans with mental health symptoms in VA primary care prior to suicide. *General Hospital Psychiatry* 38, 65-70.

Devorak J, Torres-Platas SG, Davoli MA, Prud'homme J, Turecki G, Mechawar N (2015). Cellular and molecular inflammatory profile of the choroid plexus in depression and suicide. *Frontiers in Psychiatry* 6, 138.

Ding M, Satija A, Bhupathiraju SN, Hu Y, Sun Q, Han J, Lopez-Garcia E, Willett W, van Dam RM, Hu FB (2015). Association of coffee consumption with total and cause-specific mortality in three large prospective cohorts. *Circulation* 132, 2305-2315.

dos Santos JP, Tavares M, Barros PP (2016). More than just numbers: Suicide rates and the economic cycle in Portugal (1910-2013). *SSM - Population Health* 2, 14-23.

Drake SA, Garza B, Cron SG, Wolf DA (2015). Suicide within 72 hours after discharge from health care settings: Decedent characteristics. *American Journal of Forensic Medicine and Pathology* 37, 32-34.

Ersen B, Kahveci R, Saki MC, Tunali O, Aksu I (2015). Analysis of 41 suicide attempts by wrist cutting: A retrospective analysis. *European Journal of Trauma and Emergency Surgery.* Published online: 1 December 2015. doi: 10.1007/s00068-015-0599-4.

Escolas SM, Archuleta DJ, Orman JA, Chung KK, Renz EM (2015). Postdischarge cause-of-death analysis of combat-related burn patients. *Journal of Burn Care and Research.* Published online: 1 December 2015. doi: 10.1097/BCR.0000000000000319.

Farstad SM, von Ranson KM, Hodgins DC, El-Guebaly N, Casey DM, Schopflocher DP (2015). The influence of impulsiveness on binge eating and problem gambling: A prospective study of gender differences in Canadian adults. *Psychology of Addictive Behaviors* 29, 805-812.

Fegg M, Kraus S, Graw M, Bausewein C (2016). Physical compared to mental diseases as reasons for committing suicide: A retrospective study. *BMC Palliative Care* 15, e14.

Feigelman W, Joiner T, Rosen Z, Silva C, Mueller AS (2016). Contrasts between young males dying by suicide, those dying from other causes and those still living: Observations from the national longitudinal survey of adolescent to adult health. *Archives of Suicide Research.* Published online: 11 January 2016. doi: 10.1080/13811118.2015.1104270.

Fernandez-Cabana M, Ceballos-Espinoza F, Mateos R, Teresa Alves-Perez M, Alberto Garcia-Caballero A (2015). Suicide notes: Clinical and linguistic analysis from the perspective of the interpersonal theory of suicide. *European Journal of Psychiatry* 29, 293-308.

Fountoulakis KN, Savopoulos C, Zannis P, Apostolopoulou M, Fountoukidis I, Kakaletsis N, Kanellos I, Dimellis D, Hyphantis T, Tsikerdekis A, Pompili M, Hatzitolios AI (2016). Climate change but not unemployment explains the changing suicidality in Thessaloniki Greece (2000-2012). *Journal of Affective Disorders* 193, 331-338.

Fralick M, Thiruchelvam D, Tien HC, Redelmeier DA (2016). Risk of suicide after a concussion. *Canadian Medical Association Journal.* Published online: 8 February 2016. doi: 10.1503/cmaj.150790.

Fudalej S, Kopera M, Wolynczyk-Gmaj D, Fudalej M, Krajewski P, Wasilewska K, Szymanski K, Chojnicka I, Podgorska A, Wojnar M, Ploski R (2015). Association between FKBP5 functional polymorphisms and completed suicide. *Neuropsychobiology* 72, 126-131.

Galway K, Gossrau-Breen D, Mallon S, Hughes L, Rosato M, Rondon-Sulbaran J, Leavey G (2015). Substance misuse in life and death in a 2-year cohort of suicides. *British Journal of Psychiatry* 208, 292-297.

Gillies D, Chicop D, O'Halloran P (2015). Root cause analyses of suicides of mental health clients. *Crisis* 36, 316-324.

Giupponi G, Conca A, Innamorati M, Forte A, Lester D, Erbuto D, Pycha R, Girardi P, Moller-Leimkuhler AM, Pompili M (2015). Differences among South Tyrolean suicides: A psychological autopsy study. *Wiener klinische Wochenschrift* 128, 125-130.

González-Castro TB, Hernández-Díaz Y, Tovilla-Zárate CA, González-Gutiérrez KP, Fresán A, Juárez-Rojop IE, López-Narváez L, Villar Soto M, Genis A (2015). Differences by gender in completed suicides in a Mexican population: A psychological autopsy study. *Journal of Forensic and Legal Medicine* 38, 70-74.

Gorton HC, Webb RT, Kapur N, Ashcroft DM (2016). Non-psychotropic medication and risk of suicide or attempted suicide: A systematic review. *British Medical Journal Open* 6, e009074.

Goulas E, Zervoyianni A (2016). IMF-lending programs and suicide mortality. *Social Science and Medicine* 153, 44-53.

Guldin M-B, Li J, Pedersen HS, Obel C, Agerbo E, Gissler M, Cnattingius S, Olsen J, Vestergaard M (2015). Incidence of suicide among persons who had a parent who died during their childhood: A population-based cohort study. *Journal of the American Medical Association Psychiatry* 72, 1227-1234.

Hagaman AK, Sivilli TI, Ao T, Blanton C, Ellis H, Lopes Cardozo B, Shetty S (2016). An investigation into suicides among Bhutanese refugees resettled in the United States between 2008 and 2011. *Journal of Immigrant and Minority Health*. Published online: 1 January 2016. doi: 10.1007/s10903-015-0326-6.

Harmancı FM, Mus E, Tosun H, Tascı U (2015). Why do Turkish police officers commit suicides? Analysis of suicide cases between 2001 and 2012. *European Scientific Journal* 11, 268-285.

Hawkins M, Schaffer A, Reis C, Sinyor M, Herrmann N, Lanctôt KL (2016). Suicide in males and females with cardiovascular disease and comorbid depression. *Journal of Affective Disorders* 197, 88-93.

Hodwitz O, Frey K (2016). Anomic suicide: A Durkheimian analysis of European normlessness. *Sociological Spectrum* 36, 236-254.

Hogberg G, Antonuccio DO, Healy D (2015). Suicidal risk from TADS study was higher than it first appeared. *International Journal of Risk and Safety in Medicine* 27, 85-91.

Hughes JR (2016). Varenicline as a cause of suicidal outcomes. *Nicotine & Tobacco Research* 18, 2-9.

Hung GCL, Cheng CT, Jhong JR, Tsai SY, Chen CC, Kuo CJ (2015). Risk and protective factors for suicide mortality among patients with alcohol dependence. *Journal of Clinical Psychiatry* 76, 1687-1693.

Hunt IM, Clements C, Saini P, Rahman MS, Shaw J, Appleby L, Kapur N, Windfuhr K (2015). Suicide after absconding from inpatient care in England: An exploration of mental health professionals' experiences. *Journal of Mental Health* 25, 245-253.

Hussey I, Barnes-Holmes D, Booth R (2016). Individuals with current suicidal ideation demonstrate implicit "fearlessness of death". *Journal of Behavior Therapy and Experimental Psychiatry* 51, 1-9.

Ilgen MA, Bohnert ASB, Ganoczy D, Bair MJ, McCarthy JF, Blow FC (2016). Opioid dose and risk of suicide. *Pain* 157, 1079-7084.

Inoue K, Fujita Y, Nishimura M, Fukunaga T, Tatebayashi H, Moriwaki S, Uchida T, Funo Y, Murakami Y, Matsuchika M, Okazaki Y, Fujita Y (2015). Looking at the proportion of individuals who were unemployed for a prolonged period in years before and after an abrupt increase in suicides in Japan. *International Medical Journal* 22, 288-290.

Inoue K, Fujita Y, Takeshita H, Abe S, Fujihara J, Ezoe S, Sampei M, Miyaoka T, Horiguchi J, Okazaki Y, Fukunaga T (2015). A long-term study of the association between the relative poverty rate and suicide rate in Japan. *Journal of Forensic Sciences* 61, S140-S143.

Inoue K, Fukunaga T, Okazaki Y, Amano H, Kobayashi-Miura M, Fujita Y (2015). Are trends in the number of department store staff an indicator of trends in suicide rates? Based on a study over a 20-year period in Tokyo, Japan. *International Medical Journal* 22, 136-137.

Jang SA, Sung JM, Park JY, Jeon WT (2016). Copycat suicide induced by entertainment celebrity suicides in South Korea. *Psychiatry Investigation* 13, 74-81.

Jia C-x, Zhang J (2015). Confucian values, negative life events, and rural young suicide with major depression in China. *Omega* 0, 1-12.

Johannsen BM, Larsen JT, Laursen TM, Bergink V, Meltzer-Brody S, Munk-Olsen T (2016). All-cause mortality in women with severe postpartum psychiatric disorders. *American Journal of Psychiatry*. Published online: 4 March 2016. doi: 10.1176/appi.ajp.2015.14121510.

Jokinen J, Mattsson P, Nordstrom P, Samuelsson M (2016). High early suicide risk in elderly patients after self-poisoning. *Archives of Suicide Research*. Published online: 16 March 2016. doi: 10.1080/13811118.2016.1162239.

Jones DA, Paton D (2015). How does legalization of physician-assisted suicide affect rates of suicide? *Southern Medical Journal* 108, 599-604.

Joo S-H, Wang S-M, Kim T-W, Seo H-J, Jeong J-H, Han J-H, Hong S-C (2015). Factors associated with suicide completion: A comparison between suicide attempters and completers. *Asia-Pacific Psychiatry* 8, 80-86.

Joory K, Farroha A, Moiemen N (2015). Is a self-inflicted burn part of a repeated self-harm pattern? *Annals of Burns and Fire Disasters* 28, 223-227.

Kalesan B, Mobily ME, Vasan S, Siegel M, Galea S (2016). The role of interpersonal conflict as a determinant of firearm-related homicide-suicides at different ages. *Journal of Interpersonal Violence*. Published online: 3 February 2016. doi: 10.1177/0886260516629387.

Kam D, Salib A, Gorgy G, Patel TD, Carniol ET, Eloy JA, Baredes S, Park RC (2015). Incidence of suicide in patients with head and neck cancer. *JAMA Otolaryngology Head & Neck Surgery* 141, 1075-1081.

Kawaguchi H, Koike S (2016). Association between the density of physicians and suicide rates in Japan: Nationwide ecological study using a Spatial Bayesian Model. *PLoS One*. Published online: 3 February 2016 doi: 10.1371/journal.pone.0148288.

Keadle SK, Moore SC, Sampson JN, Xiao Q, Albanes D, Matthews CE (2015). Causes of death associated with prolonged TV viewing: NIH-AARP diet and health study. *American Journal of Preventative Medicine* 49, 811-821.

Khalifeh H, Hunt IM, Appleby L, Howard LM (2015). Suicide in perinatal and non-perinatal women in contact with psychiatric services: 15 year findings from a UK national inquiry. *Lancet Psychiatry* 3, 233-242.

Kim D (2016). The associations between us state and local social spending, income inequality, and individual all-cause and cause-specific mortality: The national longitudinal mortality study. *Preventive Medicine* 84, 62-68.

Kim M-G, Ryoo J-H, Chang S-J, Kim C-B, Park J-K, Koh S-B, Ahn Y-S (2015). Blood lead levels and cause-specific mortality of inorganic lead-exposed workers in South Korea. *PLoS One* 10, e0140360.

Kimerling R, Makin-Byrd K, Louzon S, Ignacio RV, McCarthy JF (2015). Military sexual trauma and suicide mortality. *American Journal of Preventative Medicine*. Published online: 14 December 2015. doi: 10.1016/j.amepre.2015.10.019.

Klaassen Z, DiBianco JM, Jen RP, Harper B, Yaguchi G, Reinstatler L, Woodard C, Moses KA, Terris MK, Madi R (2015). The impact of radical cystectomy and urinary diversion on suicidal death in patients with bladder cancer. *Journal of Wound, Ostomy, and Continence Nursing* 43, 152-157.

Kposowa A, Hamilton D, Wang K (2016). Impact of firearm availability and gun regulation on state suicide rates. *Suicide and Life-Threatening Behavior*. Published online: 21 March 2016. doi: 10.1111/sltb.1224.

Krzyżanowska M, Steiner J, Karnecki K, Kaliszan M, Brisch R, Wiergowski M, Braun K, Jankowski Z, Gos T (2015). Decreased ribosomal DNA transcription in dorsal raphe nucleus neurons differentiates between suicidal and non-suicidal death. *European Archives of Psychiatry and Clinical Neuroscience* 266, 217-224.

Kurokouchi M, Miyatake N, Kinoshita H, Tanaka N, Fukunaga T (2015). Correlation between suicide and meteorological parameters. *Medicina* 51, 363-367.

Lariscy JT, Nau C, Firebaugh G, Hummer RA (2015). Hispanic-white differences in lifespan variability in the United States. *Demography* 53, 215-239.

Laursen TM, Musliner KL, Benros ME, Vestergaard M, Munk-Olsen T (2016). Mortality and life expectancy in persons with severe unipolar depression. *Journal of Affective Disorders* 193, 203-207.

Lee D, Lee H, Choi M (2016). Examining the relationship between past orientation and us suicide rates: An analysis using big data-driven google search queries. *Journal of Medical Internet Research* 18, e35.

Levi L, Werbeloff N, Pugachova I, Yoffe R, Large M, Davidson M, Weiser M (2016). Has deinstitutionalization affected inpatient suicide? Psychiatric inpatient suicide rates between 1990 and 2013 in Israel. *Schizophrenia Research* 173, 75-78.

Levine SZ, Levav I, Yoffe R, Becher Y, Pugachova I (2016). Genocide exposure and subsequent suicide risk: A population-based study. *PLoS One* 11, e0149524.

Lin YW, Huang HC, Lin MF, Shyu ML, Tsai PL, Chang HJ (2016). Influential factors for and outcomes of hospitalized patients with suicide-related behaviors: A national record study in Taiwan from 1997-2010. *PLoS One* 11, e0149559.

Lize SE, Scheyett AM, Morgan CR, Proescholdbell SK, Norwood T, Edwards D (2015). Violent death rates and risk for released prisoners in North Carolina. *Violence and Victims* 30, 1019-1127.

Loftfield E, Freedman ND, Graubard BI, Guertin KA, Black A, Huang WY, Shebl FM, Mayne ST, Sinha R (2015). Association of coffee consumption with overall and cause-specific mortality in a large US prospective cohort study. *American Journal of Epidemiology* 182, 1010-1022.

Mallon S, Galway K, Hughes L, Rondon-Sulbaran J, Leavey G (2016). An exploration of integrated data on the social dynamics of suicide among women. *Sociology of Health Illness* 38, 662-675.

McGinty EE, Choksy S, Wintemute GJ (2016). The relationship between controlled substances and violence. *Epidemiologic Reviews* 38, 5-31.

McPhedran S, Eriksson L, Mazerolle P, De Leo D, Johnson H, Wortley R (2015). Characteristics of homicide-suicide in Australia: A comparison with homicide-only and suicide-only cases. *Journal of Interpersonal Violence*. Published online: 8 December 2015. doi: 10.1177/0886260515619172.

Menon V, Kattimani S (2015). Suicide and serotonin: Making sense of evidence. *Indian Journal of Psychological Medicine* 37, 377-378.

Mento C, Presti EL, Mucciardi M, Sinardi A, Liotta M, Settineri S (2015). Serious suicide attempts: Evidence on variables for manage and prevent this phenomenon. *Community Mental Health Journal.* Published online: 23 September 2015. doi: 10.1007/s10597-015-9933-x.

Monsef Kasmaee V, Zohrevandi B, Asadi P, Shakouri N (2015). Non-judicial hanging in Guilan Province, Iran between 2011 and 2013. *Emergency* 3, 155-158.

Moore MD (2015). Religious heterogeneity and suicide: A cross-national analysis. *Social Compass* 62, 649-663.

Moqaddasi Amiri M, Ahmadi Livani A, Moosazadeh M, Mirzajani M, Dehghan A (2015). Seasonal pattern in suicide in Iran. *Iranian Journal of Psychiatry and Behavioral Sciences* 9, e842.

Nkhoma ET, Coumbis J, Farr AM, Johnston SS, Chu BC, Rosenblatt LC, Seekins D, Villasis-Keever A (2016). No evidence of an association between Efavirenz exposure and suicidality among HIV patients initiating antiretroviral therapy in a retrospective cohort study of real world data. *Medicine* 95, e2480.

O'Neill S, Corry C, McFeeters D, Murphy S, Bunting B (2015). Suicide in Northern Ireland. *Crisis* 37, 13-20.

Oakes-Rogers S, Slade K (2015). Rethinking pathways to completed suicide by female prisoners. *Journal of Mental Health Training, Education and Practice* 10, 245-255.

Onishi K (2015). Risk factors and social background associated with suicide in Japan: A review. *Japan-Hospitals* 2015, 35-50.

Orellana JD, Balieiro AA, Fonseca FR, Basta PC, Souza ML (2016). Spatial-temporal trends and risk of suicide in central Brazil: An ecological study contrasting indigenous and non-indigenous populations. *Revista Brasileira de Psiquiatria.* Published online: 19 January 2016. doi: 10.1590/1516-4446-2015-1720.

Pandey GN, Rizavi HS, Zhang H, Bhaumik R, Ren X (2016). The expression of the suicide-associated gene SKA2 is decreased in the prefrontal cortex of suicide victims, but not of non-suicidal patients. *International Journal of Neuropsychopharmacology.* Published online: 22 February 2016. doi: 10.1093/ijnp/pyw015.

Paraschakis A, Michopoulos I, Christodoulou C, Koutsaftis F, Douzenis A (2015). Characteristics of suicide victims who had verbally communicated suicidal feelings to their family members. *Psychiatria Danubina* 27, 230-235.

Pompili M, Innamorati M, Milelli M, Battuello M, Erbuto D, Lester D, Gonda X, Rihmer Z, Amore M, Girardi P (2016). Temperaments in completed suicides: Are they different from those in suicide attempters and controls? *Comprehensive Psychiatry* 65, 98-102.

Poorolajal J, Haghtalab T, Farhadi M, Darvishi N (2015). Substance use disorder and risk of suicidal ideation, suicide attempt and suicide death: A meta-analysis. *Journal of Public Health.* Published online: 26 October 2015. doi: 10.1093/pubmed/fdv148.

Rahu K, Rahu M, Tekkel M, Veidebaum T, Hakulinen T, Auvinen A, Bigbee WL, Hartshorne MF, Inskip PD, Boice JD (2015). Chernobyl cleanup workers from Estonia: Cohort description and related epidemiological research. *Journal of Radiological Protection* 35, r35-r45.

Rajkumar AP, Senthilkumar P, Gayathri K, Shyamsundar G, Jacob KS (2015). Associations between the macroeconomic indicators and suicide rates in India: Two ecological studies. *Indian Journal of Psychological Medicine* 37, 277-281.

Reeves A, Stuckler D (2016). Suicidality, economic shocks, and egalitarian gender norms. *European Sociological Review* 32, 39-53.

Rivera B, Casal B, Currais L (2016). Crisis, suicide and labour productivity losses in Spain. *European Journal of Health Economics.* Published online: 22 January 2016. doi: 10.1007/s10198-015-0760-3.

Roberts E, Wessely S, Chalder T, Chang CK, Hotopf M (2016). Mortality of people with chronic fatigue syndrome: A retrospective cohort study in England and Wales from the South London and Maudsley NHS Foundation Trust Biomedical Research Centre (SLaM BRC) Clinical Record Interactive Search (CRIS) Register. *Lancet* 387, 1638-1643.

Rojas Y, Stenberg S-A (2015). Evictions and suicide: A follow-up study of almost 22 000 swedish households in the wake of the global financial crisis. *Journal of Epidemiology and Community Health.* Published online: 4 November 2015. doi: 10.1136/jech-2015-206419.

Ropret S, Zupanc T, Komel R, Videtic Paska A (2015). Investigating the associations between polymorphisms in the NTRK2 and NGFR genes and completed suicide in the Slovenian sample. *Psychiatric Genetics 25, 241-248.*

Ropret S, Zupanc T, Komel R, Videti Paska A (2015). Data in support of association study of the brain-derived neurotrophic factor gene SNPS and completed suicide in the Slovenian sample. *Data in Brief 4, 529-533.*

Runeson B, Haglund A, Lichtenstein P, Tidemalm D (2016). Suicide risk after nonfatal self-harm: A national cohort study, 2000-2008. *Journal of Clinical Psychiatry* 77, 240-246.

Schinka JA, Bossarte RM, Curtiss G, Lapcevic WA, Casey RJ (2015). Increased mortality among older veterans admitted to VA homelessness programs. *Psychiatric Services* 67, 465-468.

Shahpesandy H, Oakes M, van Heeswijck A (2014). The Isle of Wight suicide study: A case study of suicide in a limited geographic area. *Irish Journal of Psychological Medicine* 31, 133-141.

Sher L (2015). Are suicide rates related to the psychiatrist density? A cross-national study. *Frontiers in Public Health* 3, e280.

Shiotsuki I, Terao T, Ishii N, Takeuchi S, Kuroda Y, Kohno K, Mizokami Y, Hatano K, Tanabe S, Kanehisa M, Iwata N, Matusda S (2016). Trace lithium is inversely associated with male suicide after adjustment of climatic factors. *Journal of Affective Disorders* 189, 282-286.

Silva C, Chu C, Monahan KR, Joiner TE (2015). Suicide risk among sexual minority college students: A mediated moderation model of sex and perceived burdensomeness. *Psychology of Sexual Orientation and Gender Diversity* 2, 22-33.

Sohn J, Kang DR, Kim HC, Cho J, Choi YJ, Kim C, Suh I (2015). Elevation of serum aminotransferase levels and future risk of death from external causes: A prospective cohort study in Korea. *Yonsei Medical Journal* 56, 1582-1589.

Steeg S, Haigh M, Webb RT, Kapur N, Awenat Y, Gooding P, Pratt D, Cooper J (2015). The exacerbating influence of hopelessness on other known risk factors for repeat self-harm and suicide. *Journal of Affective Disorders* 190, 522-528.

Stein GN, Pretorius A, Stein DJ, Sinclair H (2016). The association between pathological gambling and suicidality in treatment-seeking pathological gamblers in South Africa. *Annals of Clinical Psychiatry* 28, 43-50.

Sun BQ, Zhang J (2016). Economic and sociological correlates of suicides: Multilevel analysis of the time series data in the United Kingdom. *Journal of Forensic Sciences* 61, 345-351.

Sun Y, Lin C-C, Lu C-J, Hsu C-Y, Kao C-H (2016). Association between zolpidem and suicide: A nationwide population-based case-control study. *Mayo Clinic Proceedings* 91, 308-315.

Taktak S, Kumral B, Unsal A, Ozdes T, Aliustaoglu S, Yazici YA, Celik S (2016). Evidence for an association between suicide and religion: A 33-year retrospective autopsy analysis of suicide by hanging during the month of Ramadan in Istanbul. *Australian Journal of Forensic Sciences* 48, 121-131.

Tang KT, Lin CH, Chen HH, Chen YH, Chen DY (2015). Suicidal drug overdose in patients with systemic lupus erythematosus, a nationwide population-based case-control study. *Lupus* 25, 199-203.

Termorshuizen F, Smeets HM, Boks MP, Heerdink ER (2016). Comparing episodes of antide-pressants use with intermittent episodes of no use: A higher relative risk of suicide attempts but not of suicide at young age. *Journal of Psychopharmacology*. Published online 22 March 2016. doi: 10.1177/0269881116639752.

Thibodeau L, Lachaud J (2016). Impact of economic fluctuations on suicide mortality in canada (1926-2008): Testing the Durkheim, Ginsberg and Henry and short theories. *Death Studies* 27, 305-315.

Tondo L, Pompili M, Forte A, Baldessarini RJ (2015). Suicide attempts in bipolar disorders: Comprehensive review of 101 reports. *Acta Psychiatrica Scandinavica* 133, 174-186.

Tong Y, Phillips MR, Conner KR (2015). DSM-IV axis II personality disorders and suicide and attempted suicide in China. *British Journal of Psychiatry*. Published online: 19 November 2015. doi: 10.1192/bjp.bp.114.151076.

Trigylidas TE, Reynolds EM, Teshome G, Dykstra HK, Lichenstein R (2016). Paediatric suicide in the USA: Analysis of the national child death case reporting system. *Injury Prevention*. Published online: 18 January 2016. doi: 10.1136/injuryprev-2015-041796.

Tuck A, Bhui K, Nanchahal K, McKenzie K (2015). Suicide rates for different religious groups in the South Asian origin population in England and Wales: A secondary analysis of a national data set. *International Journal of Human Rights in Healthcare* 8, 260-266.

Turnbull P, Webb R, Kapur N, Clements C, Bergen H, Hawton K, Ness J, Waters K, Townsend E, Cooper J (2015). Variation by ethnic group in premature mortality risk following self-harm: A multicentre cohort study in England. *BMC Psychiatry* 15, e254.

Umetsu M, Otsuka K, Endo J, Yoshioka Y, Koizumi F, Mizugai A, Onuma Y, Mita T, Kudo K, Sanjo K, Fukumoto K, Nakamura H, Sakai A, Endo S (2015). Usefulness of and factors associated with Global Assessment Scale (GAS) scores in suicide attempters. *Journal of Psychiatry* 18, 203.

Vandoros S, Kavetsos G (2015). Now or later? Understanding the etiologic period of suicide. *Preventive Medicine Reports* 2, 809-811.

Vannoy SD, Andrews BK, Srebnik D (2016). Suicide after evaluation for involuntary psychiatric commitment-who gets them and what influences survival time? *Suicide and Life-Threatening Behavior*. Published online: 21 March 2016. doi: 10.1111/sltb.12245.

Vijaykumar Nair G, Nagamohan Rao BV, Jagannatha SR, Pradeep Kumar MV (2016). Profile of suicidal deaths – a retrospective study. *Journal of South India Medicolegal Association* 8, 36-40.

Villejo SJ (2015). Classification and prediction of suicidal tendencies of the youth in the Philippines: An empirical study. *Philippine Statistician* 64, 31-52.

Voros V, Osvath P, Vincze O, Pusztay K, Fekete S, Rihmer Z (2016). Word use and content analysis of the first verses of six national anthems: A transcultural aspect of suicidal behaviour. *Psychiatria Danubina* 28, 82-85.

Voshaar RCO, van der Veen DC, Hunt I, Kapur N (2016). Suicide in late-life depression with and without comorbid anxiety disorders. *International Journal of Geriatric Psychiatry* 31, 146-152.

Wada K, Eguchi H, Prieto-Merino D, Smith DR (2016). Occupational differences in suicide mortality among Japanese men of working age. *Journal of Affective Disorders* 190, 316-321.

Wang M, Bjorkenstam C, Alexanderson K, Runeson B, Tinghog P, Mittendorfer-Rutz E (2015). Trajectories of work-related functional impairment prior to suicide. *PLoS One* 10, e0139937.

Weiser M, Goldberg S, Werbeloff N, Fenchel D, Reichenberg A, Shelef L, Large M, Davidson M, Fruchter E (2015). Risk of completed suicide in 89,049 young males assessed by a mental health professional. *European Neuropsychopharmacology* 26, 341-349.

Wennerstrom EC, Simonsen J, Melbye M (2015). Long-term survival of individuals born small and large for gestational age. *PLoS One* 10, e0138594.

Werbeloff N, Dohrenwend BP, Levav I, Haklai Z, Yoffe R, Large M, Davidson M, Weiser M (2015). Demographic, behavioral, and psychiatric risk factors for suicide. *Crisis*. Published online: 23 December 2015. doi: 10.1027/0227-5910/a000359.

Yamauchi T, Inagaki M, Yonemoto N, Iwasaki M, Akechi T, Sawada N, Iso H, Noda M, Tsugane S (2016). History of diabetes and risk of suicide and accidental death in Japan: The Japan public health centre-based prospective study, 1990-2012. *Diabetes & Metabolism*. Published online: 18 January 2016. doi: 10.1016/j.diabet.2015.11.008.

Yi SW, Jung M, Kimm H, Sull JW, Lee E, Lee KO, Ohrr H (2016). Usual alcohol consumption and suicide mortality among the Korean elderly in rural communities: Kangwha cohort study. *Journal of Epidemiology and Community Health*. Published online: 17 February 2016. doi: 10.1136/jech-2015-206849.

Yin H, Pantazatos SP, Galfalvy H, Huang YY, Rosoklija GB, Dwork AJ, Burke A, Arango V, Oquendo MA, Man J (2016). A pilot integrative genomics study of GABA and glutamate neurotransmitter systems in suicide, suicidal behavior, and major depressive disorder. *American Journal of Medical Genetics Part B: Neuropsychiatric Genetics* 171, 414-426.

Prevention

Anestis MD, Anestis JC (2015). Suicide rates and state laws regulating access and exposure to handguns. *American Journal of Public Health* 105, 2049-2058.

Chung YW, Kang SJ, Matsubayashi T, Sawada Y, Ueda M (2016). The effectiveness of platform screen doors for the prevention of subway suicides in South Korea. *Journal of Affective Disorders* 194, 80-83.

Creighton GM, Oliffe JL, Lohan M, Ogrodniczuk JS, Palm E (2016). "Things I did not know": Retrospectives on a Canadian rural male youth suicide using an instrumental photovoice case study. *Health.* Published online: 15 March 2016. doi: 10.1177/1363459316638542.

Cwik MF, Tingey L, Wilkinson R, Goklish N, Larzelere-Hinton F, Barlow A (2016). Suicide prevention gatekeeper training: Can they advance prevention in Indian country? *Archives of Suicide Research.* Published online: 24 February 2016. doi: 10.1080/13811118.2015.1033122.

Langdon SE, Golden SL, Arnold EM, Maynor RF, Bryant A, Freeman VK, Bell RA (2016). Lessons learned from a community-based participatory research mental health promotion program for American Indian youth. *Health Promotion Practice* 17, 457-463.

Lee J, Lee CM, Park NK (2015). Application of sensor network system to prevent suicide from the bridge. *Multimedia Tools and Applications.* Published online: 16 December 2015. doi: 10.1007/s11042-015-3134-z

Menger LM, Stallones L, Cross JE, Henry KL, Chen PY (2015). Strengthening suicide prevention networks: Interorganizational collaboration and tie strength. *Psychosocial Intervention* 24, 155-165.

Oyama H, Sakashita T (2015). Long-term effects of a screening intervention for depression on suicide rates among Japanese community-dwelling older adults. *American Journal of Geriatric Psychiatry* 24, 287-296.

Pirkis J, Too LS, Spittal MJ, Krysinska K, Robinson J, Cheung YTD (2015). Interventions to reduce suicides at suicide hotspots: A systematic review and meta-analysis. *Lancet Psychiatry* 2, 994-1001.

VanDeusen KM, Ginebaugh KJL, Walcott DD (2015). Campus suicide prevention: Knowledge, facts, and stigma in a college student sample. *Sage Open* 5, 1-9.

VanSickle M, Werbel A, Perera K, Pak K, DeYoung K, Ghahramanlou-Holloway M (2016). Perceived barriers to seeking mental health care among United States Marine Corps noncommissioned officers serving as gatekeepers for suicide prevention. *Psychological Assessment.* Published online: 11 January 2016. doi: 10.1037/pas0000212.

Vasiliadis H-M, Lesage A, Latimer E, Seguin M (2015). Implementing suicide prevention programs: Costs and potential life years saved in Canada. *Journal of Mental Health Policy and Economics* 18, 147-155.

Wang L-J, Wu Y-W, Chen C-K (2015). Is case management effective for long-lasting suicide prevention? A community cohort study in Northern Taiwan. *Crisis* 36, 194-201.

Wilcox HC, Wyma A (2016). Suicide prevention strategies for improving population health. *Child and Adolescent Psychiatric Clinics of North America* 25, 219-233.

Postvention and Bereavement

Andriessen K, Draper B, Dudley M, Mitchell PB (2015). Pre- and post-loss features of adolescent suicide bereavement: Findings from a systematic review of the literature. *Death Studies* 40, 229-246.

Bartik W, Maple M, McKay K (2015). Suicide bereavement and stigma for young people in rural Australia: A mixed methods study. *Advances in Mental Health* 13, 84-95.

Bell J, Bailey L, Kennedy D (2015). 'We do it to keep him alive': Bereaved individuals' experiences of online suicide memorials and continuing bonds. *Mortality* 20, 375-389.

Bolton JM, Au W, Chateau D, Walld R, Leslie WD, Enns J, Martens PJ, Katz LY, Logsetty S, Sareen J (2016). Bereavement after sibling death: A population-based longitudinal case-control study. *World Psychiatry* 15, 59-66.

Cox GR, Bailey E, Jorm AF, Reavley NJ, Templer K, Parker A, Rickwood D, Bhar S, Robinson J (2016). Development of suicide postvention guidelines for secondary schools: A Delphi study. *BMC Public Health* 16, 180.

Drapeau CW, Cerel J, Moore M (2016). How personality, coping styles, and perceived closeness influence help-seeking attitudes in suicide-bereaved adults. *Death Studies* 40, 165-171.

Fhaili MN, Flynn N, Dowling S (2016). Experiences of suicide bereavement: A qualitative study exploring the role of the GP. *British Journal of General Practice* 66, e92-e98.

Groff EC, Ruzek JI, Bongar B, Cordova MJ (2016). Social constraints, loss-related factors, depression, and posttraumatic stress in a treatment-seeking suicide bereaved sample. *Psychological Trauma*. Published online: 7 March 2016. doi: 10.1037/tra0000128.

Gulfi A, Castelli Dransart DA, Heeb JL, Gutjahr E (2016). The impact of patient suicide on the professional practice of Swiss psychiatrists and psychologists. *Academic Psychiatry* 40, 13-22.

Levi-Belz Y (2016). To share or not to share? The contribution of self-disclosure to stress-related growth among suicide survivors. *Death Studies*. Published online: 10 March 2016. doi: 10.1080/07481187.2016.1160164.

Nam I (2016). Suicide bereavement and complicated grief: Experiential avoidance as a mediating mechanism. *Journal of Loss and Trauma*. Published online: 22 July 2015. doi: 10.1080/15325024.2015.1067099.

Pitman AL, Osborn DP, Rantell K, King MB (2016). Bereavement by suicide as a risk factor for suicide attempt: A cross-sectional national UK-wide study of 3432 young bereaved adults. *British Medical Journal Open* 6, e009948.

Rabalais AM, Wilks SE, Geiger JR, Bates SM (2016). Prominent feelings and self-regard among survivors of suicide: Does time heal all wounds? *Illness, Crisis and Loss*. Published online: 14 March 2016 doi: 10.1177/1054137316637189.

Spino E, Kameg KM, Cline TW, Terhorst L, Mitchell AM (2016). Impact of social support on symptoms of depression and loneliness in survivors bereaved by suicide. *Archives of Psychiatric Nursing*. Published online: 17 February 2016. doi:10.1016/j.apnu.2016.02.001.

NON-FATAL SUICIDAL BEHAVIOR

Epidemiology

Ahuja H, Mathai AS, Pannu A, Arora R (2015). Acute poisonings admitted to a tertiary level intensive care unit in Northern India: Patient profile and outcomes. *Journal of Clinical and Diagnostic Research* 9, UC01-UC04.

Amadéo S, Kõlves K, Malogne A, Rereao M, Favro P, Lam Nguyen N, Jehel L, De Leo D (2016). Non-fatal suicidal behaviours in French Polynesia: Results of the WHO/START study and its implications for prevention. *Journal of Affective Disorders* 189, 351-356.

Arat G (2015). Emerging protective and risk factors of mental health in Asian American students: Findings from the 2013 youth risk behavior survey. *Vulnerable Children and Youth Studies* 10, 192-205.

Armitage C, Abdul Rahim W, Rowe R, O'Connor R (2015). Trends in self-harm in Kuala Lumpur, 2005-2011. *Archives of Suicide Research* 20, 22-28.

Augsberger A, Yeung A, Dougher M, Hahm HC (2015). Factors influencing the underutilization of mental health services among Asian American women with a history of depression and suicide. *BMC Health Services Research* 15, 542.

Ballard ED, Kalb LG, Vasa RA, Goldstein M, Wilcox HC (2015). Self-harm, assault, and undetermined intent injuries among pediatric emergency department visits. *Pediatric Emergency Care* 31, 813-818.

Batejan KL, Swenson LP, Jarvi SM, Muehlenkamp JJ (2015). Perceptions of the functions of nonsuicidal self-injury in a college sample. *Crisis* 36, 338-344.

Bell TM, Qiao N, Jenkins PC, Siedlecki CB, Fecher AM (2016). Trends in emergency department visits for nonfatal violence-related injuries among adolescents in the United States, 2009-2013. *Journal of Adolescent Health* 58, 573-575.

Bhaskaran J, Johnson E, Bolton JM, Randall JR, Mota N, Katz C, Rigatto C, Skakum K, Roberts D, Sareen J (2015). Population trends in substances used in deliberate self-poisoning leading to intensive care unit admissions from 2000 to 2010. *Journal of Clinical Psychiatry* 76, e1583-e1589.

Brown GK, Currier GW, Jager-Hyman S, Stanley B (2015). Detection and classification of suicidal behavior and nonsuicidal self-injury behavior in emergency departments. *Journal of Clinical Psychiatry* 76, 1397-1403.

Byers AL, Lai AX, Arean P, Nelson JC, Yaffe K (2016). Mental health service use across the life course among adults with psychiatric disorders and prior suicidal behavior. *Psychiatric Services* 67, 452-455.

Caine PL, Tan A, Barnes D, Dziewulski P (2015). Self-inflicted burns: 10 year review and comparison to national guidelines. *Burns* 42, 215-221.

Carr MJ, Ashcroft DM, Kontopantelis E, Awenat Y, Cooper J, Chew-Graham C, Kapur N, Webb RT (2016). The epidemiology of self-harm in a UK-wide primary care patient cohort, 2001-2013. *BMC Psychiatry* 16, e53.

Celso BG, Pracht EE, Cuffe SP (2015). Suicide as a public health issue in the state of Florida. *Internet Journal of Public Health* 3, e22385.

Chan YC, Tse ML, Lau FL (2015). Hong Kong poison information centre: Annual report 2014. *Hong Kong Journal of Emergency Medicine* 22, 376-387.

Cheung T, Lee PH, Yip PS (2015). Suicidality among Hong Kong nurses: Prevalence and correlates. *Journal of Advanced Nursing* 72, 836-848.

Chou WJ, Liu TL, Hu HF, Yen CF (2016). Suicidality and its relationships with individual, family, peer, and psychopathology factors among adolescents with attention-deficit/hyperactivity disorder. *Research in Developmental Disabilities* 53-54, 86-94.

Clements C, Turnbull P, Hawton K, Geulayov G, Waters K, Ness J, Townsend E, Khundakar K, Kapur N (2016). Rates of self-harm presenting to general hospitals: A comparison of data from the multicentre study of self-harm in England and hospital episode statistics. *British Medical Journal Open* 6, e009749.

Ekingen E, Goktekin MC, Ardic S, Alatas OD (2015). Retrospective analysis of suicide attempt with analgesics. *Eurasian Journal of Emergency Medicine* 14, 172-176.

Fazel S, Fiminska Z, Cocks C, Coid J (2016). Patient outcomes following discharge from secure psychiatric hospitals: Systematic review and meta-analysis. *British Journal of Psychiatry* 208, 17-25.

Fekadu A, Medhin G, Selamu M, Shiferaw T, Hailemariam M, Rathod SD, Jordans M, Teferra S, Lund C, Breuer E, Prince M, Giorgis TW, Alem A, Hanlon C (2016). Non-fatal suicidal behaviour in rural Ethiopia: A cross-sectional facility- and population-based study. *BMC Psychiatry* 16, 75.

Firestone M, Smylie J, Maracle S, McKnight C, Spiller M, O'Campo P (2015). Mental health and substance use in an urban first nations population in Hamilton, Ontario. *Canadian Journal of Public Health* 106, e375-e381.

George S, Javed M, Hemington-Gorse S, Wilson-Jones N (2016). Epidemiology and financial implications of self-inflicted burns. *Burns* 42, 196-201.

Ghazanfar H, Hameed S, Ghazanfar A, Bhatti JRA, ul Haq I, Saeed R, Shafi MS, Hussain A, Javaid A, Naseem S (2015). Suicidal ideation among Pakistani medical students. *Rawal Medical Journal* 40, 458-462.

Han K-M, Won E, Paik J-W, Lee M-S, Lee H-W, Ham B-J (2016). Mental health service use in adults with suicidal ideation within a nationally representative sample of the Korean population. *Journal of Affective Disorders* 193, 339-347.

Inder ML, Crowe MT, Luty SE, Carter JD, Moor S, Frampton CM, Joyce PR (2015). Prospective rates of suicide attempts and nonsuicidal self-injury by young people with bipolar disorder participating in a psychotherapy study. *Australian and New Zealand Journal of Psychiatry* 50, 167-173.

Kadziela-Olech H, Zak G, Kalinowska B, Wagrocka A, Perestret G, Bielawski M (2015). The prevalence of nonsuisidal self-injury (NSSI) among high school students in relation to age and sex. *Psychiatria Polska* 49, 765-778.

Kalesan B, Dabic S, Vasan S, Stylianos S, Galea S (2015). Racial/ethnic specific trends in pediatric firearm-related hospitalizations in the United States, 1998–2011. *Maternal and Child Health Journal* 20, 1082-1090.

Kasinathan J (2015). Predictors of rapid reincarceration in mentally ill young offenders. *Australasian Psychiatry* 23, 550-555.

Khan N, Pérez-Núñez R, Shamim N, Khan U, Naseer N, Feroze A, Razzak J, Hyder AA (2015). Intentional and unintentional poisoning in Pakistan: A pilot study using the emergency departments surveillance project. *BMC Emergency Medicine* 15, S2.

Kim J, Kim M, Kim Y-R, Choi KH, Lee K-U (2015). High prevalence of psychotropics overdose among suicide attempters in Korea. *Clinical Psychopharmacology and Neuroscience* 13, 302-307.

Kokaliari ED (2014). An exploratory study of the nature and extent of nonsuicidal self-injury among college women. *International Journal of Population Research* 2014, e879269.

Leao SC, Araujo JFd, Silveira AR, Queiroz AAF, Souto MJS, Almeida RO, Maciel DC, Rodrigues TMdA (2015). Management of exogenous intoxication by carbamates and organophosphates at an emergency unit. *Revista da Associacao Medica Brasileira* 61, 440-445.

Leckning BA, Li SQ, Cunningham T, Guthridge S, Robinson G, Nagel T, Silburn S (2016). Trends in hospital admissions involving suicidal behaviour in the Northern Territory, 2001-2013. *Australasia Psychiatry*. Published online: 8 February 2016. doi: 10.1177/1039856216629838.

Lee JW, Hwang IW, Kim JW, Moon HJ, Kim KH, Park S, Gil HW, Hong SY (2015). Common pesticides used in suicide attempts following the 2012 paraquat ban in Korea. *Journal of Korean Medical Science* 30, 1517-1521.

Moreno MA, Ton A, Selkie E, Evans Y (2016). Secret society 123: Understanding the language of self-harm on instagram. *Journal of Adolescence Health* 58, 78-84.

Morey Y, Mellon D, Dailami N, Verne J, Tapp A (2016). Adolescent self-harm in the community: An update on prevalence using a self-report survey of adolescents aged 13-18 in England. *Journal of Public Health*. Published online: 17 February 2016. doi: 10.1093/pubmed/fdw010.

Nett RJ, Witte TK, Holzbauer SM, Elchos BL, Campagnolo ER, Musgrave KJ, Carter KK, Kurkjian KM, Vanicek CF, O'Leary DR, Pride KR, Funk RH (2015). Risk factors for suicide, attitudes toward mental illness, and practice-related stressors among US veterinarians. *Journal of the American Veterinary Medical Association* 247, 945-955.

Oladeji BD, Taiwo B, Mosuro O, Fayemiwo SA, Abiona T, Fought AJ, Robertson K, Ogunniyi A, Adewole IF (2015). Suicidal behavior and associations with quality of life among HIV/AIDS-infected patients in Ibadan, Nigeria. *JIAPAC*. Published online: 19 November 2015. doi: 10.1177/2325957415617829.

Olfson M, Wang S, Blanco C (2015). National trends in hospital-treated self-harm events among middle-aged adults. *General Hospital Psychiatry* 37, 613-619.

Onyebueke GC, Okwaraji FE (2015). Depression and suicide risk among HIV positive individuals attending an out patient HIV/AIDS clinic of a Nigerian tertiary health institution. *Journal of Psychiatry* 18, 1-8.

Oskrochi Y, Maruthappu M, Henriksson M, Davies AH, Shalhoub J (2015). Beyond the body: A systematic review of the nonphysical effects of a surgical career. *Surgery* 159, 650-664.

Pereira A, Cardoso F (2015). Suicidal ideation in university students: Prevalence and association with school and gender. *Paidéia* 25, 299-306.

Piekarska-Wijatkowska A, Kobza-Sindlewska K, Rogaczewska A, Zajdel R, Krakowiak A (2016). Intentional poisoning among elderly people-residents of a large urban agglomeration in Poland. *Human and Experimental Toxicology*. Published online: 9 February 2016. doi: 10.1177/0960327116630353.

Plener PL, Schumacher TS, Munz LM, Groschwitz RC (2015). The longitudinal course of non-suicidal self-injury and deliberate self-harm: A systematic review of the literature. *Borderline Personality Disorder and Emotion Dysregulation* 2, 2.

Qin Q, Jin Y, Zhan S, Yu X, Huang F (2015). Suicidal ideation among rural immigrant daughters-in-law with multi-roles as females, farmers and immigrants in China. *Psychology Health and Medicine* 21, 608-617.

Stiffler KA, Kohli E, Chen O, Frey JA (2015). Characterization of older emergency department patients admitted to psychiatric units. *Journal of Clinical Medicine Research* 7, 840-844.

Störmann P, Gärtner K, Wyen H, Lustenberger T, Marzi I, Wutzler S (2016). Epidemiology and outcome of penetrating injuries in a Western European urban region. *European Journal of Trauma and Emergency Surgery*. Published online: 13 January 2016. doi: 10.1007/s00068-016-0630-4.

Szmulewicz AG, Smith JM, Valerio MP (2015). Suicidality in clozapine-treated patients with schizophrenia: Role of obsessive-compulsive symptoms. *Psychiatry Research* 230, 50-55.

Tomori C, McFall AM, Srikrishnan AK, Mehta SH, Solomon SS, Anand S, Vasudevan CK, Solomon S, Celentano DD (2015). Diverse rates of depression among men who have sex with men (MSM) across India: Insights from a multi-site mixed method study. *Aids and Behavior* 20, 306-316.

Vakkalanka JP, King JD, Holstege CP (2015). Abuse, misuse, and suicidal substance use by children on school property. *Clinical Toxicology* 53, 901-907.

Weerasinghe M, Konradsen F, Eddleston M, Pearson M, Agampodi T, Storm F, Agampodi S (2016). Overdose of oral contraceptive pills as a means of intentional self-poisoning amongst young women in Sri Lanka: Considerations for family planning. *Journal of Family Planning & Reproductive Health Care*. Published online: 22 March 2016. doi: 10.1136/jfprhc-2015-101171.

Xu H, Zhang W, Wang X, Yuan J, Tang X, Yin Y, Zhang S, Zhou H, Qu Z, Tian D (2015). Prevalence and influence factors of suicidal ideation among females and males in Northwestern Urban China: A population-based epidemiological study. *BMC Public Health* 15, 961.

Yaylaci S, Genc AB, Demir MV, Cinemre H, Tamer A (2016). Retrospective evaluation of patients at follow-up with acute poisoning in intensive care unit. *Nigerian Journal of Clinical Practice* 19, 223-226.

Zarrouq B, Bendaou B, Elkinany S, Rammouz I, Aalouane R, Lyoussi B, Khelafa S, Bout A, Berhili N, Hlal H, Nejjari C, El Rhazi K (2015). Suicidal behaviors among Moroccan school students: Prevalence and association with socio-demographic characteristics and psychoactive substances use: A cross-sectional study. *BMC Psychiatry* 15, 284.

Zisman S, O'Brien A (2015). A retrospective cohort study describing six months of admissions under Section 136 of the Mental Health Act; the problem of alcohol misuse. *Medicine Science and the Law* 55, 216-222.

Zubrick SR, Hafekost J, Johnson SE, Lawrence D, Saw S, Sawyer M, Ainley J, Buckingham J (2015). Self-harm: Prevalence estimates from the Second Australian Child and Adolescent Survey of Mental Health and Wellbeing. *Australian and New Zealand Journal of Psychiatry*. Published online: 30 November 2015. doi: 10.1177/0004867415617837.

Risk and protective factors

Aaltonen K, Näätänen P, Heikkinen M, Koivisto M, Baryshnikov I, Karpov B, Oksanen J, Melartin T, Suominen K, Joffe G, Paunio T, Isometsä E (2016). Differences and similarities of risk factors for suicidal ideation and attempts among patients with depressive or bipolar disorders. *Journal of Affective Disorders* 193, 318-330.

Abdollahi A, Talib MA, Yaacob SN, Ismail Z (2016). Problem-solving skills and suicidal ideation among Malaysian college students: The mediating role of hopelessness. *Academic Psychiatry* 40, 261-267.

Adler A, Bush A, Barg FK, Weissinger G, Beck AT, Brown GK (2016). A mixed methods approach to identify cognitive warning signs for suicide attempts. *Archives of Suicide Research.* Published online: 13 January 2016. doi: 10.1080/13811118.2015.1136717.

Adrian M, Miller AB, McCauley E, Vander Stoep A (2015). Suicidal ideation in early to middle adolescence: Sex-specific trajectories and predictors. *Journal of Child Psychology and Psychiatry* 57, 645-653.

Aebi M, Barra S, Bessler C, Steinhausen HC, Walitza S, Plattner B (2015). Oppositional defiant disorder dimensions and subtypes among detained male adolescent offenders. *Journal of Child Psychology and Psychiatry.* Published online: 23 October 2015. doi: 10.1111/jcpp.12473.

Afifi TO, Taillieu T, Zamorski MA, Turner S, Cheung K, Sareen J (2016). Association of child abuse exposure with suicidal ideation, suicide plans, and suicide attempts in military personnel and the general population in Canada. *Journal of the American Medical Association Psychiatry* 73, 229-238.

Akbari M, Haghdoost AA, Nakhaee N, Bahramnejad A, Baneshi MR, Zolala F (2015). Risk and protective factor for suicide attempt in Iran: A matched case-control study. *Archives of Iranian Medicine* 18, 747-752.

Akinyemi OO, Atilola O, Soyannwo T (2015). Suicidal ideation: Are refugees more at risk compared to host population? Findings from a preliminary assessment in a refugee community in Nigeria. *Asian Journal of Psychiatry* 18, 81-85.

Al Ahwal MS, Al Zaben F, Khalifa DA, Sehlo MG, Ahmad RG, Koenig HG (2015). Depression in patients with colorectal cancer in Saudi Arabia. *Psycho-Oncology* 24, 1043-1050.

Alavi N, Roberts N, Sutton C, Axas N, Repetti L (2015). Bullying victimization (being bullied) among adolescents referred for urgent psychiatric consultation: Prevalence and association with suicidality. *Canadian Journal of Psychiatry* 60, 427-431.

Aldea Perona A, Garcia-Saiz M, Sanz Alvarez E (2016). Psychiatric disorders and montelukast in children: A disproportionality analysis of the Vigibase®. *Drug Safety* 39, 69-78.

Alpaslan AH, Soylu N, Koçak U, Guzel HI (2016). Problematic internet use was more common in Turkish adolescents with major depressive disorders than controls. *Acta Paediatrica* 105, 695-700.

Altinyazar V, Sirin FB, Sutcu R, Eren I, Omurlu IK (2016). The red blood cell acetylcholinesterase levels of depressive patients with suicidal behavior in an agricultural area. *Indian Journal of Clinical Biochemistry.* Published online: 9 February 2016. doi: 10.1007/s12291-016-0558-9.

Alvarado-Esquivel C, Hernández-Tinoco J, Sánchez-Anguiano LF (2015). Lack of association between toxocara exposure and suicide attempts in psychiatric patients. *Journal of Parasitology Research* 2015, 608604.

Ammerman BA, Burke TA, Alloy LB, McCloskey MS (2015). Subjective pain during NSSI as an active agent in suicide risk. *Psychiatry Research.* 236, 80-85.

An KO, Jang JY, Kim J (2015). Sedentary behavior and sleep duration are associated with both stress symptoms and suicidal thoughts in Korean adults. *Tohoku Journal of Experimental Medicine* 237, 279-286.

Anari AS, Bidaki R, Soltani H, Zolala H, Asadi R, Khajekari-Maddini Z, Ghannad MS, Shahrbabaki MHS, Asadpour M, Shafee A, Riahy A (2015). Frequency of suicide ideation and attempt in HIV infected patients referred to behavioral health counseling centers of Rafsanjan (RUMS) and Kerman University of Medical Sciences (KUMS). *Galen Medical Journal* 4, 33-38.

Anestis JC, Anestis MD, Rufino KA, Cramer RJ, Miller H, Khazem LR, Joiner TE (2016). Understanding the relationship between suicidality and psychopathy: An examination of the interpersonal-psychological theory of suicidal behavior. *Archives of Suicide Research*. Published online: 8 March 2016. doi: 10.1080/13811118.2015.1048399.

Anestis MD, Capron DW (2016). An investigation of persistence through pain and distress as an amplifier of the relationship between suicidal ideation and suicidal behavior. *Journal of Affective Disorders* 196, 78-82.

Annunziato RA, Kim SK, Fussner M, Ahmad T, Jerson B, Rubinstein D (2015). Utilizing correspondence analysis to characterize the mental health of cardiac patients with diabetes. *Journal of Health Psychology* 20, 1275-1284.

Antypa N, Souery D, Tomasini M, Albani D, Fusco F, Mendlewicz J, Serretti A (2015). Clinical and genetic factors associated with suicide in mood disorder patients. *European Archives of Psychiatry and Clinical Neuroscience* 266, 181-193.

Ao T, Shetty S, Sivilli T, Blanton C, Ellis H, Geltman PL, Cochran J, Taylor E, Lankau EW, Lopes Cardozo B (2015). Suicidal ideation and mental health of Bhutanese refugees in the United States. *Journal of Immigrant and Minority Health*. Published online: 28 December 2015. doi: 10.1007/s10903-015-0325-7.

Arcelus J, Claes L, Witcomb GL, Marshall E, Bouman WP (2016). Risk factors for non-suicidal self-injury among trans youth. *Journal of Sexual Medicine* 13, 402-412.

Armstrong LL, Manion IG (2015). Meaningful youth engagement as a protective factor for youth suicidal ideation. *Journal of Research on Adolescence* 25, 20-27.

Armstrong LL, Manion IG (2015). Predictors of rural and urban youth suicidal ideation by gender: A case for targeted approaches to prevention. *Vulnerable Children and Youth Studies* 10, 206-219.

Arroyo-Cobo JM (2015). Subcultural manifestations of self-injury in correctional settings. *Revista Espanola de Sanidad Penitenciaria* 17, 90-91.

Artenie AA, Bruneau J, Roy E, Zang G, Lesperance F, Renaud J, Tremblay J, Jutras-Aswad D (2015). Licit and illicit substance use among people who inject drugs and the association with subsequent suicidal attempt. *Addiction* 110, 1636-1643.

Asellus P, Nordström P, Nordström AL, Jokinen J (2016). Plasma apolipoprotein E and severity of suicidal behaviour. *Journal of Affective Disorders* 190, 137-142.

Ashrafioun L, Bonar E, Conner KR (2015). Health attitudes and suicidal ideation among university students. *Journal of American College Health* 64, 256-260.

Ashrafioun L, Pigeon WR, Conner KR, Leong SH, Oslin DW (2016). Prevalence and correlates of suicidal ideation and suicide attempts among veterans in primary care referred for a mental health evaluation. *Journal of Affective Disorders* 189, 344-350.

Ayesa-Arriola R, Alcaraz EG, Hernández BV, Pérez-Iglesias R, López Moríñigo JD, Duta R, David AS, Tabarés-Seisdedos R, Crespo-Facorro B (2015). Suicidal behaviour in first-episode non-affective psychosis: Specific risk periods and stage-related factors. *European Neuropsychopharmacology* 25, 2278-2288.

Bae SM, Lee SA, Lee S-H (2015). Prediction by data mining, of suicide attempts in Korean adolescents: A national study. *Neuropsychiatric Disease and Treatment* 11, 2367-2375.

Baer E, Barre C, Fleury C, de Montchenu C, Garre J-B, Lerolle N, Gohier B (2016). Mechanical ventilation as an indicator of somatic severity of self-poisoning: Implications for psychiatric care and long-term outcomes. *British Journal of Psychiatry* 208, 280-285.

Baetens I, Andrews T, Claes L, Martin G (2015). The association between family functioning and NSSI in adolescence: The mediating role of depressive symptoms. *Family Science* 6, 330-337.

Bagiu I, Putnoky S, Tuta-Sas I, Miloicov CB, Popa M, Vlaicu B, Bagiu R (2015). Manifestations of self-harm in relation with binge drinking to students from Timis County, Romania. *Revista Medico-Chirurgicala a Societatii de Medici si Naturalisti Din Iasi* 119, 1106-1112.

Baiden P, Fuller-Thomson E (2016). Factors associated with achieving complete mental health among individuals with lifetime suicidal ideation. *Suicide and Life-Threatening Behavior.* Published online: 26 January 2016. doi: 10.1111/sltb.12230.

Baldin E, Hesdorffer DC, Caplan R, Berg AT (2015). Psychiatric disorders and suicidal behavior in neurotypical young adults with childhood-onset epilepsy. *Epilepsia* 56, 1623-1628.

Baneshi MR, Haghdoost AA, Zolala F, Nakhaee N, Jalali M, Tabrizi R, Akbari M (2016). Can religious beliefs be a protective factor for suicidal behavior? A decision tree analysis in a mid-sized city in Iran, 2013. *Journal of Religion and Health.* Published online: 29 February 2016. doi: 10.1007/s10943-016-0215-x.

Bani-Fatemi A, Howe AS, Matmari M, Koga A, Zai C, Strauss J, De Luca V (2016). Interaction between methylation and CPG single-nucleotide polymorphisms in the HTR2A gene: Association analysis with suicide attempt in schizophrenia. *Neuropsychobiology* 73, 10-15.

Barnes MC, Gunnell D, Davies R, Hawton K, Kapur N, Potokar J, Donovan JL (2016). Understanding vulnerability to self-harm in times of economic hardship and austerity: A qualitative study. *British Medical Journal Open* 6, e010131.

Barrot C, Ortega M, Carrera C, De Alcaraz-Fossoul J, Subirana M, Salavert J, Castellà J, Mezquita J, Gené M (2015). Relationships between the molecular basis of impulsivity and suicidal behavior. *Forensic Science International* 5, e530-e531.

Barry LC, Wakefield DB, Trestman RL, Conwell Y (2015). Active and passive suicidal ideation in older prisoners. *Crisis.* Published online: 17 November 2015. doi: 10.1027/0227-5910/a000350.

Barua S, Ray P, Chakraborty S, Bhattacharjee S (2015). Relationship between disease severity and suicidal ideation: Comparison of major depression, bipolar depression and bipolar mania. *Indian Journal of Public Health Research and Development* 6, 69-73.

Bazrafshan M-R, Sharif F, Molazem Z, Mani A (2016). Exploring the risk factors contributing to suicide attempt among adolescents: A qualitative study. *Iranian Journal of Nursing and Midwifery Research* 21, 93-99.

Becerra MB, Becerra BJ, Hassija CM, Safdar N (2016). Unmet mental healthcare need and suicidal ideation among U.S.Veterans. *American Journal of Preventive Medicine.* Published online: 26 February 2016. doi: 10.1016/j.amepre.2016.01.015.

Beck-Cross C, Cooper R (2015). Micro- and macrosystem predictors of high school male suicidal behaviors. *Children and Schools* 37, 231-239.

Bentley KH, Franklin JC, Ribeiro JD, Kleiman EM, Fox KR, Nock MK (2016). Anxiety and its disorders as risk factors for suicidal thoughts and behaviors: A meta-analytic review. *Clinical Psychology Review* 43, 30-46.

Bentley KH, Sauer-Zavala S, Wilner J (2015). The unique contributions of distinct experiential avoidance domains to severity and functionality of non-suicidal self-injury. *Journal of Experimental Psychopathology* 6, 40-57.

Beristianos MH, Maguen S, Neylan TC, Byers AL (2016). Trauma exposure and risk of suicidal ideation among ethnically diverse adults. *Depression and Anxiety.* Published online: 17 March 2016. doi: 10.1002/da.22485.

Berman NC, Tung ES, Matheny N, Cohen IG, Wilhelm S (2015). Clinical decision making regarding suicide risk: Effect of patient and clinician age. *Death Studies* 40, 269-274.

Berutti M, Dias RS, Pereira VA, Lafer B, Nery FG (2015). Association between history of suicide attempts and family functioning in bipolar disorder. *Journal of Affective Disorders* 192, 28-33.

Bhatti JA, Nathens AB, Thiruchelvam D, Grantcharov T, Goldstein BI, Redelmeier DA (2015). Self-harm emergencies after bariatric surgery: A population-based cohort study. *JAMA Surgery* 151, 226-232.

Bijttebier S, Caeyenberghs K, van den Ameele H, Achten E, Rujescu D, Titeca K, van Heeringen C (2015). The vulnerability to suicidal behavior is associated with reduced connectivity strength. *Frontiers in Human Neuroscience* 9, e632.

Bischof A, Meyer C, Bischof G, John U, Wurst FM, Thon N, Lucht M, Grabe HJ, Rumpf HJ (2016). Type of gambling as an independent risk factor for suicidal events in pathological gamblers. *Psychology of Addictive Behaviors* 30, 263-269.

Bjorkenstam C, Kosidou K, Bjorkenstam E, Dalman C, Andersson G, Cochran S (2016). Self-reported suicide ideation and attempts, and medical care for intentional self-harm in lesbians, gays and bisexuals in Sweden. *Journal of Epidemiology and Community Health*. Published online: 4 March 2016. doi:10.1136/jech-2015-206884.

Björkenstam C, Tinghög P, Brenner P, Mittendorfer-Rutz E, Hillert J, Jokinen J, Alexanderson K (2015). Is disability pension a risk indicator for future need of psychiatric healthcare or suicidal behavior among MS patients- a nationwide register study in Sweden? *BMC Psychiatry* 15, 286.

Bodzy ME, Barreto SJ, Swenson LP, Liguori G, Costea G (2016). Self-reported psychopathology, trauma symptoms, and emotion coping among child suicide attempters and ideators: An exploratory study of young children. *Archives of Suicide Research* 20, 160-175.

Bonenberger M, Plener PL, Groschwitz RC, Grön G, Abler B (2015). Differential neural processing of unpleasant haptic sensations in somatic and affective partitions of the insula in non-suicidal self-injury (NSSI). *Psychiatry Research* 234, 298-304.

Boone SD, Brausch AM (2016). Physical activity, exercise motivations, depression, and nonsuicidal self-injury in youth. *Suicide and Life-Threatening Behavior*. Published online: 11 March 2016. doi: 10.1111/sltb.12240.

Borschmann R, Thomas E, Moran P, Carroll M, Heffernan E, Spittal MJ, Sutherland G, Alati R, Kinner SA (2016). Self-harm following release from prison: A prospective data linkage study. *Australian and New Zealand Journal of Psychiatry*. Published online: 24 March 2016. doi: 10.1177/0004867416640090.

Bouris A, Everett BG, Heath RD, Elsaesser CE, Neilands TB (2015). Effects of victimization and violence on suicidal ideation and behaviors among sexual minority and heterosexual adolescents. *LGBT Health* 3, 153-161.

Brackman EH, Morris BW, Andover MS (2016). Predicting risk for suicide: A preliminary examination of non-suicidal self-injury and the acquired capability construct in a college sample. *Archives of Suicide Research*. Published online: 23 March 2016. doi: 10.1080 /13811118.2016.1162247.

Bramson LM, Rickert ME, Class QA, Sariaslan A, Almqvist C, Larsson H, Lichtenstein P, D'Onofrio BM (2015). The association between childhood relocations and subsequent risk of suicide attempt, psychiatric problems, and low academic achievement. *Psychological Medicine* 46, 969-979.

Branco JC, Motta J, Wiener C, Oses JP, Pedrotti Moreira F, Spessato B, Dias L, da Silva R (2016). Association between obesity and suicide in woman, but not in man: A population-based study of young adults. *Psychology Health and Medicine*. Published online: 22 March 2016. doi: 10.1080/13548506.2016.1164870.

Brausch AM, Holaday TC (2015). Suicide-related concerns as a mediator between physical abuse and self-harm behaviors in college students. *Crisis* 36, 440-446.

Brickman LJ, Ammerman BA, Look AE, Berman ME, McCloskey MS (2014). The relationship between non-suicidal self-injury and borderline personality disorder symptoms in a college sample. *Borderline Personality Disorder and Emotion Dysregulation* 1, 14.

Brody C, Chhoun P, Tuot S, Pal K, Chhim K, Yi S (2016). HIV risk and psychological distress among female entertainment workers in Cambodia: A cross-sectional study. *BMC Public Health* 16, 133.

Bromberg MH, Law EF, Palermo TM (2016). Suicidal ideation in adolescents with and without chronic pain. *Clinical Journal of Pain.* Published online: 22 February 2016. doi: 10.1097/AJP.0000000000000366.

Bruedern J, Berger T, Michel K, Maillart AG, Held IS, Caspar F (2015). Are suicide attempters wired differently? A comparison with nonsuicidal depressed individuals using plan analysis. *Journal of Nervous and Mental Disease* 203, 514-521.

Brunstein Klomek A, Snir A, Apter A, Carli V, Wasserman C, Hadlaczky G, Hoven CW, Sarchiapone M, Balazs J, Bobes J, Brunner R, Corcoran P, Cosman D, Haring C, Kahn JP, Kaess M, Postuvan V, Sisask M, Tubiana A, Varnik A, Ziberna J, Wasserman D (2016). Association between victimization by bullying and direct self injurious behavior among adolescence in Europe: A ten-country study. *European Child and Adolescent Psychiatry.* Published online: 24 March 2016. doi: 10.1007/s00787-016-0840-7.

Bryan CJ, Griffith JE, Pace BT, Hinkson K, Bryan AO, Clemans TA, Imel ZE (2015). Combat exposure and risk for suicidal thoughts and behaviors among military personnel and veterans: A systematic review and meta-analysis. *Suicide and Life Threatening Behavior* 45, 633-649.

Bryan CJ, Ray-Sannerud B, Heron EA (2015). Psychological flexibility as a dimension of resilience for posttraumatic stress, depression, and risk for suicidal ideation among Air Force personnel. *Journal of Contextual Behavioral Science* 4, 263-268.

Buitron V, Hill RM, Pettit JW, Green KL, Hatkevich C, Sharp C (2016). Interpersonal stress and suicidal ideation in adolescence: An indirect association through perceived burdensomeness toward others. *Journal of Affective Disorders* 190, 143-149.

Burešová I, Bartošová K, Čerňák M (2015). Connection between parenting styles and self-harm in adolescence. *Procedia - Social and Behavioral Sciences* 171, 1106-1113.

Burke TA, Connolly SL, Hamilton JL, Stange JP, Abramson LY, Alloy LB (2015). Cognitive risk and protective factors for suicidal ideation: A two year longitudinal study in adolescence. *Journal of Abnormal Child Psychology.* Published online: 23 November 2015. doi: 10.1007/s10802-015-0104-x.

Burke TA, Hamilton JL, Cohen JN, Stange JP, Alloy LB (2016). Identifying a physical indicator of suicide risk: Non-suicidal self-injury scars predict suicidal ideation and suicide attempts. *Comprehensive Psychiatry* 65, 79-87.

Buron P, Jimenez-Trevino L, Saiz PA, Garcia-Portilla MP, Corcoran P, Carli V, Fekete S, Hadlaczky G, Hegerl U, Michel K, Sarchiapone M, Temnik S, Varnick A, Verbanck P, Wasserman D, Schmidtke A, Bobes J (2016). Reasons for attempted suicide in Europe: Prevalence, associated factors, and risk of repetition. *Archives of Suicide Research* 20, 45-58.

Button DM (2015). A general strain approach comparing the effects of victimization, social support, and perceived self-efficacy on LGBQ and heterosexual youth suicidality. *Criminal Justice Studies* 28, 484-502.

Calati R, Laglaoui Bakhiyi C, Artero S, Ilgen M, Courtet P (2015). The impact of physical pain on suicidal thoughts and behaviors: Meta-analyses. *Journal of Psychiatric Research* 71, 16-32.

Capron DW, Bujarski SJ, Gratz KL, Anestis MD, Fairholme CP, Tull MT (2016). Suicide risk among male substance users in residential treatment: Evaluation of the depression-distress amplification model. *Psychiatry Research* 237, 22-26.

Carlier IV, Hovens JG, Streevelaar MF, van Rood YR, van Veen T (2016). Characteristics of suicidal outpatients with mood, anxiety and somatoform disorders: The role of childhood abuse and neglect. *International Journal of Social Psychiatry*. Published online: 19 February 2016. doi: 10.1177/0020764016629701.

Carmel A, Ries R, West, II, Bumgardner K, Roy-Byrne P (2016). Suicide risk and associated demographic and clinical correlates among primary care patients with recent drug use. *American Journal of Drug and Alcohol Abuse*. Published online: 24 February 2016. doi: 10.3109/00952990.2015.1133634.

Carroll R, Metcalfe C, Steeg S, Davies NM, Cooper J, Kapur N, Gunnell D (2016). Psychosocial assessment of self-harm patients and risk of repeat presentation: An instrumental variable analysis using time of hospital presentation. *PLoS One* 11, e0149713.

Carroll R, Thomas KH, Bramley K, Williams S, Griffin L, Potokar J, Gunnell D (2016). Self-cutting and risk of subsequent suicide. *Journal of Affective Disorders* 192, 8-10.

Casiano H, Bolton SL, Hildahl K, Katz LY, Bolton J, Sareen J (2016). A population-based study of the prevalence and correlates of self-harm in juvenile detention. *PLoS One* 11, e0146918.

Cavanaugh CE, Messing JT, Eyzerovich E, Campbell JC (2015). Ethnic differences in correlates of suicidal behavior among women seeking help for intimate partner violence. *Crisis* 36, 257-266.

Celik C, Ozdemir B, Oznur T (2015). Suicide risk among perinatal women who report thoughts of self-harm on depression screens. *Obstetrics and Gynecology* 126, 216-217.

Cerel J, Maple M, van de Venne J, Moore M, Flaherty C, Brown M (2016). Exposure to suicide in the community: Prevalence and correlates in one U.S. State. *Public Health Reports* 131, 100-107.

Cha CB, Augenstein TM, Frost KH, Gallagher K, D'Angelo EJ, Nock MK (2016). Using implicit and explicit measures to predict nonsuicidal self-injury among adolescent inpatients. *Journal of the American Academy of Child and Adolescent Psychiatry* 55, 62-68.

Cha CB, Najmi S, Amir N, Matthews JD, Deming CA, Glenn JJ, Calixte RM, Harris JA, Nock MK (2016). Testing the efficacy of attention bias modification for suicidal thoughts: Findings from two experiments. *Archives of Suicide Research*. Published online: 16 March 2016.

Chakravorty S, Katy Siu HY, Lalley-Chareczko L, Brown GK, Findley JC, Perlis ML, Grandner MA (2015). Sleep duration and insomnia symptoms as risk factors for suicidal ideation in a nationally representative sample. *Primary Care Companion for CNS Disɒrders* 17, 402-422.

Chandra PS, Desai G, Reddy D, Thippeswamy H, Saraf G (2015). The establishment of a mother-baby inpatient psychiatry unit in India: Adaptation of a Western model to meet local cultural and resource needs. *Indian Journal of Psychiatry* 57, 290-294.

Cheek SM, Nestor BA, Liu RT (2015). Substance use and suicidality: Specificity of substance use by injection to suicide attempts in a nationally representative sample of adults with major depression. *Depression and Anxiety*. Published online: 22 September 2015. doi: 10.1002/da.22407.

Chin YR, Choi K (2015). Suicide attempts and associated factors in male and female Korean adolescents a population-based cross-sectional survey. *Community Mental Health Journal* 51, 862-866.

Choi JM, Yang JB (2015). Structural equation model to determine the relationship between economic hardship, depression, family relationships and suicide ideation in elderly South Koreans. *Information* 18, 3889-3895.

Choi NG, DiNitto DM, Marti CN, Choi BY (2015). Associations of mental health and substance use disorders with presenting problems and outcomes in older adults' emergency department visits. *Academic Emergency Medicine* 22, 1316-1326.

Choi NG, DiNitto DM, Marti CN, Choi BY (2015). Relationship between marijuana and other illicit drug use and depression/suicidal thoughts among late middle-aged and older adults. *International Psychogeriatrics* 28, 577-589.

Choi NG, DiNitto DM, Marti CN, Choi BY (2016). Nonsuicidal self-injury and suicide attempts among ED patients older than 50 years: Comparison of risk factors and ED visit outcomes. *American Journal of Emergency Medicine*. Published online: 26 February 2016. doi: 10.1016/j.ajem.2016.02.058.

Choi TK, Worley MJ, Trim RS, Howard D, Brown SA, Hopfer CJ, Hewitt JK, Wall TL (2016). Effect of adolescent substance use and antisocial behavior on the development of early adulthood depression. *Psychiatry Research* 238, 143-149.

Chu C, Buchman-Schmitt JM, Joiner TE, Rudd MD (2016). Personality disorder symptoms and suicidality: Low desire and high plans for suicide in military inpatients and outpatients. *Journal of Personality Disorders*. Published online: 9 March 2016. doi: 10.1521/pedi_2016_30_241.

Chu C, Podlogar MC, Hagan CR, Buchman-Schmitt JM, Silva C, Chiurliza B, Hames JL, Stanley IH, Lim IC, Joiner TE (2015). The interactive effects of the capability for suicide and major depressive episodes on suicidal behavior in a military sample. *Cognitive Therapy and Research* 40, 22-30.

Chung IW, Caine ED, Barron CT, Badaracco MA (2015). Clinical and psychosocial profiles of Asian immigrants who repeatedly attempt suicide a mixed-method study of risk and protective factors. *Crisis* 36, 353-362.

Clarkson AF, Christian WM, Pearce ME, Jongbloed KA, Caron NR, Teegee MP, Moniruzzaman A, Schechter MT, Spittal PM, Cedar Project P (2015). The CEDAR Project: Negative health outcomes associated with involvement in the child welfare system among young indigenous people who use injection and non-injection drugs in two Canadian cities. *Canadian Journal of Public Health* 106, e265-e270.

Cole-Lewis YC, Gipson PY, Opperman KJ, Arango A, King CA (2016). Protective role of religious involvement against depression and suicidal ideation among youth with interpersonal problems. *Journal of Religion and Health*. Published online: 12 February 2016. doi: 10.1007/s10943-016-0194-y.

Collett GA, Song K, Jaramillo CA, Potter JS, Finley EP, Pugh MJ (2016). Prevalence of central nervous system polypharmacy and associations with overdose and suicide-related behaviors in Iraq and Afghanistan war Veterans in VA care 2010-2011. *Drugs* 3, 45-52.

Collett N, Pugh K, Waite F, Freeman D (2016). Negative cognitions about the self in patients with persecutory delusions: An empirical study of self-compassion, self-stigma, schematic beliefs, self-esteem, fear of madness, and suicidal ideation. *Psychiatry Research* 239, 79-84.

Colman I, Kingsbury M, Sareen J, Bolton J, van Walraven C (2015). Migraine headache and risk of self-harm and suicide: A population-based study in Ontario, Canada. *Headache* 56, 132-140.

Coughlan K, Tata P, MacLeod AK (2016). Personal goals, well-being and deliberate self-harm. *Cognitive Therapy and Research*. Published online: 8 March 2016. doi: 10.1007/s10608-016-9769-x.

Cramer RJ, Bryson CN, Gardner BO, Webber WB (2016). Can preferences in information processing aid in understanding suicide risk among emerging adults? *Death Studies*. Published online: 23 March 2016. doi: 10.1080/07481187.2016.1166161.

Croen LA, Zerbo O, Qian Y, Massolo ML, Rich S, Sidney S, Kripke C (2015). The health status of adults on the autism spectrum. *Autism* 19, 814-823.

Cucchi A, Ryan D, Konstantakopoulos G, Stroumpa S, Kacar AS, Renshaw S, Landau S, Kravariti E (2016). Lifetime prevalence of non-suicidal self-injury in patients with eating disorders: A systematic review and meta-analysis. *Psychological Medicine* 46, 1345-1358.

Currier JM, Smith PN, Kuhlman S (2015). Assessing the unique role of religious coping in suicidal behavior among US Iraq and Afghanistan veterans. *Psychology of Religion and Spirituality*. Published online: 21 September 2015. doi: 10.1037/rel0000055.

Czyz EK, Berona J, King CA (2016). Rehospitalization of suicidal adolescents in relation to course of suicidal ideation and future suicide attempts. *Psychiatric Services* 67, 332-338.

Dabaghzadeh F, Jabbari F, Khalili H, Abbasian L (2015). Associated factors of suicidal thoughts in HIV-positive individuals. *Iranian Journal of Psychiatry* 10, 185-191.

Davies LE, Oliver C (2016). Self-injury, aggression and destruction in children with severe intellectual disability: Incidence, persistence and novel, predictive behavioural risk markers. *Research in Developmental Disabilities* 49-50, 291-301.

de Araújo Veras JL, Ximenes RCC, de Vasconcelos FMN, Sougey EB (2015). Prevalence of suicide risk among adolescents with depressive symptoms. *Archives of Psychiatric Nursing* 30, 2-6.

de Assis da Silva R, Mograbi DC, Bifano J, Santana CM, Cheniaux E (2016). Correlation between insight level and suicidal behavior/ideation in bipolar depression. *Psychiatric Quarterly*. Published online: 24 March 2016. doi: 10.1007/s11126-016-9432-4.

de Beer WA, Murtagh J, Cheung G (2015). Late-life self-harm in the Waikato region. *New Zealand Medical Journal* 128, 75-82.

de Cerqueira AC, Andrade PS, Godoy-Barreiros JM, e Silva ACO, Nardi AE (2015). Risk factors for suicide in multiple sclerosis: A case-control study. *Jornal Brasileiro de Psiquiatria* 64, 303-306.

De Luca SM, Franklin C, Yueqi Y, Johnson S, Brownson C (2016). The relationship between suicide ideation, behavioral health, and college academic performance. *Community Mental Health Journal*. Published online: 29 January 2016. doi: 10.1007/s10597-016-9987-4.

DeCamp W, Bakken NW (2015). Self-injury, suicide ideation, and sexual orientation: Differences in causes and correlates among high school students. *Journal of Injury and Violence Research* 8, 15-24.

DeCou CR, Skewes MC (2016). Symptoms of alcohol dependence predict suicide ideation among Alaskan undergraduates. *Crisis*. Published online: 2 February 2016. doi: 10.1027/0227-5910/a000373.

Del Bello V, Verdolini N, Pauselli L, Attademo L, Bernardini F, Quartesan R, Moretti P (2015). Personality and psychotic symptoms as predictors of self-harm and attempted suicide. *Psychiatria Danubina* 27 Suppl 1, S285-S291.

Delfabbro PH, Malvaso C, Winefield AH, Winefield HR (2015). Socio-demographic, health, and psychological correlates of suicidality severity in Australian adolescents. *Australian Journal of Psychology*. Published online: 5 November 2015. doi: 10.1111/ajpy.12104.

Dell'Osso B, Holtzman JN, Goffin KC, Portillo N, Hooshmand F, Miller S, Dore J, Wang PW, Hill SJ, Ketter TA (2015). American tertiary clinic-referred bipolar II disorder compared to bipolar I disorder: More severe in multiple ways, but less severe in a few other ways. *Journal of Affective Disorders* 188, 257-262.

Dempsey J, Dempsey AG, Guffey D, Minard CG, Goin-Kochel RP (2016). Brief report: Further examination of self-injurious behaviors in children and adolescents with autism spectrum disorders. *Journal of Autism and Developmental Disorders* 46, 1872-1879.

Denneson LM, Kovas AE, Britton PC, Kaplan MS, McFarland BH, Dobscha SK (2016). Suicide risk documented during veterans' last Veterans Affairs health care contacts prior to suicide. *Suicide and Life-Threatening Behavior*. Published online: 1 February 2016. doi: 10.1111/sltb.12226.

Dennis BB, Roshanov PS, Bawor M, ElSheikh W, Garton S, DeJesus J, Rangarajan S, Vair J, Sholer H, Hutchinson N, Lordan E, Thabane L, Samaan Z (2015). Re-examination of classic risk factors for suicidal behavior in the psychiatric population. *Crisis* 36, 231-240.

Depp CA, Moore RC, Dev SI, Mausbach BT, Eyler LT, Granholm EL (2016). The temporal course and clinical correlates of subjective impulsivity in bipolar disorder as revealed through ecological momentary assessment. *Journal of Affective Disorders* 193, 145-150.

Depp CA, Moore RC, Perivoliotis D, Holden JL, Swendsen J, Granholm EL (2016). Social behavior, interaction appraisals, and suicidal ideation in schizophrenia: The dangers of being alone. *Schizophrenia Research* 172, 195-200.

Deslauriers J, Belleville K, Beaudet N, Sarret P, Grignon S (2016). A two-hit model of suicide-trait-related behaviors in the context of a schizophrenia-like phenotype: Distinct effects of lithium chloride and clozapine. *Physiology and Behavior* 156, 48-58.

DeVylder JE, Jahn DR, Doherty T, Wilson CS, Wilcox HC, Schiffman J, Hilimire MR (2015). Social and psychological contributions to the co-occurrence of sub-threshold psychotic experiences and suicidal behavior. *Social Psychiatry and Psychiatric Epidemiology* 50, 1819-1830.

Dey M, Jorm AF (2016). Reluctance to seek professional help among suicidal people: Results from the Swiss health survey. *International Journal of Public Health*. Published online: 30 January 2016. doi: 10.1007/s00038-015-0782-8.

Dillman Carpentier FR, Parrott MS (2016). Young adults' information seeking following celebrity suicide: Considering involvement with the celebrity and emotional distress in health communication strategies. *Health Communication*. Published online: 16 March 2016. doi: 10.1080/10410236.2015.1056329.

Du Roscoät E, Legleye S, Guignard R, Husky M, Beck F (2016). Risk factors for suicide attempts and hospitalizations in a sample of 39,542 French adolescents. *Journal of Affective Disorders* 190, 517-521.

Ducasse D, Jaussent I, Olie E, Guillaume S, Lopez-Castroman J, Courtet P (2016). Personality traits of suicidality are associated with premenstrual syndrome and premenstrual dysphoric disorder in a suicidal women sample. *PLoS One* 11, e0148653.

Dugas EN, Low NC, O'Loughlin EK, O'Loughlin JL (2015). Recurrent suicidal ideation in young adults. *Canadian Journal of Public Health* 106, e303-e307.

Dutton CE, Rojas SM, Badour CL, Wanklyn SG, Feldner MT (2016). Posttraumatic stress disorder and suicidal behavior: Indirect effects of impaired social functioning. *Archives of Suicide Research*. Published online: 16 March 2016. doi: 10.1080/13811118.2016.1158680.

Eichen DM, Kass AE, Fitzsimmons-Craft EE, Gibbs E, Trockel M, Barr Taylor C, Wilfley DE (2016). Non-suicidal self-injury and suicidal ideation in relation to eating and general psychopathology among college-age women. *Psychiatry Research* 235, 77-82.

Eisen RB, Perera S, Banfield L, Anglin R, Minuzzi L, Samaan Z (2015). Association between BDNF levels and suicidal behaviour: A systematic review and meta-analysis. *Systematic Reviews* 4, 187.

Emery AA, Heath NL, Mills DJ (2015). Basic psychological need satisfaction, emotion dysregulation, and non-suicidal self-injury engagement in young adults: An application of self-determination theory. *Journal of Youth and Adolescence* 45, 612-623.

Evren C, Dalbudak E, Evren B, Bozkurt M, Demirci AC, Umut G, Can Y (2015). Psychological symptoms related with violence and its relationship with internalizing and externalizing problems among 10th grade students in Istanbul. *Dusunen Adam* 28, 344-355.

Fellows RP, Spahr NA, Byrd DA, Mindt MR, Morgello S, Manhattan HIVBB (2015). Psychological trauma exposure and co-morbid psychopathologies in HIV plus men and women. *Psychiatry Research* 230, 770-776.

Ferentinos P, Porichi E, Christodoulou C, Dikeos D, Papageorgiou C, Douzenis A (2016). Sleep disturbance as a proximal predictor of suicidal intent in recently hospitalized attempters. *Sleep Medicine* 19, 1-7.

Ferreira AD, Sponholz A, Jr., Mantovani C, Pazin-Filho A, Passos ADC, Botega NJ, Del-Ben CM (2016). Clinical features, psychiatric assessment, and longitudinal outcome of suicide attempters admitted to a tertiary emergency hospital. *Archives of Suicide Research* 20, 191-204.

Few LR, Werner KB, Sartor CE, Grant JD, Trull TJ, Nock MK, Bucholz KK, Deitz SK, Glowinski AL, Martin NG, Nelson EC, Statham DJ, Madden PA, Heath AC, Lynskey MT, Agrawal A (2015). Early onset alcohol use and self-harm: A discordant twin analysis. *Alcoholism: Clinical and Experimental Research* 39, 2134-2142.

Fletcher TM, Markley LA, Nelson D, Crane SS, Fitzgibbon JJ (2015). Pregnant adolescents admitted to an inpatient child and adolescent psychiatric unit: An eight-year review. *Journal of Pediatric and Adolescent Gynecology* 28, 477-480.

Flynn AB, Johnson RM, Bolton SL, Mojtabai R (2016). Victimization of lesbian, gay, and bisexual people in childhood: Associations with attempted suicide. *Suicide and Life Threatening Behavior*. Published online: 27 January 2016. doi: 10.1111/sltb.12228.

Ford JA, Perna D (2015). Prescription drug misuse and suicidal ideation: Findings from the national survey on drug use and health. *Drug and Alcohol Dependence* 151, 192-196.

Forkmann T, Meessen J, Teismann T, Sütterlin S, Gauggel S, Mainz V (2016). Resting vagal tone is negatively associated with suicide ideation. *Journal of Affective Disorders* 194, 30-32.

Forrest LN, Bodell LP, Witte TK, Goodwin N, Bartlett ML, Siegfried N, Eddy KT, Thomas JJ, Franko DL, Smith AR (2016). Associations between eating disorder symptoms and suicidal ideation through thwarted belongingness and perceived burdensomeness among eating disorder patients. *Journal of Affective Disorders* 195, 127-135.

Fortney JC, Curran GM, Hunt JB, Cheney AM, Lu L, Valenstein M, Eisenberg D (2016). Prevalence of probable mental disorders and help-seeking behaviors among veteran and non-veteran community college students. *General Hospital Psychiatry* 38, 99-104.

Fox KR, Franklin JC, Ribeiro JD, Kleiman EM, Bentley KH, Nock MK (2015). Meta-analysis of risk factors for nonsuicidal self-injury. *Clinical Psychology Review* 42, 156-167.

Freitas-Rosa M, Goncalves S, Antunes H (2016). Is being overweight associated with engagement in self-injurious behaviours in adolescence, or do psychological factors have more "weight"? *Eating and Weight Disorders*. Published online: 12 January 2016. doi: 10.1007/s40519-015-0251-7.

Frey LM, Hans JD, Cerel J (2016). Suicide disclosure in suicide attempt survivors: Does family reaction moderate or mediate disclosure's effect on depression? *Suicide and Life Threatening Behavior* 46, 96-105.

Friedman LE, Gelaye B, Rondon MB, Sanchez SE, Peterlin BL, Williams MA (2016). Association of migraine headaches with suicidal ideation among pregnant women in Lima, Peru. *Headache* 56, 741-749.

Gananca L, Oquendo MA, Tyrka AR, Cisneros-Trujillo S, Mann JJ, Sublette ME (2016). The role of cytokines in the pathophysiology of suicidal behavior. *Psychoneuroendocrinology* 63, 296-310.

Gandhi A, Claes L, Bosmans G, Baetens I, Wilderjans TF, Maitra S, Kiekens G, Luyckx K (2015). Non-suicidal self-injury and adolescents attachment with peers and mother: The mediating role of identity synthesis and confusion. *Journal of Child and Family Studies* 25, 1735-1745.

Gardner KJ, Dodsworth J, Klonsky ED (2016). Reasons for non-suicidal self-harm in adult male offenders with and without borderline personality traits. *Archives of Suicide Research*. Published online: 8 March 2016. doi: 10.1080/13811118.2016.1158683.

Gart R, Kelly S (2015). How illegal drug use, alcohol use, tobacco use, and depressive symptoms affect adolescent suicidal ideation: A secondary analysis of the 2011 youth risk behavior survey. *Issues in Mental Health Nursing* 36, 614-620.

Gazdag G, Belán E, Szabó FA, Ungvari GS, Czobor P, Baran B (2015). Predictors of suicide attempts after violent offences in schizophrenia spectrum disorders. *Psychiatry Research* 230, 728-731.

Geisner IM, Kirk JL, Mittmann AJ, Kilmer JR, Larimer ME (2015). College students' perceptions of depressed mood: Exploring accuracy and associations. *Professional Psychology: Research and Practice* 46, 375-383.

Geoffroy MC, Boivin M, Arseneault L, Turecki G, Vitaro F, Brendgen M, Renaud J, Seguin JR, Tremblay RE, Cote SM (2016). Associations between peer victimization and suicidal ideation and suicide attempt during adolescence: Results from a prospective population-based birth cohort. *Journal of the American Academy of Child & Adolescent Psychiatry* 55, 99-105.

Glazebrook K, Townsend E, Sayal K (2015). Do coping strategies mediate the relationship between parental attachment and self-harm in young people? *Archives of Suicide Research* 20, 2015-218.

Glenn CR, Kleiman EM, Cha CB, Nock MK, Prinstein MJ (2015). Implicit cognition about self-injury predicts actual self-injurious behavior: Results from a longitudinal study of adolescents. *Journal of Child Psychology and Psychiatry.* Published online: 18 December 2015. doi: 10.1111/jcpp.1250.

Goffin KC, Dell'osso B, Miller S, Wang PW, Holtzman JN, Hooshmand F, Ketter TA (2016). Different characteristics associated with suicide attempts among bipolar I versus bipolar II disorder patients. *Journal of Psychiatric Research* 76, 94-100.

Goldschmidt AB, Loth KA, MacLehose RF, Pisetsky EM, Berge JM, Neumark-Sztainer D (2015). Overeating with and without loss of control: Associations with weight status, weight-related characteristics, and psychosocial health. *International Journal of Eating Disorders* 48, 1150-1157.

Gonçalves AM, da Cruz Sequeira CA, Duarte JC, de Freitas PP (2015). Suicidal ideation on higher education students: Influence of some psychosocial variables. *Archives of Psychiatric Nursing* 30, 162-166.

Goncalves S, Machado B, Silva C, Crosby RD, Lavender JM, Cao L, Machado PP (2015). The moderating role of purging behaviour in the relationship between sexual/physical abuse and non-suicidal self-injury in eating disorder patients. *European Eating Disorders Review* 24, 164-168.

Gooding P, Tarrier N, Dunn G, Shaw J, Awenat Y, Ulph F, Pratt D (2015). Effect of hopelessness on the links between psychiatric symptoms and suicidality in a vulnerable population at risk of suicide. *Psychiatry Research* 230, 464-471.

Gooding P, Tarrier N, Dunn G, Shaw J, Awenat Y, Ulph F, Pratt D (2015). The moderating effects of coping and self-esteem on the relationship between defeat, entrapment and suicidality in a sample of prisoners at high risk of suicide. *European Psychiatry* 30, 988-994.

Green JD, Kearns JC, Ledoux AM, Addis ME, Marx BP (2015). The association between masculinity and nonsuicidal self-injury. *American Journal of Men's Health.* Published online: 30 December 2015.

Greene-Palmer FN, Wagner BM, Neely LL, Cox DW, Kochanski KM, Perera KU, Ghahramanlou-Holloway M (2015). How parental reactions change in response to adolescent suicide attempt. *Archives of Suicide Research* 19, 414-421.

Gujral S, Ogbagaber S, Dombrovski AY, Butters MA, Karp JF, Szanto K (2015). Course of cognitive impairment following attempted suicide in older adults. *International Journal of Geriatric Psychiatry* 31, 592-600.

Gutierrez PM, Davidson CL, Friese AH, Forster JE (2015). Physical activity, suicide risk factors, and suicidal ideation in a veteran sample. *Suicide and Life-Threatening Behavior.* Published online: 25 September 2016. doi: 10.1111/sltb.12190.

Ha JY, Kim SH, Choi HY, Ahn YM (2015). Pubertal timing, subjective health, and suicidal behaviors in Korean adolescents. *International Journal of Applied Engineering Research* 10, 39334-39337.

Hagberg KW, Li L, Peng M, Shah K, Paris M, Jick S (2016). Incidence rates of suicidal behaviors and treated depression in patients with and without psoriatic arthritis using the clinical practice research datalink. *Modern Rheumatology.* Published online: 16 February 2016. doi: 10.3109/14397595.2015.1136726.

Han B, Crosby AE, Ortega LAG, Parks SE, Compton WM, Gfroerer J (2016). Suicidal ideation, suicide attempt, and occupations among employed adults aged 18-64 years in the United States. *Comprehensive Psychiatry* 66, 176-186.

Handley TE, Kay-Lambkin FJ, Baker AL, Lewin TJ, Kelly BJ, Inder KJ, Attia JR, Kavanagh DJ (2016). Investigation of a suicide ideation risk profile in people with co-occurring depression and substance use disorder. *Journal of Nervous and Mental Disease.* Published online: 22 January 2016. doi: 10.1097/NMD.0000000000000473.

Handley TE, Ventura AD, Browne JL, Rich J, Attia JR, Reddy P, Pouwer F, Speight J (2015). Suicidal ideation reported by adults with Type 1 or Type 2 diabetes: Results from diabetes MILES-Australia. *Diabetic Medicine.* Published online: 8 December 2015. doi: 10.1111/dme.13022.

Hasking P, Rees CS, Martin G, Quigley J (2015). What happens when you tell someone you self-injure? The effects of disclosing NSSI to adults and peers. *BMC Public Health* 15, 1039.

Haviland MG, Banta JE, Sonne JL, Przekop P (2015). Posttraumatic stress disorder-related hospitalizations in the United States (2002-2011): Rates, co-occurring illnesses, suicidal ideation/self-harm, and hospital charges. *Journal of Nervous and Mental Disease* 204, 78-86.

Hawley LD, MacDonald MG, Wallace EH, Smith J, Wummel B, Wren PA (2015). Baseline assessment of campus-wide general health status and mental health: Opportunity for tailored suicide prevention and mental health awareness programming. *Journal of American College Health* 64, 174-183.

Hawton K, Bergen H, Geulayov G, Waters K, Ness J, Cooper J, Kapur N (2016). Impact of the recent recession on self-harm: Longitudinal ecological and patient-level investigation from the multicentre study of self-harm in England. *Journal of Affective Disorders* 191, 132-138.

Heath NL, Carsley D, De Riggi M, Mills D, Mettler J (2016). The relationship between mindfulness, depressive symptoms and non-suicidal self-injury amongst adolescents. *Archives of Suicide Research.* Published online: 16 March 2016. doi: 10.1080/13811118.2016.1162243.

Heerde JA, Toumbourou JW, Hemphill SA, Herrenkohl TI, Patton GC, Catalano RF (2015). Incidence and course of adolescent deliberate self-harm in Victoria, Australia, and Washington State. *Journal of Adolescent Health* 57, 537-544.

Herbert A, Li L, Gonzalez-Izquierdo A, Gilbert R (2014). Risk of future harm in adolescents admitted to hospitals in England for injury related to victimisation, self-harm, or drug or alcohol misuse: A retrospective cohort study. *Lancet* 384, 36.

Hesdorffer DC, Ishihara L, Webb DJ, Mynepalli L, Galwey NW, Hauser WA (2015). Occurrence and recurrence of attempted suicide among people with epilepsy. *Journal of the American Medical Association Psychiatry* 73, 80-86.

Hidalgo-Rasmussen C, Martín AHS (2015). Suicidal-related behaviors and quality of life according to gender in adolescent Mexican high school students. *Ciencia & Saude Coletiva* 20, 3437-3446.

Hirschtritt ME, Ordonez AE, Rico YC, LeWinn KZ (2015). Internal resilience, peer victimization, and suicidal ideation among adolescents. *International Journal of Adolescent Medicine and Health* 27, 415-423.

Hofer P, Schosser A, Calati R, Serretti A, Massat I, Kocabas NA, Konstantinidis A, Mendlewicz J, Souery D, Zohar J, Juven-Wetzler A, Montgomery S, Kasper S (2015). The impact of serotonin receptor 1A and 2A gene polymorphisms and interactions on suicide attempt and suicide risk in depressed patients with insufficient response to treatment - a European multicentre study. *International Clinical Psychopharmacology* 31, 1-7.

Holmstrand C, Bogren M, Mattisson C, Bradvik L (2015). Long-term suicide risk in no, one or more mental disorders: The Lundby study 1947-1997. *Acta Psychiatrica Scandinavica* 132, 459-469.

Hom MA, Stanley IH, Ringer FB, Joiner TE (2016). Mental health service use among firefighters with suicidal thoughts and behaviors. *Psychiatric Services*. Published online: 29 February 2016. doi: 10.1176/appi.ps.201500177.

Homaifar BY, Shura RD, Miskey HM, Yoash-Gantz RE, Rowland JA (2016). The relationship of suicidal ideation to objective and subjective executive functioning. *Military Psychology* 28, 185-191.

Homan KJ, Sim LA, Fargo JD, Twohig MP (2016). Five-year prospective investigation of self-harm/suicide-related behaviors in the development of borderline personality disorder. *Personality Disorders: Theory, Research, and Treatment*. Published online: 11 January 2016. doi: 10.1037/per0000169.

Hong L, Guo L, Wu H, Li P, Xu Y, Gao X, Deng J, Huang G, Huang J, Lu C (2016). Bullying, depression, and suicidal ideation among adolescents in the Fujian province of China: A cross-sectional study. *Medicine* 95, e2530.

Honings S, Drukker M, Groen R, van Os J (2015). Psychotic experiences and risk of self-injurious behaviour in the general population: A systematic review and meta-analysis. *Psychological Medicine* 46, 237-251.

Horgan M, Martin G (2016). Differences between current and past self-injurers: How and why do people stop? *Archives of Suicide Research* 20, 142-152.

Horton SE, Hughes JL, King JD, Kennard BD, Westers NJ, Mayes TL, Stewart SM (2015). Preliminary examination of the interpersonal psychological theory of suicide in an adolescent clinical sample. *Journal of Abnormal Child Psychology*. Published online: 14 December 2015. doi: 10.1007/s10802-015-0109-5.

Hu N, Glauert RA, Li J, Taylor CL (2016). Risk factors for repetition of a deliberate self-harm episode within seven days in adolescents and young adults: A population-level record linkage study in Western Australia. *Australian and New Zealand Journal of Psychiatry* 50, 154-166.

Huang KC, Tzeng DS, Lin CH, Chung WC (2016). Interpersonal-psychological theory and parental bonding predict suicidal ideation among soldiers in Taiwan. *Asia Pacific Psychiatry*. Published online: 2 March 2016. doi: 10.1111/appy.12236.

Huffman JC, Boehm JK, Beach SR, Beale EE, DuBois CM, Healy BC (2016). Relationship of optimism and suicidal ideation in three groups of patients at varying levels of suicide risk. *Journal of Psychiatric Research* 77, 76-84.

Hung GC, Pietras SA, Carliner H, Martin L, Seidman LJ, Buka SL, Gilman SE (2015). Cognitive ability in childhood and the chronicity and suicidality of depression. *British Journal of Psychiatry* 208, 120-127.

Hussien ZN, Solomon H, Yohannis Z, Ahmed AM (2015). Prevalence and associate factors of suicidal ideation and attempt among people with schizophrenia at Amanuel Mental Specialized Hospital Addis Ababa, Ethiopia. *Journal of Psychiatry* 18, 184.

Huz I, Nyer M, Dickson C, Farabaugh A, Alpert J, Fava M, Baer L (2016). Obsessive-compulsive symptoms as a risk factor for suicidality in U.S. College students. *Journal of Adolescence Health* 58, 481-484.

Hwang BD, Park JW, Choi R (2016). Factors influencing suicide dimensions in the elderly. *International Journal of Bio-Science and Bio-Technology* 8, 199-212.

Iskender M, Koc M, Soyer F, Colak TS, Dusunceli B, Arici N (2016). Chart of uncompleted suicide behavior regarding individual, social and psychological factors. *Studies on Ethno-Medicine* 10, 44-52.

Itzhaky L, Shahar G, Stein D, Fennig S (2015). In eating-disordered inpatient adolescents, self-criticism predicts nonsuicidal self-injury. *Suicide and Life-Threatening Behavior*. Published online: 17 October 2015. doi: 0.1111/sltb.12223.

Iverson GL (2015). Suicide and chronic traumatic encephalopathy. *Journal of Neuropsychiatry and Clinical Neurosciences* 28, 9-16.

Ivković M, Pantović-Stefanović M, Dunjić-Kostić B, Jurišić V, Lačković M, Totić-Poznanović S, Jovanović AA, Damjanović A (2016). Neutrophil-to-lymphocyte ratio predicting suicide risk in euthymic patients with bipolar disorder: Moderatory effect of family history. *Comprehensive Psychiatry* 66, 87-95.

Izci F, Findikli EK, Zincir S, Zincir SB, Koc MI (2016). The differences in temperament-character traits, suicide attempts, impulsivity, and functionality levels of patients with bipolar disorder I and II. *Neuropsychiatric Disease and Treatment* 12, 177-184.

Jahn DR, Bennett ME, Park SG, Gur RE, Horan WP, Kring AM, Blanchard JJ (2015). The interactive effects of negative symptoms and social role functioning on suicide ideation in individuals with schizophrenia. *Schizophrenia Research* 170, 271-277.

Jahn DR, DeVylder JE, Hilimire MR (2016). Explanatory risk factors in the relations between schizotypy and indicators of suicide risk. *Psychiatry Research* 238, 68-73.

Jang SI, Bae HC, Shin J, Jang SY, Hong S, Han KT, Park EC (2016). The effect of suicide attempts on suicide ideation by family members in fast developed country, Korea. *Comprehensive Psychiatry* 66, 132-138.

Jimenez E, Arias B, Mitjans M, Goikolea JM, Ruiz V, Brat M, Saiz PA, Garcia-Portilla MP, Buron P, Bobes J, Oquendo MA, Vieta E, Benabarre A (2016). Clinical features, impulsivity, temperament and functioning and their role in suicidality in patients with bipolar disorder. *Acta Psychiatrica Scandinavica* 133, 266-276.

Johnson ER, Weiler RM, Barnett TE, Pealer LN (2016). Extreme weight-control behaviors and suicide risk among high school students. *Journal of School Health* 86, 281-287.

Johnstone JM, Carter JD, Luty SE, Mulder RT, Frampton CM, Joyce PR (2016). Childhood predictors of lifetime suicide attempts and non-suicidal self-injury in depressed adults. *Australian and New Zealand Journal of Psychiatry* 50, 135-144.

Joksimović Knjisa I, Marinković L, Čobrda N (2015). Depressive disorders in student population - comparative study conducted in 2007 and 2014. *Medicinski Pregled* 68, 234-239.

Jordan JT, Samuelson KW (2015). Predicting suicide intent: The roles of experiencing or committing violent acts. *Suicide and Life-Threatening Behavior*. Published online: 29 September 2015. doi: 10.1111/sltb.12193.

Ju YJ, Han KT, Lee TH, Kim W, Park JH, Park EC (2016). Association between weight control failure and suicidal ideation in overweight and obese adults: A cross-sectional study. *BMC Public Health* 16, 259.

Jung JH, Kim DK, Jung JY, Lee JH, Kwak YH (2015). Risk factors of discharged against medical advice among adolescents self-inflicted injury and attempted suicide in the Korean emergency department. *Journal of Korean Medical Science* 30, 1466-1470.

Jylhä P, Rosenström T, Mantere O, Suominen K, Melartin T, Vuorilehto M, Holma M, Riihimäki K, Oquendo MA, Keltikangas-Järvinen L, Isometsä ET (2015). Personality disorders and suicide attempts in unipolar and bipolar mood disorders. *Journal of Affective Disorders* 190, 632-639.

Jylhä PJ, Rosenström T, Mantere O, Suominen K, Melartin TK, Vuorilehto MS, Holma MK, Riihimäki KA, Oquendo MA, Keltikangas-Järvinen L, Isometsä ET (2016). Temperament, character and suicide attempts in unipolar and bipolar mood disorders. *Journal of Clinical Psychiatry* 77, 252-260.

Kahr Nilsson K (2016). Early maladaptive schemas in bipolar disorder patients with and without suicide attempts. *Journal of Nervous and Mental Disease* 204, 236-239.

Kakounda Muallem H, Israelashvilli M (2015). Religiosity as a buffer against suicidal ideation: A comparison between Christian and Muslim-Arab adolescents. *Mental Health, Religion and Culture* 18, 838-849.

Kang CR, Bang JH, Cho SI, Kim KN, Lee HJ, Ryu BY, Cho SK, Lee YH, Oh MD, Lee JK (2015). Suicidal ideation and suicide attempts among human immunodeficiency virus-infected adults: Differences in risk factors and their implications. *AIDS Care* 28, 306-313.

Kanwal R, Aslam N (2015). Mediating role of depression in the relationship between brooding rumination and suicidal ideation. *Journal of the Liaquat University of Medical and Health Sciences* 14, 58-62.

Kaplan KJ, Harrow M, Clews K (2016). The twenty-year trajectory of suicidal activity among post-hospital psychiatric men and women with mood disorders and schizophrenia. *Archives of Suicide Research*. Published online 16 February 2016. doi: 10.1080/13811118.2015.1033505.

Kasahara-Kiritani M, Hadlaczky G, Westerlund M, Carli V, Wasserman C, Apter A, Balazs J, Bobes J, Brunner R, McMahon EM, Cosman D, Farkas L, Haring C, Kaess M, Kahn JP, Keeley H, Nemes B, Bitenc UM, Postuvan V, Saiz P, Sisask M, Värnik A, Sarchiapone M, Hoven CW, Wasserman D (2015). Reading books and watching films as a protective factor against suicidal ideation. *International Journal of Environmental Research and Public Health* 12, 15937-15942.

Kasckow J, Youk A, Anderson SJ, Dew MA, Butters MA, Marron MM, Begley AE, Szanto K, Dombrovski AY, Mulsant BH, Lenze EJ, Reynolds CF (2015). Trajectories of suicidal ideation in depressed older adults undergoing antidepressant treatment. *Journal of Psychiatric Research* 73, 96-101.

Kaur J, Bhandari A, Upmanyu VV, Chavan BS (2014). Correlates of suicide ideation in patients with depressive disorder and alcohol dependence. *Indian Journal of Social Psychiatry* 30, 43-48.

Kawada T (2015). Risk of suicidal mortality among multiple attempters. *Journal of the Formosan Medical Association*. Published online: 19 December 2015. doi:10.1016/j.jfma.2015.11.010.

Kay DB, Dombrovski AY, Buysse DJ, Reynolds CF, Begley A, Szanto K (2015). Insomnia is associated with suicide attempt in middle-aged and older adults with depression. *International Psychogeriatrics* 28, 613-619.

Kazi TB, Naidoo S (2015). Does religiosity mediate suicidal tendencies? A South African study of Muslim tertiary students. *Journal of Religion and Health* 55, 1010-1023.

Kazour F, Soufia M, Rohayem J, Richa S (2015). Suicide risk of heroin dependent subjects in Lebanon. *Community Mental Health Journal*. Published online: 30 September 2015. doi: 10.1007/s10597-015-9952-7.

Keilp JG, Stanley BH, Beers SR, Melhem NM, Burke AK, Cooper TB, Oquendo MA, Brent DA, John Mann J (2015). Further evidence of low baseline cortisol levels in suicide attempters. *Journal of Affective Disorders* 190, 187-192.

Kesinger MR, Juengst SB, Bertisch H, Niemeier JP, Krellman JW, Pugh MJ, Kumar RG, Sperry JL, Arenth PM, Fann JR, Wagner AK (2016). Acute trauma factor associations with suicidality across the first 5 years after traumatic brain injury. *Archives of Physical Medicine and Rehabilitation*. Published online: 14 March 2016. doi:10.1016/j.apmr.2016.02.017.

Khan A, Hamdan AR, Ahmad R, Mustaffa MS, Mahalle S (2015). Problem-solving coping and social support as mediators of academic stress and suicidal ideation among Malaysian and Indian adolescents. *Community Mental Health Journal* 52, 245-250.

Khazem LR, Houtsma C, Gratz KL, Tull MT, Green BA, Anestis MD (2016). Firearms matter: The moderating role of firearm storage in the association between current suicidal ideation and likelihood of future suicide attempts among United States military personnel. *Military Psychology* 28, 25-33.

Khemiri L, Jokinen J, Runeson B, Jayaram-Lindstrom N (2016). Suicide risk associated with experience of violence and impulsivity in alcohol dependent patients. *Scientific Reports* 6, 19373.

Kiekens G, Claes L, Demyttenaere K, Auerbach RP, Green JG, Kessler RC, Mortier P, Nock MK, Bruffaerts R (2016). Lifetime and 12-month nonsuicidal self-injury and academic performance in college freshmen. *Suicide and Life-Threatening Behavior*. Published online: 8 March 2016. doi: 10.1111/sltb.12237.

Kim DH, Han K, Kim SW (2016). Relationship between allergic rhinitis and mental health in the general Korean adult population. *Allergy Asthma and Immunology Research* 8, 49-54.

Kim H, Seo J, Namkoong K, Hwang EH, Sohn SY, Kim SJ, Kang JI (2015). Alexithymia and perfectionism traits are associated with suicidal risk in patients with obsessive-compulsive disorder. *Journal of Affective Disorders* 192, 50-55.

Kim HHS (2016). The associations between parental involvement, peer network, and youth suicidality in China: Evidence from the global school-based student health survey (2003). *Social Science Journal* 53, 77-87.

Kim HS, Salmon M, Wohl MJA, Young M (2016). A dangerous cocktail: Alcohol consumption increases suicidal ideations among problem gamblers in the general population. *Addictive Behaviors* 55, 50-55.

Kim J, Kim HJ, Kim SH, Oh SH, Park KN (2015). Analysis of deliberate self-wrist-cutting episodes presenting to the emergency department. *Crisis*. Published online: 23 December 2015. doi: 10.1027/0227-5910/a000361.

Kim J, Lee K-S, Kim DJ, Hong S-C, Choi KH, Oh Y, Wang S-M, Lee H-K, Kweon Y-S, Lee CT, Lee K-U (2015). Characteristic risk factors associated with planned versus impulsive suicide attempters. *Clinical Psychopharmacology and Neuroscience* 13, 308-315.

Kim JL, Kim JM, Choi Y, Lee TH, Park EC (2016). Effect of socioeconomic status on the linkage between suicidal ideation and suicide attempts. *Suicide and Life-Threatening Behavior*. Published online: 17 March 2016. doi: 10.1111/sltb.12242.

Kim NY, Lee PK, Lim MH (2015). Suicidal idea, ADHD, depression, anxiety, self-esteem and impulsiveness in Korean soldiers. *Journal of Psychiatry* 18, 314.

Kim YJ (2015). A path analysis of caregivnig stress, caregiving service and depression in suicide ideation of Korean daughters-in-law. *Information* 18, 3911-3917.

Kinyanda E, Weiss HA, Mungherera M, Onyango-Mangen P, Ngabirano E, Kajungu R, Kagugube J, Muhwezi W, Muron J, Patel V (2016). Intimate partner violence as seen in post-conflict eastern Uganda: Prevalence, risk factors and mental health consequences. *BMC International Health and Human Rights* 16, 5.

Kizilhan J (2015). Interaction of mental health and forced married migrants in Germany. *Psychiatrische Praxis* 42, 430-435.

Kjelby E, Sinkeviciute I, Gjestad R, Kroken RA, Løberg EM, Jørgensen HA, Hugdahl K, Johnsen E (2015). Suicidality in schizophrenia spectrum disorders: The relationship to hallucinations and persecutory delusions. *European Psychiatry* 30, 830-836.

Klabunde M, Saggar M, Hustyi KM, Hammond JL, Reiss AL, Hall SS (2015). Neural correlates of self-injurious behavior in Prader-Willi syndrome. *Human Brain Mapping* 36, 4135-4143.

Klibert J, LeLeux-LaBarge K, Tarantino N, Lamis D, Yancey T (2016). Procrastination and suicide proneness: A moderated-mediation model for cognitive schemas and gender. *Death Studies*. Published online: 14 January 2016. doi: 10.1080/07481187.2016.1141262.

Knorr AC, Tull MT, Anestis MD, Dixon-Gordon KL, Bennett MF, Gratz KL (2016). The interactive effect of major depression and nonsuicidal self-injury on current suicide risk and lifetime suicide attempts. *Archives of Suicide Research*. Published online: 8 March 2016. doi: 10.1080/13811118.2016.1158679.

Koenig J, Oelkers-Ax R, Parzer P, Haffner J, Brunner R, Resch F, Kaess M (2015). The association of self-injurious behaviour and suicide attempts with recurrent idiopathic pain in adolescents: Evidence from a population-based study. *Child and Adolescent Psychiatry and Mental Health* 9, 32.

Kolla NJ, Chiuccariello L, Wilson AA, Houle S, Links P, Bagby RM, McMain S, Kellow C, Patel J, Rekkas PV, Pasricha S, Meyer JH (2016). Elevated monoamine oxidase-A distribution volume in borderline personality disorder is associated with severity across mood symptoms, suicidality, and cognition. *Biological Psychiatry* 79, 117-126.

Koo CY, Soon KJ, Yu J (2014). A study on factors influencing elders' suicidal ideation: Focused on comparison of gender differences. *Journal of Korean Academy of Community Health Nursing* 25, 24-32.

Koyanagi A, Stickley A, Haro JM (2015). Psychotic-like experiences and nonsuicidal self-injury in England: Results from a national survey. *PLoS One* 10, e0145533.

Kranzler A, Fehling KB, Anestis MD, Selby EA (2016). Emotional dysregulation, internalizing symptoms, and self-injurious and suicidal behavior: Structural equation modeling analysis. *Death Studies*. Published online: 25 January 2016. doi: 10.1080/07481187.2016.1145156.

Krysinska K, Lester D, Lyke J, Corveleyn J (2015). Trait gratitude and suicidal ideation and behavior. *Crisis* 36, 291-296.

Kumar PNS, Anish PK, George B (2015). Risk factors for suicide in elderly in comparison to younger age groups. *Indian Journal of Psychiatry* 57, 249-254.

Kušević Z, Ćusa BV, Babić G, Marcinko D (2015). Could alexithymia predict suicide attempts - a study of Croatian war veterans with post-traumatic stress disorder. *Psychiatria Danubina* 27, 420-423.

Lacey KK, Parnell R, Mouzon DM, Matusko N, Head D, Abelson JM, Jackson JS (2015). The mental health of us black women: The roles of social context and severe intimate partner violence. *British Medical Journal Open* 5, e008415.

Lamis DA, Ballard ED, May AM, Dvorak RD (2016). Depressive symptoms and suicidal ideation in college students: The mediating and moderating roles of hopelessness, alcohol problems, and social support. *Journal of Clinical Psychology*. Published online: 23 March 2016. doi: 10.1002/jclp.22295.

Lara MA, Navarrete L, Nieto L, Le HN (2015). Childhood abuse increases the risk of depressive and anxiety symptoms and history of suicidal behavior in Mexican pregnant women. *Revista Brasileira de Psiquiatria* 37, 203-210.

Latina D, Giannotta F, Rabaglietti E (2015). Do friends' co-rumination and communication with parents prevent depressed adolescents from self-harm? *Journal of Applied Developmental Psychology* 41, 120-128.

Latina D, Stattin H (2016). Toward a re-interpretation of self-harm: A cross-contextual approach. *Aggressive Behavior*. Published online: 16 February 2016. doi: 10.1002/ab.21647.

Law BMF, Shek DTL (2016). A 6-year longitudinal study of self-harm and suicidal behaviors among Chinese adolescents in Hong Kong. *Journal of Pediatric and Adolescent Gynecology* 29, S38-S48.

Lawrence RE, Brent D, Mann JJ, Burke AK, Grunebaum MF, Galfalvy HC, Oquendo MA (2016). Religion as a risk factor for suicide attempt and suicide ideation among depressed patients. *Journal of Nervous and Mental Disease*. Published online: 18 February 2016. doi: 10.1097/NMD.0000000000000484.

Le Noury J, Nardo JM, Healy D, Jureidini J, Raven M, Tufanaru C, Abi-Jaoude E (2015). Restoring study 329: Efficacy and harms of paroxetine and imipramine in treatment of major depression in adolescence. *BMJ* 351, H4320.

Leal SC, Santos JC (2016). Suicidal behaviors, social support and reasons for living among nursing students. *Nurse Education Today* 36, 434-438.

Lear MK, Pepper CM (2015). Self-concept clarity and emotion dysregulation in nonsuicidal self-injury. *Journal of Personality Disorders.* Published online: 1 December 2015. doi: 10.1521/pedi_2015_29_232.

Lee J-Y, Park Y-K, Cho K-H, Kim S-M, Choi Y-S, Kim D-H, Nam G-E, Han K-d, Kim Y-H (2015). Suicidal ideation among postmenopausal women on hormone replacement therapy: The Korean National Health and Nutrition Examination Survey (KNHANES V) from 2010 to 2012. *Journal of Affective Disorders* 189, 214-219.

Lee J, Lee Y (2016). The association of body image distortion with weight control behaviors, diet behaviors, physical activity, sadness, and suicidal ideation among Korean high school students: A cross-sectional study. *BMC Public Health* 16, 39.

Lee MA (2016). Social relationships, depressive symptoms and suicidality in Korea: Examining mediating and moderating effects in men and women. *International Journal of Social Psychiatry* 62, 67-75.

Lee S-J, Kim B, Oh D, Kim M-K, Kim K-H, Bang SY, Choi TK, Lee S-H (2016). White matter alterations associated with suicide in patients with schizophrenia or schizophreniform disorder. *Psychiatry Research* 28, 23-29.

Lee WK, Lim D, Lee HA, Park H (2016). Sensation seeking as a potential screening tool for suicidality in adolescence. *BMC Public Health* 16, 92.

Lee YJ, Kim S, Gwak AR, Kim SJ, Kang SG, Na KS, Son YD, Park J (2016). Decreased regional gray matter volume in suicide attempters compared to suicide non-attempters with major depressive disorders. *Comprehensive Psychiatry* 67, 59-65.

Lehavot K, Simpson TL, Shipherd JC (2016). Factors associated with suicidality among a national sample of transgender veterans. *Suicide and Life-Threatening Behavior.* Published online: 15 February 2016. doi: 10.1111/sltb.12233.

Lewis AS, Oberleitner L, Morgan PT, Picciotto MR, McKee SA (2015). Association of cigarette smoking with interpersonal and self-directed violence in a large community-based sample. *Nicotine and Tobacco Research.* Published online: 22 December 2015. doi: 10.1093/ntr/ntv287.

Lewis SP, Seko Y (2015). A double-edged sword: A review of benefits and risks of online nonsuicidal self-injury activities. *Journal of Clinical Psychology* 72, 249-262.

Li D, Bao Z, Li X, Wang Y (2016). Perceived school climate and Chinese adolescents' suicidal ideation and suicide attempts: The mediating role of sleep quality. *Journal of School Health* 86, 75-83.

Li D, Li X, Wang Y, Bao Z (2015). Parenting and Chinese adolescent suicidal ideation and suicide attempts: The mediating role of hopelessness. *Journal of Child and Family Studies* 25, 1397-1407.

Li R, Cai Y, Wang Y, Sun Z, Zhu C, Tian Y, Jiang X, Gan F (2015). Psychosocial syndemic associated with increased suicidal ideation among men who have sex with men in Shanghai, China. *Health Psychology* 35, 148-156.

Li X, Zhang B, Li Y, Antonio AL, Chen Y, Williams AB (2016). Mental health and suicidal ideation among Chinese women who have sex with men who have sex with men (MSM). *Women Health.* Published online: 26 January 2016. doi: 10.1080/03630242.2016.1145171.

Lin CC (2015). The relationships among gratitude, self-esteem, depression, and suicidal ideation among undergraduate students. *Scandinavian Journal of Psychology* 56, 700-707.

Littlewood DL, Gooding PA, Panagioti M, Kyle SD (2015). Nightmares and suicide in posttraumatic stress disorder: The mediating role of defeat, entrapment, and hopelessness. *Journal of Clinical Sleep Medicine* 12, 393-399.

Liu HY, Fuh JL, Lin YY, Chen WT, Wang SJ (2015). Suicide risk in patients with migraine and comorbid fibromyalgia. *Neurology* 85, 1017-1023.

Lockman JD, Servaty-Seib HL (2015). College student suicidal ideation: Perceived burdensomeness, thwarted belongingness, and meaning made of stress. *Death Studies* 40, 154-164.

Lopez-Castroman J, Cerrato L, Beziat S, Jaussent I, Guillaume S, Courtet P (2016). Heavy tobacco dependence in suicide attempters making recurrent and medically serious attempts. *Drug and Alcohol Dependence* 160, 177-182.

Lucaciu LA, Dumitrascu DL (2015). Depression and suicide ideation in chronic hepatitis C patients untreated and treated with interferon: Prevalence, prevention, and treatment. *Annals of Gastroenterology* 28, 440-447.

Lutz J, Morton K, Turiano NA, Fiske A (2016). Health conditions and passive suicidal ideation in the survey of health, ageing, and retirement in Europe. *Journals of Gerontology: Series B*. Published online: 24 March 2016. doi: 10.1093/geronb/gbw019.

Lytle MC, Blosnich JR, Kamen C (2016). The association of multiple identities with self-directed violence and depression among transgender individuals. *Suicide and Life-Threatening Behavior*. Published online: 24 February 2016. doi: 10.1111/sltb.12234.

Lyu J, Shi H, Wang S, Zhang J (2016). The effect of community stress and problems on psychopathology: A structural equation modeling study. *Comprehensive Psychiatry* 65, 24-31.

Mahaki B, Mehrabi Y, Kavousi A, Mohammadian Y, Kargar M (2015). Applying and comparing empirical and full Bayesian models in study of evaluating relative risk of suicide among counties of Ilam province. *Journal of Education and Health Promotion* 4, 50.

Majid M, Tadros M, Tadros G, Singh S, Broome MR, Upthegrove R (2015). Young people who self-harm: A prospective 1-year follow-up study. *Social Psychiatry and Psychiatric Epidemiology* 51, 171-181.

Makris GD, Reutfors J, Larsson R, Isacsson G, Osby U, Ekbom A, Ekselius L, Papadopoulos FC (2015). Serotonergic medication enhances the association between suicide and sunshine. *Journal of Affective Disorders* 189, 276-281.

Mandhouj O, Perroud N, Hasler R, Younes N, Huguelet P (2016). Characteristics of spirituality and religion among suicide attempters. *Journal of Nervous and Mental Disease*. Published online: 9 March 2016. doi: 10.1097/NMD.0000000000000497.

Mandracchia J, To Y, Pichette S (2016). Suicidality in the deep south: Risks for adolescent Mississippians. *Journal of Aggression, Conflict and Peace Research* 8, 61-70.

Marappan D, Khan A, Latif AA, Yusoff AM (2016). Influence of maternal depression and sucidal thoughts: Role of spousal support during pregnancy. *Man in India* 96, 9-17.

Marco JH, Garcia-Alandete J, Perez S, Guillen V, Jorquera M, Espallargas P, Botella C (2015). Meaning in life and non-suicidal self-injury: A follow-up study with participants with borderline personality disorder. *Psychiatry Research* 230, 561-566.

Marco JH, Perez S, Garcia-Alandete J (2016). Meaning in life buffers the association between risk factors for suicide and hopelessness in participants with mental disorders. *Journal of Clinical Psychology*. Published online: 14 March 2016. doi: 10.1002/jclp.22285.

Mars B, Cornish R, Heron J, Boyd A, Crane C, Hawton K, Lewis G, Tilling K, Macleod J, Gunnell D (2016). Using data linkage to investigate inconsistent reporting of self-harm and questionnaire non-response. *Archives of Suicide Research* 20, 113-141.

Marshall BD, Socias ME, Kerr T, Zalazar V, Sued O, Aristegui I (2015). Prevalence and correlates of lifetime suicide attempts among transgender persons in Argentina. *Journal of Homosexuality*. Published online: 13 November 2015. doi: 10.1080/00918369.2015.1117898.

Martyn D, Andrews L, Byrne M (2014). Prevalence rates and risk factors for mental health difficulties in adolescents aged 16 and 17 years living in rural Ireland. *Irish Journal of Psychological Medicine* 31, 111-123.

Matheson KM, Barrett T, Landine J, McLuckie A, Soh NL, Walter G (2016). Experiences of psychological distress and sources of stress and support during medical training: A survey of medical students. *Academic Psychiatry* 40, 63-68.

May AM, Klonsky ED (2015). "Impulsive" suicide attempts: What do we really mean? *Personal Disorders*. Published online: 18 December 2015. doi: 10.1037/per000016.

May CN, Overholser JC, Ridley J, Raymond D (2015). Passive suicidal ideation: A clinically relevant risk factor for suicide in treatment-seeking veterans. *Illness Crisis and Loss* 23, 261-277.

McDermott E, Roen K, Piela A (2015). Explaining self-harm: Youth cybertalk and marginalized sexualities and genders. *Youth and Society* 47, 873-889.

McKenna Á E, Gillen AMC (2016). Direct and indirect effects of maltreatment typologies on suicidality in a representative Northern Irish sample: Psychopathology only partially mediates the relationship. *Journal of Psychiatric Research* 72, 82-90.

Meerwijk EL, Weiss SJ (2016). Does suicidal desire moderate the association between frontal delta power and psychological pain? *PeerJ* 4, e1538.

Melhem N, Munroe S, Marsland A, Krijna K, Brent D, Douaihy A, DiPietro F, Diller R, Driscoll H (2015). Biomarkers in the HPA axis and inflammatory pathways for suicidal behavior in youth. *Psychoneuroendocrinology* 61, 43.

Melhem NM, Keilp JG, Porta G, Oquendo MA, Burke A, Stanley B, Cooper TB, Mann JJ, Brent DA (2015). Blunted HPA axis activity in suicide attempters compared to those at high-risk for suicidal behavior. *Neuropsychopharmacology*. Published online: 9 October 2015. doi:10.1038/npp.2015.309.

Mellesdal L, Gjestad R, Johnsen E, Jorgensen HA, Oedegaard KJ, Kroken RA, Mehlum L (2015). Borderline personality disorder and posttraumatic stress disorder at psychiatric discharge predict general hospital admission for self-harm. *Journal of Traumatic Stress* 28, 556-562.

Menon V, Kattimani S, Sarkar S, Mathan K (2016). How do repeat suicide attempters differ from first timers? An exploratory record based analysis. *Journal of Neurosciences in Rural Practice* 7, 91-96.

Menon V, Sarkar S, Kattimani S, Mathan K (2015). Do personality traits such as impulsivity and hostility-aggressiveness predict severity of intent in attempted suicide? Findings from a record based study in South India. *Indian Journal of Psychological Medicine* 37, 393-398.

Mert DG, Kelleci M, Mizrak A, Semiz M, Demir MO (2015). Factors associated with suicide attempts in patients with bipolar disorder type I. *Psychiatria Danubina* 27, 236-241.

Mihai C, Robu V, Knieling A, Iliescu DB, Chiri R (2015). Predictors of suicide risk in incarcerated male offenders: The role of personality disorders. *Revista Medico-chirurgical a Societ tii de Medici si Naturali ti din Ia i* 119, 1133-1140.

Miller AB, Esposito-Smythers C, Leichtweis RN (2015). A short-term, prospective test of the interpersonal-psychological theory of suicidal ideation in an adolescent clinical sample. *Suicide and Life-Threatening Behavior*. Published online: 12 October 2015. doi: 10.1111/sltb.12196.

Millings A, Carnelley KB (2015). Core belief content examined in a large sample of patients using online cognitive behaviour therapy. *Journal of Affective Disorders* 186, 275-283.

Milner A, Page KM, LaMontagne AD (2016). Perception of mattering and suicide ideation in the Australian working population: Evidence from a cross-sectional survey. *Community Mental Health Journal.* Published online: 3 March 2016. doi: 10.1007/s10597-016-0002-x.

Min A, Park SC, Jang EY, Park YC, Choi J (2015). Variables linking school bullying and suicidal ideation in middle school students in South Korea. *Journal of Psychiatry* 18, 268.

Minzenberg MJ, Lesh T, Niendam T, Yoon JH, Cheng Y, Rhoades RN, Carter CS (2015). Frontal motor cortex activity during reactive control is associated with past suicidal behavior in recent-onset schizophrenia. *Crisis* 36, 363-370.

Mitchell R, Draper B, Harvey L, Brodaty H, Close J (2015). The association of physical illness and self-harm resulting in hospitalisation among older people in a population-based study. *Aging and Mental Health.* Published online: 15 October 2015. doi: 10.1080/13607863.2015.1099610.

Mitchell SM, Cukrowicz KC, Van Allen J, Seegan PL (2015). Moderating role of trait hope in the relation between painful and provocative events and acquired capability for suicide. *Crisis* 36, 249-256.

Mitchell SM, Jahn DR, Guidry ET, Cukrowicz KC (2015). The relationship between video game play and the acquired capability for suicide: An examination of differences by category of video game and gender. *Cyberpsychology, Behavior, and Social Networking* 18, 757-762.

Mitchell SM, Seegan PL, Roush JF, Brown SL, Sustaita MA, Cukrowicz KC (2016). Retrospective cyberbullying and suicide ideation: The mediating roles of depressive symptoms, perceived burdensomeness, and thwarted belongingness. *Journal of Interpersonal Violence.* Published online: 9 February 2016. doi: 10.1177/0886260516628291.

Mkrtchyan AG, Hovsepyan AA (2015). The influence of imperative hallucinations on suicidal behavior of patients with schizophrenia. *New Armenian Medical Journal* 9, 56-60.

Mondin TC, Cardoso TdA, Jansen K, Konradt CE, Zaltron RF, Behenck MdO, Mattos LDd, Silva RAd (2016). Sexual violence, mood disorders and suicide risk: A population-based study. *Ciência and Saúde Coletiva* 21, 853-860.

Montoro R, Thombs B, Igartua KJ (2015). The association of bullying with suicide ideation, plan, and attempt among adolescents with GLB or unsure sexual identity, heterosexual identity with same-sex attraction or behavior, or heterosexual identity without same-sex attraction or behavior. *Sante Mentale Au Quebec* 40, 55-75.

Moody C, Fuks N, Peláez S, Smith NG (2015). "Without this, I would for sure already be dead": A qualitative inquiry regarding suicide protective factors among trans adults. *Psychology of Sexual Orientation and Gender Diversity* 2, 266-280.

Moore SE, Scott JG, Ferrari AJ, Mills R, Dunne MP, Erskine HE, Devries KM, Degenhardt L, Vos T, Whiteford HA, McCarthy M, Norman RE (2015). Burden attributable to child maltreatment in Australia. *Child Abuse and Neglect* 48, 208-220.

Musci RJ, Hart SR, Ballard ED, Newcomer A, Van Eck K, Ialongo N, Wilcox H (2015). Trajectories of suicidal ideation from sixth through tenth grades in predicting suicide attempts in young adulthood in an urban African American cohort. *Suicide and Life-Threatening Behavior.* Published online: 23 September 2015. doi: 10.1111/sltb.12191.

Mutlu C, Ozdemir M, Yorbik O, Kilicoglu AG (2015). Possible predictors of hospitalization for adolescents with conduct disorder seen in psychiatric emergency service. *Dusunen Adam* 28, 301-308.

Naicker N, de Jager P, Naidoo S, Mathee A (2016). Household factors associated with self-harm in Johannesburg, South African urban-poor households. *PLoS One* 11, e0146239.

Nam YY, Kim CH, Roh D (2016). Comorbid panic disorder as an independent risk factor for suicide attempts in depressed outpatients. *Comprehensive Psychiatry* 67, 13-18.

Nanda P, Tandon N, Mathew IT, Padmanabhan JL, Clementz BA, Pearlson GD, Sweeney JA, Tamminga CA, Keshavan MS (2016). Impulsivity across the psychosis spectrum: Correlates of cortical volume, suicidal history, and social and global function. *Schizophrenia Research* 170, 80-86.

Nandi S, Bhattacharjee S, Chatttopadhyay S, Debnath S, Choudhury S, Roy S, Bhattacharjee A (2015). Coping styles in suicide attempters attending a peripheral medical college of West Bengal. *Indian Journal of Public Health Research and Development* 6, 193-199.

Navarro-Haro MV, Wessman I, Botella C, García-Palacios A (2015). The role of emotion regulation strategies and dissociation in non-suicidal self-injury for women with borderline personality disorder and comorbid eating disorder. *Comprehensive Psychiatry* 63, 123-130.

Nederkoorn C, Vancleef L, Wilkenhöner A, Claes L, Havermans RC (2016). Self-inflicted pain out of boredom. *Psychiatry Research* 30, 127-132.

Neufeld E, Hirdes JP, Perlman CM, Rabinowitz T (2015). Risk and protective factors associated with intentional self-harm among older community-residing home care clients in Ontario, Canada. *International Journal of Geriatric Psychiatry* 30, 1032-1040.

Niederkrotenthaler T, Tinghog P, Goldman-Mellor S, Wilcox HC, Gould M, Mittendorfer-Rutz E (2016). Medical and social determinants of subsequent labour market marginalization in young hospitalized suicide attempters. *PLoS One* 11, e0146130.

Nock MK, Ursano RJ, Heeringa SG, Stein MB, Jain S, Raman R, Sun X, Chiu WT, Colpe LJ, Fullerton CS, Gilman SE, Hwang I, Naifeh JA, Rosellini AJ, Sampson NA, Schoenbaum M, Zaslavsky AM, Kessler RC, Army SC (2015). Mental disorders, comorbidity, and pre-enlistment suicidal behavior among new soldiers in the US army: Results from the Army Study to Assess Risk and Resilience in Servicemembers (ARMY STARRS). *Suicide and Life Threatening Behavior* 45, 588-599.

Noel F, Moniruzzaman A, Somers J, Frankish J, Strehlau V, Schutz C, Krausz M (2015). A longitudinal study of suicidal ideation among homeless, mentally ill individuals. *Social Psychiatry and Psychiatric Epidemiology* 51, 107-114.

Nofziger S, Callanan VJ (2015). Predicting suicidal tendencies among high risk youth with the general theory of crime. *Deviant Behavior* 37, 167-183.

Norr AM, Allan NP, Macatee RJ, Capron DW, Schmidt NB (2016). The role of anxiety sensitivity cognitive concerns in suicidal ideation: A test of the depression-distress amplification model in clinical outpatients. *Psychiatry Research* 238, 74-80.

Norstrom T, Rossow I (2016). Alcohol consumption as a risk factor for suicidal behavior: A systematic review of associations at the individual and at the population level. *Archives of Suicide Research*. Published online: 8 March 2016. doi: 10.1080/13811118.2016.1158678.

O'Connor D, Ferguson E, Green J, O'Carroll R, O'Connor R (2015). Cortisol levels and suicidal behavior: A meta-analysis. *Psychoneuroendocrinology* 63, 370-379.

O'Donnell JK, Gaynes BN, Cole SR, Edmonds A, Thielman NM, Quinlivan EB, Shirey K, Heine AD, Modi R, Pence BW (2015). Ongoing life stressors and suicidal ideation among HIV-infected adults with depression. *Journal of Affective Disorders* 190, 322-328.

O'Dwyer ST, Moyle W, Zimmer-Gembeck M, De Leo D (2016). Suicidal ideation in family carers of people with dementia. *Aging and Mental Health* 20, 222-230.

O'Hare T, Shen C, Sherrer MV (2015). Lifetime physical and sexual abuse and self-harm in women with severe mental illness. *Violence Against Women*. Published online: 29 December 2015. doi: 10.1177/1077801215622576.

O'Hare T, Shen C, Sherrer MV (2016). Witnessing violence and self-harming behaviors in women and men with severe mental illness. *Social Work in Mental Health*. Published online: 14 December 2015. doi: 10.1080/15332985.2015.1065944.

Oexle N, Ajdacic-Gross V, Kilian R, Muller M, Rodgers S, Xu Z, Rossler W, Rusch N (2015). Mental illness stigma, secrecy and suicidal ideation. *Epidemiology and Psychiatric Sciences.* Published online: 26 November 2015. doi: 10.1017/S2045796015001018.

Okan Ibiloglu A, Atli A, Demir S, Gunes M, Kaya MC, Bulut M, Sir A (2016). The investigation of factors related to suicide attempts in Southeastern Turkey. *Neuropsychiatric Disease and Treatment* 12, 407-416.

Okusaga O, Duncan E, Langenberg P, Brundin L, Fuchs D, Groer MW, Giegling I, Stearns-Yoder KA, Hartmann AM, Konte B, Friedl M, Brenner LA, Lowry CA, Rujescu D, Postolache TT (2016). Combined Toxoplasma gondii seropositivity and high blood kynurenine - linked with nonfatal suicidal self-directed violence in patients with schizophrenia. *Journal of Psychiatric Research* 72, 74-81.

Olié E, Ding Y, Le Bars E, de Champfleur NM, Mura T, Bonafé A, Courtet P, Jollant F (2015). Processing of decision-making and social threat in patients with history of suicidal attempt: A neuroimaging replication study. *Psychiatry Research* 234, 369-377.

Olsson P, Wiktorsson S, Sacuiu S, Marlow T, Ostling S, Fassberg MM, Skoog I, Waern M (2016). Cognitive function in older suicide attempters and a population-based comparison group. *Journal of Geriatric Psychiatry and Neurology* 29, 133-141.

Otsuka K, Nakamura H, Kudo K, Endo J, Sanjo K, Fukumoto K, Hoshi K, Yagi J, Sakai A (2015). The characteristics of the suicide attempter according to the onset time of the suicidal ideation. *Annals of General Psychiatry* 14, 48.

Otsuka Y, Nakata A, Sakurai K, Kawahito J (2016). Association of suicidal ideation with job demands and job resources: A large cross-sectional study of Japanese workers. *International Journal of Behavioral Medicine.* Published online: 28 January 2016. doi: 10.1007/s12529-016-9534-2.

Ozdemiroglu F, Sevincok L, Sen G, Mersin S, Kocabas O, Karakus K, Vahapoglu F (2015). Comorbid obsessive-compulsive disorder with bipolar disorder: A distinct form? *Psychiatry Research* 230, 800-805.

Park EY, Kim JH (2016). Factors related to suicidal ideation in stroke patients in South Korea. *Journal of Mental Health* 25, 109-113.

Park JI, Yang JC, Won Park T, Chung SK (2016). Is serum 25-hydroxyvitamin D associated with depressive symptoms and suicidal ideation in Korean adults? *International Journal of Psychiatry in Medicine* 51, 31-46.

Park S, Kim J (2015). Association between smoking and suicidal behaviors among adolescents in the Republic of Korea. *Journal of Addictions Nursing* 26, 175-183.

Park S, Watanabe N, Colucci E, Taguchi M, Takizawa T, Okada S, Umeda Y (2014). Exploratory study on safe factor, anxiety stressor and coping for local elderly people in an area in North Tohoku with high rates of suicide. *Journal of Physical Education and Medicine* 15, 7-14.

Park SJ, Lee HB, Ahn MH, Park S, Choi EJ, Lee HJ, Ryu HU, Kang JK, Hong JP (2015). Identifying clinical correlates for suicide among epilepsy patients in South Korea: A case-control study. *Epilepsia* 56, 1966-1972.

Park Y-M (2015). Relationship between serotonergic dysfunction based on loudness dependence of auditory-evoked potentials and suicide in patients with major depressive disorder. *Psychiatry Investigation* 12, 421-424.

Passos IC, Mwangi B, Cao B, Hamilton JE, Wu MJ, Zhang XY, Zunta-Soares GB, Quevedo J, Kauer-Sant'Anna M, Kapczinski F, Soares JC (2016). Identifying a clinical signature of suicidality among patients with mood disorders: A pilot study using a machine learning approach. *Journal of Affective Disorders* 193, 109-116.

Peltzer K (2015). Prevalence of suicidal ideation and associated factors among postpartum HIV-positive women in health facilities, South Africa. *Journal of Psychology in Africa* 25, 547-550.

Peltzer K, Pengpid S (2015). Early substance use initiation and suicide ideation and attempts among school-aged adolescents in four Pacific Island Countries in Oceania. *International Journal of Environmental Research and Public Health* 12, 12291-12303.

Peña JB, E Masyn K, Thorpe LE, Peña SM, Caine ED (2015). A cross-national comparison of suicide attempts, drug use, and depressed mood among Dominican youth. *Suicide and Life Threatening Behavior.* Published online: 20 September 2015. doi: 10.1111/sltb.12189.

Pereira H, Rodrigues P (2015). Internalized homophobia and suicidal ideation among LGB youth. *Journal of Psychiatry* 18, 229.

Peters EM, Balbuena L, Marwaha S, Baetz M, Bowen R (2015). Mood instability and impulsivity as trait predictors of suicidal thoughts. *Psychology and Psychotherapy.* Published online: 31 December 2015. doi: 10.1111/papt.12088.

Pien FC, Chang YC, Feng HP, Hung PW, Huang SY, Tzeng WC (2015). Changes in quality of life after a suicide attempt. *Western Journal of Nursing Research* 38, 721-737.

Plener PL, Munz LM, Allroggen M, Kapusta ND, Fegert JM, Groschwitz RC (2015). Immigration as risk factor for non-suicidal self-injury and suicide attempts in adolescents in Germany. *Child and Adolescent Psychiatry and Mental Health* 9, e34.

Popovic D, Vieta E, Azorin JM, Angst J, Bowden CL, Mosolov S, Young AH, Perugi G (2015). Suicide attempts in major depressive episode: Evidence from the BRIDGE-II-Mix study. *Bipolar Disorders* 17, 795-803.

Power J, Usher AM, Beaudette JN (2015). Non-suicidal self-injury in male offenders: Initiation, motivations, emotions, and precipitating events. *International Journal of Forensic Mental Health* 14, 147-160.

Pranckeviciene A, Tamasauskas S, Deltuva VP, Bunevicius R, Tamasauskas A, Bunevicius A (2016). Suicidal ideation in patients undergoing brain tumor surgery: Prevalence and risk factors. *Support Care Cancer.* Published online: 11 February 2016. doi: 10.1007/s00520-016-3117-2.

Preuss UW, Koller G, Samochowiec A, Zill P, Samochowiec J, Kucharska-Mazur J, Wong J, Soyka M (2015). Serotonin and dopamine candidate gene variants and alcohol- and non-alcohol-related aggression. *Alcohol and Alcoholism* 50, 690-699.

Pulay AJ, Rethelyi JM (2016). Multimarker analysis suggests the involvement of BDNF signaling and microRNA biosynthesis in suicidal behavior. *American Journal of Medical Genetics Part B.* Published online: 27 February 2016. doi: 10.1002/ajmg.b.32433.

Quintanilla Montoya R, Montoya RQ, Sánchez-Loyo LM, Correa-Márquez P, Luna-Flores F (2015). Acceptance of homosexuality and homophobia associated with suicidal behavior among homosexual men. *Masculinidades y Cambo Social* 4, 1-25.

Rahme E, Low NCP, Lamarre S, Turecki G, Bonin JP, Daneau D, Habel Y, Yung ECC, Morin S, Szkrumelak N, Singh S, Renaud J, Lesage A (2015). Attempted suicide among students and young adults in Montreal, Quebec, Canada: A retrospective cross-sectional study of hospitalized and nonhospitalized suicide attempts based on chart review. *Primary Care Companion for CNS Disorders* 17, 303.

Rajapakse T, Christensen H, Cotton S, Griffiths KM (2016). Non-fatal self-poisoning across age groups, in Sri Lanka. *Asian Journal of Psychiatry* 19, 79-84.

Rajapakse T, Griffiths KM, Christensen H, Cotton S (2015). Non-fatal self-poisoning in Sri Lanka: Associated triggers and motivations. *BMC Public Health* 15, e1167.

Rajkumar RP (2016). Recurrent unipolar mania: A comparative, cross-sectional study. *Comprehensive Psychiatry* 65, 136-140.

Rasmussen S, Hawton K, Philpott-Morgan S, O'Connor RC (2016). Why do adolescents self-harm? *Crisis.* Published online: 2 February 2016. doi: 10.1027/0227-5910/a000369.

Rayner G, Warne T (2015). Interpersonal processes and self-injury: A qualitative study using bricolage. *Journal of Psychiatric and Mental Health Nursing* 23, 54-65.

Rew L, Young C, Brown A, Rancour S (2016). Suicide ideation and life events in a sample of rural adolescents. *Archives of Psychiatric Nursing* 30, 198-203.

Richard-Devantoy S, Ding Y, Lepage M, Turecki G, Jollant F (2015). Cognitive inhibition in depression and suicidal behavior: A neuroimaging study. *Psychological Medicine* 46, 933-944.

Richard-Devantoy S, Ding Y, Turecki G, Jollant F (2016). Attentional bias toward suicide-relevant information in suicide attempters: A cross-sectional study and a meta-analysis. *Journal of Affective Disorders* 196, 101-108.

Richard-Devantoy S, Olié E, Guillaume S, Courtet P (2015). Decision-making in unipolar or bipolar suicide attempters. *Journal of Affective Disorders* 190, 128-136.

Richmond S, Hasking P, Meaney R (2015). Psychological distress and non-suicidal self-injury: The mediating roles of rumination, cognitive reappraisal and expressive suppression. *Archives of Suicide Research.* Published online: 8 December 2015. doi: 10.1080/13811118.2015.1008160.

Rietschel CH, Reese JB, Hahn AP, Fauerbach JA (2015). Clinical and psychiatric characteristics of self-inflicted burn patients in the United States: Comparison with a nonintentional burn group. *Journal of Burn Care and Research* 36, 381-386.

Rimkeviciene J, O'Gorman J, De Leo D (2015). How do clinicians and suicide attempters understand suicide attempt impulsivity? A qualitative study. *Death Studies* 40, 139-146.

Rogers ML, Joiner TE, Jr. (2016). Borderline personality disorder diagnostic criteria as risk factors for suicidal behavior through the lens of the interpersonal theory of suicide. *Archives of Suicide Research.* Published online: 8 March 2016. doi: 10.1080/13811118.2016.1158681.

Roh BR, Yoon Y, Kwon A, Oh S, Lee SI, Ha K, Shin YM, Song J, Park EJ, Yoo H, Hong HJ (2015). The structure of co-occurring bullying experiences and associations with suicidal behaviors in Korean adolescents. *PLoS One* 10, e0143517.

Rood BA, Puckett JA, Pantalone DW, Bradford JB (2015). Predictors of suicidal ideation in a statewide sample of transgender individuals. *LGBT Health* 2, 270-275.

Rosiek A, Rosiek-Kryszewska A, Leksowski L, Leksowski K (2016). Chronic stress and suicidal thinking among medical students. *International Journal of Environmental Research and Public Health* 13, 212.

Rostila M, Berg L, Arat A, Vinnerljung B, Hjern A (2016). Parental death in childhood and self-inflicted injuries in young adults-a national cohort study from Sweden. *European Child and Adolescent Psychiatry.* Published online: 1 March 2016. doi: 10.1007/s00787-016-0833-6.

Rukundo GZ, Mishara B, Kinyanda E (2016). Psychological correlates of suicidality in HIV/AIDS in semi-urban South-Western Uganda. *Tropical Doctor.* Published online: 5 January 2016. doi: 10.1177/004947551562311.

Rusu C, Zamorski MA, Boulos D, Garber BG (2016). Prevalence comparison of past-year mental disorders and suicidal behaviours in the Canadian armed forces and the Canadian general population. *Canadian Journal of Psychiatry* 61, 46S-55S.

Rutkowska A, Łopuszańska U, wider K, Pac-Kozuchowska E, Makara-Studzińska M(2015). The analysis of family risk factors associated with the occurrence of suicidal attempts among girls aged 12-16 years old. A pilot study. *Psychiatria i Psychologia Kliniczna* 15, 126-130.

Saavedra J, Lopez M (2015). Risk of suicide in male prison inmates. *Revista de Psiquiatria y Salud Mental* 8, 224-231.

Sahin C, Kara M, Kara B, Sahin N, Beydilli H, Acar E (2015). Investigation of reelin, RS7341475, RS362691 AND RS12705169 gene polymorphisms in cases a with suicide attempt. *Acta Medica Mediterranea* 31, 967-972.

Sajadi SF, Arshadi N, Zargar Y, Mehrabizade Honarmand M, Hajjari Z (2015). Borderline personality features in students: The predicting role of schema, emotion regulation, dissociative experience and suicidal ideation. *International Journal of High Risk Behaviors and Addiction* 4, e20021.

Salman S, Idrees J, Hassan F, Idrees F, Arifullah M, Badshah S (2014). Predictive factors of suicide attempt and non-suicidal self-harm in emergency department. *Emergency* 2, 166-169.

Sampasa-Kanyinga H, Dupuis LC, Ray R (2015). Prevalence and correlates of suicidal ideation and attempts among children and adolescents. *International Journal of Adolescent Medicine and Health*. Published online: 10 November 2015. doi: 10.1515/ijamh-2015-0053.

Sampasa-Kanyinga H, Hamilton HA (2016). Does socioeconomic status moderate the relationships between school connectedness with psychological distress, suicidal ideation and attempts in adolescents? *Preventive Medicine* 87, 11-17.

Sánchez-Loyo L, Ventura-Martínez E, González-Garrido AA (2016). Decision making in social context in patients with suicide attempt history. *Suicide and Life Threatening Behavior*. Published online: 6 March 2016. doi: 10.1111/sltb.12239.

Sang J, Ji Y, Li P, Zhao H (2016). Effect of perceived organizational support on suicidal ideation of young employees: The mediator role of self-esteem. *Journal of Health Psychology*. Published online: 9 February 2016. doi: 10.1177/1359105315627501.

Sansone RA, Bohinc RJ, Wiederman MW (2015). History of nonsuicidal self-harm behavior and general health care adherence among primary care outpatients. *Primary Care Companion to CNS Disorders* 17, e01787.

Sansone RA, Elliott K, Wiederman MW (2015). A survey of self-directed physical aggression among perpetrators of partner violence. *Primary Care Companion for CNS Disorders* 17, 14l01703.

Saracli O, Atasoy N, Senormanci O, Atik L, Acikgoz HO, Dogan V, Sankir H, Kokturk F, Orsel S (2015). Childhood trauma and suicide risk in the population living in Zonguldak Province. *Asia Pacific Psychiatry* 8, 136-144.

Saygin C, Uzunaslan D, Hatemi G, Hamuryudan V (2015). Suicidal ideation among patients with Behcet's syndrome. *Clinical and Experimental Rheumatology* 33, S30-S35.

Scherr S, Reinemann C (2016). First do no harm: Cross-sectional and longitudinal evidence for the impact of individual suicidality on the use of online health forums and support groups. *Computers in Human Behavior* 61, 80-88.

Schlebusch L, Govender RD (2015). Elevated risk of suicidal ideation in HIV-positive persons. *Depression Research and Treatment* 2015, 609172.

Seelman KL (2016). Transgender adults' access to college bathrooms and housing and the relationship to suicidality. *Journal of Homosexuality*. Published online: 25 February 2016. doi: 10.1080/00918369.2016.1157998.

Selby EA, Gardner K (2015). A latent profile analysis of suicidal and self-injurious behavior, other dysregulated behaviors, and borderline personality disorder symptoms. *Journal of Experimental Psychopathology* 6, 356-368.

Seo H-J, Wang H-R, Jun T-Y, Woo YS, Bahk W-M (2015). Factors related to suicidal behavior in patients with bipolar disorder: The effect of mixed features on suicidality. *General Hospital Psychiatry* 39, 91-96.

Shadick R, Backus Dagirmanjian F, Barbot B (2015). Suicide risk among college student. *Crisis* 36, 416-423.

Shadick R, Dagirmanjian FB, Barbot B (2015). Suicide risk among college students: The intersection of sexual orientation and race. *Crisis* 36, 416-423.

Shafiee-Kandjani AR, Amiri S, Arfaie A, Ahmadi A, Farvareshi M (2014). Relationship between personality profiles and suicide attempt via medicine poisoning among hospitalized patients: A case-control study. *International Scholarly Research Notices* 2014, e675480.

Shah FS, Ghouri S, Shah SM (2015). Personality factors more prone towards deliberate self harm; a study on 50 patients presenting to a tertiary care hospital. *Journal of Postgraduate Medical Institute* 29, 151-155.

Shamu S, Zarowsky C, Roelens K, Temmerman M, Abrahams N (2015). High-frequency intimate partner violence during pregnancy, postnatal depression and suicidal tendencies in Harare, Zimbabwe. *General Hospital Psychiatry* 38, 109-114.

Shand FL, Proudfoot J, Player MJ, Fogarty A, Whittle E, Wilhelm K, Hadzi-Pavlovic D, McTigue I, Spurrier M, Christensen H (2015). What might interrupt men's suicide? Results from an online survey of men. *British Medical Journal Open* 5, e008172.

Sharaf AY, Thompson EA, El-Salam HF (2016). Perception of parental bonds and suicide intent among Egyptian adolescents. *Journal of Child and Adolescent Psychiatric Nursing* 29, 15-22.

Sharma B, Nam EW, Kim HY, Kim JK (2015). Factors associated with suicidal ideation and suicide attempt among school-going urban adolescents in Peru. *International Journal of Environmental Research and Public Health* 12, 14842-14856.

Sheth K, Moss J, Hyland S, Stinton C, Cole T, Oliver C (2015). The behavioral characteristics of Sotos syndrome. *American Journal of Medical Genetics Part A* 167, 2945-2956.

Shin HY, Kang G, Kang HJ, Kim SW, Shin IS, Yoon JS, Kim JM (2015). Associations between serum lipid levels and suicidal ideation among Korean older people. *Journal of Affective Disorders* 189, 192-198.

Shin JY, Roh S-G, Lee N-H, Yang K-M (2016). Risk factors related to recurrent suicide attempts in patients with self-inflicted wrist injuries. *Journal of Plastic, Reconstructive and Aesthetic Surgery* 69, 722-723.

Shorey RC, Elmquist J, Wolford-Clevenger C, Gawrysiak MJ, Anderson S, Stuart GL (2016). The relationship between dispositional mindfulness, borderline personality features, and suicidal ideation in a sample of women in residential substance use treatment. *Psychiatry Research* 238, 122-128.

Short NA, Ennis CR, Oglesby ME, Boffa JW, Joiner TE, Schmidt NB (2015). The mediating role of sleep disturbances in the relationship between posttraumatic stress disorder and self-injurious behavior. *Journal of Anxiety Disorders* 35, 68-74.

Simon GE, Coleman KJ, Rossom RC, Beck A, Oliver M, Johnson E, Whiteside U, Operskalski B, Penfold RB, Shortreed SM, Rutter C (2016). Risk of suicide attempt and suicide death following completion of the patient health questionnaire depression module in community practice. *Journal of Clinical Psychiatry* 77, 221-227.

Singh BK (2015). Suicidal hanging in urban youth: A prospective study. *Journal of Evidence Based Medicine and Healthcare* 2, 602-607.

Skopp NA, Smolenski DJ, Sheppard SC, Bush NE, Luxton DD (2016). Comparison of suicide attempters and decedents in the U.S. Army: A latent class analysis. *Suicide and Life-Threatening Behavior*. Published online: 8 January 2016. doi: 10.1111/sltb.12227.

Smith BC, Armelie AP, Boarts JM, Delahanty DL, Brazil M (2016). PTSD, depression, and substance use in relation to suicidality risk among traumatized minority lesbian, gay, and bisexual youth. *Archives of Suicide Research*. Published online: 12 January 2016. doi: 10.1080/13811118.2015.1004484.

Smith CE, Pisetsky EM, Wonderlich SA, Crosby RD, Mitchell JE, Joiner TE, Bardone-Cone A, Le Grange D, Klein MH, Crow SJ, Peterson CB (2015). Is childhood trauma associated with lifetime suicide attempts in women with bulimia nervosa? *Eating and Weight Disorders.* Published online: 13 October 2015. doi: 10.1007/s40519-015-0226-8.

Smith NB, Mota N, Tsai J, Monteith L, Harpaz-Rotem I, Southwick SM, Pietrzak RH (2016). Nature and determinants of suicidal ideation among U.S. Veterans: Results from the national health and resilience in veterans study. *Journal of Affective Disorders* 197, 66-73.

Smith PN, Stanley IH, Joiner TE, Jr., Sachs-Ericsson NJ, Van Orden KA (2016). An aspect of the capability for suicide-fearlessness of the pain involved in dying-amplifies the association between suicide ideation and attempts. *Archives of Suicide Research.* Published online: 16 March 2016. doi: 10.1080/13811118.2016.1162245.

Sobrinho AT, Campos RC, Holden RR (2016). Parental rejection, personality, and depression in the prediction of suicidality in a sample of nonclinical young adults. *Psychoanalytic Psychology.* Published online: 11 January 2016. doi: 10.1037/pap0000051.

Sokol Y, Eisenheim E (2016). The relationship between continuous identity disturbances, negative mood, and suicidal ideation. *Primary Care Companion for CNS Disorders* 18, 482-487.

Sokolowski M, Wasserman J, Wasserman D (2015). Polygenic associations of neurodevelopmental genes in suicide attempt. *Molecular Psychiatry.* Published online: 15 December 2015. doi: 10.1038/mp.2015.187.

Song HB, Lee SA (2016). Socioeconomic and lifestyle factors as risks for suicidal behavior among Korean adults. *Journal of Affective Disorders* 197, 21-28.

Southerland JL, Zheng S, Dula M, Cao Y, Slawson DL (2016). Relationship between physical activity and suicidal behaviors among 65,182 middle school students. *Journal of Physical Activity & Health.* Published online: 21 March 2016. doi: 10.1123/jpah.2015-0315.

Spiller HA, Wiles D, Russell JL, Casavant MJ (2016). Review of toxicity and trends in the use of tiagabine as reported to US poison centers from 2000 to 2012. *Human and Experimental Toxicology* 35, 109-113.

Springe L, Pulmanis T, Velika B, Pudule I, Grinberga D, Villerusa A (2016). Self-reported suicide attempts and exposure to different types of violence and neglect during childhood: Findings from a young adult population survey in Latvia. *Scandinavia Journal of Public Health.* Published online: 10 February 2016. doi: 10.1177/1403494816631394.

Srinivasagopalan, Nappinnai, Solayappan (2015). Value of studying the time of occurrence of suicide attempt in people attending hospital following suicide attempt. *International Journal of Medical Research and Health Sciences* 4, 169-177.

Stanford S, Jones MP, Loxton DJ (2016). Understanding women who self-harm: Predictors and long-term outcomes in a longitudinal community sample. *Australian and New Zealand Journal of Psychiatry.* Published online: 26 February 2016. doi: 10.1177/0004867416633298.

Stange JP, Kleiman EM, Sylvia LG, Magalhaes PV, Berk M, Nierenberg AA, Deckersbach T (2016). Specific mood symptoms confer risk for subsequent suicidal ideation in bipolar disorder with and without suicide attempt history: Multi-wave data from STEP-BD. *Depression and Anxiety.* Published online: 12 January 2016. doi: 10.1002/da.22464.

Stanley IH, Horowitz LM, Bridge JA, Wharff EA, Pao M, Teach SJ (2015). Bullying and suicide risk among pediatric emergency department patients. *Pediatric Emergency Care.* Published online: 24 September 2015. doi: 10.1097/PEC.0000000000000537.

Stefenson A, Titelman D (2016). Psychosis and suicide. *Crisis.* Published online: 2 February 2016. doi: 10.1027/0227-5910/a000372.

Stein MB, Kessler RC, Heeringa SG, Jain S, Campbell-Sills L, Colpe LJ, Fullerton CS, Nock MK, Sampson NA, Schoenbaum M, Sun X, Thomas ML, Ursano RJ, Army SC (2015). Prospective longitudinal evaluation of the effect of deployment-acquired traumatic brain injury on post-traumatic stress and related disorders: Results from the Army Study To Assess Risk and Resilience in Servicemembers (Army STARRS). *American Journal of Psychiatry* 172, 1101-1111.

Stickley A, Koyanagi A (2016). Loneliness, common mental disorders and suicidal behavior: Findings from a general population survey. *Journal of Affective Disorders* 197, 81-87.

Stickley A, Koyanagi A, Ruchkin V, Kamio Y (2015). Attention-deficit/hyperactivity disorder symptoms and suicide ideation and attempts: Findings from the Adult Psychiatric Morbidity Survey 2007. *Journal of Affective Disorders* 189, 321-328.

Stroud CH, Cramer RJ, La Guardia AC, Crosby JW, Henderson CE (2015). Personality, spirituality, suicide, and self-injury proneness among lesbian, gay, and bisexual adults. *Mental Health, Religion and Culture*. Published online: 11 November 2015. doi: 10.1080/13674676.2015.1096240.

Sublette ME, Vaquero C, Baca-Garcia E, Pachano G, Huang YY, Oquendo MA, Mann JJ (2015). Lack of association of SNPs from the FADS1-FADS2 gene cluster with major depression or suicidal behavior. *Psychiatric Genetics* 26, 81-86.

Sugden K, Moffitt TE, Pinto L, Poulton R, Williams BS, Caspi A (2016). Is toxoplasma gondii infection related to brain and behavior impairments in humans? Evidence from a population-representative birth cohort. *PLoS One* 11, e0148435.

Sukhawaha S, Arunpongpaisal S, Rungreangkulkij S (2015). Attempted suicide triggers in Thai adolescent perspectives. *Archives of Psychiatric Nursing*. Published online: 17 December 2015. doi: 10.1016/j.apnu.2015.12.005.

Sun L, Zhang J (2015). Medically serious suicide attempters with or without plan in rural China. *Journal of Nervous and Mental Disease*. Published online: 30 October 2015. doi: 10.1097/NMD.0000000000000397.

Sun Y, Farzan F, Mulsant BH, Rajji TK, Fitzgerald PB, Barr MS, Downar J, Wong W, Blumberger DM, Daskalakis ZJ (2016). Indicators for remission of suicidal ideation following magnetic seizure therapy in patients with treatment-resistant depression. *Journal of the American Medical Association Psychiatry*. Published online: 16 March 2016. doi: 10.1001/jamapsychiatry.2015.3097.

Susukida R, Wilcox HC, Mendelson T (2016). The association of lifetime suicidal ideation with perceived parental love and family structure in childhood in a nationally representative adult sample. *Psychiatry Research*. Published online: 30 March 2016. doi: 10.1016/j.psychres.2016.01.033.

Sutter M, Perrin PB (2016). Discrimination, mental health, and suicidal ideation among LGBTQ people of color. *Journal of Counseling Psychology* 63, 98-105.

Swannell S, Martin G, Page A (2015). Suicidal ideation, suicide attempts and non-suicidal self-injury among lesbian, gay, bisexual and heterosexual adults: Findings from an Australian National Study. *Australian and New Zealand Journal of Psychiatry*. Published online: 1 December 2015. doi: 10.1177/0004867415615949.

Szanto K, Bruine de Bruin W, Parker AM, Hallquist MN, Vanyukov PM, Dombrovski AY (2015). Decision-making competence and attempted suicide. *The Journal of Clinical Psychiatry* 76, e1590-e1597.

Tabaac AR, Perrin PB, Rabinovitch AE (2016). The relationship between social support and suicide risk in a national sample of ethnically diverse sexual minority women. *Journal of Gay and Lesbian Mental Health* 20, 116-126.

Talib MA, Abdollahi A (2015). Spirituality moderates hopelessness, depression, and suicidal behavior among Malaysian adolescents. *Journal of Religion and Health*. Published online: 1 October 2015. doi: 10.1007/s10943-015-0133-3.

Talih F, Warakian R, Ajaltouni J, Shehab AA, Tamim H (2016). Correlates of depression and burnout among residents in a Lebanese Academic Medical Center: A cross-sectional study. *Academic Psychiatry* 40, 38-45.

Tang GX, Yan PP, Yan CL, Fu B, Zhu SJ, Zhou LQ, Huang X, Wang Y, Lei J (2016). Determinants of suicidal ideation in gynecological cancer patients. *Psycho-Oncology* 25, 97-103.

Tang J, Yang W, Ahmed NI, Ma Y, Liu HY, Wang JJ, Wang PX, Du YK, Yu YZ (2016). Stressful life events as a predictor for nonsuicidal self-injury in Southern Chinese adolescence: A cross-sectional study. *Medicine* 95, e2637.

Tanner A, Hasking P, Martin G (2016). Co-occurring non-suicidal self-injury and firesetting among at-risk adolescents: Experiences of negative life events, mental health problems, substance use, and suicidality. *Archives of Suicide Research*. Published online: 27 July 2015. doi: 10.1080/13811118.2015.1008162.

Tanner AK, Hasking P, Martin G (2014). Effects of rumination and optimism on the relationship between psychological distress and non-suicidal self-injury. *Prevention Science* 15, 860-868.

Tanner AK, Hasking P, Martin G (2015). Suicidality among adolescents engaging in nonsuicidal self-injury (NSSI) and firesetting: The role of psychosocial characteristics and reasons for living. *Child and Adolescent Psychiatry and Mental Health* 9, 1-11.

Teismann T, Forkmann T (2015). Rumination, entrapment and suicide ideation: A mediational model. *Clinical Psychology and Psychotherapy*. Published online: 11 December 2015. doi: 10.1002/cpp.1999.

Teismann T, Forkmann T, Glaesmer H, Egeri L, Margraf J (2016). Remission of suicidal thoughts: Findings from a longitudinal epidemiological study. *Journal of Affective Disorders* 190, 723-725.

Thimmaiah R, Poreddi V, Ramu R, Selvi S, Math SB (2016). Influence of religion on attitude towards suicide: An Indian perspective. *Journal of Religion and Health*. Published online: 4 March 2016. doi: 10.1007/s10943-016-0213-z.

Thomas EG, Spittal MJ, Heffernan EB, Taxman FS, Alati R, Kinner SA (2016). Trajectories of psychological distress after prison release: Implications for mental health service need in ex-prisoners. *Psychological Medicine* 46, 611-621.

Thomson P, Jaque SV (2015). Posttraumatic stress disorder and psychopathology in dancers. *Medical Problems of Performing Artists* 30, 157-162.

Thornton LM, Welch E, Munn-Chernoff MA, Lichtenstein P, Bulik CM (2016). Anorexia nervosa, major depression, and suicide attempts: Shared genetic factors. *Suicide and Life-Threatening Behavior*. Published online: 24 February 2016. doi: 10.1111/sltb.12235.

Till B, Tran US, Voracek M, Niederkrotenthaler T (2016). Music and suicidality: A study on associations between music preferences and risk factors of suicide. *Omega* 72, 340-356.

Toudehskchuie GRG, Fereidoon M (2016). What can influence Iranian suicide attempters to go through the process of non-fatal suicide act once again? A preliminary report. *Community Mental Health Journal*. Published online 19 March 2016. doi: 10.1007/s10597-015-9958-1.

Tovilla-Zárate CA, López-Narváez ML, González-Castro TB, Juárez-Rojop I, Pool-García S, Genis A, Ble-Castillo J, Fresán A, Nicolini H (2015). Association between the SAT-1 gene and suicidal behavior in Mexican population. *Journal of Psychiatry*. Published online: 6 June 2015. doi: 10.4172/2378- 5756.S1-005.

Townsend E, Ness J, Waters K, Kapur N, Turnbull P, Cooper J, Bergen H, Hawton K (2015). Self-harm and life problems: Findings from the multicentre study of self-harm in England. *Social Psychiatry and Psychiatric Epidemiology* 51, 183-192.

Trepal HC, Wester KL, Merchant E (2015). A cross-sectional matched sample study of nonsuicidal self-injury among young adults: Support for interpersonal and intrapersonal factors, with implications for coping strategies. *Child and Adolescent Psychiatry and Mental Health*. Published online: 28 September 2015. doi: 10.1186/s13034-015-0070-7.

Tripp JC, McDevitt-Murphy ME, Henschel AV (2015). Firing a weapon and killing in combat are associated with suicidal ideation in OEF/OIF veterans. *Psychological Trauma: Theory, Research, Practice, and Policy*. Published online: 12 October 2015. doi: 10.1037/tra0000085.

Tsujimoto E, Taketani R, Yano M, Yamamoto A, Ono H (2015). Relationship between depression, suicidal ideation, and stress coping strategies in Japanese undergraduates. *International Medical Journal* 22, 268-272.

Tsukahara T, Arai H, Kamijo T, Kobayashi Y, Washizuka S, Arito H, Nomiyama T (2016). Relationships between suicidal ideation and psychosocial factors among residents living in Nagano prefecture of Japan. *Environmental Health and Preventive Medicine* 21, 164-172.

Tsypes A, Burkhouse KL, Gibb BE (2016). Classification of facial expressions of emotion and risk for suicidal ideation in children of depressed mothers: Evidence from cross-sectional and prospective analyses. *Journal of Affective Disorders* 197, 147-150.

Tsypes A, Gibb BE (2016). Cognitive vulnerabilities and development of suicidal thinking in children of depressed mothers: A longitudinal investigation. *Psychiatry Research* 239, 99-104.

Tsypes A, Lane R, Paul E, Whitlock J (2016). Non-suicidal self-injury and suicidal thoughts and behaviors in heterosexual and sexual minority young adults. *Comprehensive Psychiatry* 65, 32-43.

Turner BJ, Cobb RJ, Gratz KL, Chapman AL (2016). The role of interpersonal conflict and perceived social support in nonsuicidal self-injury in daily life. *Journal of Abnormal Psychology* 125, 588-598.

Umetsu R, Abe J, Ueda N, Kato Y, Matsui T, Nakayama Y, Kinosada Y, Nakamura M (2015). Association between selective serotonin reuptake inhibitor therapy and suicidality: Analysis of U.S. Food and Drug Administration adverse event reporting system data. *Biological and Pharmaceutical Bulletin* 38, 1689-1699.

Valderrama J, Miranda R, Jeglic E (2015). Ruminative subtypes and impulsivity in risk for suicidal behavior. *Psychiatry Research* 236, 15-21.

Valuck RJ, Libby AM, Anderson HD, Allen RR, Strombom I, Marangell LB, Perahia D (2015). Comparison of antidepressant classes and the risk and time course of suicide attempts in adults: Propensity matched, retrospective cohort study. *British Journal of Psychiatry* 208, 271-279.

Van den Broeck K, Claes L, Pieters G, Berens A, Raes F (2015). Autobiographical memory specificity and non-suicidal self-injury in borderline personality disorder. *Journal of Experimental Psychopathology* 6, 398-410.

van Geel M, Goemans A, Vedder P (2015). A meta-analysis on the relation between peer victimization and adolescent non-suicidal self-injury. *Psychiatry Research* 230, 364-368.

Vanyukov PM, Szanto K, Hallquist MN, Siegle GJ, Reynolds CF, Forman SD, Aizenstein HJ, Dombrovski AY (2016). Paralimbic and lateral prefrontal encoding of reward value during intertemporal choice in attempted suicide. *Psychological Medicine* 46, 381-391.

Vasconcelos JRO, Lôbo APS, de Melo Neto VL (2015). Risk of suicide and psychiatric comorbidities in generalized anxiety disorder. *Jornal Brasileiro de Psiquiatria* 64, 259-265.

Vega D, Vila-Ballo A, Soto A, Amengual J, Ribas J, Torrubia R, Rodriguez-Fornells A, Marco-Pallares J (2015). Preserved error-monitoring in borderline personality disorder patients with and without non-suicidal self-injury behaviors. *PLoS One* 10, 1-16.

Velkoff EA, Forrest LN, Dodd DR, A RS (2015). I can stomach that! Fearlessness about death predicts attenuated facial electromyography activity in response to death-related images. *Suicide and Life-Threatening Behavior*. Published online: 5 October 2015. doi: 10.1111/sltb.12194.

Ventorp F, Barzilay R, Erhardt S, Samuelsson M, Traskman-Bendz L, Janelidze S, Weizman A, Offen D, Brundin L (2016). The CD44 ligand hyaluronic acid is elevated in the cerebrospinal fluid of suicide attempters and is associated with increased blood-brain barrier permeability. *Journal of Affective Disorders* 193, 349-354.

Ventorp F, Gustafsson A, Traskman-Bendz L, Westrin A, Ljunggren L (2015). Increased soluble urokinase-type plasminogen activator receptor (suPAR) levels in plasma of suicide attempters. *PLoS One* 10, e0140052.

Vikström J, Sydsjö G, Hammar M, Bladh M, Josefsson A (2015). Risk of postnatal depression or suicide after in vitro fertilisation treatment: A nationwide case-control study. *BJOG*. Published online: 10 December 2015. doi: 10.1111/1471-0528.13788.

Villatte JL, O'Connor SS, Leitner R, Kerbrat AH, Johnson LL, Gutierrez PM (2015). Suicide attempt characteristics among veterans and active-duty service members receiving mental health services: A pooled data analysis. *Military Behavioral Health* 3, 316-327.

Vinson ES, Oser CB (2016). Risk and protective factors for suicidal ideation in African American women with a history of sexual violence as a minor. *Violence Against Women*. Published online: 29 February 2016. doi: 10.1177/1077801216632614.

Violanti JM, Andrew ME, Mnatsakanova A, Hartley TA, Fekedulegn D, Burchfiel CM (2015). Correlates of hopelessness in the high suicide risk police occupation. *Police Practice and Research*. Published online: 27 February 2015. doi: 10.1080/15614263.2015.1015125.

Wadman R, Clarke D, Sayal K, Vostanis P, Armstrong M, Harroe C, Majumder P, Townsend E (2016). An interpretative phenomenological analysis of the experience of self-harm repetition and recovery in young adults. *Journal of Health Psychology*. Published online: 6 March 2016. doi: 10.1177/1359105316631405.

Wakefield JC, Schmitz MF (2015). Feelings of worthlessness during a single complicated major depressive episode predict postremission suicide attempt. *Acta Psychiatrica Scandinavic* 133, 257-265.

Wang G, Fang Y, Jiang L, Zhou G, Yuan S, Wang X, Su P (2015). Relationship between cyberbullying and the suicide related psychological behavior among middle and high school students in Anhui Province. *Wei Sheng Yan Jiu* 44, 896-903.

Wang JY, Wang XT, Wang LL, Jia CX (2015). Association of brain-derived neurotrophic factor G196A and attempted suicide: A case-control study in rural China. *Neuropsychobiology* 72, 91-96.

Wang LC (2015). The effect of high-stakes testing on suicidal ideation of teenagers with reference-dependent preferences. *Journal of Population Economics* 29, 345-364.

Watts SJ (2015). 5-HTTLPR, suicidal behavior by others, depression, and criminal behavior during adolescence. *Journal of Adolescent Research* 30, 800-820.

Webb RT, Antonsen S, Pedersen CB, Mok PL, Cantor-Graae E, Agerbo E (2015). Attempted suicide and violent criminality among Danish second-generation immigrants according to parental place of origin. *International Journal of Social Psychiatry*. Published online: 26 November 2015. doi: 10.1177/0020764015615904.

Webermann AR, Myrick AC, Taylor CL, Chasson GS, Brand BL (2015). Dissociative, depressive, and PTSD symptom severity as correlates of nonsuicidal self-injury and suicidality in dissociative disorder patients. *Journal of Trauma and Dissociation*. Published online: 25 July 2015. doi: 10.1080/15299732.2015.1067941.

Wee JH, Park JH, Choi SP, Woo SH, Lee WJ, So BH, Park KN (2016). Clinical features of emergency department patients with depression who had attempted to commit suicide by poisoning. *Nigerian Journal of Clinical Practice* 19, 41-45.

Weerasinghe M, Konradsen F, Eddleston M, Pearson M, Gunne D, Hawton K, Jayamanne S, Pabasara C, Jayathilaka T, Dissanayaka K, Rajapaksha S, Thilakarathna P, Agampodi S (2015). Risk factors associated with purchasing pesticide from shops or self-poisoning: A protocol for a population-based case control study. *British Medical Journal Open.* Published online: 20 May 2015. doi: 10.1136/bmjopen-2015-007822.

Weinberg A, Perlman G, Kotov R, Hajcak G (2016). Depression and reduced neural response to emotional images: Distinction from anxiety, and importance of symptom dimensions and age of onset. *Journal of Abnormal Psychology* 125, 26-39.

Weiser M, Kapara O, Werbeloff N, Goldberg S, Fenchel D, Reichenberg A, Yoffe R, Ginat K, Fruchter E, Davidson M (2015). A population-based longitudinal study of suicide risk in male schizophrenia patients: Proximity to hospital discharge and the moderating effect of premorbid IQ. *Schizophrenia Research* 169, 159-164.

Weiss SJ, Simeonova DI, Kimmel MC, Battle CL, Maki PM, Flynn HA (2015). Anxiety and physical health problems increase the odds of women having more severe symptoms of depression. *Archives of Women's Mental Health.* Published online: 24 September 2015. doi: 10.1007/s00737-015-0575-3.

Wester KL, Ivers N, Villalba JA, Trepal HC, Henson R (2016). The relationship between nonsuicidal self-injury and suicidal ideation. *Journal of Counseling and Development* 94, 3-12.

Whalen DJ, Dixon-Gordon K, Belden AC, Barch D, Luby JL (2015). Correlates and consequences of suicidal cognitions and behaviors in children ages 3 to 7 years. *Journal of the American Academy of Child and Adolescent Psychiatry* 54, 926-937.

Whitaker K, Shapiro VB, Shields JP (2016). School-based protective factors related to suicide for lesbian, gay, and bisexual adolescents. *Journal of Adolescence Health* 58, 63-68.

Whittier AB, Gelaye B, Deyessa N, Bahretibeb Y, Kelkile TS, Berhane Y, Williams MA (2016). Major depressive disorder and suicidal behavior among urban dwelling Ethiopian adult outpatients at a general hospital. *Journal of Affective Disorders* 197, 58-65.

Whittle EL, Fogarty AS, Tugendrajch S, Player MJ, Christensen H, Wilhelm K, Hadzi-Pavlovic D, Proudfoot J (2015). Men, depression, and coping: Are we on the right path? *Psychology of Men and Masculinity* 16, 426-438.

Wiktorsson S, Berg AI, Wilhelmson K, Mellqvist Fassberg M, Van Orden K, Duberstein P, Waern M (2015). Assessing the role of physical illness in young old and older old suicide attempters. *International Journal of Geriatric Psychiatry.* Published online: 11 November 2015. doi: 10.1002/gps.4390.

Winer ES, Drapeau CW, Veilleux JC, Nadorff MR (2016). The association between anhedonia, suicidal ideation, and suicide attempts in a large student sample. *Archives of Suicide Research* 20, 265-272.

Witte TK, Zuromski KL, Gauthier JM, Smith AR, Bartlett M, Siegfried N, Bodell L, Goodwin N (2015). Restrictive eating: Associated with suicide attempts, but not acquired capability in residential patients with eating disorders. *Psychiatry Research* 235, 90-96.

Wolff H, Casillas A, Perneger T, Heller P, Golay D, Mouton E, Bodenmann P, Gétaz L (2016). Self-harm and overcrowding among prisoners in Geneva, Switzerland. *International Journal of Prisoner Health* 12, 39-44.

Wolford-Clevenger C, Elmquist J, Brem M, Zapor H, Stuart GL (2015). Dating violence victimization, interpersonal needs, and suicidal ideation among college students. *Crisis.* Published online: 1 December 2015. doi: 10.1027/0227-5910/a000353.

Wrighten SA, Al-Barwani MB, Moran RR, McKee GR, Dwyer RG (2015). Sexually violent predators and civil commitment: Is selection evidence based? *Journal of Forensic Psychiatry and Psychology* 26, 652-666.

Wu C-Y, Lee M-B, Liao S-C, Chang L-R (2015). Risk factors of internet addiction among internet users: An online questionnaire survey. *PLoS One* 10, e0137506.

Wu S, Ding Y, Wu F, Xie G, Hou J, Mao P (2015). Serum lipid levels and suicidality: A meta-analysis of 65 epidemiological studies. *Journal of Psychiatry and Neuroscience* 41, 56-69.

Wyart M, Jaussent I, Ritchie K, Abbar M, Jollant F, Courtet P (2016). Iowa gambling task performance in elderly persons with a lifetime history of suicidal acts. *American Journal of Geriatric Psychiatry* 24, 399-406.

Xavier A, Cunha M, Pinto-Gouveia J (2016). The indirect effect of early experiences on deliberate self-harm in adolescence: Mediation by negative emotional states and moderation by daily peer hassles. *Journal of Child and Family Studies* 25, 1451-1460.

Xavier A, Pinto Gouveia J, Cunha M (2016). Non-suicidal self-injury in adolescence: The role of shame, self-criticism and fear of self-compassion. *Child and Youth Care Forum*. Published online: 18 January 2016. doi: 10.1007/s10566-016-9346-1.

Xu Z, Muller M, Heekeren K, Theodoridou A, Metzler S, Dvorsky D, Oexle N, Walitza S, Rossler W, Rusch N (2016). Pathways between stigma and suicidal ideation among people at risk of psychosis. *Schizophrenia Research* 172, 184-188.

Yao S, Kuja-Halkola R, Thornton LM, Runfola CD, D'Onofrio BM, Almqvist C, Lichtenstein P, Sjolander A, Larsson H, Bulik CM (2016). Familial liability for eating disorders and suicide attempts: Evidence from a population registry in Sweden. *Journal of the American Medical Association Psychiatry* 73, 284-291.

Yeh Y-W, Ho P-S, Chen C-Y, Kuo S-C, Liang C-S, Yen C-H, Huang C-C, Shiue C-Y, Huang W-S, Ma K-H, Lu R-B, Huang S-Y (2015). Suicidal ideation modulates the reduction in serotonin transporter availability in male military conscripts with major depression: A 4-[^{18}F]-ADAM PET study. *World Journal of Biological Psychiatry* 16, 502-512.

Yen CF, Liu TL, Yang P, Hu HF (2015). Risk and protective factors of suicidal ideation and attempt among adolescents with different types of school bullying involvement. *Archives of Suicide Research* 19, 435-452.

Yim S (2015). Relationships between dietary behaviors and suicidal ideation among Korean adolescents. *Indian Journal of Science and Technology* 8, 1-5.

Yoo T, Kim S-W, Kim S-Y, Lee J-Y, Kang H-J, Bae K-Y, Kim J-M, Shin I-S, Yoon J-S (2015). Relationship between suicidality and low self-esteem in patients with schizophrenia. *Clinical Psychopharmacology and Neuroscience* 13, 296-301.

You J, Deng B, Lin MP, Leung F (2015). The interactive effects of impulsivity and negative emotions on adolescent nonsuicidal self-injury: A latent growth curve analysis. *Suicide and Life-Threatening Behavior*. Published online: 5 October 2015. doi: 10.1111/sltb.12192.

You J, Zheng C, Lin M-P, Leung F (2016). Peer group impulsivity moderated the individual-level relationship between depressive symptoms and adolescent nonsuicidal self-injury. *Journal of Adolescence* 47, 90-99.

Youssef IM, Fahmy MT, Haggag WL, Mohamed KA, Baalash AA (2016). Dual diagnosis and suicide probability in poly-drug users. *Journal of the College of Physicians and Surgeons Pakistan* 26, 130-133.

Yu S-SV, Sung HE (2015). Suicidal ideation of probationers: Gender differences. *Crisis* 36, 424-432.

Zelkowitz RL, Cole DA, Han GT, Tomarken AJ (2016). The incremental utility of emotion regulation but not emotion reactivity in nonsuicidal self-injury. *Suicide and Life-Threatening Behavior*. Published online: 6 March 2016. doi: 10.1111/sltb.12236.

Zengin Y, Calik M, Buyukcam F, Sen J, Akpinar S, Erdem AB, Ceylan A, Odabas O (2015). The relationship between suicide attempts and menstrual cycles in the emergency department and the sociodemographic and clinical characteristics of these patients. *Eurasian Journal of Emergency Medicine* 14, 118-122.

Zhang QE, Sha S, Ungvari GS, Chiu HFK, Ng CH, He HB, Forester BP, Xiang YT (2016). Demographic and clinical profile of patients with dementia receiving electroconvulsive therapy: A case-control study. *Journal of ECT.* Published online: 8 March 2016. doi: 10.1097/YCT.0000000000000314.

Zhang X, Xu H, Gu J, Lau JT, Hao C, Zhao Y, Davis A, Hao Y (2016). Depression, suicidal ideation, and related factors of methadone maintenance treatment users in Guangzhou, China. *Aids Care.* Published online: 3 February 2016. doi: 10.1080/09540121.2015.1124981.

Zhang Y, Yip PSF, Chang S-S, Wong PWC, Law FYW (2015). Association between changes in risk factor status and suicidal ideation incidence and recovery. *Crisis* 36, 390-398.

Zhong QY, Gelaye B, Miller M, Fricchione GL, Cai T, Johnson PA, Henderson DC, Williams MA (2015). Suicidal behavior-related hospitalizations among pregnant women in the USA, 2006-2012. *Archives of Women's Mental Health.* Published online: 18 December 2015. doi: 10.1007/s00737-015-0597-x.

Zhu L, Westers NJ, Horton SE, King JD, Diederich A, Stewart SM, Kennard BD (2016). Frequency of exposure to and engagement in nonsuicidal self-injury among inpatient adolescents. *Archives of Suicide Research.* Published online: 16 March 2016. doi: 10.1080/13811118.2016.1162240.

Zullig KJ (2016). The association between deliberate self-harm and college student subjective quality of life. *American Journal of Health Behavior* 40, 231-239.

Zullig KJ, Divin AL, Weiler RM, Haddox JD, Pealer N (2015). Adolescent nonmedical use of prescription pain relievers, stimulants, and depressants, and suicide risk. *Substance Use & Misuse.* Published online: 17 November 2015. doi: 10.3109/10826084.2015.1027931.

Prevention

Betz ME, Miller M, Barber C, Beaty B, Miller I, Camargo CA, Jr., Boudreaux ED (2016). Lethal means access and assessment among suicidal emergency department patients. *Depression and Anxiety.* Published online: 17 March 2016. doi: 10.1002/da.22486.

Britton PC, Kopacz MS, Stephens B, Bossarte RM (2015). Veterans crisis line callers with and without prior VHA service use. *Archives of Suicide Research.* Published online: 9 December 2015. doi: 10.1080/13811118.2015.1017681.

Carson BL, Farrelly T, Frazer R, Borthwick F (2015). Mediating tragedy: Facebook, Aboriginal peoples and suicide. *Australasian Journal of Information Systems* 19, 1-15.

Cornell D, Huang F (2016). Authoritative school climate and high school student risk behavior: A cross-sectional multi-level analysis of student self-reports. *Journal of Youth and Adolescence.* Published online: 19 January 2016. doi: 10.1007/s10964-016-0424-3

De Silva E, Bowerman L, Zimitat C (2015). A suicide awareness and intervention program for health professional students. *Education for Health* 28, 201-204.

Fekkes M, van de Sande MCE, Gravesteijn JC, Pannebakker FD, Buijs GJ, Diekstra RFW, Kocken PL (2016). Effects of the Dutch skills for life program on the health behavior, bullying, and suicidal ideation of secondary school students. *Health Education* 116, 2-15

Ferguson M, Jones M, Procter N, Martinez L, Cronin K, James L, Dollman J, Ryan B (2015). Preparing nurses to practice evidence based suicide prevention skills in the bush. *Australian Nursing and Midwifery Journal* 23, 41.

Fisher G, Foster C (2016). Examining the needs of paediatric nurses caring for children and young people presenting with self-harm/suicidal behaviour on general paediatric wards: Findings from a small-scale study. *Child Care in Practice.* Published online: 11 January 2016. doi: 10.1080/13575279.2015.1118013

Flegg M, Gordon-Walker M, Maguire S (2015). Peer-to-peer mental health: A community evaluation case study. *Journal of Mental Health Training, Education and Practice* 10, 282-293

Ford-Paz RE, Reinhard C, Kuebbeler A, Contreras R, Sanchez B (2015). Culturally tailored depression/suicide prevention in Latino youth: Community perspectives. *Journal of Behavioral Health Services and Research* 42, 519-533.

Gale J, Thalitaya MD (2015). Mental health support service for university students. *Psychiatria Danubina* 27 Supplement 1, 115-119.

Gamarra JM, Luciano MT, Gradus JL, Wiltsey Stirman S (2015). Assessing variability and implementation fidelity of suicide prevention safety planning in a regional VA healthcare system. *Crisis* 36, 433-439.

Garraza LG, Walrath C, Goldston DB, Reid H, McKeon R (2015). Effect of the Garrett Lee Smith Memorial Suicide Prevention Program on suicide attempts among youths. *Journal of the American Medical Association Psychiatry* 72, 1143-1149.

Gilhooley J, Bolger M, Charles A, Cleary E, Lane A, Malone K (2015). Young, male and feeling suicidal in Ireland: Is help or harm just one click away? *Irish Medical Journal* 108, 1-3.

Grimholt TK, Jacobsen D, Haavet OR, Sandvik L, Jorgensen T, Norheim AB, Ekeberg O (2015). Effect of systematic follow-up by general practitioners after deliberate self-poisoning: A randomised controlled trial. *PLoS One.* Published online: 2 December 2015. doi: 10.1371/journal.pone.0143934.

Gysin-Maillart A, Schwab S, Soravia L, Megert M, Michel K (2016). A novel brief therapy for patients who attempt suicide: A 24-months follow-up randomized controlled study of the Attempted Suicide Short Intervention Program (ASSIP). *PLoS Medicine* 13, e1001968.

Harmon LM, Cooper RL, Nugent WR, Butcher JJ (2016). A review of the effectiveness of military suicide prevention programs in reducing rates of military suicides. *Journal of Human Behavior in the Social Environment* 26, 15-24.

Harris FM, Maxwell M, O'Connor R, Coyne JC, Arensman E, Coffey C, Koburger N, Gusmão R, Costa S, Szekely A, Cserháti Z, McDaid D, Van Audenhove C, Hegerl U (2016). Exploring synergistic interactions and catalysts in complex interventions: Longitudinal, mixed methods case studies of an optimised multi-level suicide prevention intervention in four European countries (Ospi-Europe). *BMC Public Health* 16, 1-9.

Hashimoto N, Suzuki Y, Kato TA, Fujisawa D, Sato R, Aoyama-Uehara K, Fukasawa M, Asakura S, Kusumi I, Otsuka K (2015). Effectiveness of suicide prevention gatekeeper-training for university administrative staff in Japan. *Psychiatry and Clinical Neurosciences*. Published online: 4 October 2015. doi: 10.1111/pcn.12358.

Honeycutt A, Praetorius RT (2016). Survivors of suicide: Who they are and how do they heal? *Illness, Crisis and Loss* 24, 103-118.

Hoy J, Natarajan A, Petra MM (2016). Motivational interviewing and the transtheoretical model of change: Under-explored resources for suicide intervention. *Community Mental Health Journal*. Published online: 17 February 2016. doi: 10.1007/s10597-016-9997-2.

Hoytema van Konijnenburg EM, Diderich HM, Teeuw AH, Klein Velderman M, Oudesluys-Murphy AM, van der Lee JH (2015). Comparing policies for children of parents attending hospital emergency departments after intimate partner violence, substance abuse or suicide attempt. *Child Abuse and Neglect* 53, 81-94.

Idenfors H, Kullgren G, Renberg MS (2015). Professional care as an option prior to self-harm a qualitative study exploring young people's experiences. *Crisis* 36, 179-186.

Karras E, Lu N, Zuo G, Tu XM, Stephens B, Draper J, Thompson C, Bossarte RM (2016). Measuring associations of the department of veterans affairs' suicide prevention campaign on the use of crisis support services. *Suicide and Life-Threatening Behavior*. Published online: 16 February 2016. doi: 10.1111/sltb.12231.

Kassen GA, Ageeva LE, Bulatbayeva AA, Mukasheva AB, Onalbekov ES, Esenova KA (2016). Prevention of suicidal manifestations among youths: Art pedagogical aspect. *Research Journal of Medical Sciences* 10, 20-27.

Kelley A, Big Foot D, Small C, Mexicancheyenne T, Gondara R (2015). Recommendations from an American Indian reservation community-based suicide prevention program. *International Journal of Human Rights In Healthcare* 8, 3-13.

Kim H-S, Lee M-S, Hong J-Y (2016). Determinants of mental health care utilization in a suicide high-risk group with suicidal ideation. *Journal of Preventive Medicine and Public Health* 49, 69-78.

Kitchingman TA, Wilson CJ, Caputi P, Woodward A, Hunt T (2015). Development and evaluation of the telephone crisis support skills scale. *Crisis* 36, 407-415.

Magruder KM, York JA, Knapp RG, Yeager DE, Marshall E, DeSantis M (2015). RCT evaluating provider outcomes by suicide prevention training modality: In-person vs. E-learning. *Journal of Mental Health Training, Education and Practice* 10, 207-217.

Manuel M, Jacob V (2015). Effectiveness of school based teaching programme (SBTP) for teachers regarding 'prevention of suicide among students' in selected schools, Mangalore. *International Journal of Nursing Education* 7, 292.

Mason K, Geist M, Kuo R, Marshall D, Wines JD (2016). Predictors of clergy's ability to fulfill a suicide prevention gatekeeper role. *Journal of Pastoral Care and Counseling* 70, 34-39.

McCabe R, Garside R, Backhouse A, Xanthopoulou P (2016). Effective communication in eliciting and responding to suicidal thoughts: A systematic review protocol. *Systematic Reviews* 5, 31.

McCalman J, Bainbridge R, Russo S, Rutherford K, Tsey K, Wenitong M, Shakeshaft A, Doran C, Jacups S (2016). Psycho-social resilience, vulnerability and suicide prevention: Impact evaluation of a mentoring approach to modify suicide risk for remote Indigenous Australian students at boarding school. *BMC Public Health* 16, 1-12.

Milner A, Witt K, Burnside L, Wilson C, LaMontagne AD (2015). Contact & connect-an intervention to reduce depression stigma and symptoms in construction workers: Protocol for a randomised controlled trial. *BMC Public Health* 15, 1-6.

Miner AS, Milstein A, Schueller S, Hegde R, Mangurian C, Linos E (2016). Smartphone-based conversational agents and responses to questions about mental health, interpersonal violence, and physical health. *Journal of the American Medical Association Internal Medicine* 176, 619-625.

Mishara BL, Daigle M, Bardon C, Chagnon F, Balan B, Raymond S, Campbell J (2016). Comparison of the effects of telephone suicide prevention help by volunteers and professional paid staff: Results from studies in the USA and Quebec, Canada. *Suicide and Life-Threatening Behavior*. Published online: 6 March 2016. doi: 10.1111/sltb.12238.

Mullaney C (2016). Reshaping time: Recommendations for suicide prevention in LGBT populations reflections on "suicide and suicide risk in lesbian, gay, bisexual, and transgender populations: Review and recommendations" from Journal of Homosexuality 58(1). *Journal of Homosexuality* 63, 461-465.

Nadeem E, Santiago CD, Kataoka SH, Chang VY, Stein BD (2016). School personnel experiences in notifying parents about their child's risk for suicide: Lessons learned. *Journal of School Health* 86, 3-10.

Pasupathi M, Billitteri J, Mansfield CD, Wainryb C, Hanley GE, Taheri K (2015). Regulating emotion and identity by narrating harm. *Journal of Research in Personality* 58, 127-136.

Peterson DHM, Collings SC (2015). "It's either do it or die" the role of self-management of suicidality in people with experience of mental illness. *Crisis* 36, 173-178.

Pisani AR, Murrie DC, Silverman MM (2015). Reformulating suicide risk formulation: From prediction to prevention. *Academic Psychiatry*. Published online: 14 December 2015. doi: 10.1007/s40596-015-0434-6.

Ramberg I-L, Di Lucca MA, Hadlaczky G (2016). The impact of knowledge of suicide prevention and work experience among clinical staff on attitudes towards working with suicidal patients and suicide prevention. *International Journal of Environmental Research and Public Health* 13, 1-12.

Roberts AL, Chen Y, Slopen N, McLaughlin KA, Koenen KC, Austin SB (2015). Maternal experience of abuse in childhood and depressive symptoms in adolescent and adult offspring: A 21-year longitudinal study. *Depression and Anxiety* 32, 709-719.

Ross AM, White E, Powell D, Nelson S, Horowitz L, Wharff E (2015). To ask or not to ask? Opinions of pediatric medical inpatients about suicide risk screening in the hospital. *Journal of Pediatrics* 170, 295-300.

Santiago JL, Hanley GP, Moore K, Jin CS (2015). The generality of interview-informed functional analyses: Systematic replications in school and home. *Journal of Autism and Developmental Disorders* 46, 797-811.

Seward AL, Harris KM (2016). Offline versus online suicide-related help seeking: Changing domains, changing paradigms. *Journal of Clinical Psychology*. Published online: 29 February 2016. doi: 10.1002/jclp.22282.

Shrivastava SRBL, Shrivastava PS, Ramasamy J (2015). Public health strategies to ensure reduction in suicide incidence in middle and low income nations. *Journal of Neurosciences in Rural Practice* 6, 619-621.

Silva JAMD, Siegmund G, Bredemeier J (2015). Crisis interventions in online psychological counseling. *Trends in Psychiatry and Psychotherapy* 37, 171-182.

Skovgaard Larsen JL, Frandsen H, Erlangsen A (2016). Myplan - a mobile phone application for supporting people at risk of suicide. *Crisis.* Published online: 2 February 2016. doi: 10.1027/0227-5910/a000371.

Stanley IH, Hom MA, Joiner TE (2015). Mental health service use among adults with suicide ideation, plans, or attempts: Results from a national survey. *Psychiatric Services* 66, 1296-1302.

Steel M (2015). A nurse-led pathway to treat self-harm injuries. *Nursing Times* 111, 17-19.

Sueki H, Ito J (2015). Suicide prevention through online gatekeeping using search advertising techniques. *Crisis* 36, 267-273.

Sundvall M, Tidemalm DH, Titelman DE, Runeson B, Baarnhielm S (2015). Assessment and treatment of asylum seekers after a suicide attempt: A comparative study of people registered at mental health services in a Swedish location. *BMC Psychiatry* 15, 1-11.

Wexler L, McEachern D, DiFulvio G, Smith C, L FG, Dombrowski K (2016). Creating a community of practice to prevent suicide through multiple channels: Describing the theoretical foundations and structured learning of PC CARES. *International Quarterly of Community Health Education.* Published online: 15 February 2015. doi: 10.1177/0272684X16630886.

Wiggins S, McQuade R, Rasmussen S (2016). Stepping back from crisis points: The provision and acknowledgment of support in an online suicide discussion forum. *Qualitative Health Research.* Published online: March 1 2016. doi: 10.1177/1049732316633130.

Wilhelm K, Handley T, Reddy P (2015). Exploring the validity of the fantastic lifestyle checklist in an inner city population of people presenting with suicidal behaviours. *Australian and New Zealand Journal of Psychiatry.* Published online 16 December 2015. doi: 10.1177/0004867415621393.

Care and support

Alonzo D (2016). Suicidal individuals and mental health treatment: A novel approach to engagement. *Community Mental Health Journal*. Published online: 9 January 2016. doi: 10.1007/s10597-015-9980-3.

Amadéo S, Rereao M, Malogne A, Favro P, Nguyen NL, Jehel L, Milner A, Kõlves K, De Leo D (2015). Testing brief intervention and phone contact among subjects with suicidal behavior: A randomized controlled trial in French Polynesia in the frames of the world health organization/suicide trends in at-risk territories study. *Mental Illness* 7, 48-53.

Andreasson K (2015). Dialectical behaviour therapy with skills training seems to be more effective in reducing non-suicidal self-injury. *Evidence Based Mental Health* 18, e10.

Andreasson K, Krogh J, Wenneberg C, Jessen HK, Krakauer K, Gluud C, Thomsen RR, Randers L, Nordentoft M (2016). Effectiveness of dialectical behavior therapy versus collaborative assessment and management of suicidality treatment for reduction of self-harm in adults with borderline personality traits and disorder-a randomized observer-blinded clinical trial. *Depression and Anxiety*. Published online: 8 February 2016. doi: 10.1002/da.22472.

Armitage CJ, Abdul Rahim W, Rowe R, O'Connor RC (2016). An exploratory randomised trial of a simple, brief psychological intervention to reduce subsequent suicidal ideation and behaviour in patients admitted to hospital for self-harm. *British Journal of Psychiatry* 208, 470-476.

Ayer L, Ramchand R, Geyer L, Burgette L, Kofner A (2016). The influence of training, reluctance, efficacy, and stigma on suicide intervention behavior among NCOs in the Army and Marine Corps. *Journal of Primary Prevention* 37, 287-302.

Bantjes J, Nel A, Louw KA, Frenkel L, Benjamin E, Lewis I (2016). 'This place is making me more depressed': The organisation of care for suicide attempters in a South African hospital. *Journal of Health Psychology*. Published online: 22 February 2016. doi: 10.1177/1359105316628744.

Barnfield J (2015). A study into suicide attempt aftercare. *Australian Nursing and Midwifery Journal* 23, 51.

Benzoni O, Fàzzari G, Marangoni C, Placentino A, Rossi A (2015). Treatment of resistant mood and schizoaffective disorders with electroconvulsive therapy: A case series of 264 patients. *Journal of Psychopathology* 21, 266-268.

Bidargaddi N, Bastiampillai T, Allison S, Jones GM, Furber G, Battersby M, Richards D (2015). Telephone-based low intensity therapy after crisis presentations to the emergency department is associated with improved outcomes. *Journal of Telemedicine and Telecare* 21, 385-391.

Boudreaux ED, Camargo CA, Arias SA, Sullivan AF, Allen MH, Goldstein AB, Manton AP, Espinola JA, Miller IW (2015). Improving suicide risk screening and detection in the emergency department. *American Journal of Preventive Medicine* 50, 445-453.

Bowden CL, Singh V (2016). The use of antidepressants in bipolar disorder patients with depression. *Expert Opinion on Pharmacotherapy* 17, 17-25.

Brown GK, Karlin BE, Trockel M, Gordienko M, Yesavage J, Taylor CB (2016). Effectiveness of cognitive behavioral therapy for veterans with depression and suicidal ideation. *Archives of Suicide Research*. Published online: 16 March 2016. doi: 10.1080/13811118.2016.1162238.

Bryan CJ, Clemans TA, Hernandez AM, Mintz J, Peterson AL, Yarvis JS, Resick PA (2015). Evaluating potential iatrogenic suicide risk in trauma-focused group cognitive behavioral therapy for the treatment of PTSD in active duty military personnel. *Depression and Anxiety*. Published online: 4 December 2015. doi: 10.1002/da.22456.

Carr MJ, Ashcroft DM, Kontopantelis E, While D, Awenat Y, Cooper J, Chew-Graham C, Kapur N, Webb RT (2016). Clinical management following self-harm in a UK-wide primary care cohort. *Journal of Affective Disorders* 197, 182-188.

Cebrià AI, Pérez-Bonaventura I, Cuijpers P, Kerkhof A, Parra I, Escayola A, García-Parés G, Oliva JC, Puntí J, López D, Vallès V, Pàmias M, Hegerl U, Pérez-Solà V, Palao DJ (2015). Telephone management program for patients discharged from an emergency department after a suicide attempt. *Crisis* 36, 345-352.

Chen B-H, Shin S-J, Shiea J, Lin S-J, Chen P-Y, Su H, Lee C-W (2016). Rapid identification of pesticides in human oral fluid for emergency management by thermal desorption electrospray ionization/mass spectrometry. *Journal of Mass Spectrometry* 51, 97-104.

Chesin MS, Sonmez CC, Benjamin-Phillips CA, Beeler B, Brodsky BS, Stanley B (2015). Preliminary effectiveness of adjunct mindfulness-based cognitive therapy to prevent suicidal behavior in outpatients who are at elevated suicide risk. *Mindfulness* 6, 1345-1355.

Choi NG, Marti CN, Conwell Y (2015). Effect of problem-solving therapy on depressed low-income homebound older adults' death/suicidal ideation and hopelessness. *Suicide and Life-Threatening Behavior*. Published online: 12 October 2015. doi: 10.1111/sltb.12195.

Cracknell B (2015). Improving the quality of initial management of self harm and suicide patients in A+E at the James Paget Hospital. *British Medical Journal Quality Improvement Reports* 4, 1-4.

de Beurs DP, de Groot MH, de Keijser J, van Duijn E, de Winter RF, Kerkhof AJ (2015). Evaluation of benefit to patients of training mental health professionals in suicide guidelines: Cluster randomised trial. *British Journal of Psychiatry* 208, 477-483.

De Hert M, De Beugher A, Sweers K, Wampers M, Correll CU, Cohen D (2016). Knowledge of psychiatric nurses about the potentially lethal side-effects of clozapine. *Archives of Psychiatric Nursing* 30, 79-83.

Deshais MA, Fisher AB, Hausman NL, Kahng SW (2015). Further investigation of a rapid restraint analysis. *Journal of Applied Behavior Analysis* 48, 845-859.

Duarté-Vélez Y, Torres-Dávila P, Spirito A, Polanco N, Bernal G (2016). Development of a treatment protocol for Puerto Rican adolescents with suicidal behaviors. *Psychotherapy* 53, 45-56.

Feder MM, Diamond GM (2016). Parent-therapist alliance and parent attachment-promoting behaviour in attachment-based family therapy for suicidal and depressed adolescents. *Journal of Family Therapy* 38, 82-101.

Gale TM, Hawley CJ, Butler J, Morton A, Singhal A (2016). Perception of suicide risk in mental health professionals. *PLoS One* 11, e0149791.

Gallegos AM, Streltzov NA, Stecker T (2016). Improving treatment engagement for returning operation enduring freedom and operation Iraqi freedom veterans with posttraumatic stress disorder, depression, and suicidal ideation. *Journal of Nervous and Mental Disease* 204, 339-343.

Ghanbari B, Malakouti SK, Nojomi M, Alavi K, Khaleghparast S (2015). Suicide prevention and follow-up services: A narrative review. *Global Journal of Health Science* 8, 145-153.

Ghoncheh R, Gould MS, Twisk JW, Kerkhof AJ, Koot HM (2016). Efficacy of adolescent suicide prevention e-learning modules for gatekeepers: A randomized controlled trial. *JMIR Mental Health* 3, e8.

Grimholt TK, Jacobsen D, Haavet OR, Sandvik L, Jorgensen T, Norheim AB, Ekeberg O (2015). Structured follow-up by general practitioners after deliberate self-poisoning: A randomised controlled trial. *BMC Psychiatry* 15, 1-11.

Guille C, Zhao Z, Krystal J, Nichols B, Brady K, Sen S (2015). Web-based cognitive behavioral therapy intervention for the prevention of suicidal ideation in medical interns: A randomized clinical trial. *JAMA Psychiatry* 72, 1192-1198.

Gustavson KA, Alexopoulos GS, Niu GC, McCulloch C, Meade T, Arean PA (2016). Problem-solving therapy reduces suicidal ideation in depressed older adults with executive dysfunction. *American Journal of Geriatric Psychiatry* 24, 11-17.

Gysin-Maillart AC, Soravia LM, Gemperli A, Michel K (2016). Suicide ideation is related to therapeutic alliance in a brief therapy for attempted suicide. *Archives of Suicide Research*. Published online: 16 March 2016. doi: 10.1080/13811118.2016.1162242.

Haddock G, Davies L, Evans E, Emsley R, Gooding P, Heaney L, Jones S, Kelly J, Munro A, Peters S, Pratt D, Tarrier N, Windfuhr K, Awenat Y (2016). Investigating the feasibility and acceptability of a cognitive behavioural suicide prevention therapy for people in acute psychiatric wards (the 'INSITE' trial): Study protocol for a randomised controlled trial. *Trials* 17, 1-8.

Hassanian-Moghaddam H, Sarjami S, Kolahi AA, Lewin T, Carter G (2016). Postcards in Persia: A twelve to twenty-four month follow-up of a randomized controlled trial for hospital-treated deliberate self-poisoning. *Archives of Suicide Research*. Published online 16 March 2015. doi: 10.1080/13811118.2015.1004473.

Hatcher S, Coupe N, Wikiriwhi K, Durie SM, Pillai A (2016). Te Ira Tangata: A Zelen randomised controlled trial of a culturally informed treatment compared to treatment as usual in Maori who present to hospital after self-harm. *Social Psychiatry and Psychiatric Epidemiology*. Published online: 8 March 2016. doi: 10.1007/s00127-016-1194-7.

Hawton K, Witt KG, Taylor Salisbury TL, Arensman E, Gunnell D, Townsend E, van Heeringen K, Hazell P (2015). Interventions for self-harm in children and adolescents. *Cochrane Database Systematic Review* 12, CD012013.

Hu YD, Xiang YT, Fang JX, Zu S, Sha S, Shi H, Ungvari GS, Correll CU, Chiu HF, Xue Y, Tian TF, Wu AS, Ma X, Wang G (2015). Single I.V. ketamine augmentation of newly initiated escitalopram for major depression: Results from a randomized, placebo-controlled 4-week study. *Psychological Medicine* 46, 623-635.

Kasckow J, Zickmund S, Gurklis J, Luther J, Fox L, Taylor M, Richmond I, Haas GL (2016). Using telehealth to augment an intensive case monitoring program in veterans with schizophrenia and suicidal ideation: A pilot trial. *Psychiatry Research* 239, 111-116.

Kashani P, Yousefian S, Amini A, Heidari K, Younesian S, Hatamabadi HR (2014). The effect of intravenous ketamine in suicidal ideation of emergency department patients. *Emergency* 2, 36-39.

Kennard BD, Biernesser C, Wolfe KL, Foxwell AA, Craddock Lee SJ, Rial KV, Patel S, Cheng C, Goldstein T, McMakin D, Blastos B, Douaihy A, Zelazny J, Brent DA (2015). Developing a brief suicide prevention intervention and mobile phone application: A qualitative report. *Journal of Technology in Human Services* 33, 345-357.

Krysinska K, Batterham P, Christensen H (2016). Differences in the effectiveness of psychosocial interventions for suicidal ideation and behaviour in women and men: A systematic review of randomised controlled trials. *Archives of Suicide Research*. Published online: 16 March 2016. doi: 10.1080/13811118.2016.1162246.

Labelle R, Pouliot L, Janelle A (2015). A systematic review and meta-analysis of cognitive behavioural treatments for suicidal and self-harm behaviours in adolescents. *Canadian Psychology* 56, 368-378.

Laforgue E, Sauvaget A, Bulteau S, Vanelle JM (2015). From ketamine's antidepressant effect to ketamine for rapid reduction of suicidal ideation. *Annales Medico-Psychologiques* 174, 60-63.

Lee Cw, Su H, Chen Py, Lin Sj, Shiea J, Shin Sj, Chen Bh (2016). Rapid identification of pesticides in human oral fluid for emergency management by thermal desorption electrospray ionization/mass spectrometry (editorial). *Journal of Mass Spectrometry* 51, 97-104.

Lee Y, Syeda K, Maruschak NA, Cha DS, Mansur RB, Wium-Andersen IK, Woldeyohannes HO, Rosenblat JD, McIntyre RS (2016). A new perspective on the anti-suicide effects with ketamine treatment: A procognitive effect. *Journal of Clinical Psychopharmacology* 36, 50-56.

Lemon G, Stanford S, Sawyer AM (2016). Trust and the dilemmas of suicide risk assessment in non-government mental health services. *Australian Social Work* 69, 145-157.

Linehan MM, Korslund KE, Harned MS (2015). Dialectical behavior therapy for high suicide risk in individuals with borderline personality disorder: A randomized clinical trial and component analysis. *JAMA Psychiatry* 72, 475-482.

Lohman MC, Raue PJ, Greenberg RL, Bruce ML (2015). Reducing suicidal ideation in home health care: Results from the carepath depression care management trial. *International Journal of Geriatric Psychiatry*. Published online: 9 November 2015. doi: 10.1002/gps.4381.

Lopez-Castroman J, Jaussent I, Gorwood P, Courtet P (2016). Suicidal depressed patients respond less well to antidepressants in the short term. *Depression and Anxiety*. Published online: 16 February 2016. doi: 10.1002/da.22473.

Madsen T, Karstoft KI, Secher RG, Austin SF, Nordentoft M (2016). Trajectories of suicidal ideation in patients with first-episode psychosis: Secondary analysis of data from the OPUS trial. *Lancet Psychiatry* 3, 443-450.

Manning JC, Latif A, Carter T, Cooper J, Horsley A, Armstrong M, Wharrad H (2015). 'Our care through our eyes': A mixed-methods, evaluative study of a service-user, co-produced education programme to improve inpatient care of children and young people admitted following self-harm. *BMJ Open* 5, 1-7.

Marriott BP, Hibbeln JR, Killeen TK, Magruder KM, Holes-Lewis K, Tolliver BK, Turner TH (2016). Design and methods for the better resiliency among veterans and non-veterans with Omega-3's (BRAVO) study: A double blind, placebo-controlled trial of omega-3 fatty acid supplementation among adult individuals at risk of suicide. *Contemporary Clinical Trials* 47, 325-333.

McManama O'Brien KH (2015). Rethinking adolescent inpatient psychiatric care: The importance of integrated interventions for suicidal youth with substance use problems. *Social Work in Mental Health* 11, 349-359.

Michael K, Jameson JP, Sale R, Orlando C, Schorr M, Brazille M, Stevens A, Massey C (2015). A revision and extension of the prevention of escalating adolescent crisis events (PEACE) protocol. *Children and Youth Services Review* 59, 57-62.

Mocarski R, Butler S (2016). A critical, rhetorical analysis of man therapy: The use of humor to frame mental health as masculine. *Journal of Communication Inquiry* 40, 128-144.

Mouaffak F, Marchand A, Castaigne E, Arnoux A, Hardy P (2015). OSTA program: A French follow up intervention program for suicide prevention. *Psychiatry Research* 230, 913-918.

Patchan KM, Richardson C, Vyas G, Kelly DL (2015). The risk of suicide after clozapine discontinuation: Cause for concern. *Annals of Clinical Psychiatry* 27, 253-256.

Pratt D, Gooding P, Awenat Y, Eccles S, Tarrier N (2015). Cognitive behavioral suicide prevention for male prisoners: Case examples. *Cognitive and Behavioral Practice*. Published online: 21 October 2015. doi: 10.1016/j.cbpra.2015.09.006.

Rathus J, Campbell B, Miller A, Smith H (2015). Treatment acceptability study of walking the middle path, a new DBT skills module for adolescents and their families. *American Journal of Psychotherapy* 69, 163-178.

Ray-Griffith SL, Coker JL, Rabie N, Eads LA, Golden KJ, Stowe ZN (2016). Pregnancy and electroconvulsive therapy: A multidisciplinary approach. *Journal of ECT* 32, 104-112.

Ritschel LA, Lim NE, Stewart LM (2015). Transdiagnostic applications of DBT for adolescents and adults. *American Journal of Psychotherapy* 69, 111-128.

Rodzinski P, Rutkowski K, Sobanski JA, Murzyn A, Cyranka K, Grzadziel K, Smiatek-Mazgaj B, Klasa K, Mueldner-Nieckowski L, Dembinska E, Mielimaka M (2015). Reduction of suicidal ideation in patients undergoing psychotherapy in the day hospital for the treatment of neurotic and behavioral disorders and neurotic symptoms reported by them before the hospitalization. *Psychiatria Polska* 49, 847-864.

Rodziński P, Rutkowski K, Sobański JA, Murzyn A, Mielimaka M, Smiatek-Mazgaj B, Cyranka K, Dembińska E, Grządziel K, Klasa K, Müldner-Nieckowski Ł(2015). Reduction of suicidal ideation in patients undergoing psychotherapy in the day hospital for the treatment of neurotic and behavioral disorders and their neurotic personality traits measured before the hospitalization. *Psychiatria Polska* 49, 1303-1321.

Runyan CW, Becker A, Brandspigel S, Barber C, Trudeau A, Novins D (2016). Lethal means counseling for parents of youth seeking emergency care for suicidality. *Western Journal of Emergency Medicine* 17, 8-14.

Sampath H, Sharma I, Dutta S (2016). Treatment of suicidal depression with ketamine in rapid cycling bipolar disorder. *Asia-Pacific Psychiatry* 8, 98-101.

Schembari BC, Jobes DA, Horgan RJ (2016). Successful treatment of suicidal risk. *Crisis*. Published online: 2 February 2016. doi: 10.1027/0227-5910/a000370.

Shelef L, Tatsa-Laur L, Derazne E, Mann JJ, Fruchter E (2015). An effective suicide prevention program in the Israeli Defense Forces: A cohort study. *European Psychiatry* 31, 37-43.

Sher L (2016). Buprenorphine and the treatment of depression, anxiety, non-suicidal self-injury, and suicidality. *Acta Psychiatrica Scandinavic*. Published online: 24 March 2016. doi: 10.1111/acps.12577.

Stanley B, Chaudhury SR, Chesin M, Pontoski K, Bush AM, Knox KL, Brown GK (2016). An emergency department intervention and follow-up to reduce suicide risk in the VA: Acceptability and effectiveness. *Psychiatric Services*. Published online: 1 February 2016. doi: 10.1176/appi.ps.201500082.

Stiglmayr C, Stecher-Mohr J, Wagner T, Meibetaner J, Spretz D, Steffens C, Roepke S, Fydrich T, Salbach-Andrae H, Schulze J, Renneberg B (2014). Effectiveness of dialectic behavioral therapy in routine outpatient care: The Berlin Borderline Study. *Borderline Personality Disorder and Emotion Dysregulation* 1, 1-11.

Sueki H (2015). Willingness to pay for suicide prevention in Japan. *Death Studies* 40, 283-289.

Surgenor PWG (2015). Promoting recovery from suicidal ideation through the development of protective factors. *Counselling and Psychotherapy Research* 15, 207-216.

Surgenor PWG, Meehan V, Moore A (2016). Early attrition among suicidal clients. *British Journal of Guidance and Counselling*. Published online: 18 January 2016. doi: 10.1080/03069885.2015.1134766.

Tsai CJ, Cheng C, Chou PH, Lin CH, McInnis MG, Chang CL, Lan TH (2016). The rapid suicide protection of mood stabilizers on patients with bipolar disorder: A nationwide observational cohort study in Taiwan. *Journal of Affective Disorders* 196, 71-77.

Wachter Morris CA, Taub DJ, Servaty-Seib HL, Lee JY, Miles N, Werden D, Prieto-Welch SL (2015). Expanding capacity for suicide prevention: The ALIVE @ Purdue train-the-trainers program. *Journal of College Student Development* 56, 861-866.

Walser RD, Garvert DW, Karlin BE, Trockel M, Ryu DM, Taylor CB (2015). Effectiveness of acceptance and commitment therapy in treating depression and suicidal ideation in Veterans. *Behaviour Research and Therapy* 74, 25-31.

Ward-Ciesielski EF, Jones CB, Wielgus MD, Wilks CR, Linehan MM (2016). Single-session dialectical behavior therapy skills training versus relaxation training for non-treatment-engaged suicidal adults: A randomized controlled trial. *BMC Psychology* 4, 1-7.

Wilks CR, Korslund KE, Harned MS, Linehan MM (2016). Dialectical behavior therapy and domains of functioning over two years. *Behaviour Research and Therapy* 77, 162-169.

Wright-Hughes A, Graham E, Farrin A, Collinson M, Boston P, Eisler I, Fortune S, Green J, House A, Owens D, Simic M, Tubeuf S, Nixon J, McCabe C, Kerfoot M, Cottrell D (2015). Self-harm intervention: Family therapy (SHIFT), a study protocol for a randomised controlled trial of family therapy versus treatment as usual for young people seen after a second or subsequent episode of self-harm. *Trials* 16, 1-12.

Yovell Y, Bar G, Mashiah M, Baruch Y, Briskman I, Asherov J, Lotan A, Rigbi A, Panksepp J (2015). Ultra-low-dose buprenorphine as a time-limited treatment for severe suicidal ideation: A randomized controlled trial. *American Journal of Psychiatry* 173, 491-498.

Zor F, Aykan A, Coskun U, Aksu M, Ozturk S (2015). Late oropharyngeal functional outcomes of suicidal maxillofacial gunshot wounds. *The Journal of Craniofacial Surgery* 26, 691-695.

CASE REPORTS

Ahuja V, Ratogi P (2015). Decapitation in suicidal hanging: A case report. *Journal of Punjab Academy of Forensic Medicine and Toxicology* 15, 97-99.

Akinci E (2015). Suicide attempt with mad honey: Case report. *Dusunen Adam* 28, 387-388.

Avery AH, Rae L, Summitt JB, Kahn SA (2016). The fire challenge: A case report and analysis of self-inflicted flame injury posted on social media. *Journal of Burn Care and Research* 37, e161-e165.

Avila Alvarez AA, Parra JF, Buitrago DA, Rodriguez F, Moreno A (2014). Gastric perforation and phlegmon formation by foreign bodyingestion. *Emergency* 2, 141-143.

Azad TD, Li A, Pendharkar AV, Veeravagu A, Grant GA (2015). Junior Seau: An illustrative case of chronic traumatic encephalopathy and update on chronic sports-related head injury. *World Neurosurgery* 86, 515.E11-515.E16.

Balliet WE, Madan A, Craig ML, Serber ER, Borckardt JJ, Pelic C, Barth K, Hale A, van Bakel AB, Peura JL (2015). A ventricular assist device recipient and suicidality: Multidisciplinary collaboration with a psychiatrically distressed patient. *Journal of Cardiovascular Nursing*. Published online: 29 September 2015. doi: 10.1097/JCN.0000000000000293.

Bayram E, Durmaz FN, Akbostancı MC (2015). Uneventful recovery from a suicide attempt with tetrabenazine: A case report. *Turkish Journal of Neurology* 21, 175-176.

Biswas A, Gulati SK, Kaushal S (2015). Anesthetic management of a case of suicidal cut throat injury. *Anaesthesia, Pain and Intensive Care* 19, 181-183.

Biswas S, Bandyopadhyay C, Biswas S, Dalal D, Roy S (2015). Multiple violent suicidal attempts by one mentally ill person: A rare case. *Journal of Indian Academy of Forensic Medicine* 37, 325-327.

Borah S, McConnell B, Hughes R, Kluger B (2016). Potential relationship of self-injurious behavior to right temporo-parietal lesions. *Neurocase*. Published online: 16 February 2016. doi: 10.1080/13554794.2016.1147586.

Byard RW (2015). Evidence of premeditation in skin messages in suicide. *Journal of Forensic Sciences* 61, 566-568.

Carota A, Rimoldi F, Calabrese P (2016). Wernicke's aphasia and attempted suicide. *Acta Neurologica Belgica*. Published online: 4 March 2016. doi: 10.1007/s13760-016-0618-1.

Çelik M, Kalenderoğlu A, Almiş H, Turgut M (2016). Copycat suicides without an intention to die after watching TV programs: Two cases at five years of age. *Noropsikiyatri Arsivi* 53, 80-81.

Chen BC, Bright SB, Trivedi AR, Valento M (2015). Death following intentional ingestion of e-liquid. *Clinical Toxicology* 53, 914-916.

Chou S, Ayabe S, Sekine N (2015). Myocardial injury without electrocardiographic changes after a suicide attempt by an overdose of glimepiride and zolpidem: A case report and literature review. *Internal Medicine* 54, 2727-2733.

Cibickova L, Caran T, Dobias M, Ondra P, Vo íšek V, Cibicek N (2015). Multi-drug intoxication fatality involving atorvastatin: A case report. *Forensic Science International* 257, e26-e31.

Clark S, Catt JW, Caffery T (2015). Rapid diagnosis and treatment of severe tricyclic antidepressant toxicity. *BMJ Case Reports*. Published online: 14 October 2015. doi: 10.1136/bcr-2015-211428.

Clinebell K, Valpey R, Walker T, Gopalan P, Azzam P (2016). Self-enucleation and severe ocular injury in the psychiatric setting. *Psychosomatics* 57, 25-30.

Correa Díaz EP, Jácome Sánchez EC, Martínez BA (2015). Suicide in adolescents with depression: The need for early diagnosis. *Clinical Case Reports* 3, 962-963.

Crawford A, Wand AP, Smith MA (2015). Self-amputation of the hand: Issues in diagnosis and general hospital management. *Australasian Psychiatry*. Published online: 23 September 2015. doi: 10.1177/1039856215604479.

Dhakne R, Mishra KK, Kumar V, Khairkar P (2015). Prolonged apnea during modified electroconvulsive therapy in a patient of suicidal attempt by organophosphorus poisoning: A case report. *Journal of ECT*. Published online: 20 November 2015. doi: 10.1097/YCT.0000000000000285.

Dhooria S, Behera D, Agarwal R (2015). Amitraz: A mimicker of organophosphate poisoning. *BMJ Case Reports*. Published online: 16 September 2015. doi: 10.1136/bcr-2015-210296.

Dias D, Bessa J, Guimaraes S, Soares ME, Bastos MdL, Teixeira HM (2016). Inorganic mercury intoxication: A case report. *Forensic Science International* 259, E20-E24.

Dileep Kumar KB, Raghavendra R, Havanur B (2016). Cause of death other than asphyxia in suicidal atypical hanging - a case report. *Journal of South India Medicolegal Association* 8, 53-54.

Dinesh Kumar R, Manjula Devi AJ, Shanthi B (2015). Case report-acetaminophen poisoning. *Research Journal of Pharmaceutical, Biological and Chemical Sciences* 6, 4-7.

Dunphy L, Maatouk M, Raja M, O'Hara R (2015). Ingested cylindrical batteries in an incarcerated male: A caustic tale! *British Medical Journal Case Reports*. Published online: 29 September 2015. doi: 10.1136/bcr-2014-208922.

Elia G, Franco E, Clauser LC (2016). Multiple mandibular fractures. Treatment outlines. *Minerva Stomatologica* 65, 54-63.

Elling R, Spehl MS, Wohlfarth A, Auwaerter V, Hermanns-Clausen M (2015). Prolonged hypoglycemia after a suicidal ingestion of repaglinide with unexpected slow plasma elimination. *Clinical Toxicology*. Published online: 22 December 2015. doi: 10.3109/15563650.2015.1122793.

Emoto Y, Yoshizawa K, Shikata N, Tsubura A, Nagasaki Y (2015). Autopsy report for chemical burns from cresol solution. *Experimental and Toxicologic Pathology* 68, 99-102.

E H, Sahin MF, Emir A, Celik S (2016). Resuscitation artefact confirmed by postmortem angiography. Case report. *Romanian Journal of Legal Medicine* 24, 14-16.

Fino P, Spagnoli AM, Ruggieri M, Onesti MG (2015). Caustic burn caused by intradermal self administration of muriatic acid for suicidal attempt: Optimal wound healing and functional recovery with a non surgical treatment. *Il Giornale Di Chirurgia* 36, 214-218.

Flam B, Bendz E, Jonsson Fagerlund M, Höjer J (2015). Seizures associated with intentional severe nutmeg intoxication. *Clinical Toxicology* 53, 917.

Foley M, Cummins I (2015). Reading the death of Mrs A: A serious case review. *Journal of Adult Protection* 17, 321-330.

Gaines A, Cronin L, Hamel M (2015). An unusual method of suicide: Fluoride toxicity due to toothpaste ingestion. *American Journal of Clinical Pathology*. Published online: 1 October 2015. doi: 10.1093/ajcp/144.suppl2.018.

Galletta D, Aurino C, Sica G, Amodio A, Elce C, Micanti F (2015). Self-injurious behaviour: Self identity, impulsiveness and self-injury in patients with borderline personality disorders and bulimia. *Journal of Psychiatry* 18, 262.

Ghanbari B, Malakouti SK, Nojomi M, De Leo D, Saeed K (2015). Alcohol abuse and suicide attempt in Iran: A case-crossover study. *Global Journal of Health Science* 8, 58-67.

Green JD, Jakupcak M (2015). Masculinity and men's self-harm behaviors: Implications for non-suicidal self-injury disorder. *Psychology of Men and Masculinity* 17, 147-155.

Hassanian-Moghaddam H, Zamani N (2016). Radiopaque stomach-shaped bezoar in a suicidal patient. *Dysphagia* 31, 484-485.

Ishikawa T, Yuasa I, Endoh M (2015). Non specific drug distribution in an autopsy case report of fatal caffeine intoxication. *Legal Medicine* 17, 535-538.

Janik M, Straka L, Novomesky F, Krajcovic J, Hejna P (2016). Circular saw-related fatalities: A rare case report, review of the literature, and forensic implications. *Legal Medicine* 18, 52-57.

Joshi MC, Garg RK (2015). Examination of handwriting on an unusual surface in a suicide case: Dead persons do tell tales - conduct a forensic investigation for the cause of humanity and justice. *Problems of Forensic Sciences* 101, 50-59.

Jovi -Stoši J, Puti V, Živanovi D, Mladenov M, Brajkovi G, Djordjevi S (2016). Failure of intravenous lipid emulsion in treatment of cardiotoxicity caused by mixed overdose including dihydropyridine calcium channel blockers. *Vojnosanitetski Pregled* 73, 88-91.

Kanchan T, Raghavendra Babu YP, Atreya A, Acharya J (2016). Ligature mark on the face - forensic implications. *Medico-Legal Journal*. Published online: 11 March 2016. doi: 10.1177/0025817216630658.

Kapadia A, John JR, Gaba S, Sharma RK (2015). Primary nasal reconstruction in self-inflicted nasal injury. *Journal of Craniofacial Surgery* 26, e588-e590.

Karaoulanis SE, Syngelakis M, Fokas K (2016). Rhabdomyolysis after lamotrigine overdose: A case report and review of the literature. *Annals of General Psychiatry* 15, 6.

Karatapanis S, Lamprianou F, Ntetskas G, Kotis A (2015). Elemental mercury mixed with alcohol injected intravenously as a suicide attempt. *BMJ Case Reports*. Published online: 5 October 2015. doi: 10.1136/bcr-2014-207075.

Keles S, Dogusal G, Sönmez I (2015). Autoextraction of permanent incisors and self-inflicted oro-dental trauma in a severely burned child. *Case Reports in Dentistry* 2015, 425251.

Kim H-J, Na J-Y, Lee Y-J, Park J-T, Kim H-S (2015). An autopsy case of methanol induced intracranial hemorrhage. *International Journal of Clinical and Experimental Pathology* 8, 13643-13646.

Klavž J, Gorenjak M, Marinšek M (2016). Suicide attempt with a mix of synthetic cannabinoids and synthetic cathinones: Case report of non-fatal intoxication with AB-CHMINACA, AB-FUBINACA, alpha-PHP, alpha-PVP and 4-CMC. *Forensic Science International* 265, 121-124.

Kuchewar SV, Khetre RR, Shrigiriwar MB, Meshram RD, Gadge SJ (2015). An unusal and rare case of burn: Challenge to cause and manner of death. *Indian Journal of Forensic Medicine and Toxicology* 9, 231-235.

Kukreti P, Gautam P, Garg A (2015). An unusual case of secondary mania following hypoxia in a suicide attempt following hanging. *Indian Journal of Psychiatry* 57, S108-S109.

Kwon IJ, Kim SM, Park HK, Myoung H, Lee JH, Lee SK (2015). Successful treatment of self-inflicted tongue trauma patient using a special oral appliance. *International Journal of Pediatric Otorhinolaryngology* 79, 1938-1941.

Lalanne L, Meriot M-E, Ruppert E, Zimmermann M-A, Danion J-M, Vidailhet P (2016). Attempted infanticide and suicide inaugurating catatonia associated with hashimoto's encephalopathy: A case report. *BMC Psychiatry* 16, 13.

Landau D, Stockton S (2015). An unusual cause of suicidal ideations. *Oxford Medical Case Reports* 2015, 323-324.

Le Garff E, Delannoy Y, Mesli V, Berthezene JM, Morbidelli P, Hedouin V (2015). Homemade firearm suicide with dumbbell pipe triggering by an air-compressed gun case report and review of literature. *American Journal of Forensic Medicine and Pathology* 36, 257-261.

Lee S-H, Park SW, Han S-K, Park S-C (2015). Acute colchicine poisoning treated with granulocyte colony stimulating factor and transfusion. *Korean Society of Critical Care Medicine* 30, 207-211.

Lombardo B, Zarrilli F, Ceglia C, Vitale A, Keller S, Sarchiapone M, Carli V, Stuppia L, Chiariotti L, Castaldo G, Pastore L (2015). Two novel genomic rearrangements identified in suicide subjects using a-CGH array. *Clinical Chemistry and Laboratory Medicine* 53, E245-E248.

Lorang MR, McNiel DE, Binder RL (2016). Minors and sexting: Legal implications. *Journal of American Academy Psychiatry and the Law* 44, 73-81.

Macaluso M, Larson CA (2015). The first published case report of an adult woman who developed suicidal ideation as an adverse event related to methylphenidate use. *Primary Care Companion for CNS Disorders.* Published online: 26 March 2015. doi: 10.4088/PCC.14l01739.

Madea B, Schmidt P, Kernbach-Wighton G, Doberentz E (2015). Strangulation - suicide at the wheel. *Legal Medicine* 17, 512-516.

Martin JF, Vidas J, Baday A (2015). Acute neurocysticercosis presenting as suicidal ideation. *American Journal of Emergency Medicine* 33, 1842.e3-1842.e5.

McIntyre IM, Mallett P, Stolberg S, Haas EA, Mena O (2016). Striking increases in postmortem compared to antemortem drug concentrations in a suicidal overdose: A case report. *Australian Journal of Forensic Sciences* 48, 37-41.

Michalsen KL, Iguidbashian JP, Kyser JP, Long WB, III (2015). Low-velocity nail-gun injuries to the interventricular septum: Report of two cases, one in a child. *Texas Heart Institute Journal* 42, 393-396.

Molokwu OA, Ezeala-Adikaibe BA, Onwuekwe IO (2015). Levetiracetam-induced rage and suicidality: Two case reports and review of literature. *Epilepsy and Behavior Case Reports* 4, 79-81.

Nor FM, Das S, Naziri SZM (2015). Fatal poisoning by Malathion. *International Medical Journal* 22, 439-441.

Oke V, Schmidt F, Bhattarai B, Basunia M, Agu C, Kaur A, Enriquez D, Quist J, Salhan D, Gayam V, Mungikar P (2015). Unrecognized clozapine-related constipation leading to fatal intra-abdominal sepsis - a case report. *International Medical Case Reports Journal* 8, 189-192.

Osamu Kobori MO (2014). Cognitive-behavioral therapy for health anxiety disorder: A case report of a Japanese male suffering the after effects of apoplexy and attempted suicide. *Journal of Psychotherapy and Psychological Disorders* 2, e102.

Osawa M, Matsushima Y, Kumar A, Tsuboi A, Kakimoto Y, Satoh F (2016). Self-inflicted firearm discharge from heating using a gas burner. *Journal of Forensic Sciences* 61, 845-847.

Parashar S, Roy N, Osuagwu FC, Khalid Z, Tinklepaugh M, Mehr S, Dillon JE (2016). Trimethoprim-sulfamethoxazole–induced psychosis culminating in catastrophic self-injury: A case report. *Primary Care Companion for CNS Disorders* 1599, 70.

Patil N, Karthik Rao N, Kunder SK, Avinash A, Pathak A, Sori RK, Poojar B, Varghese G (2015). Acute clonazepam poisoning: Seeking death or attention? *Research Journal of Pharmaceutical, Biological and Chemical Sciences* 6, 1056-1058.

Ponde MP, Freire ACC (2015). Increased anxiety, akathisia, and suicidal thoughts in patients with mood disorder on aripiprazole and lamotrigine. *Case Reports in Psychiatry* 2015, 419746.

Ross LM, Dunn TM, Lozano A (2016). Suicide attempt by anaphylaxis. *Psychosomatics* 57, 226-227.

Schneir A, Rentmeester L (2016). Carbon monoxide poisoning and pulmonary injury from the mixture of formic and sulfuric acids. *Clinical Toxicology* 54, 450-453.

Schoen JC, Cain MR, Robinson JA, Schiltz BM, Mannenbach MS (2016). Adolescent presents with altered mental status and elevated anion gap after suicide attempt by ethylene glycol ingestion. *Pediatric Emergency Care.* Published online: 16 January 2016. doi: 10.1097/PEC.0000000000000606.

Scott JY (2016). Mitigating nursing biases in management of intoxicated and suicidal patients. *Journal of Emergency Nursing* 41, 296-299.

Shrivastava N, Satpati DK, Kumar A (2015). Easy confirmation of drowning by detection of diatoms in trachea. *Journal of Indian Academy of Forensic Medicine* 37, 352-354.

Smith H (2016). Self-injurious behavior in prison: A case study. *International Journal of Offender*

Therapy and Comparative Criminology 60, 228-243.

Steinritz D, Eyer F, Worek F, Thiermann H, John H (2016). Repetitive obidoxime treatment induced increase of red blood cell acetylcholinesterase activity even in a late phase of a severe methamidophos poisoning: A case report. *Toxicology Letters* 244, 121-123.

Stone T, Gould SJ (2016). Vulnerable consumers in the 'fourth age': Theoretical reflections upon the case of Sandra Bem. *Journal of Marketing Management* 32, 386-392.

Takaki S, Yamaguchi O, Morimura N, Goto T (2015). Self-inflicted oral penetration injury: An intravenous drip pole advanced from the mouth to the retroperitoneum. *International Journal of Surgery Case Reports* 16, 112-115.

Tanuj K, Alok A, Raghavendra Babu YP (2016). A case of ligature strangulation without a knot in the noose. *Journal of South India Medicolegal Association* 8, 50-52.

Tatiya HS, Jadhao VT, Taware AA, Abhijit L B (2016). Patterned injury due to flash suppressor: A case report. *Indian Journal of Forensic Medicine and Toxicology* 10, 126-128.

Teng JY, Chee CYI, Chong Y-S, Lee LY, Yong EL, Chi C, Broekman B (2016). A suicidal pregnant patient's request for premature cesarean section: Clinical and ethical challenges. *Journal of Affective Disorders* 194, 168-170.

Teng JY, Yin Ing Chee C, Chong YS, Lee LY, Yong EL, Chi C, Broekman B (2016). A suicidal pregnant patient's request for premature cesarean section: Clinical and ethical challenges. *Journal of Affective Disorders* 194, 168-170.

Türkoğlu S (2015). Paradoxical reactions related to alprazolam. *Journal of Child and Adolescent Psychopharmacology* 25, 276-276.

Uslu FI, Erdem NS, Yagan S (2015). A case with status epilepticus and cardiac arrest after bupropion overdose. *Dusunen Adam* 28, 273-275.

Veneroni L, Ferrari A, Massimino M, Alfredo CC (2015). Dying after cure: A case of suicide in an adolescent treated for cancer. *Journal of Cancer Research and Therapeutics* 11, 667.

Vilibić M, Bagarić D, Kolarić B, Radic K, Curkovic M, Zivkovic M (2015). Suicide as the first manifestation of first-episode psychosis in 21-year-old man: A case report. *Psychiatria Danubina* 27, 285-287.

Westerlund M, Hadlaczky G, Wasserman D (2015). Case study of posts before and after a suicide on a Swedish internet forum. *British Journal of Psychiatry* 207, 476-482.

Williams AC (2016). Autoextraction of twelve permanent teeth in a child with autistic spectrum disorder. *International Journal of Paediatric Dentistry* 26, 157-159.

Yadav A, Raheel MS, Kumar LR, Sharma SK, Kanwar H (2016). Cut-throat wounds: Suicidal and homicidal two case reports and review of literature. *Medicine Science and the Law* 56, 53-57.

Yadav A, Swain R, Bakshi MS, Gupta S (2015). Suicidal shotgun wound on chest: An uncommon site with an unusual track. *Journal of Indian Academy of Forensic Medicine* 37, 430-432.

Zeleny M, Pivnicka J, Sindler M, Kukleta P (2015). Unusual way of suicide by carbon monoxide. Case report. *Neuro Endocrinology Letters* 36, 147-149.

Zhang L, Ma J, Li S, Xue R, Jin M, Zhou Y (2015). Fatal diphenidol poisoning: A case report and a retrospective study of 16 cases. *Forensic Science, Medicine, and Pathology* 11, 570-575.

MISCELLANEOUS

Anonymous (2015). Alcohol misuse and self-harm. *Emergency Nurse* 23, 17.

Anonymous (2015). Correction to Anestis et al. (2014). *Journal of Abnormal Psychology* 124, 497.

Anonymous (2015). Corrections to interventions to reduce suicides at suicide hotspots: A systematic review and meta-analysis [Lancet Psychiatry, 2, (2015), 994-1001]. *Lancet Psychiatry* 2, 961.

Anonymous (2015). Elderly suicide alarming. *Australian Nursing and Midwifery Journal* 22, 17.

Anonymous (2015). Erratum for "borderline personality disorder and posttraumatic stress disorder at psychiatric discharge predict general hospital admission for self-harm". *Journal of Traumatic Stress* 29, 106.

Anonymous (2015). Erratum: Suicidal ideation and suicide attempts in five groups with different severities of gambling: Findings from the National Epidemiologic Survey on Alcohol and Related Conditions by Jacquelene F. Moghaddam, Gihyun Yoon, Daniel L. Dickerson, Suck Won Kim, and Joseph Westermeyer doi: 10.1111/ajad.12197. *American Journal on Addictions*. Published online: 29 October 2015. doi: 10.1111/ajad.12299.

Anonymous (2015). Exercise reduces suicidal thoughts and attempts in bullied students. *Journal of Psychosocial Nursing and Mental Health Services* 53, 7.

Anonymous (2015). Nurse appointed to suicide prevention programme. *Nursing New Zealand (Wellington, NZ.: 1995)* 21, 8.

Anonymous (2015). Nurses can help prevent suicides. *Nursing Standard* 13, 9.

Anonymous (2015). Suicide in America: An awful hole. *Economist* 411, 1.

Anonymous (2016). Antidepressants may double risk of suicide in younger people. *Nursing Standard* 30, 14.

Anonymous (2016). Detecting and treating suicide ideation in all settings. *Sentinel Event Alert* 56, 1-7.

Anonymous (2016). Health system screens all patients for suicide risk. *Hospital Peer Review* 41, 15-17.

Abrutyn S, Mueller AS (2016). When too much integration and regulation hurts: Reenvisioning Durkheim's altruistic suicide. *Society and Mental Health* 6, 56-71.

Adams TD, Mehta TS, Davidson LE, Hunt SC (2015). All-cause and cause-specific mortality associated with bariatric surgery: A review. *Current Atherosclerosis Reports* 17, 74.

Agoramoorthy G, Hsu MJ (2016). The suicide paradigm: Insights from ancient Hindu scriptures. *Journal of Religion and Health*. Published online: 2 February 2016. doi: 10.1007/s10943-015-0178-3.

Agyapong VIO (2015). Factors predicting the presence of impaired clinical insight in liaison psychiatric patients assessed in the emergency room. *International Journal of Psychiatry in Clinical Practice*. Published online: 19 November 2015. doi: 10.3109/13651501.2015.1107910.

Ajdacic-Gross V, Tran US, Bopp M, Sonneck G, Niederkrotenthaler T, Kapusta ND, Rössler W, Seifritz E, Voracek M (2015). Erratum: Understanding weekly cycles in suicide: An analysis of Austrian and Swiss data over 40 years (epidemiology and psychiatric sciences (2014) 10.1017/s2045796014000195)). *Epidemiology and Psychiatric Sciences* 24, 322.

Aldrich RS (2015). Using the theory of planned behavior to predict college students' intention to intervene with a suicidal individual. *Crisis* 36, 332-337.

Alonzo D, Conway A, Modrek AS (2016). Latino suicidal adolescent psychosocial service utilization: The role of mood fluctuations and inattention. *Journal of Affective Disorders* 190, 616-622.

Amoss S, Lynch M, Bratley M (2016). Bringing forth stories of blame and shame in dialogues with families affected by adolescent self-harm. *Journal of Family Therapy*. Published online: 20 January 2016. doi: 10.1111/1467-6427.12101.

Andersson A-L, Svensson K (2015). Fatalities in road traffic, a result of accidents or suicides. *Journal of Local and Global Health Science* 2015, e27.

Andersson A-L, Svensson K (2015). Suicide and accident classification methodology. *Journal of Local and Global Health Science* 2015, e28.

Andriessen K, Draper B, Dudley M, Mitchell PB (2015). Bereavement after suicide. *Crisis* 36, 299-303.

Antai-Otong D (2016). What every ED nurse should know about suicide risk assessment. *Journal of Emergency Nursing* 42, 31-36.

Arbuthnott AE, Lewis SP (2015). Parents of youth who self-injure: A review of the literature and implications for mental health professionals. *Child and Adolescent Psychiatry and Mental Health* 9, 1-20.

Arcoverde RL, de Almeida Amazonas MCL, de Lima RDM (2016). Descriptions and interpretations on self-harming. *Culture and Psychology* 22, 110-127.

Arditte KA, Morabito DM, Shaw AM, Timpano KR (2016). Interpersonal risk for suicide in social anxiety: The roles of shame and depression. *Psychiatry Research* 239, 139-144.

Arendt F, Till B, Niederkrotenthaler T (2015). Effects of suicide awareness material on implicit suicide cognition: A laboratory experiment. *Health Communication* 31, 718-726.

Artieda-Urrutia P, Delgado-Gomez D, Ruiz-Hernandez D, Manuel Garcia-Vega J, Berenguer N, Oquendo MA, Blasco-Fontecilla H (2015). Short personality and life event scale for detection of suicide attempters. *Revista de Psiquiatria y Salud Mental* 8, 199-206.

Atilola O, Ayinde O (2015). A cultural look on suicide: The Yorùbá as a paradigmatic example. *Mental Health, Religion and Culture* 18, 456-469.

Atram AR (2015). Comparison between psychiatrists and non-psychiatric physicians identifying psychiatric symptoms: A clinical study. *Journal of Psychiatry* 18, 1-5.

Austin S (2016). Working with chronic and relentless self-hatred, self-harm and existential shame: A clinical study and reflections. *Journal of Analytical Psychology* 61, 24-43.

Bachtelle SE, Pepper CM (2015). The physical results of nonsuicidal self-injury: The meaning behind the scars. *Journal of Nervous and Mental Disease* 203, 927-933.

Badoud D, Luyten P, Fonseca-Pedrero E, Eliez S, Fonagy P, Debbane M (2015). The French version of the reflective functioning questionnaire: Validity data for adolescents and adults and its association with non-suicidal self-injury. *PLoS One* 10, e0145892.

Baek JH, Heo JY, Fava M, Mischoulon D, Nierenberg A, Hong JP, Roh SW, Jeon HJ (2016). Erratum: Anxiety symptoms are linked to new-onset suicidal ideation after six months of follow-up in outpatients with major depressive disorder (J. Affect. Disord. (2015) 187 (183-187) doi: 10.1016/j.Jad.2015.08.006). *Journal of Affective Disorders* 193, 185-186.

Ballard TN, Chen X, Kim HM, Hamill JB, Pusic AL, Wilkins EG, Roth RS (2015). Managing suicidal ideation in a breast cancer cohort seeking reconstructive surgery. *Psycho-Oncology*. Published online: 22 October 2015. doi: 10.1002/pon.4017.

Bateup S (2015). On online therapies. Virtual therapies can stop the clock on suicide. *Health Service Journal* 125, 16-17.

Behera C, Krishna K, Kumar R (2016). Suicide notes and cadaveric organ donation. *Medico-Legal Journal*. Published online: 18 March 2016. doi: 10.1177/0025817216638996.

Behera C, Swain R, Bhardwaj DN, Millo T (2015). Skin suicide note written in Mehndi (Henna). *Medico-Legal Journal*. Published online: 26 November 2015. doi: 10.1177/0025817215614145.

Bell S, Russ TC, Kivimaki M, Stamatakis E, Batty GD (2015). Dose-response association between psychological distress and risk of completed suicide in the general population. *Journal of the American Medical Association Psychiatry* 72, 1254-1256.

Bell SAPFNPBC, Lori JPCNM, Redman RPRN, Seng JPCNM (2015). Psychometric validation and comparison of the self-reporting questionnaire-20 and self-reporting questionnaire-suicidal ideation and behavior among Congolese refugee women. *Journal of Nursing Measurement* 23, 393-408.

Benard V, Vaiva G, Masson M, Geoffroy PA (2016). Lithium and suicide prevention in bipolar disorder. *L'Encephale*. Published online: 19 March 2016. doi: 10.1016/j.encep.2016.02.006.

Bennett M (2015). The importance of interviewing adults on the autism spectrum about their depression and suicidal ideation experiences. *Journal of Autism and Developmental Disorders* 46, 1492-1493.

Berk MS, Hughes J (2016). Cognitive behavioral approaches for treating suicidal behavior in adolescents. *Current Psychiatry Reviews* 12, 4-13.

Berman NC, Sullivan A, Wilhelm S, Cohen IG (2015). Effect of a legal prime on clinician's assessment of suicide risk. *Death Studies* 40, 61-67.

Betz ME, Boudreaux ED (2015). Managing suicidal patients in the emergency department. *Annals of Emergency Medicine* 67, 276-282.

Beyer JL, Weisler RH (2015). Suicide behaviors in bipolar disorder. A review and update for the clinician. *Psychiatric Clinics of North America* 39, 111-123.

Bhatti JA, Nathens AB, Redelmeier DA (2016). Deliberate self-harm following bariatric surgery-reply. *JAMA Surgery*. Published online: 6 January 2016. doi: 10.1001/jamasurg.2015.5126.

Bhui K (2016). On Blackstar: Deaths, dying and dominions of discovery. *British Journal of Psychiatry* 208, 307-308.

Biddle L, Derges J, Mars B, Heron J, Donovan JL, Potokar J, Piper M, Wyllie C, Gunnell D (2015). Suicide and the internet: Changes in the accessibility of suicide-related information between 2007 and 2014. *Journal of Affective Disorders* 190, 370-375.

Blasco-Fontecilla H, Fernandez-Fernandez R, Colino L, Fajardo L, Perteguer-Barrio R, de Leon J (2016). The addictive model of self-harming (non-suicidal and suicidal) behavior. *Frontiers in Psychiatry* 7, 1-7.

Boddy J (2015). A mission to prevent suicide. *Nursing Times* 111, 27.

Bolster C, Holliday C, Shaw M (2015). Suicide assessment and nurses: What does the evidence show? *Online Journal of Issues in Nursing* 20, 2.

Bolton JM, Gunnell D, Turecki G (2015). Suicide risk assessment and intervention in people with mental illness. *BMJ* 351, h4978.

Bolton JM, Gunnell D, Turecki G (2016). Suicide risk and intervention in mental illness reply. *BMJ* 352, i268.

Bono V, Amendola CL (2015). Primary care assessment of patients at risk for suicide. *Journal of the American Academy of Physician Assistants* 28, 35-39.

Borges G, Bagge CL, Orozco R (2016). A literature review and meta-analyses of cannabis use and suicidality. *Journal of Affective Disorders* 195, 63-74.

Bornheimer LA, Nguyen D (2015). Suicide among individuals with schizophrenia: A risk factor model. *Social Work in Mental Health* 14, 112-132.

Borrill J, Mackenzie JM, Cook L, Beck A (2015). Relationships in the context of suicide risk. *Probation Journal* 62, 71-73.

Bose S, Khanra S, Umesh S, Khess CRJ, Ram D (2016). Inpatient suicide in a psychiatric hospital: Fourteen years' observation. *Asian Journal of Psychiatry* 19, 56-58.

Bowyer L, Gillett G (2015). Suicide: The lonely path. *Advances in Medical Ethics* 2, 1-10.

Bramness JG, Walby FA, Morken G, Roislien J (2015). The authors reply. *American Journal of Epidemiology* 182, 820-821.

Bramness JG, Walby FA, Morken G, Roislien J (2015). Re: "Analyzing seasonal variations in suicide with fourier poisson time-series regression: A registry-based study from Norway, 1969-2007" reply. *American Journal of Epidemiology* 182, 820-821.

Brent DA, Melhem NM, Mann JJ (2015). Pathways to offspring suicidal behavior may begin with maternal suicide attempt. *Journal of the American Academy of Child and Adolescent Psychiatry* 54, 868.

Bryan CJ, Rudd MD (2015). Brief CBT and suicide risk: Ruling out nonspecific effects of individual therapy response. *American Journal of Psychiatry* 172, 1022-1023.

Bryan CJ, Rudd MD (2016). The importance of temporal dynamics in the transition from suicidal thought to behavior. *Clinical Psychology: Science and Practice* 23, 21-25.

Bugaj TJ, Cranz A, Junne F, Erschens R, Herzog W, Nikendei C (2016). Psychosocial burden in medical students and specific prevention strategies. *Mental Health and Prevention* 4, 24-30.

Bunderla T, Kumperscak HG (2015). Altered pain perception in self-injurious behavior and the association of psychological elements with pain perception measures: A systematic review. *Psychiatria Danubina* 27, 346-354.

Burke TA, Alloy LB (2016). Moving toward an ideation-to-action framework in suicide research: A commentary on May and Klonsky (2016). *Clinical Psychology* 23, 26-30.

Butwicka A, Frisen L, Almqvist C, Zethelius B, Lichtenstein P (2016). Erratum. Risks of psychiatric disorders and suicide attempts in children and adolescents with type 1 diabetes: A population-based cohort study. Diabetes care 2015;38:453-459. *Diabetes Care* 39, 495.

Caine ED (2015). Cooling suicide hotspots. *Lancet Psychiatry* 2, 952-953.

Calati R, Artero S, Courtet P, Lopez-Castroman J (2015). Framing the impact of physical pain on suicide attempts. A reply to Stubbs. *Journal of Psychiatric Research* 72, 102-103.

Calear AL, Christensen H, Freeman A, Fenton K, Busby Grant J, van Spijker B, Donker T (2015). A systematic review of psychosocial suicide prevention interventions for youth. *European Child and Adolescent Psychiatry* 25, 467-482.

Campos RC, Holden RR, Laranjeira P, Troister T, Oliveira AR, Costa F, Abreu M, Fresca N (2016). Self-report depressive symptoms do not directly predict suicidality in nonclinical individuals: Contributions toward a more psychosocial approach to suicide risk. *Death Studies*. Published online: 18 February 2016. doi: 10.1080/07481187.2016.1150920.

Canetto SS (2015). Suicidal behaviors among Muslim women. *Crisis* 36, 447-458.

Cantrell C (2015). Liberty versus life: Suicide in the writings of Montesquieu. *Journal of Psychohistory* 43, 134-146.

Cao KO (2014). Preventing suicide among older adult Asian women. *Generations* 38, 82-85.

Carpenter B, Bond C, Tait G, Wilson M, White K (2016). Who leaves suicide notes? An exploration of victim characteristics and suicide method of completed suicides in Queensland. *Archives of Suicide Research* 20, 176-190.

Carpenter B, Tait G, Stobbs N, Barnes M (2015). When coroners care too much: Therapeutic jurisprudence and suicide findings. *Journal of Judicial Administration* 24, 172-183.

Carubia B, Becker A, Levine BH (2016). Child psychiatric emergencies: Updates on trends, clinical care, and practice challenges. *Current Psychiatry Reports* 18, 1-8.

Casey D, Choong KA (2016). Suicide whilst under GMC's fitness to practise investigation: Were those deaths preventable? *Journal of Forensic and Legal Medicine* 37, 22-27.

Castelli Dransart DA, Heeb J-L, Gulfi A, Gutjahr EM (2015). Stress reactions after a patient suicide and their relations to the profile of mental health professionals. *BMC Psychiatry* 15, 1-9.

Cea DM (2015). Make suicide prevention a national priority. *North Carolina Medical Journal* 76, 271.

Cha CB, Glenn JJ, Deming CA, D'Angelo EJ, Hooley JM, Teachman BA, Nock MK (2016). Examining potential iatrogenic effects of viewing suicide and self-injury stimuli. *Psychological Assessment*. Published online: 28 January 2016. doi: 10.1037/pas0000280.

Chakravarthy B, Yang A, Ogbu U, Kim C, Iqbal A, Haight J, Anderson C, DiMassa G, Bruckner T, Bhargava R, Schreiber M, Lotfipour S (2015). Determinants of pediatric psychiatry length of stay in 2 urban emergency departments. *Pediatric Emergency Care*. Published online: 24 September 2015. doi: 10.1097/PEC.0000000000000509.

Chandler A, King C, Burton C, Platt S (2015). General practitioners' accounts of patients who have self-harmed. *Crisis* 37, 42-50.

Chang BP, Tan TM (2015). Suicide screening tools and their association with near-term adverse events in the ED. *American Journal of Emergency Medicine* 33, 1680-1683.

Cheavens JS, Cukrowicz KC, Hansen R, Mitchell SM (2015). Incorporating resilience factors into the interpersonal theory of suicide: The role of hope and self-forgiveness in an older adult sample. *Journal of Clinical Psychology* 72, 58-69.

Chel'loob M (2016). Suicide: The last frontier in being a good Muslim: Islamic attitudes from anti-suicide to pro-suicide. *The Heythrop Journal*. Published online: 30 October 2015. doi: 10.1111/heyj.12306.

Chesin M, Interian A, Kline A, Benjamin-Phillips C, Latorre M, Stanley B (2016). Reviewing mindfulness-based interventions for suicidal behavior. *Archives of Suicide Research*. Published online: 16 March 2016. doi: 10.1080/13811118.2016.1162244.

Chiang YC, Chung FY, Lee CY, Shih HL, Lin DC, Lee MB (2016). Suicide reporting on front pages of major newspapers in Taiwan violating reporting recommendations between 2001 and 2012. *Health Communication*. Published online: 23 March 2016. doi: 10.1080/10410236.2015.1074024.

Christensen H, Cuijpers P, Reynolds CF, 3rd (2016). Changing the direction of suicide prevention research: A necessity for true population impact. *Journal of the American Medical Association Psychiatry* 73, 435-436.

Chu C, Podlogar MC, Rogers ML, Buchman-Schmitt JM, Negley JH, Joiner TE (2016). Does suicidal ideation influence memory? A study of the role of violent daydreaming in the relationship between suicidal ideation and everyday memory. *Behavior Modification*. Published online: 20 January 2016. doi: 10.1177/0145445515625189.

Coffey MJ, Coffey CE, Ahmedani BK (2015). Suicide prevention in patient and nonpatient populations. *Psychiatric Services* 66, 1119-1120.

Corbitt-Hall DJ, Gauthier JM, Davis MT, Witte TK (2016). College students' responses to suicidal content on social networking sites: An examination using a simulated Facebook newsfeed. *Suicide and Life-Threatening Behavior*. Published online: 21 March 2016. doi: 10.1111/sltb.12241.

Cousins S (2016). Nepal's silent epidemic of suicide. *Lancet* 387, 16-17.

Cross TLP (2016). Social and emotional development of gifted students. *Gifted Child Today* 39, 63-66.

Curtis A, Agarwal G, Attarian H (2016). Treatment of subjective total insomnia after suicide attempt with olanzapine and electroconvulsive therapy. *Journal of Clinical Psychopharmacology* 36, 178-180.

Curtis C (2016). Young women's experiences of self-harm: Commonalities, distinctions and complexities. *Young* 24, 17-35.

Danesh MJ, Kimball AB (2016). Brodalumab and suicidal ideation in the context of a recent economic crisis in the United States. *Journal of the American Academy of Dermatology* 74, 190-192.

Davidson CL, Anestis MD, Gutierrez PM (2016). Ecological momentary assessment is a neglected methodology in suicidology. *Archives of Suicide Research.* Published online: 29 January 2016. doi: 10.1080/13811118.2015.1004482.

Davis E (2015). We've toiled without end: Publicity, crisis, and the suicide epidemic in Greece. *Comparative Studies in Society and History* 57, 1007-1036.

De Beurs DP, Fokkema M, O'Connor RC (2016). Optimizing the assessment of suicidal behavior: The application of curtailment techniques. *Journal of Affective Disorders* 196, 218-224.

de Cates AN, Broome MR (2016). Can we use neurocognition to predict repetition of self-harm, and why might this be clinically useful? A perspective. *Frontiers in Psychiatry* 7, 1-7.

De Hepcee C, Reynaert C, Jacques D, Zdanowicz N (2015). Suicide in adolescence: Attempt to cure a crisis, but also the fatal outcome of certain pathologies. *Psychiatria Danubina* 27, S296-S299.

de Leon J, Baca-Garcia E, Blasco-Fontecilla H (2015). From the serotonin model of suicide to a mental pain model of suicide. *Psychotherapy and Psychosomatics* 84, 323-329.

de Leon J, Baca-Garcia E, Blasco-Fontecilla H (2016). Reply to the multifaceted aspects of suicide behavior by Tondo. *Psychotherapy and Psychosomatics* 85, 112-113.

de Souza MLP (2016). Indigenous narratives about suicide in Alto Rio Negro, Brazil: Weaving meanings. *Saude e Sociedade* 25, 145-159.

Depestele L, Lemmens GMD, Dierckx E, Baetens I, Schoevaerts K, Claes L (2015). The role of non-suicidal self-injury and binge-eating/purging behaviours in the caregiving experience among mothers and fathers of adolescents with eating disorders. *European Eating Disorders Review* 24, 257-260.

Deuter K, Procter N, Evans D, Jaworski K (2016). Suicide in older people: Revisioning new approaches. *International Journal of Mental Health Nursing* 25, 144-150.

Devenish B, Berk L, Lewis AJ (2016). The treatment of suicidality in adolescents by psychosocial interventions for depression: A systematic literature review. *Australian and New Zealand Journal of Psychiatry.* Published online: 19 February 2016. doi: 10.1177/0004867415627374.

Dhingra K, Boduszek D, Klonsky ED (2016). Empirically derived subgroups of self-injurious thoughts and behavior: Application of latent class analysis. *Suicide and Life-Threatening Behavior.* Published online: 19 October 2015. doi: 10.1111/sltb.12232.

Dhingra K, Boduszek D, O'Connor RC (2016). A structural test of the integrated motivational-volitional model of suicidal behaviour. *Psychiatry Research* 239, 169-178.

Di Napoli WA, Della Rosa A (2015). Suicide and attempted suicide: Epidemiological surveillance as a crucial means of a local suicide prevention project in Trento's province. *Psychiatria Danubina* 27, 279-284.

Dixon JB (2015). Self-harm and suicide after bariatric surgery: Time for action. *The Lancet Diabetes and Endocrinology* 4, 199-200.

Doran CM, Ling R, Gullestrup J, Swannell S, Milner A (2015). The impact of a suicide prevention strategy on reducing the economic cost of suicide in the New South Wales construction industry. *Crisis.* Published online: 23 December 2015. doi: 10.1027/0227-5910/a000362.

Doran N, De Peralta S, Depp C, Dishman B, Gold L, Marshall R, Miller D, Vitale S, Tiamson-Kassab M (2016). The validity of a brief risk assessment tool for predicting suicidal behavior in veterans utilizing VHA mental health care. *Suicide and Life-Threatening Behavior.* Published online: 29 January 2016. doi: 10.1111/sltb.12229.

Douglas KA, Morris CAW (2015). Assessing counselors' self-efficacy in suicide assessment and intervention. *Counseling Outcome Research and Evaluation* 6, 58-69.

Dubicka B, Cole-King A, Reynolds S, Ramchandani P (2016). Paper on suicidality and aggression during antidepressant treatment was flawed and the press release was misleading. *BMJ* 352, i911.

Ducher JL, de Chazeron I, Llorca Pm (2016). Suicide and evaluation. Review of French tools: Non-dimensional approach and self-assessment. *L'Encephale*. Published online: 19 January 2016. doi: 10.1016/j.encep.2015.12.004.

Dura H, Morar S, Cipaian CR (2015). Chemical suicide by inhalation of hydrogen sulfide in Sibiu County, Romania. Case report and literature review. *Romanian Journal of Legal Medicine* 23, 289-292.

Economou M, Angelopoulos E, Peppou LE, Souliotis K, Stefanis C (2016). Suicidal ideation and suicide attempts in Greece during the economic crisis: An update. *World Psychiatry* 15, 83-84.

Edmondson AJ, Brennan CA, House AO (2016). Non-suicidal reasons for self-harm: A systematic review of self-reported accounts. *Journal of Affective Disorders* 191, 109-117.

Eggertson L (2015). Child sexual abuse in Nunavut linked to suicide. *Canadian Medical Association Journal* 187, E463-E464.

Eggertson L (2015). Minister in charge of suicide prevention knows the crisis intimately. *Canadian Medical Association Journal* 187, E503-E504.

Eggertson L (2015). Nunavut acts on recommendations for suicide prevention. *Canadian Medical Association Journal* 187, 1346.

Eggertson L (2015). Nunavut suicide inquest: The tragedy of an 11-year-old's death. *Canadian Medical Association Journal* 187, 1-2.

Eggertson L (2015). Nunavut suicides a "public health emergency". *Canadian Medical Association Journal* 187, E462.

Eggertson L (2016). Advocates seek $100 million for youth suicide prevention. *Canadian Medical Association Journal*. Published online: 29 February 2016. doi: 10.1503/cmaj.109-5243.

Erlich MD (2016). Envisioning zero suicide. *Psychiatric Services* 67, 255.

Esfahani M, Hashemi Y, Alavi K (2015). Psychometric assessment of Beck Scale for Suicidal Ideation (BSSI) in general population in Tehran. *Medical Journal of the Islamic Republic of Iran* 29, 268.

Eskin M (2016). Turkish Imams' experience with and their attitudes toward suicide and suicidal persons. *Journal of Religion and Health*. Published online: 29 February 2016. doi: 10.1007/s10943-016-0217-8.

Eynan R, Reiss L, Links P, Shah R, Rao TSS, Parkar S, Dutt L, Kadam K, De Souza A, Shrivastava A (2015). Suicide prevention competencies among urban Indian physicians: A needs assessment. *Indian Journal of Psychiatry* 57, 397-402.

Falkowitz D (2016). In response to: Poisonings with suicidal intent aged 0-21 years reported to poison centers 2003-12. *Western Journal of Emergency Medicine* 17, 94.

Fartacek C, Schiepek G, Kunrath S, Fartacek R, Ploederl M (2016). Real-time monitoring of non-linear suicidal dynamics: Methodology and a demonstrative case report. *Frontiers in Psychology* 7, 130.

Faubert M (2015). The fictional suicides of Mary Wollstonecraft. *Literature Compass* 12, 652-659.

Faubert M, Reynolds N (2015). Introduction: Romanticism and suicide. *Literature Compass* 12, 641-651.

Ferrey AE, Hughes ND, Simkin S, Locock L, Stewart A, Kapur N, Gunnell D, Hawton K (2016). The impact of self-harm by young people on parents and families: A qualitative study. *BMJ Open* 6, e009631.

Finlayson AJR, Iannelli RJ, Brown KP, Neufeld RE, DuPont RL, Campbell MD (2016). Re: Physician suicide and physician health programs. *General Hospital Psychiatry* 40, 84-85.

Fisher G (2016). Managing young people with self-harming or suicidal behaviour. *Nursing Children and Young People* 28, 25-31.

Fiske A, O'Riley AA (2016). Toward an understanding of late life suicidal behavior: The role of lifespan developmental theory. *Aging and Mental Health* 20, 123-130.

Fitzpatrick SJ (2015). Scientism as a social response to the problem of suicide. *Journal of Bioethical Inquiry* 12, 613-622.

Florence C, Haegerich T, Simon T, Zhou C, Luo F (2015). Estimated lifetime medical and work-loss costs of emergency department-treated nonfatal injuries - United States, 2013. *Morbidity and Mortality Weekly Report* 64, 1078-1082.

Florence C, Simon T, Haegerich T, Luo F, Zhou C (2015). Estimated lifetime medical and work-loss costs of fatal injuries - United States, 2013. *Morbidity and Mortality Weekly Report* 64, 1074-1077.

Flores-Cornejo F, Kamego-Tome M, Zapata-Pachas MA, Alvarado GF (2015). Weighing the evidence for suicide prevention. *Revista Brasileira de Psiquiatria* 37, 264.

Flynn S, Gask L, Shaw J (2015). Newspaper reporting of homicide-suicide and mental illness. *BJPsych Bulletin* 39, 268-272.

Forster C (2016). The first step in preventing suicide is to ask. *Journal of Pediatrics* 170, 1-4.

Foster C, Birch L, Allen S, Rayner G (2015). Enabling practitioners working with young people who self-harm. *Journal of Mental Health Training, Education and Practice* 10, 268-280.

Foster T (2015). Schizophrenia and bipolar disorder: No recovery without suicide prevention. *British Journal of Psychiatry* 207, 371-372.

Frasquilho D, Matos MG, Salonna F, Guerreiro D, Storti CC, Gaspar T, Caldas-de-Almeida JM (2016). Mental health outcomes in times of economic recession: A systematic literature review. *BMC Public Health* 16, e115.

Freeman KR, James S, Klein KP, Mayo D, Montgomery S (2016). Outpatient dialectical behavior therapy for adolescents engaged in deliberate self-harm: Conceptual and methodological considerations. *Child and Adolescent Social Work Journal* 33, 123-135.

Freestone M, Bull D, Brown R, Boast N, Blazey F, Gilluley P (2015). Triage, decision-making and follow-up of patients referred to a UK forensic service: Validation of the DUNDRUM toolkit. *BMC Psychiatry* 15, 239-239.

Frey LM, Hans JD, Cerel J (2015). Perceptions of suicide stigma. *Crisis*. Published online: 23 December 2015. doi: 10.1027/0227-5910/a000358.

Frost M, Casey L, Rando N (2015). Self-injury, help-seeking, and the internet. *Crisis*. Published online: 17 November 2015. doi: 10.1027/0227-5910/a000346.

Fulginiti A, Pahwa R, Frey LM, Rice E, Brekke JS (2015). What factors influence the decision to share suicidal thoughts? A multilevel social network analysis of disclosure among individuals with serious mental illness. *Suicide and Life-Threatening Behavior*. Published online: 29 October 2015. doi: 10.1111/sltb.12224.

Furnivall J (2016). The gender of suicide: Knowledge production, theory and suicidology. *Sociology of Health and Illness* 38, 170-171.

Gagnon M, Oliffe JL (2015). Male depression and suicide: What NPS should know. *Nurse Practitioner* 40, 50-55.

Gandhi A, Luyckx K, Maitra S, Claes L (2015). Non-suicidal self-injury and other self-directed violent behaviors in India: A review of definitions and research. *Asian Journal of Psychiatry*. Published online: 9 October 2015. doi: 10.1016/j.ajp.2015.09.015.

Gandy J, Terrion JL (2015). Journalism and suicide reporting guidelines in Canada: Perspectives, partnerships and processes. *International Journal of Mental Health Promotion* 17, 249-260.

Geoffroy MC, Turecki G (2016). The developmental course of suicidal ideation in first-episode psychosis. *Lancet Psychiatry* 3, 395-396.

George SE, Page AC, Hooke GR, Stritzke WGK (2016). Multifacet assessment of capability for suicide: Development and prospective validation of the acquired capability with rehearsal for suicide scale. *Psychological Assessment.* Published online: 25 January 2016. doi: 10.1037/pas0000276.

Ghasemi P, Shaghaghi A, Allahverdipour H (2015). Measurement scales of suicidal ideation and attitudes: A systematic review article. *Health Promotion Perspectives* 5, 156-168.

Gholamrezaei M, De Stefano J, Heath NL (2015). Nonsuicidal self-injury across cultures and ethnic and racial minorities: A review. *International Journal of Psychology.* Published online: 8 December 2015. doi: 10.1002/ijop.12230.

Giles H (2016). The common language of homicide and suicide. *Journal of Language and Social Psychology* 35, 241-243.

Giner L, Guija JA (2015). The necessity of improvement statistical management and communication of identified suicides. *Revista de Psiquiatria y Salud Mental* 8, 250-251.

Glassmire DM, Tarescavage AM, Burchett D, Martinez J, Gomez A (2015). Clinical utility of the MMPI-2-RF SUI items and scale in a forensic inpatient setting: Association with interview self-report and future suicidal behaviors. *Psychological Assessment.* Published online: 14 December 2015. doi: 10.1037/pas0000220.

Gray BP, Dihigo SK (2015). Suicide risk assessment in high-risk adolescents. *Nurse Practitioner* 40, 30-37.

Green KL, Brown GK, Jager-Hyman S, Cha J, Steer RA, Beck AT (2015). The predictive validity of the Beck Depression Inventory suicide item. *Journal of Clinical Psychiatry* 76, 1683-1686.

Grobler C, Strumpher J, Jacobs R (2015). Overcrowding as a possible risk factor for inpatient suicide in a South African psychiatric hospital. *South African Journal of Psychiatry* 211, 107.

Guan L, Hao B, Cheng Q, Yip PS, Zhu T (2015). Identifying Chinese microblog users with high suicide probability using internet-based profile and linguistic features: Classification model. *JMIR Mental Health* 2, e17.

Guinn D, Burgermeister DM (2016). Suicide screening for prisoners: An ethical critique of research rejection. *Journal of Forensic Nursing* 12, 39-42.

Gulfi A, Heeb JL, Castelli Dransart DA, Gutjahr E (2015). Professional reactions and changes in practice following patient suicide: What do we know about mental health professionals' profiles? *Journal of Mental Health Training, Education and Practice* 10, 256-267.

Gunnell D, Derges J, Chang S-S, Biddle L (2015). Searching for suicide methods. *Crisis* 36, 325-331.

Gutierrez PM, Pease J, Matarazzo BB, Monteith LL, Hernandez T, Osman A (2016). Evaluating the psychometric properties of the interpersonal needs questionnaire and the acquired capability for suicide scale in military veterans. *Psychological Assessment.* Published online: 21 March 2016. doi: 10.1037/pas0000310.

Gvion Y, Levi-Belz Y, Hadlaczky G, Apter A (2015). On the role of impulsivity and decision-making in suicidal behavior. *World Journal of Psychiatry* 5, 255-259.

Haghdoost A, Akbari M, Zolala F (2016). Author's reply: Role of religious beliefs in preventing suicide attempts in Iran. *Archives of Iranian Medicine* 19, 235.

Halicka J, Kiejna A (2015). Differences between suicide and non-suicidal self-harm behaviours: A literary review. *Archives of Psychiatry and Psychotherapy* 17, 59-63.

Hallensleben N, Spangenberg L, Kapusta ND, Forkmann T, Glaesmer H (2016). The German version of the Interpersonal Needs Questionnaire (INQ) - dimensionality, psychometric properties and population-based norms. *Journal of Affective Disorders* 195, 191-198.

Hammerton G, Mahedy L, Mars B, Harold GT, Thapar A, Zammit S, Collishaw S (2015). Erratum: Association between maternal depression symptoms across the first eleven years of their child's life and subsequent offspring suicidal ideation (plos one (2015) 10: 8 (e0136367) doi: 10.1371/journal.Pone.0136367). *PLoS One*. Published online: 7 July 2015. doi: 10.1371/journal.pone.0131885.

Hammerton G, Zammit S, Sellers R, Thapar A, Collishaw S, Mahedy L, Pearson R (2015). Pathways to offspring suicidal behavior may begin with maternal suicide attempt reply. *Journal of the American Academy of Child and Adolescent Psychiatry* 54, 868-869.

Hammerton GB, Zammit SP, Sellers RP, Thapar AFP, Collishaw SP, Mahedy LP, Pearson RP (2015). In reply. *Journal of the American Academy of Child and Adolescent Psychiatry* 54, 868.

Han B, Compton WM (2015). Report ignores risk factor of tobacco in assessing suicidality reply. *Journal of Clinical Psychiatry* 76, 1571-1572.

Han CS, Oliffe JL (2015). Korean-Canadian immigrants' help-seeking and self-management of suicidal behaviours. *Canadian Journal of Community Mental Health* 34, 17-30.

Han JS, Lee E-H, Suh TW, Hong CH (2015). Psychometric evaluation of the suicide ideation scale in mentally ill Korean patients dwelling in communities. *Quality of Life Research* 24, 119-120.

Harper BT, Klaassen Z, DiBianco JM, Yaguchi G, Jen RP, Terris MK (2016). Suicide risk in patients with bladder cancer: A call to action. *Journal of Wound Ostomy and Continence Nursing* 43, 170-171.

Harshe DG, Vadlamani N, Tharayil HM, Andrade C (2015). Suicide lethality scale: Concerns regarding validity and scoring. *Indian Journal of Psychiatry* 57, 429-430.

Hashimoto S, Watanabe K, Takahashi T (2016). Medical intervention for attempted suicide patients in emergency room. *Nippon Rinsho* 74, 319-323.

Hasking P, Rose A (2016). A preliminary application of social cognitive theory to nonsuicidal self-injury. *Journal of Youth Adolescence*. doi: 10.1007/s10964-016-0449-7.

Heelis R, Graham H, Jackson C (2016). A preliminary test of the interpersonal psychological theory of suicidal behavior in young people with a first episode of psychosis. *Journal of Clinical Psychology* 72, 79-87.

Hegerl U, Kohls E (2016). Synergistic effects of multi-level suicide preventive interventions: Important, but difficult to disentangle. *Australian and New Zealand Journal of Psychiatry*. Published online: 7 January 2016. doi: 10.1177/0004867415621398.

Heller NR (2015). Risk, hope and recovery: Converging paradigms for mental health approaches with suicidal clients. *British Journal of Social Work* 45, 1788-1803.

Heyman I, Webster BJ, Tee S (2015). Curriculum development through understanding the student nurse experience of suicide intervention education — a phenomenographic study. *Nurse Education in Practice* 15, 498-506.

Hickey K, Rossetti J, Strom J, Bryant K (2015). Issues most important to parents after their children's suicide attempt: A pilot Delphi study. *Journal of Child and Adolescent Psychiatric Nursing*. Published online: 16 October 2015. doi: 10.1111/jcap.12124.

Hildebrand MJ (2016). The masculine sea: Gender, art, and suicide in Kate Chopin's the awakening. *American Literary Realism* 48, 189-208.

Hoffert B (2015). The suicide of Claire Bishop. *Library Journal* 140, 82-82.

Hoffmeister PA, Storer BE, Syrjala KL, Baker KS (2016). Physician-diagnosed depression and suicides in pediatric hematopoietic cell transplant survivors with up to 40 years of follow-up. *Bone Marrow Transplantation* 51, 153-156.

Hoffmire CA, Kemp JE, Thompson C (2015). Suicide prevention in patient and nonpatient populations: In reply. *Psychiatric Services* 66, 1120-1121.

Hom MA, Joiner TE, Bernert RA (2015). Limitations of a single-item assessment of suicide attempt history: Implications for standardized suicide risk assessment. *Psychological Assessment.* Published online: 26 October 2015. doi: 10.1037/pas0000241.

Hoyt T, Duffy V (2015). Implementing firearms restriction for preventing US army suicide. *Military Psychology* 27, 384-390.

Hughes ND, Locock L, Simkin S, Stewart A, Ferrey AE, Gunnell D, Kapur N, Hawton K (2015). Making sense of an unknown terrain: How parents understand self-harm in young people. *Qualitative Health Research.* Published online: 13 September 2015 doi: 10.1177/1049732315603032.

Huguet N, DeVoe JE (2015). Suicide prevention in primary care medicine. *Mayo Clinic Proceedings* 90, 1459-1461.

Hunt EJF (2015). Our encounters with self-harm. *Psychiatric Bulletin* 39, 54-55.

Ioerger M, Henry KL, Chen PY, Cigularov KP, Tomazic RG (2015). Correction: Beyond same-sex attraction: Gender-variant-based victimization is associated with suicidal behavior and substance use for other-sex attracted adolescents. *PLoS One* 10, e0139532.

Ivany CG, Hoge CW (2015). Suicide attempts in the US army. *Journal of the American Medical Association Psychiatry* 73, 176-177.

Jayasekera H, Seneviratne KACD, Narammalage HK, Embuldeniya AS, Priyadarshanie JWS, Rosana JAF, Zahriya MRF, Williams SS (2014). Psycho spiritual characteristics of persons presenting with deliberate self-harm to a suburban hospital in the western province of Sri Lanka. *Sri Lanka Journal of Psychiatry* 5, 13-18.

Jha S, Kumar R (2015). Methodological considerations in determining the effects of films with suicidal content. *British Journal of Psychiatry* 207, 562

Ji N-J, Hong Y-P, Lee W-Y (2016). Comprehensive psychometric examination of the Attitudes Towards Suicide (ATTS) in South Korea. *International Journal of Mental Health Systems* 10, 1-6.

Joiner TE, Hom MA, Hagan CR, Silva C (2015). Suicide as a derangement of the self-sacrificial aspect of eusociality. *Psychological Review* 123, 235-254

Jones H, Cipriani A (2016). Improving access to treatment for mental health problems as a major component of suicide prevention strategy. *Australian and New Zealand Journal of Psychiatry* 50, 176-178.

Jones KW (2015). Two deaths at Whittier State School: The meanings of youth suicide, 1939-1940. *Journal of the History of Childhood and Youth* 8, 403-425.

Jorm A (2016). A month for reflecting on suicide prevention. *Australian and New Zealand Journal of Psychiatry* 50, 109-110.

Jovicic M, Hinic D, Draskovic M, Obradovic A, Nikic-Duricic K, Rancic N, Perkovic-Vukcevic N, Ristic-Ignjatovic D (2016). Psychometric properties of the RASS scale in the Serbian population. *Journal of Affective Disorders* 189, 134-140.

Kahn J-P, Tubiana A, Cohen RF, Carli V, Wasserman C, Hoven C, Sarchiapone M, Wasserman D (2015). Important variables when screening for students at suicidal risk: Findings from the French cohort of the SEYLE study. *International Journal of Environmental Research and Public Health* 12, 12277-12290.

Kantha SS (2015). Suicides of 84 newsworthy Japanese between 1912 and 2015. *International Medical Journal* 22, 352-357.

Kaplan MS, Huguet N, McFarland BH, Caetano R, Conner KR, Nolte KB, Giesbrecht N (2016). Heavy alcohol use among suicide decedents: Differences in risk across racial-ethnic groups. *Psychiatric Services* 67, 258.

Kapur N, Webb R (2016). Suicide risk in people with chronic fatigue syndrome. *Lancet* 387, 1596-1597.

Karman P, Kool N, Gamel C, van Meijel B (2015). From judgment to understanding. Mental health nurses' perceptions of changed professional behaviors following positively changed attitudes toward self-harm. *Archives of Psychiatric Nursing* 29, 401-406.

Katz C, Bolton J, Sareen J (2015). The prevalence rates of suicide are likely underestimated worldwide: Why it matters. *Social Psychiatry and Psychiatric Epidemiology* 51, 125-127.

Kayman DJ, Goldstein MF, Dixon L, Goodman M (2015). Perspectives of suicidal veterans on safety planning. *Crisis* 36, 371-383.

Kazan D, Calear AL, Batterham PJ (2016). The impact of intimate partner relationships on suicidal thoughts and behaviours: A systematic review. *Journal of Affective Disorders* 190, 585-598.

Keane A (2016). Narratives of treatment outcome. *Journal of Constructivist Psychology*. Published online: 24 February 2016. doi: 10.1080/10720537.2015.1134365.

Kearns M, Muldoon OT, Msetfi RM, Surgenor PWG (2015). Understanding help-seeking amongst university students: The role of group identity, stigma, and exposure to suicide and help-seeking. *Frontiers in Psychology* 6, 1462.

Kelada L, Hasking P, Melvin G (2016). The relationship between nonsuicidal self-injury and family functioning: Adolescent and parent perspectives. *Journal of Marital and Family Therapy*. Published online: 4 January 2016. doi: 10.1111/jmft.12150.

Kene P, Brabeck KM, Kelly C, DiCicco B (2016). Suicidality among immigrants: Application of the interpersonal-psychological theory. *Death Studies*. Published online: 18 February 2016. doi: 10.1080/07481187.2016.1155675.

Kim JJ, La Porte LM, Silver RK (2015). Suicide risk among perinatal women who report thoughts of self-harm on depression screens reply. *Obstetrics and Gynecology* 126, 217.

Kitanaka J (2015). The rebirth of secrets and the new care of the self in depressed Japan. *Current Anthropology* 56, S251-S262.

Klonsky ED, Glenn CR, Styer DM, Olino TM, Washburn JJ (2015). The functions of nonsuicidal self-injury: Converging evidence for a two-factor structure. *Child and Adolescent Psychiatry and Mental Health* 9, 1-9.

Klonsky ED, May AM (2016). The importance of accuracy and care in suicidology discourse: A reply to Nock et al. *Clinical Psychology: Science and Practice* 23, 35-38.

Klonsky ED, May AM, Saffer BY (2016). Suicide, suicide attempts, and suicidal ideation. *Annual Review of Clinical Psychology* 12, 14.1-14.24.

Knipe DW, Carroll R, Thomas KH, Pease A, Gunnell D, Metcalfe C (2015). Association of socioeconomic position and suicide/attempted suicide in low and middle income countries in South and South-East Asia - a systematic review. *BMC Public Health* 15, 1-18.

Knox S, Collings SC, Nelson K (2016). Clinicians' perspectives on recruiting youth consumers for suicide research. *Mental Health and Social Inclusion* 20, 52-62.

Koenig J, Thayer JF, Kaess M (2016). A meta-analysis on pain sensitivity in self-injury. *Psychological Medicine* 46, 1597-1612.

KoKoAung E, Cavenett S, McArthur A, Aromataris E (2015). The association between suicidality and treatment with selective serotonin reuptake inhibitors in older people with major depression: A systematic review. *JBI Database of Systematic Reviews and Implementation Reports* 13, 174-205.

Kolshus EM, Kolshus EH, Gavin B, Cullen W, McNicholas F (2015). General practitioners' experience of child and adolescent suicidal ideation and behaviour – a survey. *Irish Journal of Psychological Medicine*. Published online: 2 November 2015. doi: 10.1017/ipm.2015.52.

Kõlves K, Barker E, De Leo D (2015). Allergies and suicidal behaviors: A systematic literature review. *Allergy and Asthma Proceedings* 36, 433-438.

Kopacz MS, Kane CP, Stephens B, Pigeon WR (2016). Use of ICD-9-CM diagnosis code V62.89 (other psychological or physical stress, not elsewhere classified) following a suicide attempt. *Psychiatric Services*. Published online: 14 February 2016. doi: 10.1176/appi.ps.201500302.

Kopacz MS, Rasmussen KA, Searle RF, Wozniak BM, Titus CE (2016). Veterans, guilt, and suicide risk: An opportunity to collaborate with chaplains? *Cleveland Clinic Journal of Medicine* 83, 101-105.

Kopetz C, Orehek E (2015). When the end justifies the means: Self-defeating behaviors as "rational" and "successful" self-regulation. *Current Directions in Psychological Science* 24, 386-391.

Koretsky DP (2015). "Unhallowed arts": Frankenstein and the poetics of suicide. *European Romantic Review* 26, 241-260.

Koweszko T, Gierus J, Mosiołek A, Kami ski M, Wi niewska KA, Szulc A (2015). Differences in assessment of suicidal tendencies in men and women: A pilot study. *Archives of Psychiatric Nursing* 30, 77-78.

Koyanagi A, Stickley A, Haro JM (2016). Correction: Psychotic-like experiences and nonsuidical self-injury in England: Results from a national survey. *PLoS One* 11, e0147095.

Krysinska K, Batterham PJ, Tye M, Shand F, Calear AL, Cockayne N, Christensen H (2015). Best strategies for reducing the suicide rate in Australia. *Australian and New Zealand Journal of Psychiatry* 50, 386.

Kuo DC, Tran M, Shah AA, Matorin A (2015). Depression and the suicidal patient. *Emergency Medicine Clinics of North America* 33, 765-778.

Labouliere CD, Tarquini SJ, Totura CMW, Kutash K, Karver MS (2015). Revisiting the concept of knowledge: How much is learned by students participating in suicide prevention gatekeeper training? *Crisis* 36, 274-280.

Landy G, Kripalani M (2015). Opportunities for suicide prevention in the general medical setting. *Nursing Standard* 30, 44-48.

Lappann Bott NC, Costa de Araújo LM, Costa EE, de Almeida Machado JS (2015). Nursing students attitudes across the suicidal behavior. *Investigación y Educación en Enfermería* 33, 334-342.

Large M (2016). Study on suicide risk assessment in mental illness underestimates inpatient suicide risk. *BMJ*. Published online: 20 January 2016. doi: 10.1136/bmj.i267.

Large M (2016). Suicide risk and intervention in mental illness study on suicide risk assessment in mental illness underestimates inpatient suicide risk. *BMJ*. Published online: 9 November. doi: 10.1136/bmj.h4978.

Lauw M, How CH, Loh C (2015). Authors' reply: Deliberate self-harm in adolescents. *Singapore Medical Journal* 56, 531.

Lee H, An S (2015). Social stigma toward suicide: Effects of group categorization and attributions in Korean health news. *Health Communication* 31, 468-477.

Lee SJ, Kim JS (2016). Development of a Korean Geriatric Suicidal Risk Scale (KGSRS). *Journal of Korean Academy of Nursing* 46, 59-68.

Lee SU, Park JI (2015). Ambivalence about suicide in internet: The correlation between the search for negative information about suicide and the provision of positive information. *Journal of Psychiatry* 18, 1-4.

Leeder S (2016). Preventing suicide by a systems approach. *Australian and New Zealand Journal of Psychiatry* 50, 174-175.

Lester D (2016). The death effect-is there a suicide effect? A comment on Green and Mohler. *Omega* 72, 360-361.

Lester D, Tartaro C (2015). Suicide on death row. *Psychological Reports* 117, 944-950.

Lewis KC, Meehan KB, Cain NM, Wong PS (2016). Within the confines of character: A review of suicidal behavior and personality style. *Psychoanalytic Psychology* 33, 179-202.

Lewis SP (2016). The overlooked role of self-injury scars: Commentary and suggestions for clinical practice. *Journal of Nervous and Mental Disease* 204, 33-35.

Lewis SP, Mehrabkhani S (2015). Every scar tells a story: Insight into people's self-injury scar experiences. *Counselling Psychology Quarterly.* Published online: 9 October 2015. doi: 10.1080/09515070.2015.1088431.

Lewis SP, Plener PL (2015). Nonsuicidal self-injury: A rapidly evolving global field. *Child and Adolescent Psychiatry and Mental Health* 9, 1-3.

Li A, Huang X, Hao B, O'Dea B, Christensen H, Zhu T (2015). Attitudes towards suicide attempts broadcast on social media: An exploratory study of Chinese microblogs. *PeerJ* 3, e1209.

Liu H, Wang Y, Liu W, Wei D, Yang J, Du X, Tian X, Qiu J (2015). Neuroanatomical correlates of attitudes toward suicide in a large healthy sample: A voxel-based morphometric analysis. *Neuropsychologia* 80, 185-193.

Liu Y, Sareen J, Bolton JM, Wang JL (2016). Development and validation of a risk prediction algorithm for the recurrence of suicidal ideation among general population with low mood. *Journal of Affective Disorders* 193, 11-17.

Lloyd-Richardson EE, Lewis SP, Whitlock JL, Rodham K, Schatten HT (2015). Research with adolescents who engage in non-suicidal self-injury: Ethical considerations and challenges. *Child and Adolescent Psychiatry and Mental Health* 9, 1-14.

Locklear M (2016). Drug quickly quells suicidal thoughts. *New Scientist* 229, 12.

Logue LM (2015). Elephants and epistemology: Evidence of suicide in the gilded age. *Journal of Social History* 49, 374-386.

Long M, Manktelow R, Tracey A (2015). "Knowing that I'm not alone": Client perspectives on counselling for self-injury. *Journal of Mental Health* 25, 41-46.

Lopez-Castroman J, Blasco-Fontecilla H, Courtet P, Baca-Garcia E, Oquendo MA (2015). Are we studying the right populations to understand suicide? *World Psychiatry* 14, 368-369.

Louzon SA, Bossarte R, McCarthy JF, Katz IR (2016). Does suicidal ideation as measured by the PHQ-9 predict suicide among VA patients? *Psychiatric Services* 67, 517- 522.

Lu DY, Zhu PP, Lu TR, Che JY (2016). The suicidal risks and treatments, seek medications from multi-disciplinary. *Central Nervous System Agents in Medicinal Chemistry.* Published online: 10 February 2016. doi: 10.2174/1871524916666160210142734.

Lund EM, Nadorff MR, Samuel Winer E, Seader K (2015). Is suicide an option?: The impact of disability on suicide acceptability in the context of depression, suicidality, and demographic factors. *Journal of Affective Disorders* 189, 25-35.

Luz C (2016). Family medicine: Bridge to life. *Journal of the American Board of Family Medicine* 29, 161-164.

Lv M, Li A, Liu T, Zhu T (2015). Creating a Chinese suicide dictionary for identifying suicide risk on social media. *Peerj* 3, 1-15.

Mackenzie JM, Cartwright T, Beck A, Borrill J (2015). Probation staff experiences of managing suicidal and self-harming service users. *Probation Journal* 62, 111-127.

Maeda M, Oe M, Bromet E, Yasumura S, Ohto H (2016). Fukushima, mental health and suicide. *Journal of Epidemiology and Community Health.* Published online: 9 March 2016. doi: 10.1136/jech-2015-207086.

Maksudyan N (2015). Control over life, control over body: Female suicide in early republican Turkey. *Women's History Review* 24, 861-880.

Maltsberger JT, Schechter M, Herbstman B, Ronningstam E, Goldblatt MJ (2015). Suicide studies today. *Crisis* 36, 387-389.

Manceaux P, Jacques D, Zdanowicz N (2015). Hormonal and developmental influences on adolescent suicide: A systematic review. *Psychiatria Danubina* 27, S300-304.

Marini S, Vellante F, Matarazzo I, De Berardis D, Serroni N, Gianfelice D, Olivieri L, Di Renzo F, Di Marco A, Fornaro M, Orsolini L, Valchera A, Iasevoli F, Mazza M, Perna G, Martinotti G, Di Giannantonio M (2016). Inflammatory markers and suicidal attempts in depressed patients: A review. *International Journal of Immunopathology Pharmacology*. Published online: 4 January 2016. doi: 10.1177/0394632015623793.

Martin-Fumado C, Gomez-Duran EL, Rodriguez-Pazos M, Arimany-Manso J (2015). Medical professional liability in psychiatry. *Actas Espanolas de Psiquiatria* 43, 205-212.

Martini M, Ciliberti P, Alfano L, Santi F, Schiavone M, Ciliberti R (2015). Existential suicide and pathological suicide: Historical, philosophical and ethical aspects. *Journal of Psychopathology* 21, 19-22.

Marutani M, Yamamoto-Mitani N, Kodama S (2016). Public health nurses' activities for suicide prevention in Japan. *Public Health Nursing*. Published online: 26 January 2016. doi: 10.1111/phn.12247.

Matandela M, Matlakala MC (2016). Nurses' experiences of inpatients suicide in a general hospital. *Health Sa Gesondheid* 21, 54-59.

May AM, Klonsky ED (2016). What distinguishes suicide attempters from suicide ideators? A meta-analysis of potential factors. *Clinical Psychology: Science and Practice* 23, 5-20.

McAllister S, Noonan I (2015). Suicide prevention for the LGBT community: A policy implementation review. *British Journal of Mental Health Nursing* 4, 31-37.

McAndrew S, Warne T (2015). Cutting through the red tape: Listening to the voices of young people who self-harm. *International Journal of Mental Health Nursing* 24, 30.

McCabe PJ, Christopher PP (2015). Symptom and functional traits of brief major depressive episodes and discrimination of bereavement. *Depression and Anxiety* 33, 112-119.

McCoy CE, Woo R, Anderson C, Lotfipour S (2015). Race-related healthcare disparities among California workers: Public health considerations for immigration reform. *Journal of Emergency Medicine* 50, 159-166.

McCullumsmith C (2015). Laying the groundwork for standardized assessment of suicidal behavior. *Journal of Clinical Psychiatry* 76, e1333-e1335.

McLaughlin C, McGowan I, Kernohan G, O'Neill S (2015). The unmet support needs of family members caring for a suicidal person. *Journal of Mental Health* 25, 212-216.

McNamara RF (2015). Wearing your heart on your face: Reading lovesickness and the suicidal impulse in Chaucer. *Literature and Medicine* 33, 258-278.

Medlock MM (2015). A light pierces the darkness: A reflection on spirituality and suicide. *Spirituality in Clinical Practice* 2, 282-284.

Meerwijk EL, Parekh A, Oquendo MA, Allen IE, Franck LS, Lee KA (2016). Direct versus indirect psychosocial and behavioural interventions to prevent suicide and suicide attempts: A systematic review and meta-analysis. *Lancet Psychiatry*. Published online: 24 March 2016. doi: 10.1016/S2215-0366(16)00064-X.

Melo HPM, Moreira AA, Batista E, Makse HA, Andrade JS (2015). Corrigendum: Statistical signs of social influence on suicides. *Scientific Reports* 5, 15944.

Mewton L, Andrews G (2016). Cognitive behavioral therapy for suicidal behaviors: Improving patient outcomes. *Psychology Research and Behavior Management* 9, 21-29.

Michail M, Tait L (2016). Exploring general practitioners' views and experiences on suicide risk assessment and management of young people in primary care: A qualitative study in the UK. *BMJ Open* 6, e009654.

Miller AL (2015). Introduction to a special issue dialectical behavior therapy: Evolution and adaptations in the 21(st) century. *American Journal of Psychotherapy* 69, 91-95.

Miller M, Swanson SA, Azrael D (2016). Are we missing something pertinent? A bias analysis of unmeasured confounding in the firearm-suicide literature. *Epidemiologic Reviews* 38, 62-69.

Millner AJ, Lee MD, Nock MK (2015). Single-item measurement of suicidal behaviors: Validity and consequences of misclassification. *PLoS One.* Published online: 23 October 2015. doi: 10.1371/journal.pone.0141606.

Minkkinen J, Oksanen A, Nasi M, Keipi T, Kaakinen M, Rasanen P (2015). Does social belonging to primary groups protect young people from the effects of pro-suicide sites? *Crisis* 37, 31-41.

Mirhashemi S, Motamedi MHK, Mirhashemi AH, Taghipour H, Danial Z (2016). Suicide in Iran. *Lancet* 387, 29-29.

Mishara BL, Bardon C (2015). Systematic review of research on railway and urban transit system suicides. *Journal of Affective Disorders* 193, 215-226.

Mishara BL, Weisstub DN (2015). The legal status of suicide: A global review. *International Journal of Law and Psychiatry* 44, 54-74.

Mitten N, Preyde M, Lewis S, Vanderkooy J, Heintzman J (2016). The perceptions of adolescents who self-harm on stigma and care following inpatient psychiatric treatment. *Social Work in Mental Health* 14, 1-21.

Mohan R (2015). Recent de-criminalisation of suicide attempts in the Indian sub-continent (deletion of section 309 of the Indian penal code): Thoughts of a UK-based consultant psychiatrist of Indian origin. *British Journal of Psychiatry.* Published online: 6 February 2015. doi: 10.1192/bjp.190.1.81a.

Monaghan K, Harris M (2015). Not at imminent risk. *Crisis* 36, 459-463.

Montreuil M, Butler KJD, Stachura M, Pugnaire Gros C (2015). Exploring helpful nursing care in pediatric mental health settings: The perceptions of children with suicide risk factors and their parents. *Issues in Mental Health Nursing* 36, 849-859.

Moor S, Crowe M, Luty S, Carter J, Joyce PR (2016). Erratum: Effects of comorbidity and early age of onset in young people with bipolar disorder on self harming behaviour and suicide attempts (Journal of Affective Disorders (2011)136:3 (1212-1215) doi: 10.1016/j.Jad. 2011.10.018). *Journal of Affective Disorders* 190, 894.

Moore MM, Cerel J, Jobes DA (2015). Fruits of trauma? *Crisis* 36, 241-248.

Moradinazar M, Amini S, Baneshi M, Najafi F, Abbasi N, Ataee M (2016). Survival probability in self immolation attempters: A prospective observational cohort study. *Ulusal Travma Ve Acil Cerrahi Dergisi* 22, 23-28.

Moxham L, Patterson C (2015). Getting men to talk about suicide. *Australian Nursing and Midwifery Journal* 23, 39.

Mula M, McGonigal A, Micoulaud-Franchi JA, May TW, Labudda K, Brandt C (2016). Validation of rapid suicidality screening in epilepsy using the NDDIE. *Epilepsia.* Published online: 25 March 2016. doi: 10.1111/epi.13373.

Murphy JA, Lee MT, Liu X, Warburton G (2015). Factors affecting survival following self-inflicted head and neck gunshot wounds: A single-centre retrospective review. *International Journal of Oral and Maxillofacial Surgery* 45, 513-516.

Nadler S (2015). Spinoza on lying and suicide. *British Journal for the History of Philosophy* 24, 257-278.

Nadorff MR, Pearson MD, Golding S (2016). Explaining the relation between nightmares and suicide. *Journal of Clinical Sleep Medicine* 12, 289-290.

Namratha P, Kishor M, Rao TSS, Raman R (2015). Mysore study: A study of suicide notes. *Indian Journal of Psychiatry* 57, 379-382.

Newland C, Barber E, Rose M, Young A (2015). Critical stress. Survey reveals alarming rates of EMS provider stress and thoughts of suicide. *JEMS* 40, 30-34.

Niaura R (2015). Varenicline and suicide: Reconsidered and reconciled. *Nicotine & Tobacco Research*. Published online: 12 November 2015. doi: 10.1093/ntr/ntv247.

Nicholl E, Loewenthal D, Gaitanidis A (2015). 'What meaning does somebody's death have, what meaning does somebody's life have?' psychotherapists' stories of their work with suicidal clients. *British Journal of Guidance and Counselling*. Published online: 23 September 2015. doi: 10.1080/03069885.2015.1089430.

Niederkrotenthaler T, Arendt F, Till B (2015). Predicting intentions to read suicide awareness stories. *Crisis* 36, 399-406.

Nock MK, Kessler RC, Franklin JC (2016). Risk factors for suicide ideation differ from those for the transition to suicide attempt: The importance of creativity, rigor, and urgency in suicide research. *Clinical Psychology: Science and Practice* 23, 31-34.

Noh D, Park Y-S, Oh EG (2016). Effectiveness of telephone-delivered interventions following suicide attempts: A systematic review. *Archives of Psychiatric Nursing* 30, 114-119.

Nordentoft M (2016). Listen to the patient: Challenges in the evaluation of the risk of suicidal behaviour. *Acta Psychiatrica Scandinavica* 133, 255-256.

Oliffe JL, Ogrodniczuk JS, Gordon SJ, Creighton G, Kelly MT, Black N, Mackenzie C (2016). Stigma in male depression and suicide: A Canadian sex comparison study. *Community Mental Health Journal* 52, 302-310.

Omar H (2016). Positive youth development, part 3. Youth suicide prevention is everybody's business. *Journal of Pediatric and Adolescent Gynecology* 29, 77-78.

Ong SH (2015). Comment on: Deliberate self-harm in adolescents. *Singapore Medical Journal* 56, 530.

Oppliger M, Mauermann E, Ruppen W (2016). Are transdermal opioids contraindicated in patients at risk of suicide?: An underappreciated problem. *European Journal of Anaesthesiology*. Published online: 4 January 2016. doi: 10.1097/EJA.0000000000000393.

Oquendo MA (2015). Suicidal behavior: Measurement and mechanisms. *Journal of Clinical Psychiatry* 76, 1675-1675.

Orlando CM, Broman-Fulks JJ, Whitlock JL, Curtin L, Michael KD (2015). Nonsuicidal self-injury and suicidal self-injury: A taxometric investigation. *Behavior Therapy* 46, 824-833.

Osazuwa-Peters N, Adjei Boakye E, Walker RJ, Varvares MA (2016). Suicide: A major threat to head and neck cancer survivorship. *Journal of Clinical Oncology*. Published online: 19 January 2016. doi: 10.1200/JCO.2015.65.4673.

Ostacher MJ, Nierenberg AA, Rabideau D, Reilly-Harrington NA, Sylvia LG, Gold AK, Shesler LW, Ketter TA, Bowden CL, Calabrese JR, Friedman ES, Iosifescu DV, Thase ME, Leon AC, Trivedi MH (2015). A clinical measure of suicidal ideation, suicidal behavior, and associated symptoms in bipolar disorder: Psychometric properties of the Concise Health Risk Tracking Self-Report (CHRT-SR). *Journal of Psychiatric Research* 71, 126-133.

Otsuka K, Sakai A (2015). The psychology and medical education of those who have the risk of committing suicides. *Journal of Psychiatry* 18, 1-2.

Owen R, Gooding P, Dempsey R, Jones S (2016). The experience of participation in suicide research from the perspective of individuals with bipolar disorder. *Journal of Nervous and Mental Disease*. Published online: 24 February 2016. doi: 10.1097/NMD.0000000000000487.

Owens C (2016). Hotspots and copycats: A plea for more thoughtful language about suicide. *Lancet Psychiatry* 3, 19-20.

Owens C, Hansford L, Sharkey S, Ford T (2015). Needs and fears of young people presenting at accident and emergency department following an act of self-harm: Secondary analysis of qualitative data. *British Journal of Psychiatry* 208, 286-291.

Parisot E (2015). Living to labour, labouring to live: The problem of suicide in charlotte Smith's elegiac sonnets. *Literature Compass* 12, 660-666.

Park S, Choi KH, Oh Y, Lee HK, Kweon YS, Lee CT, Lee KU (2015). Clinical characteristics of the suicide attempters who refused to participate in a suicide prevention case management program. *Journal of Korean Medical Science* 30, 1490-1495.

Pease JL, Billera M, Gerard G (2016). Military culture and the transition to civilian life: Suicide risk and other considerations. *Social Work* 61, 83-86.

Perlis ML, Grandner MA, Chakravorty S, Bernert RA, Brown GK, Thase ME (2015). Suicide and sleep: Is it a bad thing to be awake when reason sleeps? *Sleep Medicine Reviews* 29, 101-107.

Peters K, Cunningham C, Murphy G, Jackson D (2016). 'People look down on you when you tell them how he died': Qualitative insights into stigma as experienced by suicide survivors. *International Journal of Mental Health Nursing*. Published online: 18 February 2016. doi: 10.1111/inm.12210.

Petroni S, Patel V, Patton G (2015). Why is suicide the leading killer of older adolescent girls? *The Lancet* 386, 2031-2032.

Phillips GA (2015). He never said anything: A critical poetic response to suicide among young gay men. *Cultural Studies-Critical Methodologies* 15, 112-118.

Pirkis J (2016). The population-level effectiveness of suicide prevention strategies that might be used in a systems-based approach. *Australian and New Zealand Journal of Psychiatry* 50, 179-180.

Pirkis J, Krysinska K, Cheung YTD, Too LS, Spittal MJ, Robinson J (2016). "Hotspots" and "copycats": A plea for more thoughtful language about suicide - authors' reply. *Lancet Psychiatry* 3, 20.

Podlogar MC, Rogers ML, Chiurliza B, Hom MA, Tzoneva M, Joiner T (2015). Who are we missing? Nondisclosure in online suicide risk screening questionnaires. *Psychological Assessment*. Published online: 30 November 2015. doi: 10.1037/pas0000242.

Pompili M (2015). Our empathic brain and suicidal individuals. *Crisis* 36, 227-230.

Pompili M, Goracci A, Giordano G, Erbuto D, Girardi P, Klonsky ED, Baldessarini RJ (2015). Relationship of non-suicidal self-injury and suicide attempt: A psychopathological perspective. *Journal of Psychopathology* 21, 348-353.

Pon N, Asan B, Anandan S, Toledo A (2015). Special considerations in pediatric psychiatric populations. *Emergency Medicine Clinics of North America* 33, 811-824.

Ponnudurai R (2015). Suicide in India - changing trends and challenges ahead. *Indian Journal of Psychiatry* 57, 348-354.

Power J, Smith HP, Beaudette JN (2016). Examining Nock and Prinstein's four-function model with offenders who self-injure. *Personal Disorders: Theory, Research, & Treatment*. 15 February 2016. doi: 10.1037/per0000177.

Pozzi M, Radice S, Clementi E, Molteni M, Nobile M (2016). Antidepressants and, suicide and self-injury: Causal or casual association? *International Journal of Psychiatry in Clinical Practice* 20, 47-51.

Presson B, Rambo C (2015). Claiming, resisting, and exempting pathology in the identities of self-injurers. *Deviant Behavior* 37, 219-236.

Price JH (2015). The conceptual transfer of human agency to the divine in the second temple period: The case of Saul's suicide. *Shofar* 34, 107-130.

Pridmore S, Pridmore C (2016). Suicidal thoughts in the novel Don Quixote. *Malaysian Journal of Medical Sciences* 23, 65-69.

Pritchard C (2015). Under-reported suicides hiding or compounding the tragedy? *Mental Health Today,* May/June 2015, 18-19.

Procter N, Ferguson M (2015). Are there warning signs for suicide? *Australian Nursing and Midwifery Journal* 23, 31.

Pullen JM, Gilje F, Tesar E (2015). A descriptive study of baccalaureate nursing students' responses to suicide prevention education. *Nurse Education in Practice* 16, 104-110.

Quinlivan L, Cooper J, Davies L, Hawton K, Gunnell D, Kapur N (2016). Which are the most useful scales for predicting repeat self-harm? A systematic review evaluating risk scales using measures of diagnostic accuracy. *BMJ Open* 6, e009297.

Ramchandani P, Reynolds S, Cole-King A, Dubicka B (2016). Re: Suicidality and aggression during antidepressant treatment: Systematic review and meta-analyses based on clinical study reports (Sharma et al, 352:I65, 2016). *BMJ* 352, i65.

Rao AL, Hong ES (2015). Understanding depression and suicide in college athletes: Emerging concepts and future directions. *British Journal of Sports Medicine* 50, 136-137.

Rauh SH (2015). The tradition of suicide in Rome's foreign wars. *Transactions of the American Philological Association* 145, 383-410.

Read M, McCrae N (2016). Preventing suicide in lesbian, gay, bisexual, and transgender prisoners: A critique of U.K. Policy. *Journal of Forensic Nursing* 12, 13-18.

Reardon S (2015). Brain study seeks roots of suicide. *Nature* 528, 19.

Recker NL, Moore MD (2015). Durkheim, social capital, and suicide rates across us counties. *Health Sociology Review* 25, 78-91.

Regehr C, Bogo M, LeBlanc VR, Baird S, Paterson J, Birze A (2015). Suicide risk assessment: Clinicians' confidence in their professional judgment. *Journal of Loss and Trauma* 21, 30-46.

Reilly-Harrington NA, Shelton RC, Kamali M, Rabideau DJ, Shesler LW, Trivedi MH, McElroy SL, Sylvia LG, Bowden CL, Ketter TA, Calabrese JR, Thase ME, Bobo WV, Deckersbach T, Tohen M, McInnis MG, Kocsis JH, Gold AK, Singh V, Finkelstein DM, Kinrys G, Nierenberg AA (2016). A tool to predict suicidal ideation and behavior in bipolar disorder: The concise health risk tracking self-report. *Journal of Affective Disorders* 192, 212-218.

Reko A, Bech P, Wohlert C, Noerregaard C, Csillag C (2015). Usage of psychiatric emergency services by asylum seekers: Clinical implications based on a descriptive study in Denmark. *Nordic Journal of Psychiatry* 69, 587-593.

Reyes-Foster BM, Kangas R (2016). Unraveling Ix Tab: Revisiting the "suicide goddess" in Maya archaeology. *Ethnohistory* 63, 1-27.

Reynolds CF, 3rd (2015). Preventing suicidal ideation in medical interns. *JAMA Psychiatry* 72, 1169-1170.

Rice TR, Sher L (2015). Adolescent suicide and testosterone. *International Journal of Adolescence Medicine and Health.* Published online: 16 September 2015. doi: 10.1515/ijamh-2015-0058.

Rice TR, Sher L (2015). Preventing plane-assisted suicides through the lessons of research on homicide and suicide-homicide. *Acta Neuropsychiatrica.* Published online: 23 December 2015. doi: 10.1017/neu.2015.67.

Richard-Devantoy S, Turecki G, Jollant F (2016). Neurobiology of elderly suicide. *Archives of Suicide Research.* Published online: 8 January 2016. doi: 10.1080/13811118.2015.1048397.

Richards T (2016). There is no longer a law against suicide. *New Scientist* 229, 53.

Rimkeviciene J, Hawgood J, O'Gorman J, De Leo D (2015). Assessment of acquired capability for suicide in clinical practice. *Psychology, Health and Medicine.* Published online: 27 November 2015. doi: 10.1080/13548506.2015.1115108.

Roaten K, Khan F, Brown K, North CS (2015). Development and testing of procedures for violence screening and suicide risk stratification on a psychiatric emergency service. *American Journal of Emergency Medicine* 34, 499-504.

Roberson C (2015). Suicide assessment and prevention. *The Alabama Nurse* 42, 8-14.

Robinson I (2015). Adolescent suicide: A primary care issue. *International Journal of Nursing Education* 7, 286.

Rockett IRH, Caine ED (2015). Self-injury is the eighth leading cause of death in the United States it is time to pay attention. *Journal of the American Medical Association Psychiatry* 72, 1069-1070.

Rockett IRH, Hobbs GR, Wu D, Jia H, Nolte KB, Smith GS, Putnam SL, Caine ED (2015). Correction: Variable classification of drug-intoxication suicides across us states: A partial artifact of forensics? (PLoS One (2015) 10(9): E0137933 doi:10.1371/journal.Pone.0137933). *PLoS One.* Published online 3 September 2015. doi: 10.1371/journal.pone.0137933.

Rocos B, Acharya M, Chesser TJS (2015). The pattern of injury and workload associated with managing patients after suicide attempt by jumping from a height. *Open Orthopaedics Journal* 9, 395-398.

Rogers ML, Tucker RP, Law KC, Michaels MS, Anestis MD, Joiner TE (2016). Manifestations of overarousal account for the association between cognitive anxiety sensitivity and suicidal ideation. *Journal of Affective Disorders* 192, 116-124.

Rosenbaum PJ (2016). How self-harmers use the body as an interpretive canvass. *Culture and Psychology* 22, 128-138.

Rosenthal D (2015). Victims of seductive and unfortunate lives: Jewish suicide in interwar Poland. *Jewish History* 29, 301-330.

Rudd MD (2015). The last and greatest battle: Finding the will, commitment, and strategy to end military suicides. *American Journal of Psychiatry* 172, 1164.

Ruzhenkov VA, Ruzhenkova VV, Boeva AV, Moskvitina US (2015). Stigmatization and self-stigmatization by persons with mental disorders and suicidal behavior. *Research Journal of Medical Sciences* 9, 168-170.

Ryan CJ, Large M, Gribble R, Macfarlane M, Ilchef R, Tietze T (2015). Assessing and managing suicidal patients in the emergency department. *Australasian Psychiatry* 23, 513-516.

Sachs-Ericsson N, Van Orden K, Zarit S (2015). Suicide and aging: Special issue of aging and mental health. *Aging & Mental Health* 20, 110-112.

Salvatore T (2015). Suicide risk in homebound elderly individuals what home care clinicians need to know. *Home Healthcare Now* 33, 476-481.

Samarasinghe D (2013). Falling suicide rates in Sri Lanka: Lessons and cautions. *Sri Lanka Journal of Psychiatry* 4, 1-3.

Samraj B, Gawron JM (2015). The suicide note as a genre: Implications for genre theory. *Journal of English for Academic Purposes* 19, 88-101.

Santaella-Tenorio J, Cerda M, Villaveces A, Galea S (2016). What do we know about the association between firearm legislation and firearm-related injuries? *Epidemiologic Reviews* 38, 140-157.

Schaffer A, Sinyor M (2016). Building an evidence base for national suicide prevention strategies. *Australian and New Zealand Journal of Psychiatry.* Published online: 7 January 2016. doi: 10.1177/0004867415622274

Scheeringa MS (2016). Validity of measurement of suicidal ideas in very young children. *Journal of the American Academy of Child Adolescent Psychiatry* 55, 243-245.

Schrier AC, Beekman AT (2016). Letter on ethnic density and suicide: Interpretation of results as a protective ethnic density effect is premature. *Social Psychiatry and Psychiatric Epidemiology* 51, 787-788.

Scocco P, Toffol E, Preti A (2016). Psychological distress increases perceived stigma toward attempted suicide among those with a history of past attempted suicide. *Journal of Nervous and Mental Disease* 204, 194-202.

Scott M, Underwood M, Lamis DA (2015). Suicide and related-behavior among youth involved in the juvenile justice system. *Child and Adolescent Social Work Journal* 32, 517-527.

Sertbas M, Sertbas Y, Ordu O, Berber E, Ozen B, Ozdemir A (2016). Myocardial injury and acute renal failure associated with lactic acidosis due to suicide attempt with metformin. *Journal of the Pakistan Medical Association* 66, 223-225.

Shapiro SE, Pinto M, Evans DD (2016). Suicidality risk assessment in adolescents and young adults. *Advanced Emergency Nursing Journal* 38, 4-9.

Sharma T, Guski LS, Freund N, Gotzsche PC (2016). Suicidality and aggression during antidepressant treatment: Systematic review and meta-analyses based on clinical study reports. *BMJ*. Published online: 27 January 2016. doi: 10.1136/bmj.i65.

Sheikh S (2016). Response to comments on "poisonings with suicidal intent aged 0-21 years reported to poison centers 2003-12". *Western Journal of Emergency Medicine* 17, 94-96.

Shepard DS, Gurewich D, Lwin AK, Reed GA, Silverman MM (2015). Suicide and suicidal attempts in the United States: Costs and policy implications. *Suicide and Life-Threatening Behavior*. Published online: 29 October 2015. doi: 10.1111/sltb.12225.

Shepphird J (2015). Suicide rate high in patients with head and neck cancer. *Oncology Report* 11, 21.

Sher L (2015). Parental alienation and suicide in men. *Psychiatria Danubina* 27, 288-289.

Shetty P, Kumar A, Nayak VC, Patil N, Avinash A, Shashidhara S, Karthik Rao N, Rao R (2016). A rare case of neem oil ingestion as a suicidal modality. *Research Journal of Pharmaceutical, Biological and Chemical Sciences* 7, 1253-1255.

Signoracci GM, Stearns-Yoder KA, Holliman BD, Huggins JA, Janoff EN, Brenner LA (2015). Listening to our patients: Learning about suicide risk and protective factors from veterans with HIV/AIDS. *Journal of Holistic Nursing*. Published online: 16 November 2015. doi: 10.1177/0898010115610688.

Silva DSD, Tavares NVS, Alexandre ARG, Freitas DA, Brêda MZ, de Albuquerque MCS, de Melo Neto VL (2015). Depression and suicide risk among nursing professionals: An integrative review. *Revista da Escola de Enfermagem* 49, 1023-1031.

Simkhada P, Teijlingen EV, Winter RC, Fanning C, Dhungel A, Marahatta SB (2015). Why are so many Nepal women killing themselves? A review of key issues. *Journal of Manmohan Memorial Institute of Health Sciences* 1, 43-49.

Singaravelui V, Stewart A, Adams J, Simkin S, Hawton K (2015). Information-seeking on the internet an investigation of websites potentially accessed by distressed or suicidal adolescents. *Crisis* 36, 211-219.

Singh R, Verdolini N, Agius M, Moretti P, Quartesan R (2015). Comparison of assessment and management of suicidal risk for acute psychiatric assessment between two states sponsored hospitals in England and Italy. *Psychiatria Danubina* 27, 292-295.

Sinniah A, Oei TPS, Chinna K, Shah SA, Maniam T, Subramaniam P (2015). Psychometric properties and validation of the Positive and Negative Suicide Ideation (PANSI) inventory in an outpatient clinical population in Malaysia. *Frontiers in Psychology* 6, 1934-1934.

Slade K, Forrester A (2015). Shifting the paradigm of prison suicide prevention through enhanced multi-agency integration and cultural change. *Journal of Forensic Psychiatry and Psychology* 26, 737-758.

Sledge W, Plakun EM, Bauer S, Brodsky B, Caligor E, Clemens NA, Deen S, Kay J, Lazar S, Mellman LA, Myers M, Oldham J, Yeomans F (2014). Psychotherapy for suicidal patients with borderline personality disorder: An expert consensus review of common factors across five therapies. *Borderline Personality Disorder and Emotion Dysregulation* 1, 1-8.

Sloan KA (2016). Death and the city: Female public suicide and meaningful space in modern Mexico City. *Journal of Urban History* 42, 396-418.

Slomski A (2015). Online therapy reduces suicide ideation in medical interns. *JAMA* 314, 2608.

Slovak K, Pope ND, Brewer TW (2015). Geriatric case managers' perspectives on suicide among community-dwelling older adults. *Journal of Gerontological Social Work* 59, 3-15.

Solla P, Fasano A, Cannas A, Marrosu F (2015). Suicide and dopamine agonist withdrawal syndrome in Parkinson's disease. *Movement Disorders* 30, 1859-1860.

Spangenberg L, Hallensleben N, Friedrich M, Teismann T, Kapusta ND, Glaesmer H (2016). Dimensionality, psychometric properties and population-based norms of the German version of the revised Acquired Capability for Suicide Scale (ACSS-FAD). *Psychiatry Research* 238, 46-52.

Spence W, Millott J (2016). An exploration of attitudes and support needs of police officer negotiators involved in suicide negotiation. *Police Practice and Research* 17, 5-21.

Stankiewicz BW, Smith EG, Herz L (2015). Brief CBT and suicide risk: Ruling out nonspecific effects of individual therapy. *American Journal of Psychiatry* 172, 1022.

Stanley IH, Hom MA, Joiner TE (2016). A systematic review of suicidal thoughts and behaviors among police officers, firefighters, emts, and paramedics. *Clinical Psychology Review* 44, 25-44.

Stanley IH, Hom MA, Rogers ML, Hagan CR, Joiner TE, Jr. (2016). Understanding suicide among older adults: A review of psychological and sociological theories of suicide. *Aging and Mental Health* 20, 113-122.

Stefansson J, Nordstrom P, Runeson B, Asberg M, Jokinen J (2015). Combining the suicide intent scale and the Karolinska interpersonal violence scale in suicide risk assessments. *BMC Psychiatry* 15, 1-8.

Stevenson O (2015). Suicidal journeys: Attempted suicide as geographies of intended death. *Social and Cultural Geography* 17, 189-206.

Stone M (2016). Suicidality and aggression during antidepressant treatment: Authors misinterpreted earlier paper from the FDA. *BMJ* 352, i906.

Stroebe W (2015). Firearm availability and violent death: The need for a culture change in attitudes toward guns. *Analyses of Social Issues and Public Policy*. Published online: 23 November 2015. doi: 10.1111/asap.12100.

Stroehmer R, Edel MA, Pott S, Juckel G, Haussleiter IS (2015). Digital comparison of healthy young adults and borderline patients engaged in non-suicidal self-injury. *Annals of General Psychiatry* 14, 47.

Subica AM, Allen JG, Frueh BC, Elhai JD, Fowler JC (2015). Disentangling depression and anxiety in relation to neuroticism, extraversion, suicide, and self-harm among adult psychiatric inpatients with serious mental illness. *British Journal of Clinical Psychology*. Published online: 30 December 2015. doi: 10.1111/bjc.12098.

Sunderland N, Wong S, Lee CK (2015). Fatal insulin overdoses: Case report and update on testing methodology. *Journal of Forensic Sciences*. Published online: 24 September 2015. doi: 10.1111/1556-4029.12958.

Swanson JW, Bonnie RJ, Appelbaum PS (2015). Getting serious about reducing suicide: More "how" and less "why". *JAMA* 314, 2229-2230.

Syme KL, Garfield ZH, Hagen EH (2016). Testing the bargaining vs. Inclusive fitness models of suicidal behavior against the ethnographic record. *Evolution and Human Behavior* 37, 179-192.

Tait G, Carpenter B, De Leo D, Tatz C (2015). Problems with the coronial determination of 'suicide'. *Mortality* 20, 233-247.

Tanner R, Cassidy E, O'Sullivan I (2014). Does using a standardised mental health triage assessment alter nurses assessment of vignettes of people presenting with deliberate self-harm. *Advances in Emergency Medicine* 2014, 1-9.

Tavares A, Volpe FM (2015). Attempted suicide by breaking pre-electroconvulsive therapy fasting. *Journal of ECT*. Published online 5 December 2015. doi: 10.1097/YCT.0000000000000283.

Taylor JD, Ibanez LM (2015). Sociological approaches to self-injury. *Sociology Compass* 9, 1005-1014.

Teague-Palmieri EB, Gutierrez D (2016). Healing together: Family therapy resource and strategies for increasing attachment security in individuals engaging in nonsuicidal self-injury. *Family Journal* 24, 157-163.

Tenhouten WD (2016). Normlessness, anomie, and the emotions. *Sociological Forum*. Published online: 14 March 2016. doi: 10.1111/socf.12253.

Termorshuizen F, Braam AW (2016). Response to "letter on ethnic density and suicide: Interpretation of results as a protective ethnic density effect is premature". *Social Psychiatry and Psychiatric Epidemiology* 51, 789-790.

Thapa P, Sung Y, Klingbeil DA, Lee C-YS, Klimes-Dougan B (2015). Attitudes and perceptions of suicide and suicide prevention messages for Asian Americans. *Behavioral Sciences* 5, 547-564.

Thomas SP (2015). Suicide: Old problem, new solutions needed. *Issues in Mental Health Nursing* 36, 847-848.

Thompson N, Allan J, Carverhill PA, Cox GR, Davies B, Doka K, Granek L, Harris D, Ho A, Klass D, Small N, Wittkowski J (2016). The case for a sociology of dying, death, and bereavement. *Death Studies* 40, 172-181.

Till B, Niederkrotenthaler T (2015). Methodological considerations in determining the effects of films with suicidal content: Authors' reply. *British Journal of Psychiatry* 207, 562-563.

Tobar RAT, Prieto BLA, Castrillón DA (2016). Design and psychometric analysis of the Hopelessness and Suicide Ideation Inventory "IDIS". *International Journal of Psychological Research* 9, 52-63.

Tondo L (2016). The multifaceted aspects of suicide behavior. *Psychotherapy and Psychosomatics* 85, 111.

Tosh S (2015). Depression and goth culture. *Emergency Nurse* 23, 15.

Towl G, Walker T (2015). Learning lessons about suicides in prison. *Psychologist* 28, 887-889.

Towl G, Walker T (2015). Prisoner suicide. *Psychologist* 28, 886.

Travasso C (2015). Maharashtra government launches mental health programme to reduce suicide in farmers. *BMJ* 351, h5234.

Trogan C (2015). Reclaiming the existential discourse of suicide: Literary and philosophical approaches to suicide and why they matter. *International Journal of Literary Humanities* 13, 27-32.

Troister T, D'Agata MT, Holden RR (2015). Suicide risk screening: Comparing the Beck Depression Inventory-II Beck Hopelessness Scale, and Psychache Scale in undergraduates. *Psychological Assessment* 27, 1500-1506.

Trossman S (2015). A matter of life or death. Offering competencies to address suicide prevention, management. *American Nurse* 47, 1-8.

Tucker RP, Michaels MS, Rogers ML, Wingate LR, Joiner TE (2015). Construct validity of a proposed new diagnostic entity: Acute suicidal affective disturbance (ASAD). *Journal of Affective Disorders* 189, 365-378.

Tuft M, Gjelsvik B, Nakken KO (2015). Ian Curtis: Punk rock, epilepsy, and suicide. *Epilepsy and Behavior* 52, 218-221.

Uleman J (2016). No king and no torture: Kant on suicide and law. *Kantian Review* 21, 77-100.

Umubyeyi A, Mogren I, Ntaganira J, Krantz G (2015). Help-seeking behaviours, barriers to care and self-efficacy for seeking mental health care: A population-based study in Rwanda. *Social Psychiatry and Psychiatric Epidemiology* 51, 81-92.

Ursano RJ, Kessler RC, Stein MB (2015). Suicide attempts in the US Army-reply. *Journal of the American Medical Association Psychiatry* 73, 176-177.

Van Orden KA, Smith PN, Chen T, Conwell Y (2016). A case controlled examination of the interpersonal theory of suicide in the second half of life. *Archives of Suicide Research.* Published online: 28 July 2015. doi: 10.1080/13811118.2015.1025121.

van Wijngaarden E, Leget C, Goossensen A (2016). Caught between intending and doing: Older people ideating on a self-chosen death. *BMJ Open* 6, 1-11.

Vaz JS, Kac G, Nardi AE, Hibbeln JR (2016). Erratum: Omega-6 fatty acids and greater likelihood of suicide risk and major depression in early pregnancy (Journal of Affective Disorders (2014) 152:154(76-82)). *Journal of Affective Disorders* 190, 893.

Ventura A (2015). Scratching: Girls' suicides. *Medico E Bambino* 34, 623.

Vogel L (2015). Podcast: 10 questions with Canada's prison watchdog. *Canadian Medical Association Journal* 187, E511.

Volpe FM (2015). Re: "Analyzing seasonal variations in suicide with fourier poisson time-series regression: A registry-based study from Norway, 1969-2007". *American Journal of Epidemiology* 182, 820.

von Glischinski M, Teismann T, Prinz S, Gebauer JE, Hirschfeld G (2016). Depressive symptom inventory suicidality subscale: Optimal cut points for clinical and non-clinical samples. *Clinical Psychology and Psychotherapy.* Published online: 8 February 2016. doi: 10.1002/cpp.2007.

Vukčevič NP, Ercegovič, Šegrt Z, Djordjevič S, Stošič JJ(2016). Benzodiazepine poisoning in elderly. *Vojnosanitetski Pregled* 73, 234-238.

Wachtel SDP, Siegmann PM, Ocklenburg CM, Hebermehl LM, Willutzki UP, Teismann TP (2015). Acquired capability for suicide, pain tolerance, and fearlessness of pain - validation of the pain tolerance scale of the German Capability for Suicide Questionnaire. *Suicide and Life-Threatening Behavior* 45, 541-555.

Wald C (2016). What I forgot to mention in my suicide note. *American Journal of Nursing* 116, 57.

Walsh J (2015). Recovering from the suicide of a client with schizophrenia: Recommendations for case managers. *Care Management Journals* 16, 188-194.

Walsh PC (2011). Re.: Suicide risk in men with prostate-specific antigen-detected early prostate cancer: A nationwide population-based cohort study from PCBaSe Sweden. *Journal of Urology* 185, 1706-1707.

Ward S, Outram S (2016). Medicine: In need of culture change. *Internal Medicine Journal* 46, 112-116.

Waters S (2015). Suicide as protest in the French workplace. *Modern and Contemporary France* 23, 491-510.

Weisz GM (2015). Secondary guilt syndrome may have led Nazi-persecuted Jewish writers to suicide. *Rambam Maimonides Medical Journal* 6, 1-9.

Westlund Schreiner M, Klimes-Dougan B, Begnel ED, Cullen KR (2015). Conceptualizing the neurobiology of non-suicidal self-injury from the perspective of the research domain criteria project. *Neuroscience & Biobehavioral Reviews* 57, 381-391.

Whalen DJ, Belden AC, Luby JL, Barch D, Dixon-Gordon K (2016). Validity of measurement of suicidal ideas in very young children reply. *Journal of the American Academy of Child and Adolescent Psychiatry* 55, 243-245.

Whisenhunt JL, Chang CY, Brack GL, Orr J, Adams LG, Paige MR, McDonald CPL, O'Hara C (2015). Self-injury and suicide: Practical information for college counselors. *Journal of College Counseling* 18, 275-288.

Widger T (2015). Suicide and the 'poison complex': Toxic relationalities, child development, and the Sri Lankan self-harm epidemic. *Medical Anthropology: Cross Cultural Studies in Health and Illness* 34, 501-516.

Williams JM, Steinberg ML (2015). Report ignores risk factor of tobacco in assessing suicidality. *Journal of Clinical Psychiatry* 76, 1570-1571.

Williams MN, Hill SR, Spicer J (2015). Erratum to: Will climate change increase or decrease suicide rates? The differing effects of geographical, seasonal, and irregular variation in temperature on suicide incidence. *Climatic Change* 134, 341.

Williams S (2015). Establishing a self-harm surveillance register to improve care in a general hospital. *British Journal of Mental Health Nursing* 4, 20-25.

Winterrowd E, Canetto SS, Benoit K (2015). Permissive beliefs and attitudes about older adult suicide: A suicide enabling script? *Aging & Mental Health*. Published online: 23 October 2015. doi: 10.1080/13607863.2015.1099609.

Wise J (2015). Army suicide attempts are most likely among enlisted soldiers on first tour of duty and female soldiers, US study finds. *BMJ* 351, h3702.

Wise J (2015). Suicide screening should be given to patients who have bariatric surgery, study recommends. *BMJ* 351, h5367.

Wise J (2016). Antidepressants may double risk of suicide and aggression in children, study finds. *BMJ* 352, i545.

Wolfson JA, Teret SP, Frattaroli S, Miller M, Azrael D (2016). The U.S. Public's preference for safer guns. *American Journal of Public Health* 106, 411-413.

Wright N, Roesler J, Heinen M (2015). The unequal burden of suicide among Minnesotans: Three strategies for prevention. *Minnesota Medicine* 98, 37-39.

York A, Heise B, Thatcher B (2016). Child suicide screening methods: Are we asking the right questions? A review of the literature and recommendations for practice. *Journal for Nurse Practitioners*. Published online: 24 February 2016. doi: 10.1016/j.nurpra.2016.01.003.

You JY, You J (2015). Pain regulation in nonsuicidal self-injury. *Journal of Psychological Abnormalities in Children* 4, e102.

Youngstrom EA (2015). Using standardized methods to assess suicidal behavior: The need is even greater than it looks. *Journal of Clinical Psychiatry* 76, e1331-e1332.

Youngstrom EA, Hameed A, Mitchell MA, Van Meter AR, Freeman AJ, Perez Algorta G, White AM, Clayton PJ, Gelenberg AJ, Meyer RE (2015). Direct comparison of the psychometric properties of multiple interview and patient-rated assessments of suicidal ideation and behavior in an adult psychiatric inpatient sample. *Journal of Clinical Psychiatry* 76, 1676-1682.

Zalpuri I, Rothschild AJ (2016). Does psychosis increase the risk of suicide in patients with major depression? A systematic review. *Journal of Affective Disorders* 198, 23-31.

Zamani M, Vahedi A (2016). Role of religious beliefs in preventing suicide attempts in Iran. *Archives of Iranian Medicine* 19, 235.

Zeller BE (2015). Sacred suicide. *Journal of Religious History* 39, 458-459.

Zetterqvist M (2015). The DSM-5 diagnosis of nonsuicidal self-injury disorder: A review of the empirical literature. *Child and Adolescent Psychiatry and Mental Health* 9, 31.

Ziebell L (2015). Facial emotion recognition and reaction in a non-suicidal self-injury population. *Canadian Journal of Experimental Psychology-Revue Canadienne De Psychologie Experimentale* 69, 356.

Zolala F, Akbari M, Haghdoost A (2016). Role of religious beliefs in preventing suicide attempts in Iran: An authors' response to a letter by Zamani M, et al. *Archives of Iranian Medicine* 19, 235.

www.ingramcontent.com/pod-product-compliance
Lightning Source LLC
Chambersburg PA
CBHW080418270326
41929CB00018B/3078